# WESTMINSTER AND EUROPE

*Also by Philip Giddings*

MARKETING BOARDS AND MINISTERS
PARLIAMENTARY ACCOUNTABILITY: A Study of Parliament and
Executive Agencies (*editor*)

*Also by Gavin Drewry*

LEGISLATION AND PUBLIC POLICY (*co-author*)
THE CIVIL SERVICE TODAY (*co-author*)

# Westminster and Europe

## The Impact of the European Union on the Westminster Parliament

Edited by

**Philip Giddings**
*Lecturer in Politics*
*University of Reading*

and

**Gavin Drewry**
*Professor of Public Administration and*
*Head of the Department of Social Policy and Social Sciences*
*Royal Holloway, University of London*

for the Study of Parliament Group

First published in Great Britain 1996 by
**MACMILLAN PRESS LTD**
Houndmills, Basingstoke, Hampshire RG21 6XS
and London
Companies and representatives
throughout the world

A catalogue record for this book is available
from the British Library.

ISBN 0–333–64980–X

First published in the United States of America 1996 by
**ST. MARTIN'S PRESS, INC.,**
Scholarly and Reference Division,
175 Fifth Avenue,
New York, N.Y. 10010

ISBN 0–312–15964–1

Library of Congress Cataloging-in-Publication Data
Westminster and Europe : the impact of the European Union on the
Westminster Parliament / edited by Philip Giddings and Gavin Drewry
for the Study of Parliament Group.
p. cm.
Includes bibliographical references and index.
ISBN 0–312–15964–1
1. Great Britain. Parliament. 2. European Union—Great Britain.
I. Giddings, Philip James. II. Drewry, Gavin. III. Study of
Parliament Group.
JN550 1996
328.41'07—dc20
96–1324
CIP

Selection and editorial matter © Philip Giddings and Gavin Drewry 1996
Chapters 1–13 © Macmillan Press Ltd 1996

10  9   8   7   6   5   4   3   2   1
05  04  03  02  01  00  99  98  97  96

Printed and bound in Great Britain by
Antony Rowe Ltd, Chippenham, Wiltshire

# Contents

*Page*

Preface . . . . . . . . . . . . . . . . . . . . . . . . . . . . . . . . . vii

Contributors . . . . . . . . . . . . . . . . . . . . . . . . . . . . . . xi

1. Introduction: *Philip Giddings and Gavin Drewry* . . . . . . . 1

## Part I: Setting the Scene

2. The Development of the European Community, 1973–95:
   *David Miers* . . . . . . . . . . . . . . . . . . . . . . . . . . . . . 9
3. The Constitutional Background: *Alan Page* . . . . . . . . . . 31
4. The Evolution of the Scrutiny System in the House of
   Commons: *Priscilla Baines* . . . . . . . . . . . . . . . . . . . 49
5. The House of Lords and the European Community: the
   Evolution of Arrangements for Scrutiny: *Donald Shell* . . . 91

## Part II: The Westminster Parliament in Action

6. The House of Commons and the European Community,
   1990–91: *Philip Giddings and Priscilla Baines* . . . . . . . 113
7. The House of Lords and the European Community,
   1990–91: *Donald Shell* . . . . . . . . . . . . . . . . . . . . . 159
8. Parliament and the Common Agricultural Policy, 1990–92:
   *Priscilla Baines* . . . . . . . . . . . . . . . . . . . . . . . . . 191
9. The Welfare of Farm Animals: *Priscilla Baines* . . . . . . . 223
10. The Road to Maastricht: Parliament and the
    Intergovernmental Conferences of 1991: *Richard Ware* . . 241
11. Legislation and Ratification: the Passage of the European
    Communities (Amendment) Act 1993: *Richard Ware* . . . 261

## Part III: Conclusions

12. Scrutiny without power? The Impact of the European
    Community on the Westminster Parliament:
    *Philip Giddings and Gavin Drewry* . . . . . . . . . . . . . . 299
13. The Way Forward? *David Millar* . . . . . . . . . . . . . . . 317

## Appendix

Scrutiny of European Community Affairs by National
Parliaments: *David Millar* . . . . . . . . . . . . . . . . . . . . . . 333

**Bibliography** . . . . . . . . . . . . . . . . . . . . . . . . . . . . . . . . 353
**Index** . . . . . . . . . . . . . . . . . . . . . . . . . . . . . . . . . . . . . 361

# Preface

The Study of Parliament Group was founded in 1963, bringing together academics concerned with parliamentary affairs and officers of both Houses, with the aim of studying and conducting research into Parliament. The Group's interest has however never been confined entirely to the British Parliament, and since 1970 it has from time to time debated, and published studies on, the impact of the European Community (EC) on Westminster.

At the Group's annual meeting in January 1990 it was decided to form a study group on Parliament and the EC. It will be recalled that in June 1989 the European Council in Madrid adopted the objective of creating an economic and monetary union, while in December of that year 11 member states (the United Kingdom dissenting) signed the Social Charter. By 1989 also, it was clear that the aim of achieving a single European market, founded on 285 proposals by the Commission, would almost certainly be realised by the target date of December 1992.

These major developments in the EC seemed to present a challenge—at the time only reluctantly admitted—to the role and status of parliament in the unwritten British constitution and within the framework of the European Community.

A study group was formed under the convenorship of Ann Robinson, then Head of the Policy Unit at the Institute of Directors, and with Priscilla Baines of the House of Commons Library as secretary. By July 1990 Ann Robinson found that her other commitments precluded her from continuing to act as convenor and David Millar succeeded her. As work progressed, Priscilla Baines and he became co-convenors, she continuing also to act as a secretary without whose imagination, efficiency and persistence the project could not have been realised. The task of welding the authors' contributions into a whole was undertaken by Philip Giddings and Gavin Drewry as editors, with considerable assistance from Priscilla Baines.

Apart from the present authors, David Beamish, George Cubie, Dermot Englefield, Carol Harlow, Ann Robinson, Michael Rush, Philippa Tudor and Simon Young made helpful contributions to the work of the study group and the eventual shape and content of the book. Paul Silk, Vaughne Miller and Robert Rogers also read and commented on some of the individual chapters. The editors wish to express their thanks to them and also to Lisa Hasell, who prepared the copy for printing and to Sue Martin for preparing the index.

During 1990 and 1991, the study group sought to inform itself on the manner in which government departments handled EC legislation and legislative proposals in relation to Parliament. Several senior government officials gave generously of their time to inform members of the study group, which stands much in their debt for their clear and comprehensive explanations.

Three MPs and several clerks, together with a representative of an interest group, took considerable pains to meet the study group and to assist it with their expertise and personal opinions. The study group benefited greatly from a rewarding visit to the European Parliament in Brussels in September 1993, arranged by Dr Martyn Bond, Head of the Parliament's London Office, to whom the study group wishes to record its warmest thanks.

Almost all these briefings were conducted on a non-attributable basis, for which reason acknowledgements of their value must remain in general terms. None of those who assisted the study group in this way bears any responsibility for the contents of the book.

The study group could not have functioned at all without the generosity of the Nuffield Foundation Small Grants scheme, which the authors acknowledge with gratitude. The scheme is one of the best examples known to the editors of the timely provision of a peck of seed corn enabling the reaping of a bushel of grain.

There are several reasons why this work has taken five years to come to fruition. First the forecasts made by various authors of the aspects of the EC activities which the Commons were likely to debate between 1990 and 1992 and which lay within their field of study proved to be wide of the mark. Thus the original plan for detailed studies of the work of both Houses in these years to be matched by case studies of proceedings on specific EC legislative proposals became impossible to realise.

In the second place, the unexpectedly prolonged proceedings on the bill to amend the European Communities Act 1972 and to authorise ratification of the Treaty on European Union called for detailed study of the exceptionally difficult issues raised.

In the final part of the book we have included some proposals for reform. We should make it clear that these proposals are advanced by the (academic) authors of the particular chapters concerned and are not intended to represent the corporate view of the Study of Parliament Group.

Finally, the editors would like to express their sincere thanks to colleagues on the study group and particularly to the authors, whose contributions to the many meetings they attended added greatly to their value and opened avenues along which the project was able to advance. The formation in latter months of a small editorial committee greatly assisted the editors to weld the chapters into a reasonably coherent whole.

The content of individual chapters is the responsibility of the authors of these chapters. The co-editors are answerable for all matters of editorial policy, including the structure of the book as a whole, and for the material in the sections for which they are individually responsible.

Edinburgh University,                                      David Millar
February 1995

# Contributors

**Priscilla Baines** is Deputy Librarian of the House of Commons. She joined the Economic Affairs Section of the Research Division of the Library in 1968, became head of section in 1977, head of the Science and Environment Section in 1988 and then Head of the Parliamentary Division. Her publications include contributions to the Study of Parliament Group's *Parliament and Economic Affairs* (1980) and to G Drewry (ed), *The New Select Committees: a Study of the 1979 Reforms* (Oxford University Press, 2nd edition, 1989).

**Gavin Drewry** is a Professor of Public Administration, and Head of the Department of Social Policy and Social Science at Royal Holloway, University of London. He has published widely on parliament and the legislative process, on civil service reform and on aspects of public law. He has contributed chapters to several Study of Parliament Group publications, and edited, on the Group's behalf, *The New Select Committees: A study of the 1979 Reforms* (Oxford University Press, 2nd edition, 1989). His other books include *Legislation and Public Policy* (Macmillan, 1981), co-authored with Ivor Burton, and *The Civil Service Today* (Blackwell, 2nd edition, 1991), co-authored with Tony Butcher. He is currently Deputy Chairman of the Study of Parliament Group.

**Philip Giddings** lectures in Politics at the University of Reading. He is author of *Marketing Boards and Ministers* (Saxon House, 1974) and a number of articles on Parliament and public agencies. He edited *Parliamentary Accountability: A Study of Parliament and Executive Agencies* (Macmillan, 1995) and has contributed to several Study of Parliament Group publications, including *The New Select Committees: a Study of the 1979 Reforms* (Oxford University Press, 2nd edition, 1989) and *Parliamentary Questions* (Oxford University Press, 1993), and published articles on the Parliamentary and Health Service Commissioners.

**David Miers** is Professor of Law and Director of the Centre for Professional Legal Studies, Cardiff Law School. He has written extensively on the preparation and interpretation of legislation. He is co-author (with Alan Page) of *Legislation* (Sweet & Maxwell, 2nd edition, 1990) and is a member of the Editorial Board of the *Statute Law Review*. He has been a member of the Study of Parliament Group since 1988.

**David Millar** worked as a Clerk in the House of Commons, being responsible latterly for the work of the Select Committee on Procedure. On British accession to the European Communities in 1973 he transferred to the Directorate of Research in the Secretariat of the European Parliament. His main fields of work there were European elections, inter-institutional relations, foreign policy and human rights.

After retiring in 1989, David Millar became an Honorary Fellow of the Europa Institute in the University of Edinburgh. He has contributed to several books and has published several articles in academic journals.

**Donald Shell** lectures in Politics at the University of Bristol. He wrote *The House of Lords* (Harvester Wheatsheaf, 2nd edition, 1992), and co-edited and was principal contributor to *The House of Lords at Work* (Oxford University Press for the Study of Parliament Group, 1993). He also co-edited and contributed to *The British Prime Minister* (C Hurst, 1995) and he writes frequent journal articles on parliamentary themes and constitutional questions.

**Alan Page** is Professor of Public Law at the University of Dundee. He has acted as a specialist adviser in legal matters to the Select Committee on Scottish Affairs and is a member of the Tax Law Review Committee which is examining ways of simplifying tax legislation. He is the author (with D R Miers) of *Legislation* (Sweet & Maxwell, 2nd edition 1989) and (with R B Ferguson) of *Investor Protection* (1992). He is currently working on a study of the constitutional implications of executive self-regulation in the United Kingdom, which includes an examination of the impact of EU membership on executive initiative and discretion.

**Richard Ware** is head of the International Affairs and Defence Section at the House of Commons Library and was joint editor of *Parliament and International Relations* (Open University Press, 1991).

# 1

# Introduction

### Philip Giddings and Gavin Drewry

The role and powers of the Westminster Parliament have been at the heart of the controversy about the United Kingdom's relationship with the European Community. When the United Kingdom joined the Community in 1973 it accepted amongst the obligations of membership certain restrictions on national parliaments, including our own. These restrictions were extended when the scope of the Community's powers, and the remit of the European Parliament, were extended by the Single European Act. The controversy about the significance of these and subsequent measures emerged again in a particularly acute form in the debates about the Treaty of Maastricht and the establishment of the European Union in 1993. Moreover, it looks likely to feature strongly again when the next inter-governmental conference is convened in 1996. The Westminster Parliament's relationship with the European Community, therefore, continues to be a matter of intense political controversy, and one that cuts sharply across party lines.

In this book we have set out to do three things: first, to provide an authoritative description of how the British Parliament has adapted itself, and particularly its procedures, in response to the changed constitutional position arising from British accession to the EC; secondly, to illustrate the variety of ways in which the two Houses have actually used their procedures to deal with European business since accession; and thirdly, to assess the effectiveness of the Westminster Parliament's response to the challenges posed by an ever-growing EC agenda. In this way we provide a context for the continuing controversy about the role of national parliaments in the Community in the run-up to the next set of inter-governmental conferences.

In a book written by several authors it is necessary to explain at the outset how we have proceeded. The group has included academics from the disciplines of law and political science and officers from both Houses of the Westminster Parliament (it should be made clear that these have contributed purely in a personal capacity). Early on the group decided on a two-pronged methodology: first, to monitor what Parliament was actually doing; and secondly, to learn at first hand from those in Parliament, in Government departments and interest groups who were actually engaged in the process of doing European business. As explained in the Preface, this was achieved by inviting outside experts to address the study group. Subsequently, the group also decided that it would be helpful to view this activity from a European angle and accordingly, with generous assistance from the European Parliament, a series of seminars was held in Brussels at which we were informed about and debated the EC's legislative and administrative processes.

Monitoring the Westminster Parliament proved to be a more difficult exercise than we had envisaged. Our original intention was to take one session, identify the main issues concerning the EC that arose during the session, and focus our monitoring upon them. However, our original plan ran into some practical difficulties. We were not successful in prophesying what would be the key issues, as some issues failed to materialise, whereas others which we had not foreseen did. Moreover, it also soon became apparent that while one session is a natural time period for the Westminster Parliament it does not necessarily fit in with the schedule and politics of European business.

What therefore had seemed at the outset to be a neat scheme for monitoring had to be substantially amended. We identified retrospectively the (European) issues which had commanded most attention at Westminster and whilst some chapters are focused upon one session (1990–91), we have not stuck rigidly to that time period, particularly if there have been significant developments since. We believe that this more flexible time-scale gives a fuller and richer picture of Westminster's handling of Euro-business, not least because it has enabled us to include the holding of the inter-governmental conferences which culminated in the Treaty of Maastricht and the consequential legislation brought before the Westminster Parliament.

The primary focus of our work has been upon Westminster as *a national parliament*. Although we refer to the processes of the institutions of the European Community, particularly the Council of Ministers and the European Parliament, our concern with them has been from the perspective of an evaluation of the work of the Parliament at Westminster, not a study of the workings of the European institutions themselves. It is, of course, necessary to an evaluation of the Westminster processes to take into account the workings of the European institutions with which those processes are engaged and, in particular, the timetable of decision-making which those institutions impose.

The first part of the book is concerned with description. In it we set the scene with four chapters which give the context for Westminster's European business: the evolution of the Community itself, the constitutional consequences of accession for the United Kingdom, and the procedural mechanisms adopted in Parliament. This part of the book provides the institutional and procedural background necessary to an understanding of what the Westminster Parliament is able to do with regard to European business, of how it has set about doing that business and to an assessment of its effectiveness in doing it.

Thus in Chapter 2 David Miers describes how the European Community has evolved since British accession in 1972. In the more than two decades of British membership, the Community has further expanded, the Single Market has become an economic reality, and the Community has transformed itself into the European Union. This chapter provides an account of the aims, structure and legal characteristics of the Community within which the UK Parliament has sought to find and develop its appropriate role as a national parliament.

The character of the Community posed some well-known problems for British constitutional law and practice when Britain joined. In Chapter 3 Alan Page explains what those difficulties were thought to be, sets out the solutions to them adopted in the European Communities Act 1972 and traces their legal and constitutional consequences for the three branches of government.

The consequences for Parliament's scrutiny mechanisms are set out in Chapters 3 and 4, dealing separately with the two Houses. Priscilla Baines and Donald Shell describe how the Commons and Lords respectively evolved their distinctive forms of scrutiny for European legislation in the light of their differing memberships and cultures. In both cases particular attention is given to the committees which the Houses have set up to deal with European business and, in the Commons, to the implications of the Single European Act and majority voting in the Council of Ministers. The two Houses adopted different forms of scrutiny mechanism and in the Commons in particular there has been dissatisfaction with the way the mechanism worked, particularly after the adoption of the Single European Act in 1987. Significant changes were made in 1991 and more may be needed as the Maastricht Treaty comes into force and the next round of inter-governmental conferences gets under way.

It must be borne in mind that the Westminster Parliament's scrutiny mechanisms were still evolving as the research for this book was being conducted and that process of evolution will continue. In this respect at least, Westminster's treatment of European business has followed the traditional incremental pattern of British parliamentary culture: adaptation and evolution—critics might say muddling through—are the watchwords.

Part II of the book illustrates what Westminster had done. In it we provide an account of the two Houses at work. Here we have adopted a three-pronged method of attack. First, we look at the work of each House for one session—1990–91, as typical as any session can be given the fast moving nature of modern political life—against the background of the evolving Community. The purpose of looking at a whole session is to show the variety of the business, the wide range of opportunities for raising 'matters European' in addition to the specially created European procedures, and the way in such business has to be set in the context of the politics of the day (it will be recalled that the session began with Mrs Thatcher's fall from office). Thus Giddings and Baines begin Chapter 6 by setting the 1990–91 session in the context of contemporary events and then look in detail at the use MPs made of procedural opportunities to raise and exploit European issues. The variety of opportunity—questions, statements, legislative scrutiny, select committees, financial procedures, adjournment debates, early day motions—is considerable and the chapter presents significant empirical material about the way MPs used the procedural devices available to them.

To give more focus to the way such procedural opportunities have been used, Giddings and Baines examine how the Commons dealt with two prominent policy issues during the 1990–91 session—fisheries policy and the run-up to the inter-governmental conferences. (Two other issues —reform of the CAP and animal welfare—are dealt with separately in Chapters 8 and 9). The debates on these issues illustrate the problems the House faced in dealing with European business and the chapter as a whole shows how MPs have been carrying out their classic Parliamentary roles of scrutiny, representation and legislation in the European context.

For the House of Lords, as Donald Shell shows, the emphasis is very much upon scrutiny. Chapter 7 looks in detail at the work of the Lords' Select Committee on the European Communities and its six sub-committees, analysing the areas chosen for inquiry, the reports made and the follow-up to them. Drawing on interviews with some of the most closely involved, Shell assesses the influence of the committee upon the House, the government and major EC institutions.

Although the contrast between the highly politicised context of the Commons and the more detached scrutiny attempted by the Lords is very evident from the comparison of Chapters 6 and 7, Priscilla Baines' examination of Parliament's handling of the Common Agricultural Policy in Chapter 8 shows how the different procedures of the two Houses can complement one another. The CAP is a central feature of the European Community and one which has presented particular difficulties for British policy-makers. It therefore provides a litmus test of the effectiveness of Parliament's scrutiny procedures for European policies and legislation. The two sessions covered in Chapter 8 were dominated by negotiations on agricultural trade in the GATT Uruguay Round and consideration of proposals for major reform of the CAP but the chapter also considers how other, more routine, European agricultural business was dealt with.

The mixture of scrutiny procedures available would appear to give Parliament ample opportunities to provide input at a relatively early stage of the policy-making process. However, Chapter 8 illustrates the difficulties caused for the scrutiny machinery by the vagaries of the timetabling of EC legislation in Brussels as well as demonstrating the tactical difficulties faced by the Opposition at Westminster in areas of Community policy for the authorship of which UK ministers are not responsible. This is also evident in Chapter 9 in the case of animal welfare, a subject of great sensitivity to the British public but viewed rather differently across the channel.

The inter-governmental conferences presented a different kind of challenge to Westminster's procedures. The negotiations at the two conferences were concerned with a wide range of questions about the political and economic decision-making processes of the EC. For the British government and parliament, and the political parties within them, this developed into a protracted debate about sovereignty and its possible transfer from British to European institutions. As Richard Ware shows in Chapters 10 and 11, a considerable amount of parliamentary time was devoted to these negotiations. Opinion in the Commons, and within the political parties, was very sharply divided. Ware identifies the main strands of argument deployed and describes the way in which the government sought to maintain parliamentary support for its negotiating position, particulary on the very controversial issue of a common currency.

In Chapter 11 Ware examines the legal and constitutional problems presented by the treaty which emerged from the inter-governmental conferences and describes the twists and turns of the saga of the social protocol which culminated in a government defeat in July 1993, which was reversed in a vote of confidence the following day. It is evident from this chapter that the abstruse, legal and procedural debates reflected the extreme complexity of the post Maastricht European Union treaty system and did little to enhance the reputation of either the European institutions or the Westminster Parliament. There must be better ways of handling parliamentary consideration of the implementation and ratification of Treaty amendments, which could be an important issue as the 1996 inter-governmental conference approaches.

Part III of the book is concerned with assessment. In it we draw together the material which has emerged from the earlier chapters' examination of how parliament has organised itself and what it has actually done in the two decades since accession. We assess the effectiveness of this activity in two ways: for the House of Commons in terms of the three classic functions of scrutiny, legislation and representation; for the Lords as a chamber of influence. We then suggest some ways in which Westminster could extend its influence or deploy it more effectively. In the final chapter David Millar gives a personal view of the way forward in the post-Maastricht era.

An appendix, also by David Millar, outlines the arrangements that have been made in other national parliaments for dealing with European business and describes mechanisms that have been developed to secure a degree of collaboration between those parliaments. The variety of these arrangements, and the histories of their development, inevitably reflects the diversity of the constitutions and political systems of the member states concerned.

Description, illustration, assessment: we offer this analysis of the first two decades of Westminster's relationship with the European Community as an indispensable context for the public and parliamentary debates about what the next two decades may bring.

# PART I

## Setting the Scene

# 2

# The Development of the European Community 1973–1995

## David Miers

## Introduction

Upon its accession to the European Economic Community (EEC) on 1 January 1973, the United Kingdom became subject to a political regime whose distinctive aspirational, institutional and legal characteristics had been established with the coming into force in July 1952, under the Treaty of Paris, of the first of the three Communities, the European Coal and Steel Community (ECSC). The Community's aspirations, like those of the European Atomic Energy Community (Euratom) and the EEC (both coming into force on January 1 1958 under separate Treaties of Rome), were to bring about integration between its member states concerning the matters within the scope of the founding treaty.

The purpose of this chapter is to provide a summary of the main developments that have taken place within the Community from the time of the accession of the United Kingdom in 1973 to the enactment of the European Communities (Amendment) Act 1993 by which Parliament gave effect to the Treaty on European Union that was signed at Maastricht in February 1992. The first section reviews what was envisaged by the EEC Treaty as 'closer union among the peoples of Europe'; the second, the expansion in Community membership that has occured over the past 22 years. The third section describes the background to and main provisions of the Single European Act 1986 (SEA), while the final section outlines the principal features of the Maastricht Treaty. This part also previews very briefly the difficulties created for the United Kingdom by the powerful desire on the part of the majority of member states to achieve both political and economic union.[1]

---

[1] For general guides see H Arbuthnott and G Edwards, *A Common Man's Guide to the Common Market*, London: Macmillan, 1989; N Colchester and D Buchan, *Europe Relaunched: Truths and Illusions on the Way to 1992*, London: Hutchinson, 1990;

## The Aims, Structure and Legal Characteristics of the European Community

In the case of the EEC, 'closer union among the peoples of Europe'[2] contemplated a market internal to the Community involving the abolition of all tariffs and quantitative restrictions on trade; the creation of a common external tariff subjecting all imported goods to the same conditions irrespective of their place of entry into the Community; the prohibition of practices distorting competition within the Community; and the harmonisation of laws to the extent necessary to achieve a common market. In addition to the free movement of the four primary incidents of member states' economies—goods, persons (in particular, workers), services and capital—which would be brought about by these measures, the treaty envisaged other areas of integration, for example in agriculture and transport, as well as an approximation of economic policies. This last now finds further expression in the promotion of economic and monetary union under the Treaty on European Union (TEU).

The working out of both the principles and the detail of 'closer union' in these matters has been a controversial and complex process involving lengthy negotiation and agreement upon individual, national and collective interests. The process has on occasion been acrimonious, involving decisions of acute political sensitivity, as exemplified by the recurring eruptions of 'lamb wars' between the United Kingdom and France[3] and the conflict between the United Kingdom and Spain over fishing rights which, in January 1995, presented the Conservative 'Euro-rebels' with the opportunity to embarrass the government on a Commons vote. Later chapters in this book describe the bitter divisions that this process has generated within the United Kingdom government and Parliament. Nevertheless, under the terms of the SEA which was signed by the heads of government of the 12 member states on 17 February 1986, the completion of the internal market was almost entirely achieved by 31 December 1992.

---

D Freestone and J Davidson, *The Institutional Framework of the European Communities*, London: Croom Helm, 1988; S George, *An Awkward Partner: Britain in the European Community*, Oxford: The University Press, 1990; and W Nicoll and T Salmon, *Understanding the European Communities*, London: Philip Allan, 1990.

[2] EEC Treaty Preamble para 1.

[3] See F Snyder, *New Directions in European Community Law*, London: Weidenfeld and Nicolson, 1990, pp 25–26, 76.

The founders of the treaties recognised that to achieve their aspirations it would be necessary to create an institutional framework that met two basic criteria. The first was to divide power, in a balanced way, between the two groups principally responsible for formulating Community obligations and for securing compliance with them, that is, the central executive and the member states, at the expense of democratic accountability to their citizens. The second was to ensure that member states, upon whose political tractability success would inevitably depend, enjoyed sufficient representation at the policy making stage. These constraints were, in each of the three Communities, translated into essentially the same institutional configuration: one body to represent Community interests (the Commission, and in the case of the ECSC, the High Authority), one to represent national interests (the Council of Ministers), one to provide a limited measure of democratic accountability (the European Assembly), and the fourth to provide authoritative rulings on the interpretation of Community law (the Court of Justice). From 1958 each European Assembly (known as the European Parliament from 1962) and the Court of Justice of the European Communities (CJEC) became common to all three; in 1965, what is generally known as the 'Merger Treaty' established one European Commission and one Council of Ministers to serve the three Communities.[4] As a result in particular of the concentration of these legislative and executive functions into two, rather than six, institutions, it became common to refer to the three Communities collectively as the European Community, even though each remained technically separate. In this chapter, references to the Community are, unless otherwise indicated, references to the EEC.

The treaties thus formally distribute executive, legislative and judicial power among four bodies; but the distribution of functions does not mirror exactly that to be found in the United Kingdom. Modelled on the French Conseil d'Etat, the CJEC dispenses judicial power in a manner that resembles a constitutional court, laying down propositions concerning the interpretation of Community law that are final and that cannot be reversed by legislation, only by amendment of the treaty provision in issue. While its express functions make comparisons with the role of the courts in the United Kingdom an exercise of limited value, the CJEC's approaches to the interpretation of legal texts are by no means unfamiliar. On the other hand, comparisons between the European and the United Kingdom

---

[4] The Treaty Establishing a Single Council and a Single Commission of the European Communities.

Parliaments are misleading. While its consultative role has been enhanced by the co-operation procedure introduced by the SEA and its decision making role enhanced by the negative assent procedure provided by the TEU, the European Parliament (EP) has limited law-making functions.

The third distinctive characteristic of the European Communities is that they created what the CJEC called a 'new legal order'.[5] An international agreement, which was the device by which each treaty was concluded, typically does no more than create mutual obligations for the signatories; in the case of the United Kingdom, these obligations become part of domestic law only when incorporated into it by legislation. The Community treaties, however, established legal rights and duties that were, without more ado, directly applicable in each member state and capable of being invoked by individuals. Moreover, Community law is not just an additional part of domestic law, like each new Act of Parliament. If this were so, the courts would be at liberty to determine the priority to be accorded to one source of law over another where they are apparently irreconcilable. It is a fundamental tenet of Community law that it is a legal system independent of, and different from, domestic law, and that it takes priority over domestic law; if this were not so, the aspirations of the treaties would inevitably founder on the national interests of each member state. As one writer puts it:

> [the signatories] were limiting their own sovereign rights, transferring them to institutions over which they had no direct control and endowing them with powers they did not always possess themselves. Furthermore they were not only binding the states they represented to assume new rights and obligations, they were also directly including their citizens, who became subjects of the Community.[6]

## The Expansion in Community membership

The aspirations of the Treaty of Rome were unambiguous in their contemplation of an increasing Community involvement in the economic and social affairs of member states. These aspirations were 'to promote

---

[5] *Van Gend en Loos v Nederlandse Administratie der Belatstingen Case* 26/62 [1963] ECR 1, 12.

[6] P Mathijsen, *A Guide to European Community Law*, London: Sweet and Maxwell, 1990, p 1.

throughout the Community a harmonious development of economic activities, a continuous and balanced expansion, an increase in stability, an accelerated raising of the standard of living and closer relations between the States belonging to it.'[7] Notwithstanding the vagueness with which the Treaty of Rome described the means by which these aspirations were to be realised, which, apart from the creation of a common market, involved the progressive approximation of member states' economic policies, the Community now seeks to exert control over matters for which authority has only recently been provided by the SEA and the TEU. These new policy areas are outlined in the third and fourth sections of this chapter. Like these qualitative extensions of Community influence, the quantitative expansion brought about by the increase from six member states in 1972 to 15 from 1 January 1995 have posed difficult and novel issues that on occasion have seriously threatened the stability of the Community.

For the first 15 years of its existence, the Community comprised the original six signatories: Belgium, the Federal Republic of Germany, France, Italy, Luxembourg and the Netherlands. In the following 13 years, following the decision taken by the heads of government at their meeting at the Hague in 1969 to enlarge the Community, its membership doubled: Denmark and Ireland became member states under the same treaty of accession that admitted the United Kingdom, Greece entered the Community in 1981, Portugal and Spain in 1986. This expansion inevitably disturbed the balance of economic and political power that had been established within the Community; it is simply more difficult to convince eleven than five other partners of the wisdom of a preferred option. Whether such disturbance is, from the standpoint of existing member states, desirable or, as General de Gaulle considered when objecting to the United Kingdom's applications for entry in 1961 and 1967, not, is a question that assumed renewed significance during the negotiations in 1994 that led to the accession of Austria, Finland and Sweden on 1 January 1995.

By contrast with the two relatively lengthy periods of stability in the 1960s and 1970s, the past few years have seen both the potential for and the further expansion of the Community. In late 1990 Sweden became the second (after Austria in 1989) of the EFTA (European Free Trade Association) countries to apply to join the Community. By virtue of their membership of the European Economic Area (EEA, comprising the

---

[7] EEC, Article 2.

member states and the EFTA countries) which commenced on 1 January 1994, EFTA countries have enjoyed a much closer relationship with the Community, and in March 1994 negotiations were completed for the accession of Austria and the Scandinavian countries.[8] In addition to these, Turkey (1987), Cyprus (1990), Malta (1990), Hungary (1994) and Poland (1994) have all formally applied for membership. Beyond these clear cases, the implications of the construction of a new Federal Republic of Germany as the largest member state have yet to be worked out, as have those of any further expansion likely to be brought about by the inclusion of any of the newly liberated eastern European states. A major issue which is raised by the rearrangement following the end of the cold war of Europe's geopolitical map is whether the Community should seek to widen (that is, expand) or deepen (that is, create a federal state of existing member countries) its economic and political influence. Disagreement as to which of these two possibilities was to be preferred comprised part of the context within which the Maastricht Treaty was negotiated: Euro-sceptics (especially the United Kingdom) argued that more was to be gained by assisting the former communist republics to achieve economic and political independence;[9] the federalists (especially Germany and France) argued that while those countries were in principle welcome to join, more urgent was the strengthening of the Community itself.

The first obvious consequence of these enlargements is that the Community has, by becoming bigger, become a very much more influential political and economic unit. The Community contains the most powerful western European states; together with the EFTA countries, the EEA has an internal market of 380 million people. The Community is the world's major commercial power, accounting until recently for just over one fifth of the total volume of world trade (not counting trade within the Community); this will amount to some 45 percent within the EEA. The use of this power can be controversial, as the protracted negotiations between 1986 and 1993 with the United States, other developed countries

---

[8] Norway was part of these negotiations, but in a subsequent referendum, the Norwegian population voted against entry.

[9] See Lord Waddington, HL Deb 18 December 1991 c 1334.

and the economies of the Third World concerning the proposed new terms of the General Agreement on Tariffs and Trade (GATT) attest.[10]

A second feature of the Community is the variation in the political preferences displayed by member states. In the first place, these may, as was the case with the applications by Greece, Portugal and Spain, delay entry. By reason of the terms of article 237, which provides that 'Any European State may apply to become a member of the Community', and the related Declaration on Democracy 1978 agreed between the EP, the Commission and the Council, it was not until the demise in the mid 1970s in each of these countries of essentially dictatorial regimes that their entry could be a matter for serious consideration. Similarly, the democratic deficit obtaining in the political arrangements of some eastern European countries may delay their entry.

Once within the Community, these political preferences will have an impact, sometimes negative, upon its institutions and practices. One example of this is the opposition of successive United Kingdom governments (both Labour and Conservative) to any form of proportional representation for direct elections to the EP. These were first held in 1979, but not, as the treaty envisaged, on a uniform basis.[11] Nor, for the same reason, were the subsequent elections in 1984, 1989 and 1994. A second example is the way in which the Community's political agenda for the 1970s, which included the creation of closer ties between member states by 1980, was subverted by the aggressive stance adopted by the United Kingdom, in particular when Mrs Thatcher became prime minister, towards the question of its contributions to the Community budget. This issue occupied the Community for some ten years before being resolved in 1984, a resolution not assisted by Mrs Thatcher's resentment about what she perceived to be the patronising manner of the French and Germans and their tendency to regard the Community as their own club. A third matter concerns member states' own political stability; where governments are ephemeral or indecisive, it is correspondingly more difficult for them to settle to the Community's formal and informal routines.

Another important feature is the variation in economic strength of existing, new and proposed member states. The impact that an enlarged

---

[10] On the EC's impact on the Uruguay round of the GATT talks, see S Woodcock, 'Trade diplomacy and the European Community', in J Story (ed), *The New Europe*, Oxford: Blackwell, 1993, pp 292-313.

[11] The Act concerning the election of the representatives of the Assembly by direct universal suffrage.

membership may have upon the Community's economic agenda can be seen, for example, in the way in which the balance of agricultural interests has changed since the accession of Greece and the Iberian countries. This is of importance at a time when the older, northern European member states have been endeavouring to curb the excesses of the Common Agricultural Policy (CAP). The inclusion of poorer, less industrialised member states 'has produced pressures for a reorientation of the [CAP] away from northern temperate products towards Mediterranean products, and also for more redistributive policies which will directly assist economic development in the south.'[12] Concern about these pressures was one reason for the Community's insistence on a long transitional period in agriculture preceding the entry of Portugal and Spain, and apart from political considerations, Greece's entry was delayed because its economy was for a time considered incapable of sustaining the obligations of membership. By contrast, the entry of Austria and the Scandinavian countries was welcome, first, because the strength of their economies meant that they would be net contributors to the Community budget; and, second, because they might therefore be expected to oppose the spending ambitions of the poorer countries. Even if the political arrangements obtaining in the independent states in Eastern Europe should comply with Community requirements, their economic deficiencies may mean that they would be required to occupy something less than full membership until closer convergence prevailed between their economies and those in the EEA.

The economic implications of the accession of new member states are, however, complex. Economic strengths and weaknesses are not divided equally between north and south. Both within and between member states there are areas of relative development and of prosperity: northern Italy is highly industrialised, whereas the south is poor and dependent on agriculture and fishing; Ireland is relatively under-industrialised, and some areas of the United Kingdom are relatively poor. The strength of Spain's fishing fleet was an important factor in the negotiations leading to its accession, and as the *Factortame* litigation in the United Kingdom shows,[13] the threat it posed has not solely been of an economic nature. Nor do such realignments of economic power only pose threats to the

---

[12] N Nugent, *The Government and Politics of the European Community*, London: Macmillan, 1989, p 49.

[13] *R v Secretary of State, ex p Factortame* [1991] 3 All E.R. 769 (CJEC). See Chapter 3.

existing membership. France, with its substantial Mediterranean economy, and more obviously Italy, may benefit from a more pronounced Mediterranean interest in the working out of Community policy.

In short, enlarged membership has brought and constantly threatens change. Decision-making has become more complex and more tortuous as more interests and preferences affect agenda issues. For example, the boundaries between the four Community institutions whose responsibilities were conceived in the Treaty of Rome as discrete elements, have become blurred. No longer is the Council of Ministers confined to deciding upon what the European Commission proposes; it has also assumed a policy-making role. This was perhaps inevitable given that its creation was to ensure that Treaty objectives were realised at a pace acceptable to the member states. A further development has been the gradual entrenchment, formally recognised by the SEA and the Maastricht Treaty, of the European Council, the regular 'summit' meetings of the member states' heads of government. The tendency to refer all matters of significance upon which the Council of Ministers fails to agree to this body underlines the erosion of the treaty's conception of a precise institutional balance between the interests of the member states (the Council of Ministers) and those of the Community (the Commission). This diversification in decision-making has in turn encouraged the proliferation of groups representing every conceivable interest that is touched by the Community, whose sole function is to monitor and to seek to influence Community policy.

The most recent expansion of the Community also raised difficult questions concerning the formal voting influence that each member state should have; these difficulties are discussed below in the context of the system of qualified majority voting.

## The Single European Act

### *The background*

During the Community's first ten years many aspects of the Treaty of Rome's principal features were set in place, for example the CAP and the customs union, while its institutions and budgetary arrangements assumed a relatively settled shape. The economic progress achieved by the six founding states was substantially due to the fact that these developments coincided with their own national interests. However, largely owing to

General de Gaulle's opposition, little headway was made towards the realisation of the goal of closer union between the member states. With his departure, the six heads of government, persuaded by the new leaders of the French and German governments, Georges Pompidou and Willy Brandt, agreed at their 1969 meeting at the Hague to set about the completion of the Community. This did not prove readily compatible with the goal of an enlarged membership, also agreed at that meeting. One of the first consequences of the accession of the United Kingdom was, as has been noted, the protracted and difficult negotiations concerning its budgetary contribution. This was always going to be a problem given its historic trading pattern, and it brought the United Kingdom into conflict with France over the application of the CAP to the production of lamb and mutton, culminating in the trade wars of 1978–80.[14] The question of its budgetary contribution was superficially dealt with by the Labour government's 'renegotiation' during 1974 and 1975 of the United Kingdom's membership of the Community, a process that further obstructed discussion on wider issues and was not finally resolved for another ten years. Factors beyond the Community also contributed to a period of some difficulty. Whereas the 1960s had seen widespread and sustained economic growth, the substantial increases in the price of oil in 1973–74 and again in 1979–80 encouraged a world-wide recession. Progress towards closer union during the 1970s was therefore modest, with procedural activity acting as a substitute for policy.[15]

By contrast, greater success was achieved in the objective of enlarging the Community. In the early 1980s, buoyed by the successful completion of entry negotiations with Greece, Portugal and Spain respectively and by the completion of the common fisheries policy, attention once more returned to the question of European Union. A bland draft European Act promoted by the West German and Italian foreign ministers, Hans-Dietrich Genscher and Emilio Colombo, led to a Solemn Declaration that was agreed at the heads of government meeting at Stuttgart in June 1983, but the first significant move was a proposal approved by the EP in 1984 advocating a European Union to replace the Treaty of Rome. The instrument was drafted by a specially appointed committee and contemplated a radically reformed Community having explicit federal implications. In this it reflected the aspirations of one of the veterans of

---

[14] Snyder, op cit.
[15] See E Regelsberger, 'European political cooperation', in J Story (ed), *The New Europe*, Oxford: Blackwell, 1993, pp 270–291.

European integration, Altiero Spinelli. Under the European Union Treaty (EUT), the EP's decision-making role was to be enhanced at the expense of that of the member states, and many areas then within the exclusive jurisdiction of national governments, such as internal security, the suppression of terrorism, disarmament, health, welfare, and economic and monetary policy were to be brought within the Community's ambit.

Not surprisingly, some of the member states had serious reservations concerning this proposal, involving as it did a substantial accretion of Community power. However, sufficient of them were prepared to examine the proposals in detail. Encouraged by their resolution at Fontainebleau in June 1984 of the United Kingdom's budget contribution, the heads of government established two ad hoc committees to prepare background papers. In terms of its implications for the Community, the more important of these was the report of the committee chaired by the former Irish foreign minister, James Dooge, on 'Institutional Affairs'. In order to limit the opportunities for member states to use their veto under the Luxembourg Compromise (discussed below), it advocated the adoption of further occasions on which majority voting within the Council of Ministers would be permissible. It also took up the EUT proposals to increase the powers of the EP. On the policy side, it stressed the need for the Community to develop, for example, regional policies, and to establish a genuine internal market. As with the EUT proposals, these recommendations did not command complete support, Denmark, Greece and the United Kingdom in particular expressing so many reservations that they became known as 'the footnote countries'.

Nevertheless, the inter-governmental conference which the Dooge Committee recommended as the next step took place in Luxembourg in 1985, from which emerged the SEA. Reflecting the divisions of opinion that preceded it, the Act turned out to be a diluted version of the 1984 draft instrument, amending rather than replacing the Treaty of Rome, and, because of ratification difficulties in Ireland and Denmark, not coming into force until 1987.

*The Act's main provisions*

The main provisions of the SEA can be divided into those affecting the procedures of the Community's institutions, and those extending the Community's reach over member states' economic and political activities.

First, the Act gave recognition to the European Council. Though these regular meetings of the heads of government had over the years acquired increasing significance in terms of the promotion and realisation of Community policy, they had, until then, no official status within the Community's institutional framework as the treaty specified the Council of Ministers as the forum in which national interests would be represented. Even with the European Council's further enhancement in the TEU, the Council of Ministers retains its role, as no proposal agreed by the former will progress unless the latter has approved it.

Secondly, the SEA introduced changes to the powers of the EP. Under the 'co-operation procedure', proposals by the Commission based on certain treaty articles may be amended at first reading by the EP, and become the subject of a 'common position' achieved by the Council, if necessary on the basis of a qualified majority vote. The EP then has three months within which to consider and return the proposal (with or without amendment) after second reading, taking account also of the Commission's views upon it. Should the EP reject the proposal, the Council may only proceed with it if it is unanimous. If the EP proposes amendments to the common position, the proposal is re-examined by the Commission (along with the EP's objections to the common position), returning it within a month to the Council with its own recommendations. The Council in turn may accept the re-examined proposal by a qualified majority, or if it wishes to amend it further, by a unanimous vote. While complex, the co-operation procedure is a modest advance in the EP's involvement in the making of Community law. Although proving a disappointment to those who wished to see it given a more prominent role, the procedure offers the EP a greater say without giving it a decisive voice.

Thirdly, in order to ensure that individual member states could not obstruct progress towards completion of the internal market, the SEA introduced changes to the rules governing voting in the Council of Ministers. The treaty specifies occasions on which unanimity is required; for example, on finance and taxation, the accession of new members, the election of a new President of the Commission, and where the Council, acting on a proposal from the Commission, wishes to adopt an act constituting an amendment to the proposal. The Treaty also provides that voting on all other matters is by simple majority unless otherwise specified.[16] In fact, on many issues of importance (for example, the internal market, health, the environment) the treaty does otherwise specify, in a procedure known as qualified majority voting. This weights the votes

---

[16] Art 148(1).

of the member states (for example, the largest, France, Germany, Italy and the United Kingdom are valued at 10, the smallest, Luxembourg, at 2; the total weighting of all 15 member states being 87), and then imposes conditions to be met if a majority vote is to carry a proposal.[17] In the commonest instance, where the Council is voting on a proposal from the Commission, the majority must be at least 62.

These procedures have meant that the four largest members cannot dictate to the others. They also meant, prior to the accession of the three new member states on 1 January 1995, when the total weighting was 76 and the majority 54, that the blocking vote of 23 could be achieved by the votes of two of the largest member states and one of those weighted at three (Denmark and Ireland). But during the negotiations in March 1994 concerning the accession of these new member states, the Commission proposed that, with the forthcoming increase in the weighted total to 87, there should be an increase in the blocking vote to 26 (these figures would have been 90 and 27 if Norway had not voted against membership later in 1994). This increase would then require (in the instance given) the vote of a fourth member state (and a fifth if one of the four were Luxembourg) for a block to be effective. The proposal caused the United Kingdom considerable difficulty during these negotiations, since its effect would be to weaken the influence of any one of the largest member states to obstruct the Commission's wishes.

With Spain, the United Kingdom argued for the retention of the 23 vote threshold, but in the face of the adamant position taken by the other 10 member countries, settled for the compromise suggested by the Greek presidency at the foreign ministers' meeting at Ioannina in March 1994. Under this compromise, the blocking minority threshold was increased as agreed by the majority, but with the condition that if 23 blocking votes were cast, 'the Council will do all in its power to reach, within a reasonable time and without prejudicing obligatory time limits ... a satisfactory solution that could be adopted by at least 68 votes.'

In practice, the Council has usually reached a consensus; a blocking vote has been effective on only a few occasions since the United Kingdom's accession to the Community. In part this reflects a desire to reach agreement, and in part the effect of the arrangements concluded at Luxembourg in 1966. These were designed to break the deadlock caused by General de Gaulle's refusal to accept the automatic transfer of national

---

[17] Art 148(2).

agricultural levies and duties to the Community as its 'own resources' (as required by article 201) in place of the Community being financed by national contributions voted by each member state. The Commission's proposal to implement article 201 was accompanied by two related proposals, to complete the financing arrangements of the CAP and to give the EP control over the budget. Despite his interest in finalising the CAP, de Gaulle was strongly opposed to the diminution in member states' autonomy that these increases in the Community's influence implied. Unable to disentangle the three proposals, France boycotted the Council, and for six months Community decision making at this level was at a standstill. French grievances were resolved by what is generally known as the Luxembourg Compromise, which provides that:

> Where, in the case of decisions which may be taken by majority vote on a proposal of the Commission, very important interests of one or more partners are at stake, the Members of the Council will endeavour, within a reasonable time, to reach solutions which can be adopted by all the Members of the Council while respecting their mutual interests and those of the Community, in accordance with Article 2 of the Treaty.

The arrangement noted that there 'is a divergence of views on what should be done in the event of failure to reach complete agreement', though the French view has been that discussion should continue until unanimity is achieved. It should also be noted that there was no definition of what constitutes 'very important interests', but unilateral attempts by member states to provide their own definition when invoking the Compromise have largely been unsuccessful. The other member states have required the objecting member to convince them that its objection is indeed based on a vital national interest, and that the use of the Compromise is appropriate.

Despite efforts by the United Kingdom in 1986 to formalise this agreement to disagree, the Luxembourg Compromise remains just that, involving no change to the treaty provisions on voting in the Council. Both France and the United Kingdom have, in recent years, continued to express support for its continued potential, but set against the extended provisions on qualified majority voting in the SEA and the Maastricht Treaty, it seems unlikely that it will be successfully invoked again.

The SEA extends the qualified majority procedure to six articles of the treaty which have hitherto required unanimity, and to amendments introduced by the Act. One of the most important of these is article 100A which deals principally with the internal market. As majority voting has become more common, the opportunities for member states to insist upon their own interests have become, as was intended, fewer. This in turn has on occasion prompted states who have been outvoted to challenge the legality of a measure before the Court of Justice, if they can find a legal technicality, as for example, did the United Kingdom on the hormones and battery hen directives. It has, secondly, led to disputes concerning the legal base of Community measures, as in the hormones case where the United Kingdom argued that the directive should have been based on article 100 (requiring unanimity) and not article 43 (qualified majority).

On the policy side, the SEA is probably most widely known for its requirement that the internal market was to be completed by 1 January 1993. This timetable was proposed by a 'White Paper' prepared by the Commission in 1985 under the chairmanship of the British vice-president, Lord Cockfield. What was required was the removal of all physical, technical and fiscal barriers to the free movement of goods, persons, services and capital. This objective was strongly backed, in particular by the larger and more influential transnational commercial and financial interests.[18] But while the deregulation and liberalisation of markets was especially attractive to the United Kingdom governments of the 1980s, they maintained some substantial reservations. Contemplating the implications of the absence of border controls, for example, Mrs Thatcher observed, 'I didn't join Europe to have the free movement of terrorists, criminals, drugs, plant and animal diseases and rabies, and illegal immigrants.'[19] In February 1995 a junior minister (Charles Wardle MP) at the Department of Trade and Industry (and former junior Minister at the Home Office) resigned over what he perceived to be the threat of uncontrolled immigration into the United Kingdom implied by the abolition of passport controls within the Community. Despite the government's assurances, this issue continues to be politically controversial.

The SEA also authorised other important extensions in the Community's reach over member states' affairs in the pursuit of 'ever closer union': research and technological development, the environment, economic and social cohesion (better known as regional policy), economic and monetary

---

[18] See A Bressand, 'The 1992 breakthrough and the global economic agenda', in J Story (ed) *The New Europe*, Oxford: Blackwell, 1993, pp 314–327.

[19] Quoted in G Edwards, 'Britain and Europe', in J Story (ed) *The New Europe*, Oxford: Blackwell, 1993, pp 187–227, 222.

union, and foreign policy. As in its earlier history, these qualitative accretions to Community power have proved controversial both in their determination and their implementation.

During the 1980s the heads of government came to accept that a condition of European political union was the development of a common foreign policy. Article 30/7a of Title III of the SEA requires that member states 'shall endeavour to adopt common positions on subjects covered by this Title'; other paragraphs enjoin member states not to be subversive of the agreed position on foreign affairs matters (article 30/3c), but to work towards making the Community a 'cohesive force in international relations' (article 30/2d) and to implement joint action in appropriate cases (article 30/2a). On some matters, such as its attitude to the Gulf war, the Arab-Israeli conflict, South Africa and the Balkans conflict, the Community has achieved *acquis politique* (an agreed position), but national divisions necessarily persist. The United Kingdom adopted a very different response to that initially taken by the rest of the Community to the invasion by Argentinian troops of the Falkland Islands in 1982, and its 'special relationship' with the United States meant that the United Kingdom government did not join member states in condemning the air raids on Libya that were launched by the US air force from British mainland bases.[20]

## The Treaty on European Union

The United Kingdom has always been cast as a reluctant member of the Community. A declining industrial base together with the economic consensus of Butskellism meant that upon its accession in 1973, the United Kingdom joined the Community under very different economic conditions and with a different outlook than obtained among the six founding states. Subsequent differences over its budgetary contribution, together with its (declining) role within the Commonwealth and successive governments' desire to maintain the 'special relationship' with the United States, have meant that the United Kingdom has never approached the Community's long term political aspirations with enthusiasm. Mrs Thatcher's antipathy to what she perceived to be the erosion of sovereignty implied by political union was, during the late 1980s, tempered by her pragmatic support for

---

[20] On these issues see E Regelsberger, 'European political cooperation', in J Story (ed) *The New Europe*, Oxford: Blackwell, 1993, pp 270–291.

the completion of the internal market. Economic and monetary union were, however, very far removed from the vision of a Europe of sovereign states economically liberal, deregulated and interdependent, and based on political co-operation but not integration which she described in her Bruges speech in September 1988.[21] Nevertheless, the United Kingdom did become a member of the European Monetary System (EMS) and entered the negotiations on economic and monetary union, even if some senior Cabinet members took the view that the EMS was a Franco-German plot. The United Kingdom's subsequent enforced withdrawal in September 1992 from membership of the exchange rate mechanism (ERM) merely confirmed for the Euro-sceptics the folly of joining the EMS in the first place.[22]

The United Kingdom's suspicions about the long term implications of closer union between the member states were forcefully and divisively brought to a head by the intergovernmental conferences which took place during 1991 and which culminated in agreement being reached at Maastricht on 11 December of that year, and the TEU being signed on 7 February 1992.[23] This treaty, which covers a variety of matters, seeks to advance European union on two broad fronts: European political co-operation (leading to political union) and economic and monetary union.

While relatively modest by comparison with economic and monetary union, the more particular means by which European political co-operation is to be achieved goes some way beyond the conception of closer union contemplated by the Community's founders. One of these ways, as has been noted above, is the identification of a Community foreign policy. It is envisaged that the Community will speak with one voice on international affairs (for example, the conflict in Bosnia), eventually developing a common defence policy co-ordinated by the Western European Union.

---

[21] See G Edwards, 'Britain and Europe', in J Story (ed) *The New Europe*, Oxford: Blackwell, 1993, pp 187–227.

[22] To understand the impetus for EMU, it is necessary to understand the mutual interests in stable and linked exchange rates for Germany as the prime exporting country within the Community, and for France as its main trading partner. For the French, stable exchange rates are necessary to ensure predictability in farm prices under the CAP. For Germany, the link established by the ERM with the weaker European currencies means that a strong Deutschmark is less likely to advance against the dollar, with adverse consequences for the price competitiveness of German products on international markets. See J Story and M de Cecco, 'The politics of monetary union: 1985–1991', in J Story (ed) *The New Europe*, Oxford: Blackwell, 1993, pp 328–354.

[23] On these divisions see Chapter 10.

Secondly, member states' citizens will become European citizens. Amongst other consequences, citizenship will entitle them to vote or stand in elections to the EP, wherever in the Community they happen to reside. In addition, European citizens will be able to petition the Parliament and appeal against administrative malpractice to a Community Ombudsman. Political co-operation also implies common positions on home and legal affairs, notably transnational crime and immigration. The treaty also effects some changes in the locus of decision-making. Under article 189b, the EP will be able to negotiate directly with the Council of Ministers and, through a negative assent procedure, may block certain types of legislation if an absolute majority of its members vote against them. This introduces a kind of co-decision between the EP and the Council.

Another significant shift in decision making is implied by the principle of subsidiarity, introduced in article 3b. Regarded by Euro-sceptics as a victory for decentralisation rather than federalism,[24] this is intended to give effect to the treaty's express recognition of the constitutional traditions, rights and duties and the 'national identity' of member states (in a manner reminiscent of the 'states' rights' clause in article 30 of the German Basic Law). Article 3b reads:

> This Community shall act within the limits of the powers conferred on it by this Treaty and of the objectives assigned to it therein. In areas which do not fall within its exclusive competence, the Community shall take action, in accordance with the principle of subsidiarity, only if and so far as the objectives of the proposed action cannot be sufficiently achieved by the Member States and can therefore, by reason of the scale or effects of the proposed action, be better achieved by the Community. Any action by the Community shall not go beyond what is necessary to achieve the objectives of this Treaty.

While the principle of subsidiarity can be readily expressed, that decisions should be taken 'as closely as possible to the citizen' (the preamble to the treaty), there are significant areas of doubt about its application. One concerns the exemption to which article 3b refers. If a matter falls within the Community's exclusive competence, the question of subsidiarity does not arise; but neither the Treaty of Rome nor the TEU make any explicit

---

[24] But this depends on what concept of federalism is employed; see N Emiliou, 'Subsidiarity: panacea or fig-leaf?' in D O'Keefe and P Twomey (eds), *Legal Issues of the Maastricht Treaty*, London: Chancery Lane Publishing, 1994, pp 65–83.

distinction between exclusive and non-exclusive areas of competence. One view is that such exclusivity can only apply to matters on which the Community has already legislated, since if it were to apply to post-treaty legislation, the principle's purpose would be substantially undermined.[25]

A second area of doubt concerns the relationship between the subsidiarity principle as expressed in article 3b, and the proportionality principle expressed in its final sentence. The subsidiarity principle seeks to deal with two matters: to assess whether there is a need for Community action in a given area and, if the need is established, to control the exercise of such Community action as is taken. It is well established that the Community should exercise such powers as most efficiently achieve its objectives. But efficiency may contemplate a more extensive exercise of power than would follow from the adoption of the competing, and equally well established Community principle, proportionality. This is expressed in article 3b as dependent on what is necessary to achieve the objective. The proportionality principle may, therefore, be seen as a secondary constraint on the exercise of Community power. At its meeting at Edinburgh in 1992, the European Council approved the following guidelines for the interpretation of article 3b:

(1)   is the proposed action within the limits of the powers conferred on the Community by the Treaty and aimed at meeting one or more of the Treaty objectives?

(2)   if so, can the objectives of the proposed action not be sufficiently achieved by Member States?

(3)   if not, what should be the nature and intensity of Community action?

Critics argue that these guidelines introduce no greater specificity, and that it will be possible to formulate the 'proposed action' in such a way that it will satisfy both those who wish to invoke and those who wish to

---

[25] See J Steiner, 'Subsidiarity under the Maastricht Treaty', in D O'Keefe and P Twomey (eds), *Legal Issues of the Maastricht Treaty*, London: Chancery Lane Publishing, 1994, pp 49–64, 58.

deny article 3b's application in any given case.[26] Moreover, there is serious doubt as to the justiciability of subsidiarity before the CJEC.[27]

'A stage in the realisation of ever closer Union between the peoples' of the Community, Maastricht was, like the SEA, a compromise between deeply felt and often unmoving positions, in particular concerning state autonomy. For the United Kingdom, the government hailed the elimination of the 'F' word (federalism) as a considerable triumph of negotiation, which also saw the concession on the opt-out on the Social Chapter. For France and Germany, on the other hand, the federal goal has merely been postponed, to be secured with the completion of economic and monetary union. The treaty binds member states to an irreversible commitment to monetary union by 1997–99. It envisages this to be achieved in three stages. The first entails the creation of a system of central banks whose principal function will be to foster price stability within the Community. This 'basic fitness exercise', in which member states will be urged to demonstrate budgetary control, is to be followed by a three year period during which they are expected to bring their economies to convergence.[28] The final stage is the irrevocable fixing of exchange rates, leading to a single European currency.

The United Kingdom's ambivalence about monetary union and its political implications have continued to create divisions both within the Community and the Conservative government. In readiness for the 1996 intergovernmental conference, the French and German foreign ministers, Alain Juppe and Klaus Kinkel, confirmed their view that the Community could proceed to monetary union recognising that some member states would take longer than others to meet the conditions for convergence. But the notion of a 'two-tier' Europe, in which Franco-German interests appear to drive the Community agenda, only served to fuel the Tory Euro-sceptics' opposition, and led to the removal of the whip following their abstention on a government motion in the Commons. The divisions that appeared between the Prime Minister, the Chancellor of the Exchequer and other Cabinet ministers in early 1995 as to the constitutional significance of a single currency were, for many commentators,

---

[26] T Hartley, 'Constitutional and institutional aspects of the Maastricht agreement' *International and Comparative Law Quarterly*, vol 42, 1992, pp 213–237.

[27] A Toth, 'A legal analysis of subsidiarity', in D O'Keefe and P Twomey (eds), *Legal Issues of the Maastricht Treaty*, London: Chancery Lane Publishing, 1994, pp 37–48.

[28] D Arter, *The Politics of European Integration in the Twentieth Century*, London: Dartmouth, 1993, p 210.

reminiscent of the divisions that were evident during Mrs Thatcher's third term of office. Taking a longer view, they reflect the fundamental issues about the United Kingdom's position within and attitude towards the Community that have been constant features of the parliamentary history of its membership of the European Community.

# 3

# The Constitutional Background

## Alan Page

### Introduction

Revolutions, for the lawyer, the late JDB Mitchell once observed, 'come in all sorts of shapes and ways.'[1] According to Mitchell, the United Kingdom's accession to the European Communities was a revolution, one destined to leave its imprint on constitutional theory.[2] In the same way as legal theory had caught up with the political reality of the dismantling of the Empire and its replacement by the Commonwealth, so too it would catch up with the political reality reflected in the United Kingdom's membership of what is now the European Union. It may well be that with the passage of time accession will come to be seen as having marked a watershed in our constitutional development, but for the moment we occupy the European Union equivalent of the 'half-world' between Empire and Commonwealth of which Mitchell wrote.[3] It follows that the doctrinal consequences of membership are impossible to state with certainty. Concern with doctrine, however, should not obscure the consequences of membership for the legislative, executive and judicial branches of government. It is with these consequences that we are here concerned.

### Parliament

The conventional shorthand way of describing parliament's position within the constitution before accession was to say that it was 'sovereign'. By this was meant that its legislative competence was unlimited, and that there

---

[1] J D B Mitchell, 'The Sovereignty of Parliament and Community Law: The Stumbling Block That Isn't There' *International Affairs,* vol 55, January 1979, pp 33–46.

[2] See also J D B Mitchell, 'British Law and British Membership' *Europarecht,* vol 6, April 1971, pp 97–118; 'What Happened To The Constitution On 1st January 1973' *Cambrian Law Review,* vol 11, 1980, pp 69–86.

[3] 'British Law And Membership', p 104.

was no other body whose legislative competence rivalled or exceeded that of parliament. Dicey, the most renowned exponent of the doctrine, wrote:

> The principle of Parliamentary sovereignty means neither more nor less than this ... namely, that Parliament ... has, under the English constitution, the right to make or unmake any law whatever; and, further, that no person or body is recognised by the law of England as having a right to override or set aside the legislation of Parliament.[4]

Thus defined, the sovereignty of parliament was 'the dominant characteristic of our political institutions', and 'the very keystone of the law of the constitution.'[5]

The origins of the doctrine of parliamentary sovereignty as expounded by Dicey may be traced to the 17th century constitutional conflict between the Crown on the one hand and parliament and the courts on the other. Parliament emerged from that conflict occupying a uniquely powerful position in the constitution. The basis of that position was that its approval, expressed in the form of legislation, was required to change the law and to raise taxes.[6] The combined effect of these requirements was that there were few aspects of *domestic* policy that did not require the legislatively expressed sanction of parliament.

Parliament never succeeded in asserting the same degree of control over government in the field of *foreign* policy. The making and subsequent ratification of treaties, for example, continued to be treated as executive acts. There too, however, parliament's role in the legislative process—its monopoly of law-making—was protected by the rule that a treaty had first to be incorporated by statute if it was to have the force of law in the United Kingdom. The position was explained by Lord Atkin in *A-G for Canada* v *A-G for Ontario:*[7]

> Within the British Empire there is a well-established rule that the making of a treaty is an executive act, while the performance of its obligations, if they entail alteration of the existing domestic law, requires legislative action. Unlike some other countries, the stipulations

---

[4] A Dicey, *An Introduction to the Study of the Law of the Constitution,* London and Basingstoke: Macmillan, 10th ed, 1959, pp 39–40.

[5] Ibid, pp 39 and 70.

[6] *Case of Proclamations* (1611) 12 Co Rep 74; Bill of Rights 1689, Art 4.

[7] [1937] AC 326.

of a treaty duly ratified do not within the Empire, by virtue of the treaty alone, have the force of law. If the national executive, the government of the day, decide to incur the obligations of a treaty which involve alteration of law they have to run the risk of obtaining the assent of Parliament to the necessary statute or statutes.[8]

Were the executive not to be obliged to obtain parliamentary approval to incorporating legislation, it would be in a position to alter individual rights and duties without submitting itself to the disciplines, in the form of the need to explain and defend its proposals and to secure the repeated support of a majority for them, inherent in the legislative process.

Against this background, the major consequence of membership for parliament is that its approval is no longer a pre-requisite of the making of legislation having domestic legal effect. One of the features of the European Communities, as we saw in the last chapter, is that the institutions—the Council of Ministers and to a lesser extent the Commission—have power under the Treaties to adopt measures which automatically become law in member states. Such measures have the force of law in the United Kingdom by virtue of the European Communities Act 1972, section 2(1) of which provides that 'enforceable Community rights', *ie* rights which 'in accordance with the Treaties are without further enactment to be given legal effect or used in the United Kingdom', are to be 'recognised and available in law, and ... enforced, allowed and followed accordingly.' In contrast to the provisions of a treaty, which as we have seen must first be incorporated by statute if they are to be given domestic legal effect, Community legislation thus has effect without any intervening act on the part of the Westminster parliament being necessary or indeed, according to the European Court, permissible.[9]

Although the European Communities Act gave the force of law to Community legislation in the United Kingdom, it did not seek to impose any restriction on parliament's legislative competence. There were good reasons for this. The rule that parliament's legislative competence was unlimited was commonly held to be subject to the exception that no parliament could bind its successors; were it to have the power to do so, the result would be to limit their (unlimited) legislative competence.[10] An

---

[8] [1937] AC at 347.

[9] *Variola* v *Amministratzione Italiana delle Finanze* [1973] ECR 981.

[10] Dicey, op cit, pp 64–70; *Ellen Street Estates Ltd* v *Minister of Health* [1934] 1 KB 590.

attempt to restrict the legislative freedom of future parliaments would thus have been of questionable legal effect, as well as politically inflammatory. It was in any case unnecessary. All that was necessary, given that legislation in the United Kingdom is by and large a function of government,[11] was that the government should refrain from promoting legislation inconsistent with the United Kingdom's obligations as a member of the Communities. So long as this self-imposed limitation is observed, the result is a reduction in the practical scope of the exercise of parliament's theoretically unlimited legislative power.

In contrast to the member states, the Communities (and the Union) only have such powers as are conferred on them by the Treaties. The practical scope of the exercise of parliament's legislative competence is therefore only restricted within the boundaries of the Communities' competence; outside those boundaries the scope for the exercise of its competence remains undisturbed. When the Communities were first established the boundaries of their legislative competence were relatively narrowly drawn: in *Costa* v *ENEL,* the European Court spoke of the member states having limited their sovereign rights, 'albeit within limited fields'.[12] The effect of the Single European Act and the Treaty on European Union, however, has been markedly to extend those boundaries. The loss of law-making power parliament has experienced as a result of accession has therefore increased.[13]

Although the practical scope of the exercise of parliament's legislative competence has been reduced as a result of membership, parliament has not renounced all say in matters concerning the Union. Amendments to the treaties, including the EC Treaty and the Treaty on European Union, must be ratified in accordance with member states' constitutional requirements before they enter into force.[14] In the United Kingdom, as we have seen, ratification is a matter for the executive, but where the obligations to be assumed under a treaty entail changes in domestic law, those changes must be made by statute. Rather than run the risk of parliament refusing to give its sanction to required changes, and thus of being unable to fulfil

---

[11] D Miers and A Page, *Legislation,* London: Sweet and Maxwell, 2nd ed, 1990, pp 5–7.

[12] [1964] ECR 585 at 593.

[13] It was in response to this narrowing of the legislative competence of the member states that the principle of subsidiarity was incorporated in the EC Treaty: see above, pp 26–28.

[14] See eg Article 236 EC.

obligations assumed under a treaty, the practice is for the executive to refrain from ratifying a treaty until the necessary changes in domestic law have been made by parliament.[15] As a matter of constitutional practice, therefore, parliamentary approval of any consequential changes to domestic law is a pre-condition of executive ratification of an amending treaty.

Under the European Communities Act some consequential changes to domestic law may be made by way of subordinate legislation. Section 1(3) of the Act empowers the government to declare that a treaty is to be regarded as one of the 'Community Treaties'—with the result that rights created by or under the treaty must in accordance with section 2(1) of the Act be given effect in the United Kingdom—by Order in Council approved in draft by both Houses of Parliament. In theory, therefore, it is open to the executive to curtail the scope for parliamentary discussion by relying on Orders in Council under section 1(3) of the 1972 Act rather than primary legislation. In practice this has not happened. The two enlargement Treaties and the Single European Act as well as the Treaty on European Union and the Agreement on the European Economic Area have all been given effect by Act of Parliament.[16] This in turn creates an expectation that any changes in domestic law required by future amending treaties will likewise be made by primary legislation.

That expectation has been reinforced by the introduction of specific safeguards of parliament's position. The prototype of such safeguards is contained in section 6 of the European Parliamentary Elections Act 1978. This provision, which was introduced in response to fears that any increase in the powers of the Strasbourg Parliament would be at the expense of its Westminster counterpart, fetters the executive's treaty-making power by requiring a treaty which provides for an increase in the powers of the European Parliament to be approved by Act of Parliament before it is ratified by the United Kingdom. Since both the Single European Act and the Treaty on European Union provided for an increase in the powers of the European Parliament, the government was thus obliged to obtain parliamentary approval of those Treaties in the form of

---

[15] HC Deb 15 February 1993 c 31.

[16] By the European Communities (Greek Accession) Act 1979, the European Communities (Spanish and Portuguese Accession) Act 1985, the European Communities (Amendment) Act 1986, the European Communities (Amendment) Act 1993 and the European Economic Area Act 1993.

an Act of Parliament before ratifying them.[17] The example set by section 6 of the 1978 Act has now been followed in the European Communities (Amendment) Act 1993, section 2 of which stipulates that no notification is to be given to the Council of Ministers that the United Kingdom intends to move to the third stage of economic and monetary union unless, *inter alia*, a draft of the notification has first been approved by Act of Parliament.

Apart from questions relating to the future development of the Union and the United Kingdom's place within it, parliament also has a continuing role in the implementation of Community obligations, not all of which are directly applicable in the sense of taking effect without any intervening act on the part of the national legislature being necessary.[18] An efficiency scrutiny set up to examine ways of minimising the burden on business imposed by EC law estimated that over a third of existing United Kingdom legislation (including subordinate legislation) arose from an obligation to implement Community law.[19] Most Community obligations are implemented by subordinate legislation but primary legislation may, and in certain cases must, be used: the Directive on Product Liability, for example, was implemented by the Consumer Protection Act 1987.[20] In contrast to primary legislation that has no Community dimension, however, the scope for amendment is confined by the binding nature of the obligations assumed. As Mitchell observed, the legislature can play

> only a limited and automatic role. It is cut out of any real choice as to substance (which is governed by the directive) and is confined, at most, to a technical role more appropriate to a Parliamentary Draftsman. While one can appreciate the reasons for adopting directives one can see the problems of Parliamentary *amour propre* to which they can give rise.[21]

---

[17] European Communities (Amendment) Act 1986, s.3(4); European Communities (Amendment) Act 1993, s 1(2). As regards the latter, the Divisional Court, in *R v Secretary of State for Foreign and Commonwealth Affairs, ex parte Rees-Mogg*, rejected a claim that by ratifying the protocol on social policy the United Kingdom government was in breach of section 6 of the 1978 Act: *The Times Law Reports* 31 July 1993.

[18] Directly applicable Community legislation may also require to be supplemented.

[19] Department of Trade and Industry, *Review of the Implementation and Enforcement of EC Law in the UK* (1993) Introduction, para 1.

[20] And see below, pp 38–40.

[21] 'British Law and British Membership', p 106.

The effect of membership has thus been to diminish parliament's role in the legislative process overall, an effect which has been reinforced by the Single European Act and the Treaty on European Union. To the extent that Parliament's role in the constitution depends on its legislative role, therefore, it is difficult to avoid the conclusion that its importance has been diminished. However, its importance has not been diminished to the extent, implicit in the European Communities Act, that it has proved possible to give domestic legal effect to amending treaties by subordinate legislation. Instead primary legislation has been used, and parliament's position has been strengthened by the requirement of its approval expressed in the form of primary legislation in respect of increases in the power of the European Parliament and movement to the third stage of economic and monetary union.

## The Executive

The executive, in contrast to parliament, emerged from the 17th century constitutional conflict with few inherent powers, dependent on the sanction of parliament for changing the law, raising taxes and (later) spending money. Its position was to be transformed by the rise of representative, and with it, party government, so that by virtue of its command of a majority on which it could normally rely to vote in its favour it could be confident of getting what it wanted by way of legislation. The sovereignty of parliament became the sovereignty of the executive. Nevertheless it remained the case that it required parliamentary approval to legislate, to raise taxes and to spend money.

When the United Kingdom first joined the Communities, the consequence for the executive upon which most emphasis was placed was the increased freedom it had acquired to act, in combination with governments of other member states, without the domestic consequences of that action being subject to the need for parliamentary approval or the degree of discussion and scrutiny formerly associated with the legislative process. As the Select Committee on European Legislation observed:

... the Executive itself by agreeing with the other Member governments to a proposal for legislation makes the law, *ie* has assumed the constitutional function and power of Parliament ...[22]

In this respect the executive had escaped the confines of the 17th century constitutional settlement.

This theme of increased freedom was underscored by the vastly increased power of delegated law-making the executive assumed under the European Communities Act for the purpose of implementing Community obligations. Section 2(2) of the Act empowers the government to legislate for the purpose of:

(a)    implementing the Community obligations of the United Kingdom or enabling such obligations to be implemented,

(b)    enabling rights enjoyed or to be enjoyed by the United Kingdom under or by virtue of the Treaties to be exercised, or

(c)    dealing with matters arising out of or related to such obligations or rights (or the operation from time to time of section 2(1)).

Such legislation may include 'any such provision (of any such extent) as might be made by Act of Parliament'.[23] Section 2(2) also provides that in the exercise of other delegated law-making powers regard may be had to the objects of the Communities and to enforceable Community rights, thereby enabling directives to be implemented and regulations supplemented under other delegated law-making powers appropriate to the subject matter of the directive or regulation in question.[24]

The European Communities Act imposes limits on the power to make delegated legislation in the implementation of Community obligations, which reflect 'a general understanding of what is inappropriate to statutory instruments'.[25] Under Schedule 2 to the Act the power conferred by section 2(2) may not be used to make provisions:

---

[22] Second Report from the Select Committee on European Secondary Legislation, 1972–73, HC 463, para 34.

[23] European Communities Act, s 2(4).

[24] In certain limited circumstances directives may be implemented by administrative action.

[25] J Mitchell, S Kuipers and B Gall, 'Constitutional Aspects of the Treaty and Legislation Relating to British Membership' *Common Market Law Review,* vol 9, 1972, p 140.

(a)   imposing or increasing taxation,

(b)   having retrospective effect,

(c)   sub-delegating the power to legislate, other than a power to make procedural rules for courts or tribunals, or

(d)   creating new criminal offences punishable with more than two years' imprisonment or, on summary conviction, with more than three months' imprisonment or a fine exceeding the statutory maximum.[26]

Where these restrictions apply, primary legislation must be used.

Where subordinate legislation is used, the scope for parliamentary discussion is at the discretion of the government. Schedule 2(2) to the Act provides that an instrument made under section 2(2) shall be subject to annulment by resolution of either House unless a draft has been approved by each House before it was made. Unless, therefore, the government invites parliament expressly to approve an instrument, there is no guarantee that it will be discussed, since it has become extremely difficult to find time to debate instruments subject to negative resolution procedure.[27] This in turn has generated criticisms of substantial obligations being imposed without parliamentary debate; the Joint Committee on Statutory Instruments, for example, has criticised the use of negative resolution procedure for instruments involving considerable sums of expenditure or substantially amending Acts of Parliament.[28]

While readily understandable, this criticism in a sense misses the point, which is that the scope for discussion and rejection of instruments, like that for the discussion and amendment of primary legislation enacted in implementation of Community obligations, is limited by the binding and inescapable nature of the obligations to which effect is being given.[29] It

---

[26] Sched 2, para 1(1).

[27] Only 25 out of 114 'prayers' tabled in the 1990–91 session were debated: see *Making the Law: The Report of the Hansard Commission on the Legislative Process,* London: The Hansard Society, 1993, paras 364–384; and J Griffith and M Ryle, *Parliament,* London: Sweet and Maxwell, 1989, pp 345–350.

[28] First Special Report from the Joint Committee on Statutory Instruments, 1977–78, HC 169, HL 51, para 36.

[29] See above; there is of course no scope for the amendment of subordinate legislation, though instruments may be withdrawn and revised in response to points made.

is not clear therefore that increasing the scope for the parliamentary discussion of subordinate legislation implementing Community obligations would serve any purpose beyond perhaps reminding MPs of their lack of voice in the Community legislative process, in much the same way as increasing the opportunities for the scrutiny of the Scottish administration is sometimes said to merely underline the powerlessness of the official Opposition in Scotland.

As regards practice, the efficiency scrutiny found that section 2(2) has traditionally been used as a method of implementation of last resort.[30] The scrutiny attributed this partly to assurances given during the course of the parliamentary proceedings on the bill that the 'Clause 2(2) powers'—including the power to amend earlier Acts of Parliament by statutory instrument—would not normally be used instead of primary legislation in relation to matters of 'major substance',[31] partly to the 'strict interpretation' which has been applied to it by the Standing (sic) Committee on Statutory Instruments,[32] and partly to the relatively low level of penalties which, because of the Schedule 2 restrictions, can be imposed in the exercise of the power conferred by it. The scrutiny pointed out, however, that departments varied in their use of the power as a matter of policy, and recommended that revised guidance should be issued on its use.

More recently, however, the emphasis on the executive's increased freedom of action *vis a vis* parliament has been replaced by a persistent concern with the restrictions to which the executive finds itself subject as a result of membership. The trigger of that concern has been the shift to qualified majority voting which took place after the Single European Act came into force in July 1987.[33] This has opened the door to something that was always conceived as an integral part of the Communities, distinguishing them from purely intergovernmental organisations, namely the possibility of a member state being bound against its will by the majority vote of its partners. The executive thus finds itself in what is for

---

[30] *Review of the Implementation and Enforcement of EC Law in the UK*, op cit, para 4.10.

[31] G Howe, 'The European Communities Act 1972' *International Affairs*, vol 49, January 1973, p 11; HC Deb 9 February 1995 c 460.

[32] See eg Sixth Report from the Joint Committee on Statutory Instruments, 1993–94, drawing special attention to the Transfrontier Shipment of Radioactive Waste Regulations 1993 SI 1993/3031, HC 19–iv, HL 22, February 1994.

[33] Seventeenth Report from the Select Committee on the European Communities, 1990–91, *Political Union: Law-Making Powers and Procedures*, HL 80, para 63.

it the unaccustomed position of not having the final say in the decision-making process.

Although it is relatively rare for the United Kingdom to be outvoted,[34] the shift has had profound implications for the negotiating positions adopted by member states. In particular, it has increased the likelihood of the adoption of blocking tactics leading to a member state being marginalised. As the efficiency scrutiny noted:

> EC Commission officials are motivated to achieve the directive. Under qualified majority voting they concentrate their attentions on meeting the difficulties of those who support their proposal in principle. If they can secure this without the doubters, they will. While it is recognised that blocking tactics may be necessary on some major political issues, they also sour relationships and remove opportunities to secure worthwhile concessions during negotiations.[35]

The obligations to which the executive finds itself involuntarily subject as a result of being outvoted by other member states constitute only a minute fraction of the obligations entailed by membership. The wider significance of these obligations is to circumscribe the executive's freedom of action. As Daintith explains in relation to economic policy, the field where Union membership bears most heavily on executive decision-making:

> The effect of such constraints may sometimes be to rule out consideration of substantive policy choices at national level altogether; if they are to be pursued at all, they must be pursued at Community level ... No less often the impact of Community membership is to impose special restrictions on instrument choice at State level: Community legal norms may require the use of given instruments of policy at State level (for example, the use of production quotas in agriculture or of direct control instead of reliance on self-regulation),

---

[34] According to the House of Lords Select Committee, the United Kingdom was outvoted only five times on single market legislation: ibid, para 65.

[35] Op cit, para 3.19.

or may determine the acceptable content of given instruments if a State decides to use them (as by the operation of non-discrimination rules).[36]

Moreover, many of these restrictions are, as a result of the doctrine of direct effect, enforceable at the instance of individuals as well as the Commission and other member states. Given that the executive's domination of parliament has meant that it has seldom been subjected to restrictions to which it is opposed, one of the most important consequences of membership, from a constitutional point of view, has been the transformation it has effected in the individual's position *vis a vis* the executive through the conferral of rights which national courts are obliged to uphold.

While membership has thus increased the executive's freedom of action in relation to parliament, it has also subjected it to a growing web of restrictions, not all of which, it is reasonable to assume, are to its liking. That the shoe is beginning to pinch is suggested in a variety of ways, including most obviously the negotiation of the protocol on social policy and the argument over the number of votes required to form a blocking minority, but also by the concern, which lay behind the setting up of the efficiency scrutiny, 'that the UK may have tended to exceed its obligations under EC law, imposing as a consequence unnecessary burdens on business and damaging international competitiveness.'[37] In these circumstances it is not beyond the bounds of possibility that the executive may feel driven to ignore its self-denying ordinance and to unfurl the banner of the sovereignty of parliament by securing the enactment of legislation which runs directly counter to the United Kingdom's Community obligations. Were it to do so, the key question would be whether the courts would give effect to that legislation or to Community law.

---

[36] T Daintith, 'Regulation' in *The International Encyclopedia of Comparative Law*, vol xvii, 'Law, State and Economy', Tubingen: Mohr, 1995, para 53.

[37] *Introduction,* para 1. The Review found that while there was little evidence to support the allegation that the UK deliberately adds obligations when transposing EC law, UK implementing legislation does tend to go beyond the requirements of directives, first, because there is a tendency to carry over existing national provisions, wider scope and tougher penalties than in other Member States, and, second, because the UK drafting tradition is dominated by a search for certainty, which may be unattainable in an EC context: *Executive Summary,* para 2.

## The Courts

The 17th century constitutional settlement was a victory not just for parliament but also the courts. The courts, however, occupied a subordinate position to parliament. In Bacon's famous phrase they were 'lions under the throne'. Consistent with their subordinate position their task in relation to Acts of Parliament was limited to interpreting and applying them. The positive meaning of the doctrine of parliamentary sovereignty, Dicey wrote, is that 'any Act of Parliament, or part of an Act of Parliament, which makes new law, or repeals or modifies an existing law, will be obeyed by the courts.'[38] The courts could not therefore refuse to obey or give effect to an Act of Parliament; nor, because it was the supreme law, could they hold an Act of Parliament to be invalid.

... it is fundamental to our (unwritten) constitution that it is for Parliament to legislate and for the judiciary to apply and interpret the fruits of Parliament's labours. Any attempt to interfere with primary legislation would be wholly unconstitutional.' [39]

Community law, however, envisages a wider role for the courts. In particular it envisages that in cases of conflict the courts will give effect to Community law over national law, regardless of the fact that it may take the form of an Act of Parliament. In the *Simmenthal* case[40] the European Court stated:

A national court which is called upon, within the limits of its jurisdiction, to apply provisions of Community law is under a duty to give full effect to those provisions, if necessary refusing of its own motion to apply any conflicting provisions of national legislation, even if adopted subsequently, and it is not necessary for the court to request or await the prior setting aside of such provisions by legislative or other constitutional means.[41]

---

[38] Op cit, p 40.
[39] [1989] 2 CMLR 353 at 397, per Lord Donaldson MR.
[40] *Amministratzione delle Finanze dello Stato* v *Simmenthal Spa (No 2)* [1978] ECR 629.
[41] [1978] ECR at 645–46.

From a United Kingdom constitutional point of view, ensuring the primacy of Community law over national law was seen as a less tractable problem than that of ensuring that effect was given to Community law in the United Kingdom. The 'stumbling block'[42] in the eyes of most commentators was the doctrine of the sovereignty of parliament which, as we have seen, was widely interpreted as meaning that no parliament could bind its successors and that the courts were powerless to review the validity of an Act of Parliament. Since effect could only be given to Community law in the United Kingdom by means of an Act of Parliament, one difficulty anticipated by some commentators was that the courts might treat a later Act of Parliament which was inconsistent in its application with Community law as impliedly repealing the provisions of the Act giving effect to Community law. Another was that faced with a conflict between Community law and an Act of Parliament the courts would regard themselves as bound to give effect to the Act.

The European Communities Act sought to forestall these difficulties by enjoining the courts to interpret and apply domestic law in a manner consistent with Community law. Section 2(4) of the Act provides that '... any enactment passed or to be passed ... shall be construed and have effect subject to the foregoing provisions of this section'; those foregoing provisions include section 2(1), which gives the force of law in the United Kingdom to those provisions of Community law which, under the Treaties, are to be given legal effect without further enactment.[43] The Act does not therefore attempt to deny parliament the power to enact legislation which is in conflict with Community law. As was pointed out above, such a provision would have been of questionable legal effect as well as politically inflammatory. Instead, it seeks to deny effect to such legislation by controlling the way in which the courts construe and give effect to it.

Although section 2(4) appears to open up the possibility of effect being denied to inconsistent provisions of national law, the preferred approach of the courts to those conflicts that have arisen has been to resolve them by interpretative means. In *Garland* v *British Rail Engineering Ltd*,[44]

---

[42] J Mitchell, 'The Sovereignty of Parliament and Community Law: The Stumbling Block that Isn't There' op cit.

[43] Section 3(1) of the Act also provides that any question as to the meaning or effect of any of the Treaties, or as to validity, meaning or effect of any Community instrument, is to be treated as a question of Community law to be determined either by the European Court or in accordance with the principles laid down by it.

[44] [1983] 2 AC 751.

Lord Diplock took as his starting point the basic principle of statutory construction that where the words of a statute relating to the United Kingdom's treaty obligations were 'reasonably capable' of bearing a meaning consistent with those obligations, they should be given that meaning. This principle, he said, applied with special force to Community obligations, and he went on to question whether, in view of the direction as to the construction of enactments 'to be passed' contained in section 2(4) of the 1972 Act, anything short of 'an express positive statement' in a later Act that parliament intended to legislate in defiance of Community law would justify a court in interpreting that statute in a manner inconsistent with Community law, 'however wide a departure from the prima facie meaning of the language of the provision might be needed in order to achieve consistency.'[45]

In pursuance of this approach the courts have shown themselves to be willing to supply the omission of the legislature (and of the executive) by in effect re-writing implementing legislation in order to achieve its stated purpose. In *Pickstone* v *Freemans plc*[46] the House of Lords was faced with a question of the construction of the Equal Pay (Amendment) Regulations 1983 which had been made in order to repair shortcomings in the Equal Pay Act revealed in enforcement proceedings before the European Court. On a literal interpretation they failed to do so. The House of Lords, however, held that in order that their 'manifest purpose' might be achieved and effect given to the 'clear but inadequately expressed intention of Parliament' certain words were to be read in to them 'by necessary implication.'[47] To interpret the Regulations otherwise, Lord Keith said, would mean that the United Kingdom had failed 'yet again' fully to implement its obligations, a failure which it was plain parliament could not possibly have intended.[48]

In *Factortame* v *Secretary of State for Transport*,[49] however, the

---

[45] [1983] 2 AC at 771.

[46] [1989] AC 66.

[47] [1990] 1 AC at 554, per Lord Keith of Kinkel.

[48] [1989] AC at 111–112; For the parliamentary proceedings on the Equal Pay (Amendment) Regs (SI 1983/1794), see HC Deb 20 July 1983 cc 480–500, and A Clark, *Diaries*, London: Weidenfeld and Nicolson, 1993. See also *Litster* v *Forth Dry Dock and Engineering Co Ltd* [1990] 1 AC 546. The need for the courts to supply the omission of the legislature in this way calls into question the value of implementing legislation.

[49] [1990] 2 AC 85; *Factortame* v *Secretary of State for Transport (No 2)* [1991] 1 AC 603.

courts found themselves faced squarely with the question of denying effect
to an Act of Parliament allegedly incompatible with Community law. The
Merchant Shipping Act 1988 introduced a new system of registration for
British fishing vessels. To be entered on the register vessels had to be
British owned, a requirement designed to preserve the benefit of United
Kingdom quotas for the British fishing industry. Spanish owners and
operators whose vessels were registered under the old register argued that
this requirement discriminated against them contrary to Community law.
In judicial review proceedings they sought an order restraining the
Secretary of State from enforcing the Act against them pending a ruling
on its compatibility with Community law by the European Court. The
House of Lords held that as a matter of national law the courts had no
power to suspend the effect of an Act of Parliament, but referred to the
European Court the question whether Community law empowered or
obliged a national court to provide effective interim protection of rights
claimed under Community law. The Court replied that if the only obstacle
to the granting of relief in order to protect directly effective Community
rights was a rule of national law prohibiting it from doing so, the national
court must as a matter of Community law set that rule aside. The House
of Lords then took the unprecedented step of restraining the Secretary of
State from applying the Act pending a ruling on its compatibility with
Community law by the European Court.

Parliamentary reaction to the European Court's ruling was perhaps
predictable. Richard Shepherd described the ruling as setting aside our
constitution 'as we have understood it for several hundred years',[50] and
Teddy Taylor asked the Prime Minister whether it was not 'a dangerous
development that the court is effectively taking on the power to suspend
sections of laws passed by this Parliament?', a concern which she
indicated she shared.[51] Lord Bridge referred to that reaction when the
House of Lords gave its reasons for granting relief:

> Some public comments on the decision of the European Court of
> Justice, affirming the jurisdiction of the courts of member states to
> override national legislation if necessary to enable interim relief to be
> granted in protection of rights under Community law, have suggested
> that this was a novel and dangerous invasion by a Community

---

[50] HC Deb 20 June 1990 c 926.
[51] HC Deb 21 June 1990 c 1108.

institution of the sovereignty of the United Kingdom Parliament. But such comments are based on a misconception. If the supremacy within the European Community of Community law over the national law of member states was not always inherent in the EEC Treaty it was certainly well established in the jurisprudence of the European Court of Justice long before the United Kingdom joined the Community. Thus, whatever limitation of its sovereignty Parliament accepted when it enacted the European Communities Act 1972 was entirely voluntary. Under the terms of the Act of 1972 it has always been clear that it was the duty of a United Kingdom court, when delivering final judgment, to override any rule of national law found to be in conflict with any directly enforceable rule of Community law ... Thus ... to insist that, in the protection of rights under Community law, national courts must not be inhibited by rules of national law from granting interim relief in appropriate cases is no more than a logical recognition of that supremacy.[52]

Lord Bridge's analysis is unquestionably correct. It must therefore be an unfavourable reflection on the United Kingdom political process, and to an extent also the legal process, that some twenty years after accession there should remain so much confusion—some of it no doubt deliberate—about the legal and constitutional consequences of membership.

In Lord Bridge's analysis the supremacy of Community law over an Act of the United Kingdom Parliament rests on the European Communities Act 1972. His analysis does not therefore address the possibility, raised above, of legislation enacted in defiance of Community law which makes it plain that the courts are to give effect to it notwithstanding the European Communities Act 1972. In an earlier case Lord Denning suggested that:

If the time should come when our Parliament deliberately passes an Act with the intention of repudiating the Treaty or any provision in it or intentionally of acting inconsistently with it and says so in express terms then I should have thought that it would be the duty of courts to follow the statute of our Parliament.[53]

---

[52] [1991] 1 AC at 658–59.
[53] *Macarthys* v *Wendy Smith* [1979] 3 All ER 325 at 329.

The meaning of legislation, however, is a matter ultimately for the courts. The possibility cannot be excluded, therefore, that they might give a different meaning to such legislation to that which on its face was intended. Were they to do so, the executive would have lost, in theory as well as practice, the power to legislate contrary to Community law. The fact that such a power is now within the grasp of the courts, whether or not they choose to exercise it, indicates the extent to which their position within the constitution has been transformed as a result of membership.

# 4

# The Evolution of the Scrutiny System in the House of Commons

*Priscilla Baines*[1]

## Introduction: the origins of the system

One of the most prominent and widespread concerns throughout the prolonged and sometimes stormy debates which led to the United Kingdom's entry to the European Economic Community in 1973 was the loss of national sovereignty which, it was held, membership would entail. Community membership was the subject of acute internal divisions within both major parties, but it was evident to both pro- and anti-Marketeers in the House of Commons that the transfer of legislative powers to the Community would result in a significant reduction in parliament's traditional legislative functions, while the Community's own decision-making procedures gave national parliaments no formal role. They could not, and cannot, amend, and it is unnecessary for them to approve, Community legislation, although there are circumstances in which national parliaments may have to legislate in order to implement Community law.[2] Community law-making machinery also largely reflected (and continues to reflect) continental practice which differs markedly from that in Britain. Legislation normally reaches the British parliament in a fairly final form and is only rarely significantly amended during its parliamentary stages whereas Community legislative proposals are the subject of negotiation at all stages up to their final adoption by the Council of Ministers and major changes at almost any point are common.[3] In addition, the essentially

---

[1] I am very grateful to the Clerk to the Select Committee on European Legislation, Robert Rogers, for his helpful comments and suggestions on this chapter.
[2] St John Bates, Chapter 10 'Scrutiny of Administration' in Michael Ryle and Peter G Richards (eds) *The Commons Under Scrutiny* London: Routledge, 1988 p 206.
[3] Vernon Bogdanor, Chapter 1, 'Britain and the European Community' in Jeffrey Jowell and Dawn Oliver (eds) *The Changing Constitution* (3rd edn) Oxford: Clarendon Press, 1994 p 9.

adversarial approach of proceedings on the floor of the House of Commons is in many respects inherently unsuited to informing ministers negotiating on Britain's behalf in Brussels.[4]

Before EC entry, it was widely recognised, not least by the government, that parliament would have to adapt its procedures to meet a situation in which its relationship with the executive had fundamentally changed and legislation directly applicable in the United Kingdom would be made in completely different ways. The machinery which was eventually devised by both Houses consisted largely of adaptations of existing procedures and has in many respects proved both durable and resilient but it can also be seen as a series of *ad hoc* expedients designed to reconcile conflicting practices and approaches. As one group of commentators put it, 'the ... adjustment of Parliament's procedure and organisation, which as is normal was mainly the responsibility of the executive, was greatly influenced by the desire to appease opponents and to re-assure waverers'.[5]

Differences between the two main parties prevented the setting up of machinery to consider Community legislative proposals prior to EC accession. The Chancellor of the Duchy of Lancaster, Geoffrey Rippon, pointed out in the debate on the second reading of the European Communities Bill on 15 February 1972 that all the existing procedures, such as questions and debates, for ensuring the accountability of ministers when taking part in the Council of Ministers would still be available. The government was concerned that parliament, as well as ministers, should play its full part when future Community policies were being formulated, and 'in particular that Parliament should be informed about and have an opportunity to consider at the formative stage those Community instruments which, when made by the Council, will be binding in this country.'[6] The House would need special arrangements to keep it informed of draft regulations and directives before they went to the Council of Ministers and he proposed the setting up forthwith of an *ad hoc* committee of both Houses, rather than the Procedure Committee, to consider what would be the most suitable method of ensuring adequate parliamentary scrutiny of draft Community legislation.

---

[4] See the contribution by a Labour backbencher, John Mackintosh, to the debate on 24 January 1974—HC Deb c 1947.

[5] Hansard Society, *The British People: their voice in Europe*, Farnborough, Hants: Saxon House, 1977 p 26.

[6] HC Deb 15 February 1972 c 274.

That suggestion was not immediately pursued, mainly because the Labour party, which was strongly opposed both to Community membership and to the way in which the government handled the European Communities Bill, refused to take part. A Special Report by the Procedure Committee in July 1973 recommended that either the Procedure Committee itself or a specially constituted select committee should examine the procedural problems which it had identified, implicitly rejecting the idea that existing machinery would be adequate for the purpose. The short report, to which the government never responded, concluded that the 'entry of Britain into the Communities presents a profound challenge to many of the established procedures of Parliament which, if not adequately dealt with, could leave Parliament substantially weaker vis a vis the executive.'[7]

By the time the European Communities Act received the Royal Assent on 17 October 1972, no committee had been set up. Mr Rippon's suggestion of a joint committee of both Houses had proved unworkable for two main reasons: the roles of the two Houses, though complementary, were 'different and separate' and there was less pressure on the time of peers and on time for debate in the Lords; and political views on the EEC diverged widely between the two Houses, there being comparatively few members of the House of Lords who were actively hostile to British entry. The two Houses therefore had to proceed separately and the composition of the two committees which were eventually set up by the two Houses reflected this.[8]

## The Foster Committee

On 18 December 1972, a few days before the United Kingdom was due to join the European Community, the government tabled a motion to set up a select committee 'to consider procedures for scrutiny of proposals for European Community Secondary Legislation and to make

---

[7] Third Special Report from the Select Committee on Procedure, 1971–72, HC 448: *Procedural Consequences of Entry into the European Communities*.

[8] J R Rose, 'Westminster and European Communities Legislation' *The Table* Vol XLII, 1974, p 74; see also HC Deb 24 January 1974 c 1944 where it was claimed by John Mackintosh, a member of the Procedure Committee, that the Procedure Committee had not been permitted to consider the adaptation of parliamentary procedure to cope with the problems of British membership of the EEC because its membership 'lacked ... anti-Market fervour and ... a special committee of more orthodox people would be set up'.

recommendations'. The motion was briefly debated on 21 December when the Leader of the House, James Prior, emphasised the importance of speedy establishment of the new procedures and denied that the government had been responsible for the delay in setting up the committee. He also pointed out that the terms of reference had been based on an amendment tabled by the opposition to the European Communities Bill (and rejected by the government at the time). The motion to set up the committee was approved without a vote.[9]

The committee was chaired by a Conservative QC, Sir John Foster, a self-confessed 'federalist,'[10] and became known as the Foster Committee. Its thirteen members (seven Conservative, five Labour and one Liberal) included anti-marketeers from both major parties, notably Eric Deakins, Michael Foot and Peter Shore from the opposition. As its clerk subsequently described, with its Lords equivalent it faced a potentially daunting task. The two committees had to establish what was meant by 'proposals for European Community Secondary Legislation' and to examine the procedures by which such proposals were prepared. They also had to consider a range of wider questions, most notably

> Could or should [the United Kingdom Parliament] exercise influence or control on its own Government before decisions were taken in the Council of Ministers, bearing in mind the secret and negotiatory nature of Council decision-making and the prospect at some future date of majority decisions there?[11]

The Foster Committee published its unanimous first report on 13 February 1973.[12] The report was primarily concerned with what was seen as the essential basis for considering Community proposals: how the House and Members were to be informed about draft legislation, forthcoming Council business and the outcome of Council meetings. It started by defining Community secondary legislation (primary legislation being the treaties themselves) as including regulations, decisions,

---

[9] HC Deb 21 December 1972 cc 1741–53.
[10] HC Deb 24 January 1974 c 1928; see also Martin Kolinsky, 'Parliamentary Scrutiny of European Legislation', *Government and Opposition* Winter 1975 pp 47–69.
[11] J R Rose, 'Westminster and European Communities Legislation', *The Table*, vol XLII, 1974 pp 73–80.
[12] First Report from the Select Committee on European Community Secondary Legislation, 1972–73. HC 143.

directives, the Community budget and instruments concluding treaties. Its recommendations were concerned with the 300 or so proposals for legislation in those categories which were agreed each year by the Council and about which the Committee was aware 'of the immediate need for greater Parliamentary control over the policies and legislative proposals that are already flowing from the European Communities'.[13]

The Committee reviewed the arrangements for supplying Community documents to the House and providing briefing on Community matters and recommended that in order 'to give Members early information as to the scope and importance of proposed European secondary legislation', for each proposal the government should issue a written statement explaining the general effect and the legal and policy implications of the proposal, the government department with primary responsibility, and the date of likely consideration by the Council of Ministers. The Committee also recommended that the government should publish a monthly list giving the agenda of forthcoming Council meetings, and make an oral statement on it in the House as well as making regular reports to the House after each Council meeting. 'Armed with this information, individual Members could inform themselves of Community proposals, and then use the existing procedures of the House for further action.'[14]

The Leader of the House announced on 13 March 1973 that the government had accepted the recommendation on explanatory memoranda on Community legislative proposals, to be prepared by the responsible government department following the model in the Committee's report. The two other recommendations were only partially accepted. The government agreed to place a list in the Vote Office each month of subjects likely to be discussed that month so that questions could be tabled or debates arranged but not to the proposed oral statements as that would lead to 'an excess of statements.' Instead, as previously, ministers would make statements to the House after Council meetings 'whenever the substance of the meeting warrants it.'[15]

Both the exchanges which followed the announcement and the half-day debate subsequently conceded on 18 April 1973 showed that, although for the anti-marketeers at least, the main argument about Community membership might have been lost, many battles remained to be fought,

---

[13] Ibid, para 2.
[14] J R Rose op cit, p 75.
[15] HC Deb 13 March 1973 c 1115–6.

particularly over how to influence or control ministers negotiating in Brussels. Michael Foot and Peter Shore (among others) argued that placing statements of forecast business in the Vote Office was very different from giving the House opportunities to question ministers on such statements and Michael Foot added that 'we are considering a matter which concerns the power that this House can still retain over decisions made by legislative bodies outside this country.'[16] Several of the speakers in the debate on 18 April were members of the Foster Committee but, although the report had been unanimous, their views differed about the government's response to it. Anti-marketeers argued that the government should have implemented the report in full, mainly because a requirement for monthly oral statements about forthcoming business and routine oral statements after Council meetings would have provided opportunities for questioning ministers about their negotiating position in the Council. Sir John Foster made it clear, however, that the unanimity had arisen mainly from the need to agree a report quickly on the matters of most pressing urgency and other solutions might have to be found if the report's proposals did not work.

The Foster Committee made its final report, again unanimous, on 25 October. Notwithstanding the provisions of the Community's treaties, an underlying theme of the report was the need for parliament to retrieve some of the powers which had been taken away from it, especially by holding ministers to account. The supremacy of Community law over United Kingdom law and the way in which the executive, in conjunction with ministers from other member states, had assumed the constitutional functions and power of parliament, particularly in relation to Community regulations, meant that 'new and special procedures' were required in order to ensure that control of the law making process remained with parliament—and ultimately with the elected members of it. The objective must be 'to restore to Parliament responsibilities for, and opportunities to exercise its constitutional rights' in respect of law-making. The government therefore had to accept that some of the freedom of action enjoyed by the executive since UK entry into the EEC would have to disappear while parliament had to accept that the scope, means and degree of scrutiny and control must all be attuned to the fact that it was dealing

---

[16] Ibid, c 1118.

with a new way of making laws which was very different from that to which it is accustomed.[17]

The Committee was 'adamantly opposed'[18] to any suggestion that the executive should have the right without the support of the House to establish or modify laws in negotiations with other governments in the Council. Moreover, as long as the weighted majority rule in the EEC Treaty was in abeyance, and as long as the practice of unanimity was required, it should be possible to exert at least as much control over Community legislation as was currently available in respect of delegated legislation in the United Kingdom. The Committee's main concerns were therefore to ensure the provision of adequate information for the House about proposed Community legislation and to find a means of reaching and expressing conclusions on particular measures before the Council made a final decision.

The Committee's 'special procedures' followed the lines suggested by the Procedure Committee in 1973: a new and different committee, for the House of Commons only, with all the powers of a select committee and otherwise totally flexible procedures, to act as a sifting mechanism, to identify legislative and other proposals of legal and/or political importance and to make recommendations as to their further consideration. It would have the services available to it of a legal adviser, possibly a second Speaker's Counsel, as well as clerks. It was envisaged that much of its initial sifting of the proposals laid before it would be undertaken by the committee's staff, but it was also recognised that the committee's members would have to undertake a considerable volume of work.

> The object of the Committee will be to inform the House as to any proposals of legal or political importance and to make recommendations as to their further consideration. Its task would not be to debate the reasons for or against a proposal but to give the House the fullest information as to why it considered the particular proposal of importance and to point out the matter of principle or policy which it affects and the changes in UK law involved.[19]

---

[17] Second Report from the Select Committee on European Community Secondary Legislation (the Foster Committee), 1972–73, HC 463.

[18] Kolinsky op cit.

[19] Foster Report, para 69.

The committee was expected to meet fortnightly when the House was sitting and to have the power to report to the House at any time. It was left to the government to determine how any 'further consideration' of proposals should be achieved, although a proposal classified by the committee as being of 'extreme urgency and importance' should be debated within two weeks of the committee's report. No recommendations for changes in the House's Standing Orders were made: the government had to accept 'that it will not cause or permit the law of the UK to be changed contrary to a resolution of the House.'[20]

In Part III of the report, the Committee looked at debates and questions on Community matters. It recommended that the government should make twice-yearly reports to the House 'on EEC matters generally' and that there should be two days in government time for debating the reports. In addition, there should be provision by sessional or standing order for four days each session to enable debates on EEC matters, with the actual subject for debate on two of the days to be chosen by the opposition. It was also recommended that there should be a specific slot in the rota for questions relating wholly to EEC matters.

The report was debated on 24 January 1974 when Mr Prior announced that the government had accepted the main recommendation for a House sifting committee with all the normal powers of a select committee, although some of the detailed recommendations were rejected, and reservations expressed about others. The debate showed that there was still a great deal of concern, especially among anti-marketeers, about what was described by the Chancellor of the Duchy of Lancaster (John Davies), who wound up for the government, as 'the question of ministerial responsibility, responsibility to Parliament and the Committees, and ... the problem of Ministers being in a position of having the assent and authority of Parliament in what they do in the Council of Ministers'.[21]

The minority Labour government which took office after the February 1974 election was committed to renegotiating the United Kingdom's terms of entry to the Community but in the meantime had to address itself to the question of scrutiny procedures. The new Leader of the House, Edward Short, said when he wound up the debate on the Queen's speech on 18 March 1974 that the renegotiation commitment did not weaken the case for parliament's effectively scrutinising proposals for Community legislation

---

[20] Ibid, para 80.
[21] HC Deb 24 January 1974 c 2022.

which were coming forward. He saw the Foster Report as 'a means of restoring to the House the sovereignty that has been eroded since the Treaty of Accession' and that the government would bring forward as soon as possible detailed plans for implementing the major proposals in the Report 'to restore the sovereignty of the House in EEC matters.'[22]

Those proposals were announced in a written statement on 2 May 1974. A motion had been tabled on 29 April to set up the proposed new scrutiny committee and ministers and departments would do all they could to assist it. Almost all the Foster Committee's other recommendations, with the exception of the appointment of a third law officer, a committee of officials to do an initial sift of Commission drafts and the presence of a Minister at all Committee meetings, were implemented more or less as they stood, including oral statements about forthcoming Council business and after Council meetings. The new arrangements were 'a further important step in the construction of an effective system of parliamentary scrutiny over proposals for Community secondary legislation.'[23] The motion to appoint the new committee was agreed to on 7 May 1974, without a debate or vote. The terms of reference were somewhat wider than had been envisaged by the Foster Committee in that they allowed the Committee to consider all published documents submitted by the Commission to the Council, not just proposals for secondary legislation:

> That a Committee be appointed to consider draft proposals by the Commission of the European Economic Community for secondary legislation and other documents published by the Commission for submission to the Council of Ministers, and to report their opinion as to whether such proposals or other documents raise questions of legal or political importance, to give their reasons for their opinion, to report what matters of principle or policy may be affected thereby, and to what extent they may affect the laws of the United Kingdom, and to make recommendations for the further consideration of such proposals and other documents by the House.[24]

---

[22] HC Deb 18 March 1974 cc 796–798.
[23] HC Deb 2 May 1974 cc 523-5w.
[24] HC Deb 7 May 1973 cc 361-2.

## The scrutiny system in operation

The different elements of the scrutiny machinery originally proposed by the Foster Committee thus came fully into operation nearly eighteen months after Britain had joined the Community. In many respects, the Committee's proposals proved both workable and realistic, although the system of allowing a specific twenty-minute 'slot' for EC matters during the four-weekly Foreign and Commonwealth Office questions was dropped in 1986 because it was considered that it gave undue prominence to EC matters.[25] The practice of making oral statements after all Council meetings rapidly proved unworkable, although they continued to be made after all Foreign Affairs Councils until 1986. The publication by the government of a six-monthly White Paper on *Developments in the European Communities* started in November 1974 and still happens in the mid-1990s. There are also still twice-yearly debates on EC matters which include consideration of the White Papers but the scope of those debates was considerably widened in 1990, following a report by the Procedure Committee in 1989 (see below p 77). The proposal that there should also be four further days allocated to debating EC matters, with the subjects of debate chosen by the opposition on two of the days, was never fully implemented through lack of time.

The most significant element in the legislative scrutiny system, the Select Committee on European Secondary Legislation, &c, started work under the chairmanship of John Davies, the former Conservative Chancellor of the Duchy of Lancaster with specific responsibility for EC matters, with sixteen members including some committed anti-marketeers. The basic pattern of its work has changed remarkably little, although the volume of documents to be scrutinised has increased very substantially. There have also been continuing problems connected with certain aspects of the Committee's work which have recurred at intervals since it was first set up. Those problems have been documented in some detail in the Special Reports containing reviews of its work which the Committee originally initiated in 1974, as well as in two reviews of the scrutiny system which were carried out by the Procedure Committee in 1977–78 and 1988–89.

---

[25] Crispin Poyser in Chapter 2 of Charles Carstairs and Richard Ware (eds) *Parliament and International Relations*, Buckingham: Open University Press, 1991, p 25.

The Foster Committee had argued that it seemed 'to be entirely within the power of a government to give full effect to the recommendations without any such changes (to Standing Orders), eg by undertaking to provide, and providing, time as required by the recommendations of the new Committee ... and by accepting, as any Government must, that it will not cause or permit the law of the UK to be changed contrary to a resolution of the House.'[26] The Labour government which eventually implemented the Foster Committee's report accepted these implications for the scrutiny machinery. In the statement on 2 May 1974, the Leader of the House (Edward Short) said that 'Provided the scrutiny committee makes its views known in sufficient time, I can assure the House that it is the government's firm intention that the debate of any proposal which the committee regards as being of extreme urgency and importance should take place before a decision is taken in the Council of Ministers.'[27]

This undertaking was subsequently confirmed by the Foreign Secretary, James Callaghan, in a debate on 11 June 1974 when he said that the government was bound not to assent in the Council of Ministers to any legislative instrument recommended by the Committee for debate until after a debate had been held.[28] The undertakings, although a vital element in the scrutiny system, at first caused both the government and the Committee considerable problems, mainly because of the backlog of Commission proposals which the Committee faced and the consequent need for large numbers of debates for which little, if any, time was available. In a special report published in August 1974, the Committee drew particular attention to the difficulties caused by the unpredictability of Council agendas and the size of the backlog which had been significantly reduced only because of the large number of documents which had been adopted before the Committee could consider them. There had been serious difficulties in keeping track of revisions to the documents and in obtaining up to date explanatory memoranda from government departments. The Committee's workload was heavy and lack of time and staff had prevented it from giving reasons for its opinions or from reporting what matters of principle or policy might be affected by Community documents. The Committee's successor should be set up as early as possible in the new session to prevent further backlogs, and it

---

[26] Foster Report 1972-73, HC 463, para 80.

[27] HC Deb 2 May 1974 c 525w.

[28] HC Deb 11 June 1974 cc 1425-9; this undertaking was subsequently repeated on 4 November 1974—HC Deb cc 691-2 and on 27 November 1974 HC Deb cc 447-8.

should be set up for the duration of a Parliament, with sufficient staff and accommodation. However, the Committee felt that in some respects its position was secure:

> The undertaking given by the Government not to give their consent to legislative proposals until debate has taken place, when that has been called for by the Committee, constitutes the basis upon which its effectiveness largely depends. This gives real force to the meaning of scrutiny.[29]

The Committee was set up again on 18 November 1974, immediately after the start of the new Parliament, with additional staff and for the duration of that Parliament. By February 1975, the backlog which had built up during the dissolution had been reduced to insignificant proportions. As the Second Special Report of the 1974–75 session described, in future the Committee would concentrate more on the occasions when it thought that, in accordance with its terms of reference, it should give reasons for its opinion about whether instruments raised matters of legal or political importance and report on what matters of principle or policy might be raised and their impact on United Kingdom law. It would therefore have to choose which instruments to consider in more detail and would seek both more detailed information from the government department concerned and oral evidence from interested outside bodies. The Committee was anxious that such outside bodies should make their interest in specific instruments known to it and the reports on the instruments selected for more detailed scrutiny would be longer than the normal ones.[30]

While the Committee was tackling its backlog, the Procedure Committee examined other matters which had already arisen in connection with the scrutiny of European legislation, especially in relation to debates in the House. These included the difficulties of keeping up with the documentation and tracing the progress of successive revisions of draft legislation in the Community and the consequent problems of timing of consideration of proposals by the House. The volume of documents was very large (estimated at 650 to 700 a year—more than double the 300

---

[29] Second Special Report from the Select Committee on European Secondary Legislation &c, 1974, HC 258–II.

[30] Second Special Report from the Select Committee on European Secondary Legislation &c, 1974–75, HC 234.

which had been estimated at the time of EEC entry) and although only very small numbers had been recommended for debate, there were problems connected with both the timing of debates in relation to Council meetings and the hour at which debates were held, almost all of them having happened after 10.00 pm and for only an hour and a half. There had also been problems, particularly of timing, associated with consideration of the Community Budget.

The Procedure Committee's main recommendation was that documents which the European Secondary Legislation Committee recommended for further consideration could be referred to a standing committee where they could be debated on a substantive, amendable, motion, with the debate not subject to specific time limits.[31] The report was debated on 3 November 1975, after the 'renegotiation' referendum was over. The Leader of the House, Peter Shore, announced that, although the government had accepted the recommendation that EEC documents could be referred to a standing committee for debate, by analogy with the normal procedure on statutory instruments such debates would be on formal motions for consideration of the document(s) in question and should be limited to a duration of an hour and a half.[32] In the debate, speakers from all sides, almost all of them members of the European Secondary Legislation Committee or the Procedure Committee, disagreed with the government's approach but the proposed amendment to Standing Orders was nevertheless agreed to.

In practice, the new procedure was hardly used: as the then chairman of the European Legislation Committee, Sir John Eden, told the 1977–78 Procedure Committee, government motions to refer 'all but the least significant EEC documents' to standing committees had been blocked.[33] He nevertheless thought that, after the initial difficulties caused by the backlog, the European Legislation Committee had generally established a *modus vivendi* and was a 'relative success', although practical problems remained about the Community's business timetable and the need to keep track of successive revisions of Commission proposals.

Sir John listed a litany of by then familiar complaints about the continuing difficulties experienced in debating EEC documents, some already identified by the 1974–75 Procedure Committee but still

---

[31] First Report from the Select Committee on Procedure, 1974–75, HC 294.
[32] HC Deb 3 November 1975 cc 29–39.
[33] First Report from the Select Committee on Procedure, 1977–78, HC 588–II p 196.

unresolved and the 'aspect of the procedures for the control of legislation which continues to give most cause for concern.'[34] He underlined the 'vital part of the whole system of control' played by the government's undertaking, most recently restated on 4 August 1976,[35] that where the Committee recommended an EEC document for further consideration by the House, time would be found for such a debate before the document was finally adopted by the Council. However, although the government had stuck to the letter of the undertaking, many of the earlier criticisms of the arrangements for debates on the floor of the House were still being made, both by the Committee and by individual Members, as well as by outside commentators.[36] Despite some recent improvements, the arrangements for debates would need to be considerably further improved before it could safely be assumed that the floor of the House (and standing committees) was the best place for the discussion of the merits of important EEC legislation.[37]

In its report, the Procedure Committee considered both the nature of the government's undertaking about allowing debates in the House before Community instruments were adopted by the Council and the need for improving the arrangements for debates. The form of the 1976 undertaking by the Leader of the House, Michael Foot, was more circumscribed and gave ministers more discretion than that given by his predecessor in the May 1974 statement and subsequently confirmed on 11 June 1974 by the Foreign Secretary.[38] In a debate on a Private Member's motion moved by Nigel Spearing on 28 November 1977 Mr Foot had agreed in principle that the undertaking should take the form of a resolution of the House.[39] The Procedure Committee recommended that there should be a 'declaratory resolution' which should embody a 'firm commitment' that the government should not give its final approval to legislation prior to

---

[34] First Report from the Select Committee on Procedure 1977–78, HC 588–II p 196; see also the evidence to the Committee from the Leader of the House, Michael Foot, on 20 December 1976 Q 210.

[35] HC Deb 4 August 1976 cc 802–3w.

[36] First Report from the Select Committee on Procedure 1977–78, HC 588–II p 195.

[37] Ibid, p 196.

[38] HC Deb 11 June 1974 c 1547.

[39] Special Report from the Select Committee on European Legislation &c, 1977–78 HC 642, para 23.

debate in the House or in standing committee, where debate had been recommended by the European Legislation Committee.[40]

The Procedure Committee recognised that the great majority of instruments recommended for debate by the European Legislation Committee had actually been debated, even though very few of the debates had been in standing committee. In view of the difficulties associated with such debates, the Committee recommended that in future they should normally take place on a government motion 'to approve, to approve with modifications or qualifications, or to disagree with the Commission proposals concerned.'[41] It was also recommended that, in order to relieve pressure of time on the floor of the House and to allow more time for debates on Community proposals, the relevant standing orders should be amended so as to give effect to the 1974–75 Procedure Committee's recommendations.[42]

Following the change of government in 1979, the Procedure Committee's recommendations on European legislation were debated and agreed to on 30 October 1980. The Leader of the House, Mr Norman St.John-Stevas, said he believed that 'the House would value a voluntary undertaking being framed as a declaratory resolution of the House.'[43] In conjunction with the European Legislation Committee, the text of a resolution had been agreed, but one which departed from the suggestion of the Procedure Committee as it was not totally binding on ministers—'I consider that the provision that a Minister must at the first opportunity explain to the House the reason for giving agreement prior to a debate should safeguard that exceptions to the general rule are made only when it is absolutely necessary.'[44]

Mr St.John-Stevas also accepted the recommendation that amendable motions on Community proposals should be allowed to be debated in standing committee and on the floor of the House and to allow standing committee debates to last for two and a half hours. Shortly after the debate, the European Legislation Committee published a review of its work in which it welcomed the procedural changes and again drew attention to the crucial importance for the effectiveness of the scrutiny

---

[40] First Report from the Select Committee on Procedure, 1977–78, HC 588–I, para 4.13.

[41] Ibid, para 4.15.

[42] Ibid, para 4.17.

[43] HC Deb 30 October 1980 c 729.

[44] Ibid.

machinery of the government's undertaking about the holding of debates in response to Committee recommendations. It was therefore regretted that the Resolution did not require a minister who had had to agree to a decision by the Council without a recommended debate being held to make an oral statement to the House, rather than, as was commonly the practice, a written answer. The government was urged 'to ensure that the convention is at least established that ... "when such occasions occur, oral statements are generally made."' Following the decision to allow debates in standing committee to take place on substantive and amendable motions, the Committee intended to revert to its former practice of distinguishing between proposals thought suitable for debate on the floor of the House and those which could be considered in standing committee.[45]

The Committee reviewed its work during the three sessions before the 1983 election (1980–81, 1981–82 and 1982–93) in a special report published shortly before the election.[46] The House's Standing Orders had recently been revised to bring the Committee's terms of appointment into the main body of standing orders (the '&c' was dropped from the Committee's title at the same time, the 'Secondary' having been dropped in December 1976). The report revealed a high level of activity (well over 700 instruments reported on in 1980–81 and 1981–82) and commented that 'the framework established by the House for dealing with European documents is now broadly satisfactory', although concern was also expressed about the circumstances in which documents were approved by the Council before being considered by the Committee.[47] It was considered that such documents should be brought within the terms of the Resolution of 30 October 1980. It was also argued (again) that ministers should use oral rather than written statements when they had agreed to an instrument recommended for debate before a debate had been held 'in order that the Minister may be questioned about the special reasons which caused him not to withhold his agreement to the instrument.'[48]

---

[45] First Special Report from the Select Committee on European Legislation, &c, 1980–81, HC 50.
[46] First Special Report from the Select Committee on European Legislation, 1982–83, HC 367.
[47] Ibid, para 8.
[48] Ibid, para 9.

In June 1984, the Committee reviewed its operations during its first ten years.[49] It concluded that its terms of reference and working methods had become 'broadly non-controversial' and its current workload of about 700 documents a year was 'not indigestible' but the report contained several admonitions to the government about recurring areas of concern—the timing of debates which were often arranged too near the final stage of negotiations, the increasing number of instruments which were adopted before they reached the Committee for scrutiny, and the apparent diminishing awareness among ministers and officials of the strict requirements of the resolution of 30 October 1980, 'as suggested by a recent serious lapse in its operation' which had shown 'clear disregard of the scrutiny system' by a minister and his officials.[50] It was also remarked that although the Leader of the House (John Biffen, who had given evidence to the Committee) had accepted the principle that debates should be held earlier rather later, that principle 'had not always been implemented by the Government's business managers.'[51]

The Committee considered in some detail the question of the adoption of documents before scrutiny which, it pointed out, could provide a loophole which would undermine the scrutiny system altogether if the practice became too frequent. Documents which had been recommended for debate but adopted before one was held were also still a problem, despite the many earlier strictures by the Committee and its predecessors on the subject. The Committee recognised that there were circumstances where it might be impossible to arrange a debate before adoption but it clearly felt that in at least the one recent case described at length in the report, the Minister concerned had gone too far:

> ... if a document, still awaiting debate after many weeks, is finally adopted because British objections are removed, such a situation threatens the scrutiny rights of Parliament. A Minister's statement of the attractions of a proposal should not be confused with the reasons why a debate should not be held before adoption. It is an explanation

---

[49] First Special Report from the Select Committee on European Legislation, 1983–84, HC 527.

[50] Ibid, para 1 and para 8(ii) The document in question was concerned with the European Strategic Programme for Research and Development in Information Technology (ESPRIT) which had been recommended for debate but the debate had been delayed; the Minister of State at the Department of Trade and Industry had lifted the scrutiny reserve without informing the House and agreed to its approval in the Council.

[51] Ibid.

of the latter which the Committee, and we believe, the House, expect from any Minister who takes advantage of exception (b) to the Resolution by invoking "special reasons".[52]

In examining the future prospects of the scrutiny system, the Committee drew attention to the continuing underlying concern about the 'restraints which the Community methods of work place on the normal constitutional relationship between Ministers and Parliament and on the powers that each exercises.' The Committee saw a need for stronger action but not solely as a matter for government initiative: the House itself and, more particularly, select committees, could show a greater interest in the European affairs and in Community documents.[53]

Most of the recommendations in the report consisted of exhortations to the government, mainly to ensure that both the spirit and the letter of the 1980 resolution were followed. The government's response to the report came in the form of a letter of 23 August 1984 from the Leader of the House to the Committee's chairman, Nigel Spearing, later reproduced as a written answer.[54] Mr Biffen stated that 'The government accept that special care is needed to ensure the continued involvement of the House in the Community decision-making process.' Many of the detailed responses consisted of undertakings to tighten up existing procedures in order to ensure that ministers and departments did as the Committee sought in relation to both the adoption of documents before scrutiny and adoption of documents after scrutiny but before debate, but without tying the government's hands too tightly. Mr Biffen did, however, accept the Committee's desire for debates to be held as early as possible and subsequently paid particular attention to that point.[55] In relation to the adoption of documents before scrutiny, Mr Biffen gave what the Committee subsequently saw as a vital undertaking:

By convention, Ministers are able to agree to certain confidential, routine or trivial proposals before the scrutiny process has been completed. So far as other proposals are concerned, while in principle the Resolution of the House of 30 October 1980, being addressed solely

---

[52] Ibid, para 17.
[53] Ibid, para 29.
[54] HC Deb 29 October 1984 cc 800–802w.
[55] See memorandum of evidence by the Leader of the House to the Procedure Committee in 1988–89, HC 622–II p 14.

to documents that the Committee has recommended for debate, does not bear on proposals yet to be scrutinised, the Government consider that its spirit should apply to all proposals. Departments will therefore be asked to ensure in future that, when consideration is being given to the adoption of unscrutinised proposals, exception (b) of the Resolution of 30 October 1980 is satisfied.[56]

The Single European Act in 1986 introduced a new procedure for draft European Community legislation (the co-operation procedure) in which the European Parliament would be much more closely involved than hitherto. In February 1986, the Committee published a special report in which it examined both the Act itself and its implications for parliamentary scrutiny of European Community documents.[57] The Committee observed rather sourly that the 'developments in the Community which have led to the drafting of the Single Act have been outside the scrutiny powers of the Committee' because the relevant documentation had been outside its terms of reference—an important point to which it was subsequently to return. However, it could, and therefore did, look at the implications of the Act for the scrutiny process. Proposals for Community legislation in the fields affected by the Single Act would both become more frequent and move faster, particularly those related to the internal market. There would therefore be more recommendations for debates and debates would more often have to be arranged at short notice. In addition, the increase in the number of cases subject to majority voting

could reduce the power of any individual Member State to put any sort of brake on progress ... This would not affect the accountability of Ministers to the House of Commons for their actions in Council; but it would underline the necessity for seeking a view from the House before any particular proposal reaches a critical stage.[58]

Where the co-operation procedure was used, there might have to be additional scrutiny stages and the initial explanatory memoranda prepared by government departments should make it clear when that might happen.

---

[56] HC Deb 29 October 1984 cc 800–802w.
[57] First Special Report from the Select Committee on European Legislation, 1985–86, HC 264: *The Single European Act and Parliamentary Scrutiny*.
[58] Ibid.

There might also be further difficulties over the already vexed question of the timing of debates, especially if proposals moved fast under the influence of time limits. How such developments would affect an already 'complex legislative procedure in a Community of Twelve' was not entirely clear. Furthermore:

> How precisely all of this would, in practice, reflect on the parliamentary scrutiny machinery in the United Kingdom remains to be seen; but it is clear that the whole area will need to be watched carefully.[59]

Later in that session, the Committee conducted a detailed review of its work since the 1983–84 special report.[60] That review revealed again many procedural and other concerns about the operation of the scrutiny machinery. The government's undertaking in response to the earlier report about documents adopted before scrutiny was warmly welcomed but a warning note was also sounded about how, in normal circumstances, ministers informed the Committee, but not the House, why adoption before scrutiny had happened. 'The House should be aware of the existence of this limitation on the full implementation of the 1980 Resolution in respect of instruments adopted prior to scrutiny.'[61] There was a further complaint about a case where a minister in the Department of Trade and Industry—the department which had incurred the Committee's displeasure for the same reason in 1983–84—had agreed to the adoption of an undebated proposal and subsequently given a very inadequate explanation. The department was again rebuked:

> Yet the fact that the ... case could still occur after the new instructions had been issued to Departments shows that what we identified in the [1983–84] Special Report as "diminishing awareness among Ministers and officials of the strict requirements of the Resolution of the House of 30 October 1980" ... has still not been remedied.[62]

---

[59] Ibid, para 33.

[60] Second Special Report from the Select Committee on European Legislation, 1985–86, HC 400.

[61] Ibid, para 9.

[62] Ibid, para.16.

Other difficulties remained, particularly in relation to government departments' responsibilities for the scrutiny process. The supply of the full text of documents to the Committee in time for them to be considered before their final consideration by the Council was a difficulty which had arisen throughout the Committee's existence. It was recognised that there was often no easy solution, although departments mostly did their best to keep the Committee as well informed as they could. Departments were taken to task for several other inadequacies in the information they supplied in explanatory memoranda and insufficient attention to detail including, for example, how they identified whether or not proposals were of 'legal importance', and whether correct procedures were being followed.[63]

The Committee also drew attention to the inadequacy of its own procedures in relation to the negotiation of treaties and other international agreements, a matter where parliamentary scrutiny often could not take place early enough to be relevant or effective and sometimes no information could be supplied to parliament before completion of negotiations.[64] Another concern was the effect of the Single European Act on the Committee's work, the subject of the earlier report that session which had also been referred to twice in recent debates. Some helpful developments were noted: the government had accepted that the co-operation procedure would impose additional pressures on the Committee and the House had passed a resolution urging the government to improve procedures so that scrutiny by the House could be maintained. In the debate on 23 April 1986 on the second reading of the European Communities (Amendment) Bill (the bill to implement the Single European Act), the government had also accepted the Committee's earlier recommendation that explanatory memoranda should specifically identify cases subject to the co-operation procedure, including the Treaty powers used and the procedure and voting procedures applicable. Departments would also be ready to issue supplementary explanatory memoranda where proposals had significantly changed since they were first considered by the Committee.[65]

As the report emphasised, a debate on 5 March 1986 on the six-monthly White Paper had 'highlighted dissatisfaction within the House

---

[63] Ibid, paras 30–39.

[64] Ibid, paras 43–44.

[65] Ibid, para 50.

about inadequate involvement in European Community affairs.'[66] The Committee's own role as a 'sifting agent' was essential but still left a gap in relation to 'a comprehensive and well-informed political examination' of important Community proposals. Debates which were intended to ensure that ministers took full account of the views of the House were often too generalised or held too late to have an impact. The Single European Act had also illustrated an inherent weakness in the system, caused by the limitation on the Committee's terms of reference which meant that the House had no opportunity to examine the Act until it had been agreed by the member states. The Committee had been unable to report on the Act or on the inter-governmental conference in the autumn of 1985 which produced it. As in some other cases, the House had suddenly been faced with a major development and the Committee's terms of reference had meant that the document concerned was not subject to scrutiny procedure.

The Committee saw the answer to these (and other) difficulties in adapting its own role by allowing a 'relatively simple change' in its terms of reference. The elimination of the constraint limiting it to particular categories of documents or proposals would permit 'occasional investigations into broader issues' about which the House might wish to be informed but which were not being otherwise covered, thus allowing the Committee an 'exploratory role' in the European field. The Committee's work would thus develop in three ways: its traditional scrutiny function; reports on general developments in the Community of which the House should be aware, with a brief assessment of their likely significance for the United Kingdom; and more detailed reports on selected documents or matters based on inquiries similar to those by departmental select committees or the House of Lords Select Committee on the European Communities.[67]

Governments had generally reacted sympathetically towards the Committee's anxieties to ensure that its scrutiny functions were properly carried out and that recommended debates were held at an appropriate time. They had endorsed the Committee's criticisms of government departments (and ministers) and accepted the need for correct procedures and due vigilance on the part of departments. Reactions to suggestions that the Committee's powers should be extended or its terms of reference

---

[66] Ibid, para 50.
[67] Ibid, para 59.

significantly altered had been much more wary and the response to the Second Special Report in 1985–86 was no exception. It was short and endorsed most of the Committee's concerns but 'The Government is of the opinion that now would not be the right time to change the existing arrangements (for the Committee's terms of reference) in the way proposed.'[68]

The Committee nevertheless persisted in its efforts to get its terms of reference extended, as well as to remove new procedural loopholes in the scrutiny process which had emerged. Its First Special Report in 1988–89 consisted of an exchange of correspondence with the Leader of the House (John Wakeham) about its terms of reference and other matters.[69] The Committee regretted that the government was still not prepared to extend the Committee's powers in the way proposed in 1985–86, but welcomed the Leader of the House's willingness to provide a greater range of documents to the Committee, 'thus *de facto* extending the scope of scrutiny.' The Committee was prepared to proceed on that basis provided that the government was prepared to keep the position under review and to take steps 'wherever possible to remove any procedural impediments ... to any such documents being considered by the House as if they were "European Community Documents" within the meaning of its Standing Orders.'

Concern had also arisen again over the operation of the October 1980 Resolution in relation to the co-operation procedure, and the Committee continued to seek watertight undertakings from the government that the terms of the Resolution would not be undermined by procedural developments in the Community. It welcomed the steps which the Leader of the House had taken to ensure early debates after recommendations by the Committee. However,

> It would also welcome a formal understanding that, for proposals subject to the co-operation procedure ... the Government will treat agreement by the Council on a common position as "agreement ... to [a] proposal for European Legislation" but without prejudice to the Resolution also applying to any recommendation the Committee may

---

[68] *Observations by the Government on the Second Special Report from the House of Commons Select Committee on European Legislation, Session 1985–86*—Cm 123, April 1987.

[69] First Special Report from the Select Committee on European Legislation, 1988–89, HC 533.

make regarding debate on any subsequent Commission re-examined proposal.[70]

There was a further category of document which was escaping the Committee's net, those which were not proposals for European legislation but 'in respect of which any Council decision relating to these documents may substantially pre-empt consideration of future legislative proposals.' Such documents included the Delors Committee report on Economic and Monetary Union which had preceded the recent Madrid Council which had approved the first stage of economic and monetary union, thus pre-empting discussions of principle of the legislative steps to be taken. The Committee sought a similar informal extension to the scope of the Resolution to that agreed in response to the 1983–84 Special Report so that it could consider such proposals.

In his response to the report, the Leader of the House said that the government was prepared 'to adopt a liberal interpretation of the Committee's Terms of Reference' and accepted that some documents, notably the Commission's Work Programme and drafts of those Council resolutions which were not published in draft form, might cause difficulties for the Committee. He undertook to ask his colleagues to supply the Committee, on request, with such documents and explanatory memoranda and

> wherever possible, to consider any request to remove any procedural impediments to such documents being further considered by the House. If the Committee does not find the position satisfactory the Government will be willing to consider whether the arrangements might need to be changed in the light of experience.[71]

Mr Wakeham reaffirmed once more the government's commitment to the spirit of the 1980 Resolution in relation to common positions adopted by the Council but was less accommodating about debates on non-legislative proposals:

> A debate will always be held at the time the Government consider most appropriate. In that context, the Government will naturally give careful

---

[70] Ibid, p iv.
[71] Ibid, p v.

consideration to the extent to which a Council decision may substantially pre-empt discussion of future legislative proposals and the implications for timing of the debate. That said, it remains the case that the Opposition can seek to secure a debate on a specific occasion by negotiation through the usual channels.[72]

## The 1988–89 Procedure Committee inquiry

The Procedure Committee's inquiry in 1988–89 into *The Scrutiny of European Legislation* was the first such review since the earlier Procedure Committee report in 1977–78. It took place when the system was under increasing strain as a result of the co-operation procedure and the introduction of qualified majority voting and when widespread concern had emerged about how the House was considering European matters.[73] The European Legislation Committee's succession of Special Reports since 1983–84 had underlined that Committee's continuing concerns about the detailed operation of the scrutiny system. The increasing volume of Community legislation recommended for debate had also led to a substantial number of debates on the floor of the House, many of them held after 10.00 pm and often sparsely attended, other than by longstanding partisans who used each occasion to reopen fundamental arguments over Community membership.

The Procedure Committee was at pains to dispel some of the misconceptions which had emerged from the evidence received. In particular, and contrary to the views of some witnesses, the volume of Community legislation was not on a sharply rising trend, although there were peaks and troughs. The number of documents recommended by the Scrutiny Committee for further consideration by the House had remained remarkably steady since 1978, while the number of documents adopted prior to the completion of the scrutiny process was not negligible but not so large as to suggest that the scrutiny safeguards were being by-passed on an substantial scale. Some genuine causes for concern nevertheless remained (some of them of long standing): the absolute volume of European legislation was considerable and hard for the House to digest; some important documents were adopted before scrutiny was complete; too

---

[72] Ibid, p v.
[73] Fourth Report from the Select Committee on Procedure, 1988–89, HC 622-I-II *The Scrutiny of European Legislation*.

many debates on European legislation were held late at night in a sterile and unproductive atmosphere; and the extension of qualified majority voting had further reduced the areas in which a single member state could prevent the enactment of legislation; 'this means that, in such areas, Ministers can be pressed to take a position on a timescale not of their own choosing; this in turn means that Parliament's views may be pre-empted.'[74]

The Committee endorsed the view that the European Legislation Committee's sifting function was indispensable. It also endorsed that Committee's desire for its terms of reference to be amended so that it could consider consultative and similar documents, as well as report on trends and developments in broad European policy areas. It criticised the former Leader of the House (John Wakeham) for his refusal to do as the Committee had sought in this respect on the grounds that 'the Government is blocking a proposal designed to improve Parliament's scrutiny of the Executive.'[75] Sympathy was also expressed with the Committee's wish to be notified of legislative proposals at the earliest possible stage.

Not surprisingly, the Procedure Committee devoted a substantial amount of attention to the timing and frequency of debates on European legislative proposals, particularly in the context of the co-operation procedure and the unsatisfactory nature of any debates held after a 'common position' had been adopted by the Council. The 'basic precondition for effective scrutiny (was) that the House should be able to express its views on a Community legislative proposal *before* it is finally approved in the Council of Ministers'.[76] The timing of debates was 'a matter of the utmost sensitivity to the House', with particular concern having been expressed in evidence about the 'futility of debates held after the event' and 'late scrutiny [being] effectively no scrutiny'.[77] Ministers should interpret the criteria of the 1980 Resolution strictly while the European Legislation Committee should exercise vigilance on behalf of the House to ensure that the convention about not withholding consent for proposals of a 'confidential, routine or trivial nature' was not abused. Other recommendations were also intended to ensure that ministers rigorously observed the spirit and the letter of the 1980 Resolution, with the government being urged to continue to err on the side of earliness in

---

[74] Ibid, para 16.
[75] Ibid, para 22.
[76] Ibid, para 27.
[77] Ibid, para 31.

arranging debates, but also to be prepared to be flexible over timing—even though it was pointed out that the House had long abandoned any idea of mandating ministers as a realistic objective.

The most substantial of the Procedure Committee's recommendations were concerned with the arrangements for debates on European legislation. The unpopularity of late night debates and the resentment they generated were recognised, although it was also acknowledged that there were circumstances in which debates on the floor of the House were essential and the European Legislation Committee's criticisms of the government for not allowing a debate in advance of the Madrid Summit were strongly endorsed as a 'serious breakdown' in the scrutiny system. The six-monthly retrospective debates on the White Papers on *Developments in the Community* were largely wasted opportunities and should be replaced by one-day debates immediately before the half-yearly European summits..[78]

The Committee's main proposal was for an enhanced role for standing committees in debating European Community proposals, building on the existing system of Standing Committees on European Community Documents. There should be five European Standing Committees, each responsible for a specific subject area and with ten members, nominated for a session, with the power to hear initial statements from ministers 'and thereafter to cross-examine them about a document before any Motion relating to that document has been made.'[79] It was hoped that, in order to make scrutiny of European legislation by standing committees more effective, and thus more acceptable as a means of reducing pressure on the Chamber, the European Legislation Committee would feel able to refer more documents for debate in standing committee, although automatic referral of documents for debate in standing committee was rejected in favour of increasing the minimum number of Members who could block a motion for referral. Motions for debate should also be 'more pointed' so that the debates were 'lively' and the government's position on individual documents was made clear.

Some attention was also given to the possible extension of the role of select committees in relation to European legislation, including proposals from the former Leader of the House, John Biffen, for a European Affairs Committee and from the then chairman of the Liaison Committee, Terence Higgins, for European Business Sub-Committees of the departmental select

---

[78] Ibid, para 51.
[79] Ibid, para 63.

committees. Both suggestions were rejected, mainly because in their different ways they would separate consideration of European business from that of related domestic policy issues. Any additional burdens on select committees would also be unacceptable to those committees and require extra staff, as would a European Affairs Committee. The chairmen of the departmental select committees were not enthusiastic about taking on specific responsibilities for examining European legislation, although in several cases their committees had conducted inquiries with a substantial 'European' content. The Committee considered that departmental select committees both could and should play a much larger part than hitherto in the scrutiny of European legislation but, like its predecessor in 1978, stopped short of recommending that the House should have specific powers to refer such legislation to the appropriate select committee—'we do not believe that it would be sensible for the House to seek formally to direct the priorities of departmentally-related Select Committees in this way.'[80]

The Procedure Committee also examined the question of relations with the European Parliament because the introduction of the co-operation procedure had given that Parliament an enhanced role.[81] Formal involvement of MEPs in the scrutiny process at Westminster (other than as witnesses) would require legislation and was summarily rejected but there was much more enthusiasm for the cultivation of informal contacts, mainly through party organisations, particularly in order to obtain early warning of forthcoming legislation. It was also suggested that the House should take various practical steps to make communication with the European Parliament easier.[82]

In the concluding summary of the report, the Procedure Committee repeated its earlier acknowledgment of 'the inevitable constraints imposed by the United Kingdom's treaty commitments on the House's ability to improve the effectiveness of scrutiny and the corresponding need to approach the subject with realistically modest expectations.' It also uttered a strong reminder about unrealistic expectations about what the scrutiny process might achieve:

> ... those seeking from this Report some form of procedural antidote to the legal and political limitations imposed on scrutiny by this country's

---

[80] Ibid, para 100.
[81] Ibid, para 107.
[82] Ibid, para 115.

treaty obligations will be disappointed ... it was never envisaged that the House would be able to exercise the same degree of control over the final form of European legislation as it does over its domestic equivalent. By the same token, it has never seriously been contended that United Kingdom Ministers can be mandated to adhere rigidly, on pain of censure by the House, to a single specific negotiating stance in the Council of Ministers. The subsequent political evolution of the Community and its institutions has further reinforced those constraints on the House's influence. Nevertheless, the House has always expected, entirely with reason, that Ministers should not, save in the most exceptional circumstances, enter into negotiations in the Council without at least knowing, and taking fully into account, the collective views of Members.[83]

The Committee's report was published in November 1989 and the Government's response was followed in May 1990.[84] Despite the Committee's generally modest recommendations and the desire for improvements often expressed by the Leader of the House, John Wakeham,[85] on most of the major points of principle about the operation of the scrutiny system the government preferred to maintain the status quo, while acknowledging the need to ensure effective national parliamentary scrutiny procedures 'to deal with the volume and significance of European legislation now emerging, for example in relation to the Single Market programme.'[86] The European Legislation Committee's desire for its terms of reference to be extended was almost entirely rejected, on the grounds that that Committee performed a valuable function very effectively. Any shift of activity into major policy areas 'might tend to detract from the Committee's present effectiveness in its primary scrutiny function.' A minor concession was made in the form of a promised amendment to the Committee's terms of reference to allow it to consider consultative documents and horizontal issues (ie issues which recurred in several documents). 'This function would, however, continue to be related

---

[83] Ibid, para 125.

[84] *Fourth Report from the House of Commons Select Committee on Procedure Session 1988–89 The Scrutiny of European Legislation:Government Response* Cm 1081; May 1990.

[85] Mr Wakeham was replaced as Leader of the House by Sir Geoffrey Howe at the end of July 1989.

[86] Ibid, p 1.

to specific Community documents deposited in Parliament rather than involving free-standing studies of broad policy issues which might tend to duplicate the work of other Committees.' The government did undertake to help the House as far as it could to be involved at an earlier stage in the Community legislative process by providing access to Commission pre-legislative working documents.

On the 'vexed question' of the timing of debates on proposals for European legislation and the operation of the scrutiny reserve,[87] the government was at its most cautious and in effect reserved its position, arguing that the spirit of the 1980 Resolution had generally been strictly observed, and would continue to be, but it was necessary for ministers to have some discretion about its operation. It was, however, agreed that the Resolution should be amended to incorporate the undertakings given in 1987 and 1989 about the adoption of a common position under the co-operation procedure.

The government was at its least cautious where it had least to lose—or most to gain. It positively welcomed the recommendation that the six-monthly debates on the *Developments in the Community* White Papers should be replaced by general debates before each twice-yearly heads of government meetings, with the debates held later in the six-month period. The intention behind the creation of special standing committees on European Community documents—a significant shift away from debate on the floor of the House—was also welcomed and the recommendation accepted in principle, including the suggested opening statements and question and answer sessions with ministers, but with some modifications. Five such committees were considered to be too many because it would not be possible to find sufficient Members to serve on them, so three were proposed, initially on an experimental basis for one session and with some of the detailed aspects of their procedure to be decided after the Procedure Committee's report and the government's response had been debated.

The suggestion that the minimum number of Members needed to block a reference to standing committee should be increased from 20 to 40 was rejected in favour of automatic referral unless, after discussion through the usual channels, the government put down a motion for debate on the floor of the House, in order to ensure the majority of instruments recommended for debate were considered in the special standing committees. The need for motions for debate to be 'more pointed' was viewed rather cagily:

---

[87] 1988–89 HC 622–I para 120.

'other features of the new system such as the fact that members of the Standing Committees may have an interest in the subject area and are to be given an opportunity to question Ministers about it, will be more important in encouraging attendance.' The government also endorsed the Procedure Committee's cautious approach to any extension of the role of select committees in relation to European legislation. It 'remain[ed] to be convinced' that the creation of sub-committees to consider European legislation was necessary and agreed 'that the House should not seek formally to direct the priorities of departmentally-related Select Committees towards enhanced scrutiny of European legislation.'

The European Legislation Committee made its own response to the Procedure Committee's report in June 1990[88] in which it welcomed the Procedure Committee's support for its work in general and for the need for its terms of reference to be amended. It also welcomed most aspects of the government's response, in particular the agreement to amend its terms of reference, but disagreed with the proposal for automatic referral of Community documents to standing committee, arguing that such a reference should be made by the House.

The Procedure Committee's report, the government's response and the European Legislation Committee's Special Report were debated for a full day on 28 June 1990 when the Leader of the House, Sir Geoffrey Howe, emphasised that the main reason for reducing the proposed number of standing committees from five to three was strictly practical.[89] Most speakers commended the European Legislation Committee for its work and supported the proposed creation of the European Standing Committees, although some opposition speakers, including the shadow Leader of the House, Dr John Cunningham, repeated their preference, expressed in evidence to the Procedure Committee, for a European Grand Committee. The debate was wide-ranging, with the long-standing EC opponent, Teddy Taylor, arguing that the Procedure Committee's report ignored the reality that power was 'slipping away' from the House of Commons and the standing committees would if anything make matters worse rather than better. The Chairman of the European Legislation Committee, Nigel Spearing, urged the government to think again about both widening his committee's terms of reference and automatic referral of documents to standing committee.

---

[88] First Special Report from the Select Committee on European Legislation, 1989–90, HC 512.
[89] HC Deb 28 June 1990 c 528.

The government returned to the House on 24 October 1990 with specific motions to amend standing orders to set up the proposed three new European Standing Committees, each with ten members, to refer EC documents recommended for debate automatically to one of the new standing committees, and to amend both the European Legislation Committee's terms of reference and the 1980 Resolution. After a short debate, all the motions were agreed to but it soon became clear that the government was having difficulties in setting up the committees. On 22 January 1991, the Leader of the House (by then John MacGregor) moved another motion to amend the revised Standing Order 102 by reducing the number of committees from three to two, because of problems over their composition, but with thirteen members each instead of ten and a corresponding reallocation of subjects between them. Each committee was expected to need to meet about twice a month. He emphasised that the government was anxious for the committees to be set up as quickly as possible, because in their absence all scrutiny debates since the start of the session had had to be held on the floor of the House.

Several speakers in the subsequent short debate questioned how the potential members of the committees had been selected. Replying to the debate, Mr MacGregor repeated that the work of the committees would be reviewed at the end of the session and, following a point raised by several speakers both then and in the October 1990 debate, assured the House that any Member would be able to attend the committees' debates. If they were not on the committee, they would be able to speak and move amendments but not move actual motions or vote. The further amendments to standing orders were agreed without a vote. European Standing Committee A first met on 30 January 1991 and Standing Committee B on 29 January 1991. Details of their proceedings for the remainder of that session are described in Chapter 6. A simplified diagrammatic representation of the scrutiny system as currently operated is shown in Table 4.1.

The promised review of the European Standing Committees was conducted by the Procedure Committee at the start of the 1991–92 session and the Committee reported to the House in December 1991.[90] The report reiterated the Committee's original aims in relation to the standing committees and contained a reminder about their role:

---

[90] First Report from the Select Committee on Procedure, 1991–92, HC 31, *Review of European Standing Committees*.

the new Committees were intended to remain firmly as a deliberative part of the House's *legislative* role, distinct and separate from the investigative activities of Select Committees. Hence our firm recommendation against equipping European Standing Committees with powers to send for persons, papers and records.[91]

The government's difficulties in setting up the committees were described in some detail and some other criticisms and disappointments were voiced. Almost all the Committee's witnesses had, however, regarded the new committees as a success, partly because of the shift of business from late night debates on the floor of the House to morning meetings, but also because 'of the positive effect of the quality of scrutiny of a more systematic and coherent period of questioning before the consideration of a substantive motion.'[92] The committees were generally given a clean bill of health, with recommendations only for minor changes, although the Leader of the House was urged to think again about increasing their number to three, with ten members each, in order to spread the burden of work among more Members.

Perhaps not surprisingly, the Procedure Committee also returned to the 'overriding importance' of the government's undertaking in what had by then become the October 1990 Resolution on adoption before scrutiny of legislative proposals was complete:

> We hope that the Government will continue to make every effort to bring documents forward for debate, whether in Committee or on the floor of the House, in time to allow the House's views to be taken into account by Ministers before final approval is given in the Council of Ministers. The importance of this undertaking cannot be overstated since it underpins and gives purpose and meaning to the entire machinery of scrutiny which the House has developed.[93]

The government's response to the Procedure Committee's report was published as a further report by the Committee, shortly before Parliament

---

[91] Ibid, para 3.
[92] Ibid, para 7.
[93] Ibid, para 44.

was dissolved for the 1992 general election.[94] Predictably, the report was welcomed and the absence of any need for fundamental change accepted without demur. Most of the detailed recommendations were also accepted, at least on a 'best endeavours' basis. The suggestion that the number of committees should be increased was, however, deferred for further consideration 'in the new Parliament'.

## Conclusion

Although there have been numerous changes of detail in the Commons' system for scrutinising EC legislation, the European Legislation Committee has hardly changed its manner of operation since it was first set up in 1974. It is appointed for the duration of a Parliament. It has always had sixteen members and been chaired by an opposition backbencher. It usually meets weekly while the House of Commons is sitting and reports to the House after each meeting, thus making around thirty reports in a session of normal length.

The Committee's proceedings follow very closely the pattern envisaged by the Foster Committee: examining EC documents and reporting its opinion on the legal and political importance of each such document and on any matters of principle, policy or law which may be affected. The categories of document which the Committee may consider have been the subject of a good deal of debate and their scope has been somewhat extended, to the point where in 1994 they included all legislative proposals to be considered by the Council as well as a wide range of Commission Communications and other reports submitted to the Council. They still, however, follow the Foster Committee's recommendation in excluding legislation approved by the Commission.

The volume of documents considered by the Committee has fluctuated over time but has grown steadily. The Foster Committee estimated in 1973 that there would be about 300 a year but by 1975 the annual total was already between 650 and 700,[95] and it remained at that level until the early 1980s by which time the number averaged over 700 a year. By

---

[94] Third Report from the Select Committee on Procedure, 1991–92, HC 331: *The Government's Response to the Procedure Committee's Review of European Standing Committees.*

[95] First Report from the Select Committee on Procedure, 1974–75, HC 294.

1988, the number had risen to an annual average of 840[96] and by the mid-1990s it had reached about 1,000. The peaks have generally coincided with specific events such as Community enlargement and the implementation of the Single European Act.

The Committee's sifting function requires it to give an opinion on the legal and political importance of each document before it. There are no specific criteria against which to judge the political or legal importance of a document, so each case has to be assessed individually. Some documents are of obvious importance, while others may be important to particular sectors or interests. They may also raise issues of Community competence or unusual uses of treaty powers—both matters in which the Committee has a particular interest.

The Committee's reports usually follow the same general format. There are summaries of the contents of anything between four and twelve documents, or groups of documents on the same topic, considered to raise matters of legal or political importance. The summaries generally draw on explanatory memoranda by the Commission and government departments and they have tended to become more detailed, as Community legislation has grown in complexity and scope. The Committee does not have to give the reasons for its decision about the significance of a particular document or proposal but normally does so. It often comments on the handling of a proposal, either by the UK government or by the Community institutions, and has been particularly vigilant in seeking adequate time for national parliamentary scrutiny. It often comments on the practicality and cost of a proposal, its drafting, and its consistency with other EC policies. It may also give the reactions of those affected by a proposal, especially where it has sought written evidence from 'relevant interests'. There may be comments by the Committee's legal adviser, especially where there are doubts about the treaty base of a proposal or where questions of Community competence arise. Documents not considered to be of political or legal importance—about two-thirds of the total—are simply listed at the end of each report.

The volume of documents before the Committee means that it has to be selective, both about the documents on which it decides to seek written evidence and those which it recommends for further consideration by the House. The need to be selective has grown as more proposals, particularly those subject to the co-operation procedure, have had to be re-examined

---

[96] Fourth Report from the Select Committee on Procedure, 1988–89, HC 622–I *The Scrutiny of European Legislation* para 11.

after they have been subject to major revisions. The likely timescale of individual proposals may determine whether or not it is feasible to seek further evidence. The decision about further consideration by the House, whether by a European Standing Committee or, exceptionally, on the floor of the House, has to take account of several factors, including the timing of any forthcoming consideration by the Council of Ministers and the availability of time for debate. Some documents more or less automatically qualify for debate but with others account has to be taken of what parliamentary consideration would (or would not) achieve, particularly where it is known that a proposal is likely to be modified or where the issues raised are controversial but too narrow to justify debate.

The Committee's method of working has remained unique within the Commons and examination of its reports shows that it is not as mechanistic as it may appear. In the course of its routine work, it has to scrutinise and report on very large amounts of paper, some inevitably concerned with the nuts and bolts of Community activity but also dealing with proposals with far-reaching implications for member states. Much of the Committee's work can only be described as a hard grind, as the then chairman, Nigel Spearing, acknowledged in June 1990.[97] A great deal of the preliminary work is done by the staff but for a conscientious member, to be on the Committee represents a substantial workload, most of all for the chairman. The nature of its proceedings, which are almost all carried out in private deliberative sessions, as well as the style and content of its reports, mean that the Committee's activities seldom achieve a high public profile, even when the subject matter being considered is of intense public concern.

Whatever strictures may have been uttered about other aspects of the scrutiny system, the European Legislation Committee has generally been seen as a success. The Procedure Committee has found little to criticise and such recommendations as have been made have been concerned mainly with strengthening the Committee's powers. The Committee has been not only durable and resilient but also able to adapt its proceedings to changing circumstances both in the EC and at Westminster and to handle an ever-increasing volume of paper. Its history shows, however, that its success has been achieved not only by hard work and efficiency but also by constant vigilance and persistence in ensuring that successive governments, as well as individual government departments, fulfil their

---

[97] HC Deb 28 June 1990 c 545.

own responsibilities for the operation of the scrutiny system in relation to such mundane but vital matters as the timely supply of the documents which are the basis of its work. Much of this vigilance has been exercised behind the scenes and emerges publicly from time to time only in the special reports.[98]

Both the European Legislation Committee itself and the Procedure Committee have frequently stated that the Committee's effectiveness depends crucially on the government's honouring its undertaking not to agree to the adoption of EC legislation before the scrutiny process was complete including, where required, a debate in the House. Without that undertaking, the scrutiny process would have little point. Because they cannot be seen to oppose the principle of ministerial accountability to the House, ministers have been forced, at least outwardly, to adhere to the undertaking. There has nevertheless always been an underlying tension between the need to observe the terms of the undertaking and ministers' desire not to have their freedom of manoeuvre in negotiations unnecessarily restricted, particularly in the political environment of Brussels where compromises and trade-offs are an essential element in the negotiating process and where decisions often have to be taken in circumstances where references back to national parliaments are impossible.

It is therefore not surprising that, while acknowledging the importance of the principle embodied in it, governments have generally resisted efforts to strengthen the undertaking or to make it more restrictive. The experiences of the early 1980s showed that even with the undertaking embodied in a resolution of the House, ministers could not always be relied on to abide by it—and when they failed to do so, the Committee could do little more than make a fuss. In its 1983–84 Special Report, the Committee itself quoted a remark made in evidence by the then Leader of the House, John Biffen that

> in the circumstances of our relationship with the European Community, Government has retained its sphere of authority more effectively than has Parliament.[99]

---

[98] See, in particular, First Special Report, 1983–84, HC 527; and Second Special Report, 1985–86, HC 400.

[99] First Special Report from the Select Committee on European Legislation, 1983–84, HC 527, para 26.

As the Committee commented, this places 'an obligation on the Government to take special care to involve the House in the Community decision-making process.'[100] In practice, Leaders of the House have generally supported the Committee's efforts to ensure that government departments fulfil correctly and without delay their obligations to supply documents to the Committee, particularly during Mr Biffen's term.[101] They have also been content to rely on the Committee's vigilance in relation to some aspects of the operation of the scrutiny system, such as ensuring that ministers observed the provisions of the 1980 Resolution in relation to 'confidential, routine or trivial' legislative proposals[102] and to the adoption of proposals before a debate was held. They have, however, been less willing to make concessions to the Committee's often-expressed concern that ministers should observe the letter as well as the spirit of the Resolution over the occasions when debates could not be held or oral statements made.[103]

Governments have also been anxious to maintain as far as they can their power of initiative in relation to the consideration of EC business, hence their reluctance to agree to any extension of the European Legislation Committee's terms of reference to include different categories of document and thus the scope of scrutiny by the House. This has been interpreted by one observer as arising from a desire to preserve their role as 'gatekeeper' between the EC and the domestic political system.[104] The categories of document which the Committee may consider have gradually been extended to include both pre-legislative and some non-legislative proposals but this has been achieved largely by a process of attrition and reluctant concessions. It took very strongly worded criticism by the Procedure Committee in its 1988–89 report for the government to agree to a relatively limited amendment to the Committee's terms of reference, rather than the earlier promise by the Leader of the House to adopt a liberal interpretation of the documents covered by the terms of reference.

---

[100] Ibid, para 27; see also Mr Biffen's response to the 1983–84 First Special Report, HC Deb 29 October 1984 cc 800–2w.

[101] See, for example, the response to the Committee's Second Special Report, 1985–86, HC—Cm 123; April 1987.

[102] See, for example, the response to the 1988–89 Procedure Committee Report—Cm 1081, May 1990.

[103] Ibid.

[104] Stephen George in Chapter 4, 'The Legislative Dimension' of Stephen George (ed) *Britain and the European Community—The Politics of Semi-Detachment* Oxford: Clarendon Press, 1992 p 94.

As the terms of Standing Order 127 show, the European Legislation Committee has never been 'just another select committee'. It has very different functions and methods of operation from other Commons select committees and is subject to particular constraints in that its agenda is almost entirely dictated by documents generated within the EC and transmitted to it by government departments rather than by its own choice. The Committee is also unique as a select committee in that it is an essential element in the House's legislative processes, but its role relates to legislation which is not of domestic origin and over which the government has very little direct control. This is in distinct contrast to the tight control which governments normally exercise over both the domestic legislative programme and the rest of the House's business. Extension of the Committee's competence, particularly into non-legislative areas, not only weakens the government's 'gatekeeper' role, but also potentially weakens its normal control over the Commons' agenda because of the commitment to allow debates on documents recommended by the Committee for consideration by the House. It is therefore understandable that governments have resisted efforts to extend the Committee's competence outside legislative or pre-legislative areas. The Madrid Summit (and other episodes) may have shown the risks for a government of *not* allowing debates on matters of intense political concern, but there may equally be risks in being forced to hold such debates at moments or on topics not of the government's own choosing—and what is perceived as good for the government may not be good for parliament or the public interest.

The efforts in the latter part of the 1980s, following the Single European Act, to extend the scope of scrutiny by widening the Committee's terms of reference may be seen partly as yet another episode in the traditional conflict between parliament and the executive. At a more practical level, they also reflect the growth of Community competence and greater awareness, both inside and outside the House, of the significance of EC matters. One observer has also seen 'a new determination on the part of many MPs to prevent further leakage of sovereignty by default, and a drive to regain as much control as possible over a widening range of legislative matters that are being determined at EC level.'[105]

The basic principles of the scrutiny system, as originally laid down by the Foster Committee, are to ensure that the House is kept properly

---

[105] Stephen George, op cit, p 95.

informed of Community initiatives and has the necessary opportunities to ensure that ministers are aware of its views. That system was devised at a time when the existence of the veto in the EC Council put ministers in a more clear-cut position than they are today when Community decision-making procedures often involve qualified majority voting and are considerably more complex, particularly the co-decision procedure. So far the system has survived with its principles essentially unchanged but, as David Miers observes in Chapter 2, post-Maastricht it not only has to keep up with the intricacies of the co-decision procedure but also faces the challenge of new areas of inter-governmental activity and the prospect of a much-enlarged Community.

---

**Key to Table 4.1**

(1) The Select Committee may indicate that Ministers need not withhold agreement pending consideration.

(2) The Select Committee may also *either* not recommend debate at this stage *or* not come to a decision.

(3) Standing Committee A covers the Ministry of Agriculture Fisheries and Food, the Department of Transport and the Environment and the Forestry Commission, together with the analagous responsibilities of the territorial departments (the Northern Ireland, Scottish and Welsh Offices) Standing Committee B covers all other departments.

---

**Table 4.1**
**House of Commons Consideration of EC Documents**
**(Simplified Flow Chart)**

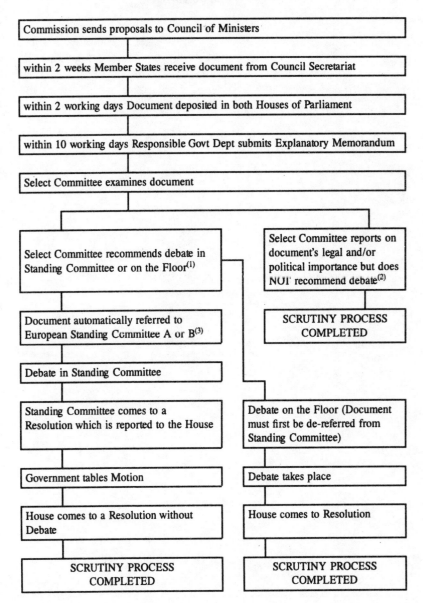

# 5

# The House of Lords
# and the European Community:
# the Evolution of Arrangements for Scrutiny

## *Donald Shell*[1]

The House of Lords has displayed considerable diligence in developing its scrutiny of European Community matters, especially through its Select Committee on the European Communities. When first established in 1974 there was no expectation that this committee would become not only the predominant select committee in the upper House, but also the major forum for parliamentary scrutiny of Community policy within Britain. Nor was it anticipated that its careful, thorough, and non-partisan approach to scrutiny would contribute so much to the enhanced reputation of the House of Lords.

The European Communities Committee, with its several subject based sub-committees, has regularly involved from 60 to 100 peers and has produced around twenty reports a session, many of them substantial documents. For a significant proportion of the more active members of the House experience as members of this Committee has helped develop their interest in and knowledge of Community policy-making. Many of the reports are debated on specific motions on the floor of the House. But even where the work of the Committee is not brought explicitly before the House, its reports never seem to be far from the minds of peers. The reports the Committee has produced have undoubtedly added depth to the consideration given to Community issues in the other proceedings of the House. Debate on domestic legislation, for example to do with environmental concerns, regional policy, employee protection and many other matters, almost invariably draws forth reference to a European Community dimension. Questions in the House produce regular references

---

[1] The author wishes to acknowledge the generous help and advice given by Dr Philippa Tudor, Clerk in the House of Lords, formerly attached to the European Communities Committee Office. Responsibility for any errors of fact, and for all judgement and opinions expressed, rests solely with the author.

to Community concerns—and to reports from the Select Committee. When the House has debated major developments within the Community, notably the Single European Act and the Maastricht Treaty, reports from the Committee have illuminated its debates. The activities of the Committee have helped to ensure that consideration of Community concerns in the Lords has predominantly taken place in a very straight-forward, matter-of-fact way, with peers eager to explore the practical consequences of policy proposals, to find solutions to problems, and to influence decision makers wherever they happen to be located.

Before examining the evolution of the Lords scrutiny system it is worth considering for a moment some features of the House of Lords which have been significant in shaping its general approach to European Community issues.

## The Character of the House

The clear subordinate status of the House as well as the nature of its membership give it a character very different from the House of Commons. Three aspects are worth emphasising. First, the whole party battle is played out in a much lower key in the House of Lords than it is in the Commons. There is neither the same temptation so relentlessly to pursue party advantage in the upper chamber, nor the same remorseless drive to ensure party cohesion. The forces which insist that the vast majority of issues which come before the Commons become subject to some degree of inter-party conflict do not operate in the same irresistible manner in the Lords. Secondly, the membership of the House consists predominantly of part-timers. Even those who are classified as regular attenders often have major interests, and in many cases full-time careers, to pursue outside the House. Among the consequences of this is the ability of peers to bring to their work in the House perspectives derived from first hand experience of business, industry and the professions, all to a degree far beyond that found in the contemporary House of Commons. Thirdly, the fact that the House is in its proceedings generally untroubled by any pretence of exercising power and readily understands that it is no more than a chamber of influence, makes it in many respects more suited to engage with European Community draft legislation than the Commons. MPs feel they ought to be exercising power, and are troubled when they experience not simply the practical removal of that power, but even the denial of its existence. Peers have no such aspirations; if they talk about sovereignty, then they know it is not any 'sovereignty' possessed by their chamber that is at stake.

These features of the House have been reflected in its approach to European Community issues.[2] Most obvious has been a markedly more favourable attitude towards the Community than that which has generally prevailed in the Commons. Opinion in the Lords has always been overwhelmingly 'pro-Europe'. In 1971 peers voted 451 to 58 for a motion approving the United Kingdom's entry to the European Communities, whilst the identical motion in the Commons was carried by 356 votes to 244. The majority opinion on the floor of the House has remained solidly supportive of the European Community. Peers who have consistently criticised European integration have been in a minority and—with only a few exceptions—recognised 'Euro-sceptics' have not played much part on the European Communities Committee; they have confined their criticisms to the floor of the House or to activities outside it, including television appearances. The sensitivities which have inhibited procedural developments in respect of the scrutiny of Community legislation in the Commons have not been evident in the Lords. Nor has the temptation to obtain some party political advantage through the treatment of Community matters been a distraction to the House, as it has frequently been to the House of Commons.

The sharp polarisation of opinion within the Conservative Party on the development of the Community following the fall of Mrs Thatcher and the negotiation of the Maastricht Treaty found expression in the House of Lords, with the added ingredient of Thatcher herself and some of her chief acolytes being by then members of the House. But hopes on the part of the Euro-sceptics that the House would somehow upset the Maastricht apple cart were decisively disappointed. This reflected not only the basically pro-Europe stance of most peers, but also a sense on the part of the House as a whole of its own political weakness. On the really big questions of politics the House is in no position to add to the heat of battle—though it may certainly attempt to shed light on what is being fought over. But on more mundane, day-to-day matters the House is well-placed to seek to exert a little gentle influence. And this it has consistently done, especially through its select committee.

---

[2] On the House of Lords generally see Donald Shell *The House of Lords*, Philip Allan, 2nd edition 1992 and Donald Shell and David Beamish (eds), *The House of Lords at Work*, Clarendon Press, 1993.

## The Decision to Establish a Select Committee

In December 1972, only a few days before Britain's formal accession to the European Community, the House of Lords established a select committee to 'consider procedures for scrutiny of proposals for European Community instruments'. Under the chairmanship of Lord Maybray-King, a former Speaker of the House of Commons, the Committee clearly saw its task as both urgent and important. By the time it first met in January 1973, Britain was already a member of the European Community; legislation was being enacted by the Council of Ministers, but parliament had devised no special means to ensure such legislation received some form of scrutiny. In March the Committee produced an interim report recommending as a matter of urgency that 'a Select Committee should be appointed at once to "sift" the proposals, that is to distinguish between the majority, proposals which deal with minor or technical matters, and the minority, to which the attention of Parliament ought to be drawn, because of their special importance'.[3] Despite the urging of the Committee nothing was done to implement this recommendation. The Committee, however, pursued its task with vigour, meeting in all 28 times before producing its final report in July.[4] Evidence taken by the Committee was exchanged with evidence taken by the parallel Commons committee. Most witnesses to the Lords' committee, including government ministers, very much favoured a joint select committee between the two Houses which, it was argued, would make the best use of available resources, not least in terms of members of both Houses willing and able to give their time to this new task. But as Lord Maybray-King commented to one witness: 'the other Committee is not looking favourably on joint meetings', and in the event not only were no joint meetings held, but it was clear by the time that the Maybray-King Committee reported that the Commons were not disposed to agree to any joint committee activity in this area.

For the Government Lord Jellicoe, Leader of the House, advocated the establishment of a standing committee, arguing that 'the investigatory and inquisitorial procedures of a Select Committee' were not really appropriate because such a committee would take too long, would be difficult to staff, and would preclude the participation of all but a small number of specialist

---

[3] First Report by the Select Committee on Procedures for Scrutiny of Proposals for European Instruments, 1972–73, HL 67, March 1973, para 6.

[4] Second Report by the Select Committee on Procedures for Scrutiny of Proposals for European Instruments, 1972–73, HL 194, July 1973.

peers.[5] These arguments reflected the tone adopted by the Leader of the Commons in evidence given to the parallel Commons Committee. But overwhelmingly other witnesses pressed for a select committee, and with one dissident member the Maybray-King Committee strongly urged the use of a select committee.[6] Furthermore this new select committee should have the power to appoint sub-committees, one of which should deal particularly with law and legal points. The power to co-opt other peers to membership of sub-committees should also be given to the main committee. Because the chairmanship of the new committee was recognised as likely to be an onerous task, it was recommended that a new salaried post should be created, the occupant of which would become chairman of the committee. Assistance should be provided by a legal adviser (another new post), and the sub-committees should have the right to appooint specialist advisers. Finally, the new committee should be able to appoint a Parliamentary Observer in Brussels to 'serve as a source of information and to inform the Select Committee of important Community proposals while they are in the formative stage' and to keep in contact with the Court of Justice.

Though made in July 1973 the report of the Maybray-King Committee was not debated until December, by which time many peers were emphasizing the desirability of acting quickly to establish some means to ensure appropriate parliamentary scrutiny of Community instruments. In a maiden speech Lord Crowther-Hunt, the Oxford political scientist who had formerly been an adviser to the Labour Government on constitutional matters, referred to the 252 Regulations that had been adopted by the Community in the eleven months since Britain had become a member. Lord Brooke of Cumnor said the Danes, who had joined at the same time as the UK, had established appropriate parliamentary machinery within seven weeks of accession. The law lord, Lord Diplock, stressed the urgency of the situation. But speaking for the Government Lord Windlesham gave the report a very guarded welcome, arguing that the House should think very carefully before taking on commitments on a scale that may be difficult to sustain, and that it may well be easier to have one main committee rather than a number of sub-committees; for these reasons he recommended that the report be referred to the House's Select

---

[5] Ibid, evidence given on 13 February 1973, Q 124.

[6] Ibid, para 109. The dissident committee member was Lord Diamond (a former Labour Treasury minister, who subsequently became the first chairman of the House of Lords Select Committee on the European Communities), see p lxvi of the Report.

Committee on Procedure.[7] This was done, and the Procedure Committee quickly offered its support to the Maybray-King Committee's recommendations.[8] The change of government in March 1974 slowed things down, but eventually in May 1974, over 16 months after entry to the Community, the House agreed to the establishment of a select committee to examine Community legislation.[9] The one proposal about which considerable doubt had been expressed in debate was that for a Parliamentary Observer in Brussels, and this was duly dropped.

The terms of reference recommended for the new select committee, which were subsequently adopted, were as follows:

> to consider Community proposals, whether in draft or otherwise, to obtain all necessary information about them, and to make reports on those which, in the opinion of the Committee, raise important questions of policy or principle, and on other questions to which the Committee consider that the special attention of the House should be drawn.

These terms of reference were significantly wider than those of the Commons select committee in two main respects: first, they empowered the Lords' Committee to report on proposals in a substantive way, rather than directing it primarily to identify proposals which raised important questions; secondly, they permitted the Committee to report on matters not directly tied to draft Community legislation, giving it the capacity to conduct broader inquiries into Community developments if it so wished.

In line with the recommendations of the Maybray-King Committee the new select committee was given freedom to decide its own sub-committee structure and to co-opt additional peers to serve on the sub-committees it chose to establish. The new post of Principal Deputy Chairman of Committees was established as a salaried officer of the House, its holder becoming in effect the full-time chairman of the European Communities Committee. At the same time a professional legal adviser was appointed, followed later by a legal assistant. In retrospect, what is striking about the recommendations made by the Maybray-King Committee is the extent to which the arrangements devised and adopted then have endured with very little change.

---

[7] HL Deb 6 December 1973 cc 759–839.

[8] First Report from the Select Committee on Procedure 1973–74, HL 58, January 1974.

[9] HL Deb 7 May 1974 cc 369–70.

## The structure and method of work of the Select Committee

When established the European Communities Committee (ECC) initially set up five subject based sub-committees, and remitted to these the actual work of detailed scrutiny. To begin with 35 peers were involved, either as members of the main committee or co-opted to sub-committees. The second report of the EEC stated that 'the number, subject matter, and co-opted membership of the Sub-Committees will be kept under consideration'.[10] The number of sub-committees subsequently grew to seven by 1975, but was reduced to six in 1986–87 to allow for the appointment of *ad hoc* sub-committees. The total number of peers serving on the select committee and its sub-committees rose to about 100 in the early 1980s, but then fell back to just under 80 ten years later.[11] Given that the House had no regular investigatory select committees prior to the early 1970s, this represented a very considerable investment by the House in what was for peers a new form of parliamentary activity. From 1979 onwards a Select Committee on Science and Technology has existed alongside the EEC, while the House has also made increasing use of ad hoc investigatory select committees on various subjects. Growing demands placed on the House, both by its select committees and by an increased burden of legislation, led to a review of all committee work in 1991–92, followed by a cut back in the ECC, which by 1993 had only 60 members and five sub-committees (see below p 105).

It is worth noting that when the EEC was first formed in the 1970s the House had for over a decade benefited from a higher rate of recruitment following the 1958 Life Peerages Act. An increase in the active members of the House gave it the capacity to develop this new role. Furthermore, for many peers the demands imposed by select committee work constituted a more congenial form of parliamentary activity than business taken on the floor of the House. Committee work has a steady rhythm and predictable hours (which can be booked into a diary long in advance), whereas the timing and duration of debates on the floor of the House are often surrounded by unpredictability. Some peers active in committee work take virtually no part in debates on the floor of the House. A rotation rule has required peers to leave the committee or a particular sub-committee after five sessions' membership (in 1992 reduced to four), and not return to that

---

[10] Second Report from the European Communities Committee 1973–74, HL 62.
[11] See *Report from the Select Committee on the Committee Work of the House*, 1991–92, HL 35, February 1992, vol ii p 28.

committee or sub-committee for at least a session, though they were free immediately to join a different sub-committee. The number of peers involved in the ECC, and the turnover of members, has ensured that a sizable proportion of the House had by this means some experience of the European Communities.[12] The first chairman of the EEC, occupying the post of Principal Deputy Chairman of Committees, was the then Labour peer, Lord Diamond, formerly Chief Secretary to the Treasury in the Labour cabinet prior to the 1970 election. But he very soon took up another post, and so gave way to Baroness Tweedsmuir of Belhelvie, who in both Houses had held non cabinet offices in Conservative administrations. Thereafter a succession of former Labour ministers held this post, until in 1994 the former Liberal Democrat Chief Whip in the House, Lord Tordoff, became chairman of the Committee.[13]

The Committee quickly established a method of work which has been retained with little variation. The main committee has exercised a broad supervisory role. It offers guidance and advice to the chairman who has special responsibilities (see below); it helps keep the sub-committees in touch with each other; it can act as a sounding board for ideas which the sub-committee chairmen may wish to ventilate; it keeps the sub-committee structure under review, and it represents the interests of the committee and sub-committees to the House as a whole. The main committee receives and approves the reports of sub-committees.

The chairman receives all documents deposited by the government in parliament relating to Community legislation; this includes all Commission proposals submitted to the Council of Ministers, and some other documents put forward by Community institutions—all told about 800 documents annually. Within 14 days of the receipt of each document the lead government department submits a memorandum, signed by a minister, indicating the legal, financial and policy implications of the proposal, and also offering some guidance as to the timetable the government envisages for the proposal's consideration and possible adoption. As there are far too many proposals for detailed scrutiny, and as many are of comparatively small importance, the Chairman sifts the more significant from the less

---

[12] Over 200 of those attending the House in the 1988–89 session had served on the ECC or one of its sub-committees; see Donald Shell 'The European Communities Committee' in *the House of Lords at Work*, eds Donald Shell and David Beamish, Clarendon Press, Oxford, 1993.

[13] Following Lord Greenwood of Rossendale were Baroness White, Baroness Llewelyn-Davies of Hastoe, Baroness Serota and Lord Boston of Faversham.

important (see Table 5.1). In 1980 the government gave an undertaking that, save where the Committee has indicated that agreement need not be withheld and in certain other closely defined circumstances, no minister would vote for proposals in the Council of Ministers which are still subject to parliamentary scrutiny or awaiting debate. This is known as the parliamentary reserve.

The main Committee then confirms this sift, which is reported to the House by means of a fortnightly document published while the House is sitting entitled *Progress of Scrutiny*. This not only indicates which documents have been sifted where, but also shows what stage the scrutiny of documents has reached. The proportion sifted for scrutiny has varied a good deal, but in recent years has been around one-third. In 1992 the chairman recommended that documents sifted to sub-committees should be divided into those for possible scrutiny and those sifted to sub-committees for information purposes only; the latter would not be subject to the parliamentary reserve. This reflects the feeling within the EEC that it is helpful for sub-committees to see a wide range of documents within their subject area.

The sub-committees must then decide which documents should be the focus of an enquiry, and indeed the depth and range of such enquiries. In practice enquiries have been conducted on only about one in ten of the documents sifted to sub-committees, though in recent years a further twenty to thirty documents annually have been the subject of correspondence with ministers. Sub-committees act in the main as autonomous free standing committees, though all reports are formally made through the main committee to the House, and occasionally the main committee has referred a report back, perhaps for clarification on a particular point.

Reports are made to the House and published. Each report is recommended as being either for information only or for debate, with the latter usually being debated fairly soon, though there can be delays. Some complaints to the effect that debates tend to be arranged at 'off-peak times', such as the last day before a recess, have been heard.[14] However, it is worth emphasising that all reports recommended for debate do in fact receive such debate (unless unusually the request for debate has been withdrawn); the House has not hitherto had to restrict the opportunity for

---

[14] See HL Deb 28 January 1991 cc 488–9.

**Table 5.1**
**System of Scrutiny**

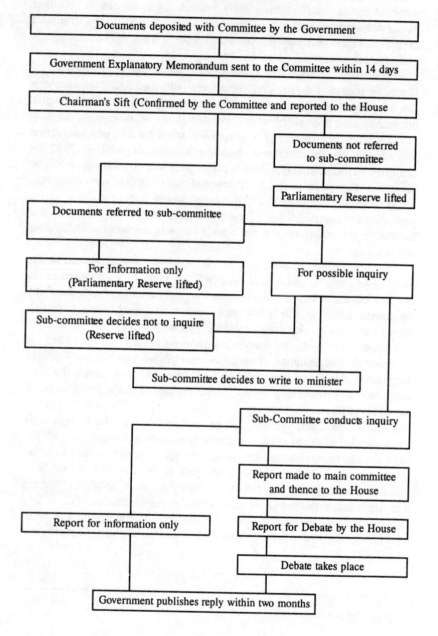

debate as has been the case in the Commons for so long. Government replies to reports have either been made through ministerial contributions to debates, or by means of a written response to the Committee. Gradually the conventions about government replies have been tightened up. Complaints about unacceptably long delays, sometimes six months or more, have been heard. Furthermore the fact that only an oral reply might be made to a report recommended for debate, meant that in some cases the more important reports appeared to receive the less satisfactory form of reply. By 1990 written replies were made as a matter of course to all reports, and in 1992 the Government committed itself wherever possible to make such replies within two months of the publication of a report.[15]

Sub-committees have been structured so as to cover broad subject areas, though one sub-committee has always had terms of reference specifically dealing with the legal implications of proposals, namely:

to consider and report on:

(a) any Community proposal which would lead to significant changes in UK law, or have far reaching implications for areas of UK law other than those to which it is immediately directed,

(b) the merits of such proposals as are referred to it by the select committee,

(c) whether any important developments have taken place in Community law, and

(d) any matters which they consider should be drawn to the attention of the Committee concerning the vires of any proposal.

Normal practice has been for this sub-committee to be chaired by a Lord of Appeal in Ordinary. In recent years an area of particular concern for this sub-committee has been the treaty base on which draft legislation has been made. It has been responsible for a high proportion of the letters sent to ministers, not infrequently concerning itself with some legal aspect of a proposal while policy considerations relating to the same proposal have been examined by another sub-committee.

---

[15] See First Report from the Select Committee on Procedure, 1992–93, HL 11, June 1992.

### Table 5.2
### 'Ad Hoc' Sub Committees of the Lords'
### European Communities Committee

| Date | Title/Reference |
|---|---|
| Jul 1978 | *Relations with the European Parliament after Direct Elections* HL 256, 1977–78 |
| Jul 1979 | *European Economic Community Passport Union* HL 58, 1979–80 |
| Dec 1979 | *Policies for Rural Areas* HL 129, 1979–80 |
| Apr 1980 | *European Air Fares* HL 235, 1979–80 |
| Oct 1980 | *Human Rights* HL 362, 1979–80 |
| Jul 1981 | *Outward Processing of Textiles and Clothing* HL 269, 1980–81 |
| Jan 1983 | *A Uniform Electoral Procedure for the European Parliament* HL 64, 1982–83 |
| Jun 1984 | *Agriculture and the Environment* HL 247, 1983–84 |
| Jul 1985 | *European Union* HL 226, 1984–85 |
| Mar 1988 | *Staffing of Community Institutions* HL 66, 1987–88 |
| Feb 1989 | *Fraud Against the Community* HL 27, 1988–89 |
| Jul 1990 | *European Company Statute* HL 71, 1989–90 |
| Oct 1990 | *Economic and Monetary Union and Political Union* HL 88, 1989–90 |
| Nov 1993 | *Scrutiny of Inter-Governmental Pillars of the European Union* HL 124, 1992–93 |

As well as the regular sub-committees, ad hoc committees have been established from time to time to look at issues which cross normal sub-committee boundaries. Arguably this has been one of the most useful aspects of the Committee's work. Some reports from such ad hoc committees, notably that on *Economic and Monetary and Political Union* in 1990 and the 1989 report on *Fraud against the Community*, have received considerable attention. Table 5.2 contains a complete list of such ad hoc committees; from this it can be seen that the use of such committees has at times been more in the nature of an expansion of an existing sub-committee, but in recent years the tendency has been to use ad hoc committees for more fundamental and wide ranging enquiries.

In the 1994–95 session a further ad hoc committee was established to inquire into proposals being put forward for the 1996 Inter-Governmental Conference. The Committee has generally expressed itself satisfied with its own structures and methods of work. In evidence given to the Select Committee on the committee work of the House in 1991, the chairman of the ECC commented that the Committee's terms of reference were 'wide enough to enable the Committee to carry out almost any enquiry it chooses', and that they had allowed the Committee at times 'to adopt a more pro-active broader brush approach', as had been demonstrated in its enquiry into *Fraud against the Community*.[16]

## Recent Developments

As already indicated increased demands being made on the House resulted in the appointment in April 1991 of a select committee to consider the committee work of the House. The Committee became known as the 'Jellicoe' Committee after its chairman, a former Leader of the House. The ECC had already—in late 1990—formed a working group consisting of six of its most senior members to consider its own future. Drawing on the deliberations of this group the chairman of the ECC, Baroness Serota, gave evidence to the 'Jellicoe' Committee showing how the work of the ECC had increased, partly in response to the quickened tempo of Community legislation occasioned by the advent of the Single Market.[17] Until the mid 1980s most sub-committees were meeting fortnightly; by 1990 the general practice was to meet weekly. The total number of documents circulated to members had increased by almost 50 per cent since 1982. Reports from the sub-committees had become longer, with the average number of paragraphs in each report increasing from 29 in 1976 to 94 in 1990.

---

[16] *Report from the Select Committee on the Committee Work of the House*, 1991–92, HL 35–ii, paras 30–31, pp 25–26.

[17] Ibid, especially summary of evidence at paragraphs 66–68.

The Jellicoe Report paid tribute to the achievements of the ECC and to the reputation which it had established both in the UK and among Community institutions, in the following terms:

> It has made a unique contribution to the process of European scrutiny by national parliaments, a process now recognised as important not only by the Government but by the Heads of State who agreed a specific declaration on the role of National Parliaments at the Conference on Political Union in Maastricht in December 1991. More generally the Committee has over the years demonstrated conclusively the value and distinctive qualities of Lords' select committee work. It has come to play an essential role ...[18]

Whilst recognising these achievements, and recommending no change in the ECC's wide terms of reference, the Jellicoe Committee recommended that the Committee's scrutiny function should be exercised with greater speed and more selectivity. It also called for a reduction in the number of sub-committees, and suggested that in place of some eighty peers being involved in its work the number should be cut to about fifty. To monitor the committee work of the House, and to organise the allocation of resources between committees, it recommended that a new steering committee be established.

These recommendations appeared to surprise and even to pain some peers. Members of the ECC re-constituted their own 'working group' to consider how to respond. When the Jellicoe Committee report was debated in the House several members and former members of the ECC spoke up in defence of its activities and suggested not unreasonably that, if the problem was a shortage of resources, then ought not more resources to be provided to enable their committee to continue with its significant parliamentary role? If the Committee incurred a net cost of some £500,000 a year, was it not possible to increase funding to enable its good work to continue? Should the House not 'invest in success' asked Lord Shepherd, who went on to claim that the ECC did 'a great deal for the Community as a whole' and for relatively small sums of money.[19]

---

[18] Ibid, para 137.
[19] See HL Deb 3 June 1992 cc 899–1017.

However, the Select Committee on Procedure broadly endorsed the Jellicoe recommendations.[20] To oversee the committee work of the House a liaison committee rather than a steering committee was established with a remit to co-ordinate rather than supervise in any way the work of select committees, entailing for example decisions about the allocation of resources between committees. In its first report the Liaison Committee recommended that the ECC should be reduced from six sub-committees to five.[21] In support of this proposal it argued that such a reduction would permit the establishment of some other select committees and would mean that, instead of consuming some three-quarters of the resources of the House available for committee work, the ECC would consume only two-thirds. This recommendation was greeted by a marked lack of enthusiasm when debated on the floor of the House. Lord Aldington, a senior member of the House, and chairman of one of the ECC sub-committees, pressed an amendment to a division. The result was a tie with 106 peers voting in each lobby, which meant under the standing orders of the House that the amendment was not carried.[22] The House thus approved the change. But the moral victory appeared to lie with Lord Aldington who had nearly defeated a principal recommendation of a report endorsed by the government.

Several peers argued that it was folly to curtail the work of the Committee on the European Communities at the very time when widespread argument on the ratification of the Maastricht Treaty was developing. The Foreign Secretary, Douglas Hurd, was quoted as having recently said that: 'there is a real opportunity now for national parliaments to involve themselves more closely in Community business', yet this was the very moment when the House of Lords appeared to be scaling down its involvement. Nevertheless in January 1993 the scaling down took place. Five sub-committees were re-appointed in place of the six which had previously been in operation, and only 40 peers were co-opted to serve on them alongside the twenty full members of the select committee.[23]

---

[20] See First Report from the Select Committee on Procedure, 1992–93, HL 11, June 1992.

[21] First Report from the Liaison Committee, 1992–93, HL 40, November 1992.

[22] HL Deb 7 December 1992 cc 11–36.

[23] The new structure was sub-committee A: Finance, Trade and External Relations; B: Energy, Industry and Transport; C: Environment and Social affairs; D: Agriculture and Food; E: Law and Institutions. For the previous sub-committee structure see below p 12, Chapter 7.

The argument for slimming down the scale of the ECC's operation in the House was based on several factors. In giving evidence to the Jellicoe Committee the then Leader of the House, Lord Waddington, had revealed one of the government's concerns when he suggested that 'there may sometimes be a danger that a report will become too much a critique of domestic policy in isolation from its European context'; he went on to say that the 'unique contribution of the European Communities Committee is in producing reports which focus sharply on the most significant European issues'.[24] But it is worth noting why apologists for the Committee defended its lengthy reports. Among peers active in the work of the ECC something akin to professional pride seems to motivate them in the desire to produce thorough reports drawing on a comprehensive analysis of the subject of inquiry. Examining Community proposals without paying considerable attention to the domestic context could easily result in a failure to appreciate the likely impact of such a proposal. Short reports focusing sharply on matters demanding more or less immediate decision may be seen by ministers and their civil servants as the most useful. But this may simply reflect the perspective of those caught up in the urgency of day-to-day government decision-making rather than the position of those examining policy from the more detached parliamentary perspective as found in the second chamber.

Other complaints about the work of the ECC had been heard, including the fact that the membership of its sub-committees was insufficiently clearly defined. The whole question of participation in Lords' committees was indeed somewhat opaque. Peers who were not members or even co-optees could attend sessions when evidence was being taken and ask questions of witnesses, though unless formally co-opted they could not vote in deliberative sessions of the committee. Peers who wished to attend evidence sessions could request all the papers of a committee, and such circulations of papers could be both substantial and frequent. Furthermore, there appeared to have been a tendency to welcome as co-opted members some peers who contributed very little, and who in a few cases attended scarcely at all. Against the background of fewer peers being available to take part in the work of the Committee, peers had been encouraged to contribute almost, it seemed, wherever and whenever they could, for

---

[24] See *Report from the Select Committee on the Committee Work of the House*, 1991–92, HL 35–ii, p 104, para 10. In his oral evidence this point was confirmed when he said that he had gone to great pains to establish that he spoke for the whole government on that point (See Q 202).

example by remaining members of a sub-committee even though they were unable to take a regular and sustained part in its work.[25] This may seem a trivial point, yet it probably helped to feed a feeling that a certain laxity had developed in the workings of the Committee, an approach becoming less appropriate in a busier and more professionalised House.

Probably of more significance was the fact that some peers actively sought the establishment of other select committees dealing with quite different subjects. Shortly after the cut-back in the ECC had taken place two new select committees (one on Medical Ethics and the other on Delegated Powers) were established, developments for which strong lobbies had existed within the House for some time. But there had been real doubts about the capacity of the House to sustain more such committee work. Its legislative burdens had increased, and the supply of active new members had diminished. Hence the reduction in the ECC was seen as necessary to pave the way for new developments.

But it would be easy—yet mistaken—to draw a false conclusion from this. The House remained highly satisfied with the work of the European Communities Committee. And for its part the Committee showed itself eager to continue to develop its role in response to the changing European Community context of the 1990s.

## From European Community to European Union

By 1991–92 the need for perhaps more fundamental change was being recognised. The broadened competence of Community institutions, the development of co-decision procedures between the Council of Ministers and the European Parliament, as well as other changes embodied in the Maastricht Treaty, seemed likely to stimulate changes within national parliaments. Prominent among the new concerns was the need to ensure the existence of an appropriate means for the scrutiny of decisions taken under the two new pillars of the European Union, concerning foreign and security policy and justice and home affairs respectively. In practice the terms of reference of the House of Lords scrutiny committee had been wide enough to allow for investigations into areas which hitherto had not

---

[25] Attendance in the 1988–89 session at the six standing sub-committees had varied between 50 and 65 per cent; see Donald Shell 'The European Communities Committee' in *The House of Lords at Work*, eds Donald Shell and David Beamish, Clarendon Press, Oxford: 1993.

lain clearly within the European Community's legal competence, but which were now firmly placed within the structure of the European Union's new pillars. For example in 1978–79, and again in 1992–93, a sub-committee had inquired into the possible accession of the Community to the European Convention on Human Rights, and in 1988–89 reports on border controls on people, and on voting rights in local elections had been issued, all issues now covered by the justice and home affairs pillar. On several occasions too sub-committees had tackled questions concerned with the external relations of the Community or its enlargement. But following the Treaty of European Union the question arose as to what systematic scrutiny of decisions reached under the two new pillars would take place.

The ECC set up an ad hoc sub-committee to investigate and report on this area.[26] While acknowledging that much scrutiny under the two new pillars could be seen simply as a development of its existing role, this committee clearly wanted to ensure that scrutiny in the areas covered by the new pillars should be properly systematised. Thus it recommended that the ECC's terms of reference should be altered specifically to include the new pillars, and that draft proposals being considered should be available to the Committee, as with draft Community legislation. Furthermore the Committee argued that the criteria to determine whether proposals should be subject to scrutiny should be either significance, or eventual need for United Kingdom legislation, or imposition of legal commitments on the United Kingdom. Above all the report asserted that it was essential that the work of the inter-governmental pillars be supervised by national parliaments.

In its reply the government flatly refused to agree to provide drafts of proposals made under the foreign and security policy pillar on the grounds that these frequently involved both speed and secrecy and rarely the need for domestic legislation.[27] Under the justice and home affairs pillar the government stated that it 'would provide the first full text of any convention or proposal which would, if agreed, require later primary legislation'. When the House debated this report the government was pressed by peers on these points but refused to give ground.[28]

---

[26] Twenty-Eighth Report from the Select Committee on the European Communities 1992–93, HL 124 *House of Lords Scrutiny of the Inter-Governmental Pillars of the European Union*, November 1993.

[27] Cm 2471, February 1994.

[28] HL Deb 12 April 1994 cc 1470–1506.

The way in which decision-making under the two new pillars has been kept insulated from the procedures established for European Community decision-making presents a clear challenge to national parliaments. If, instead of creating the European Union, the competence of existing Community institutions had simply been extended to embrace the areas now covered by the new pillars, then existing scrutiny arrangements could likewise have taken on board policy-making in the new areas. Such a development would, however, have been seen as far too 'federalist'. Hence the new structure. But this may also be seen by ministers as a convenience in that the new pillars are not subject to the existing scrutiny arrangements in national parliaments. Perhaps the European Parliament will fill the gap, though it was notable that ministers in evidence to the Lords sub-committee considering this subject were eager to emphasise that they saw national parliaments as the proper forum for scrutiny of policy made under the new pillars rather than the European Parliament. Certainly in the British case one is tempted to think the reason for such emphasis was that they saw national parliaments as so much less threatening and more controllable than the European Parliament. In tackling this subject the Lords Select Committee on the European Communities had shown its willingness to continue to take very seriously the need for scrutiny of the whole European dimension to policy making, and its readiness to try to push the government gently but firmly in the direction of allowing more effective parliamentary scrutiny.

## Conclusion

Within the House the ECC has been widely viewed as a resounding success. Prior to its establishment in 1974 investigative select committees were not a regular feature of the House of Lords, though the capacity of the House to develop such a parliamentary role had been readily acknowledged.[29] By the early 1990s it had become unthinkable that such committees could be abolished; instead their role has been extended. At a time when the House of Commons had its own reasons for not developing a system for the detailed scrutiny of Community policy making, the House of Lords invested its resources to this end. By 1992 the lower House in setting up the European Standing Committees was showing a greater

---

[29] See especially *Reform of the House of Lords*, Cmnd 3799, 1968, Appendix 2, para 10.

readiness to grasp the nettle it had previously avoided. The House of Lords, while not in any sense abandoning its role in relation to the European Communities, had demonstrated its flexibility and its desire to seek a complementary role to the Commons by adjusting the way in which its own European Communities Committee operated.

The European Communities Committee of the House of Lords has since 1989 taken a leading part in the six monthly meetings of scrutiny committees of the parliaments of member countries, entitled the Conference of Committees specialising in European Affairs. Fostering cross-national contacts with parliamentarians and officials of the Community had always been part of its activities. Increasingly in recent years it has found itself being visited by parliamentarians from other European Community countries and being asked for advice about the role scrutiny committees might develop. Perhaps the extent of its work had been more widely recognised outside the UK rather than here at home. Few could have foreseen such a role for a committee of the House of Lords when Britain first joined the Community.

# PART II

# The Westminster Parliament in Action

# 6

# The House of Commons and the EC 1990–91

## Philip Giddings and Priscilla Baines

Part I of this book has set the scene with an account of the development of the European Community since British accession and of the way in which both Houses of Parliament have evolved systems for scrutinising the Community's work. In Part II we look at the two Houses in action, beginning with an account of a particular parliamentary session (1990–91), and then considering some policy issues and the run-up to, and consequences of, the Maastricht Intergovernmental Conferences.

## 1. The context

We look first at the House of Commons in the 1990–91 session. But before we consider it in any detail, we need to place it in context in three respects—the unique circumstances of contemporary events; the constitutional context provided by membership of the Community; and the political context provided by the divisions of opinion within and between the political parties.

While every parliamentary session might have some claim to be considered unique, in the context of matters European, the 1990–91 session was certainly extra-ordinary. It ran from November 1990 to October 1991. At its start the Prime Minister was forced out of office, at least in part because of her European policy. In January hostilities broke out in the Gulf. Throughout the session the Intergovernmental Conferences were taking place, as were what were hoped to be the concluding sessions of the Uruguay round GATT negotiations. And all this was taking place in a world still adjusting to the consequences of the collapse of Soviet hegemony in Eastern Europe, which was to lead to the collapse of the Soviet Union itself after the failure of the coup against Gorbachev in August 1991. In world, European and national terms these were months of high political drama. And it is against the background of those particular events that the House of Commons' handling of matters European has to be considered.

Secondly, as explained in Part I, since Britain became a member of the European Community in 1973, and particularly since the adoption of the Single European Act in 1986, the powers of the Westminster parliament have been significantly constrained: for the extensive range of matters covered by the Communities' treaties, legislative power resides in the Council of Ministers in Brussels, not the UK parliament at Westminster, and British ministers must act in concert with their Community colleagues. This does not, however, mean that there is nothing for Westminster to discuss!

Indeed, an important consequence of Community membership is the need to make appropriate provision in British law and practice to implement Community decisions. And British ministers remain accountable to parliament for the actions they take and the positions they adopt in the Community's decision-making process. Thus, even without the particular circumstances in 1990-91 of the intergovernmental conferences and the GATT negotiations, the House of Commons would have had a significant amount of business to conduct arising from Community membership - but much of that business (and particularly the legislative aspects) has to be conducted differently from other domestic business because of the constitutional context created by Community membership.

Thirdly, as events before and since this particular session have shown, Britain's relationship with the European Community is a matter of acute political controversy and the focus for continuing power struggles within and between the parties. Given the heavy penalties the British electoral system and political culture can exact for party disunity, it is inevitable that potential divisions of opinion within the parties will be seized upon and exploited by opponents. The Westminster parliament is the principal forum for the political struggle between and within the parties, and a continuing battle-ground for the hearts and minds of the electorate. For much of this session European issues provided the raw material for those struggles, particularly following the change in Conservative Party leadership and in anticipation of a general election. Throughout the session, then, even more than usual the political struggle was very much to the fore.

## 2. The opportunities

Notwithstanding the restricted competence of the House of Commons in these matters, its procedures provide no shortage of opportunities for raising European issues and in the 1990–91 session many MPs were keen to exploit them. These opportunities can be considered under eight headings: questions; statements; Euro-legislation; financial procedures; delegated legislation; adjournment debates; early day motions and the work of committees.

*Questions* Question time is a natural opportunity for the exploitation of political issues. POLIS (the House of Commons Library's database) has identified 774 questions concerning EC action or EC law during the 1990–91. Of these 69 received oral answers (including supplementaries) and a further 13 were questions for oral answer which were not reached. Of the remaining 692 written answers, 54 were vehicles for ministerial statements either on meetings of councils of ministers or on proposed European policy action.

Written questions are not used by all MPs: the 705 questions identified by POLIS as on European matters which received written answers in the 1990–91 session were asked by just 207 MPs. And of those 705 Questions, 43% were asked by just 20 MPs. Not surprisingly opposition members are proportionately more active in putting questions: 12 of the 20 most active questioners were Labour MPs and only 6 Conservative. 48% of the WPQs were asked by Labour MPs, compared with 40% by Conservatives and 7% by Liberal Democrats.

**Table 6.1**
**Written Questions Analysed by Party**

| Party | MPs asking WPQs | WPQs asked (%) |
|-------|-----------------|----------------|
| Labour | 83 | 339 (48%) |
| Conservative | 98 | 279 (40%) |
| Liberal Democrat | 12 | 49 (7%) |
| Plaid Cymru | 3 | 18 |
| SNP | 4 | 7 |
| UUP | 3 | 7 |
| SDLP | 2 | 2 |
| SDP | 1 | 2 |
| UPUP | 1 | 2 |

Paul Flynn (Labour—44) led the way in tabling WPQs by some distance, with Ron Davies (Labour front-bench agriculture spokesman—30), Tony Favell (Conservative—30) and Rhodri Morgan (Labour—28) also some way ahead of the field. At the other end of the scale of 'Euroquestioners', 74 MPs asked just one WPQ on European related matters (allowing for Ministers, about 360 MPs asked none).

There is no evidence of 'anti-EC' MPs being particularly prominent questioners. Amongst the Conservatives, whereas Teddy Taylor asked 19 and Tim Janman 9, Nicholas Winterton and Richard Body asked only 2, and Nicholas Budgen and Bill Cash asked none. Similarly, some prominent Labour 'antis' asked few 'Euro-Questions': Ron Leighton (3), Nigel Spearing (2), Peter Shore (1) and Dennis Skinner (0).

Nor are questions evenly distributed amongst departments. Over half of the WPQs were answered by just three departments—Environment, Trade and Industry and Agriculture, Fisheries and Food. These same three departments also lead the table for oral answers. (See Table 6.4)

Questions vary a good deal. But the following, taken from the first week after the Christmas recess, are probably typical:

Tam Dalyell asked MAFF to comment on the negotiations for the adoption of comprehensive Community rules setting higher welfare standards for animals during all stages of transport;[1]

Tam Dalyell also asked the Department of Energy about plans for a further reduction in sulphur dioxide emissions during negotiations on the new European protocol;[2]

Elliot Morley asked the Department of Environment when the Humber Estuary & Ramsar site would be designated a special protection site under the European Community directive;[3]

Margaret Ewing asked the Secretary of State for Scotland to review the question of access to salmon fishing in Scotland in the light of European Community law;[4]

---

[1] HC Deb 14 January 1991 c 394w.

[2] Ibid, c 360w.

[3] Ibid, c 444w.

[4] Ibid, c 446w.

Teddy Taylor asked the Foreign Secretary about the views of HMG on the concept of a Community Ombudsman;[5]

**Table 6.2**
**Most Active Questioners by Party**

| Conservative | | Labour | |
|---|---|---|---|
| Favell, Tony | 30 | Flynn, Paul | 44 |
| Taylor, Teddy | 19 | Davies, Ron | 30 |
| Nicholson, Emma | 17 | Morgan, Rhodri | 28 |
| Janman, Tim | 9 | Cohen, Harry | 12 |
| Bottomley, Peter | 8 | Clark, David | 11 |
| Butler, Chis | 8 | Dalyell, Tam | 11 |
| | | Michael, Alun | 11 |
| **Liberal Democrat** | | **Other** | |
| Hughes, Simon | 17 | Jones, Ieuan Wyn (PC) | 10 |
| Kirkwood, Archy | 6 | Thomas, Dafydd Ellis (PC) | 5 |
| Maclennan, Robert | 5 | Beggs, Roy (UUP) | 3 |
| Carlile, Alex | 4 | Taylor, John D (UUP) | 3 |
| Fearn, Ronnie | 3 | Wigley, Dafydd (PC) | 3 |
| Steel, David | 3 | | |

**Table 6.3**
**Distribution of 'Euro-WPQs'**

| Number of WPQs (N=705) | Number of Questions (N=207) |
|---|---|
| 10 or more | 14 |
| 5–9 | 24 |
| 4 | 9 |
| 3 | 24 |
| 2 | 61 |
| 1 | 74 |

[5] Ibid, c 383w.

**Table 6.4**
**Questions Analysed by Department**

| Written Questions | | Questions for Oral Answer* | |
|---|---|---|---|
| Environment | 139 | Trade & Industry | 17 |
| Trade & Industry | 121 | Enviroment | 16 |
| Agriculture, Fisheries | | Agriculture, Fisheries | |
| & Food | 97 | & Food | 13 |
| Transport | 54 | Employment | 9 |
| Home Office | 41 | Foreign & Commonwealth | |
| Employment | 38 | Office | 7 |
| Energy | 38 | Prime Minister | 5 |
| Health | 34 | Leader of the House | 4 |
| Foreign & Commonwealth | | Home Office | 3 |
| Office | 30 | Energy | 2 |
| Treasury | 28 | Scottish Office | 2 |
| Scottish Office | 23 | Welsh Office | 2 |
| Welsh Office | 21 | Attorney-General | 1 |
| Social Security | 13 | Health | 1 |
| Northern Ireland Office | 12 | Treasury | 1 |
| Prime Minister | 11 | | |
| Leader of the House | 4 | | |
| Education & Science | 3 | | |
| Defence | 2 | | |
| Attorney-General | 1 | | |

\* including 13 questions put down for oral answer but not reached (DoE 4; DTI 3; DE 2; FCO 2; Leader of House 1; Scottish Office 1)

Teddy Taylor also asked the Transport Secretary for what reasons the Government had agreed that the Commission's proposals on excise duties should be resolved by the European Council by 30 June, and to summarise the proposals submitted by the Commission.[6]

James Wallace asked the DES whether the Council of Ministers intended to extend the Tempus Scheme to promote the development of

---

[6] Ibid, c 402w.

the higher education system in the countries of central and eastern Europe to countries in addition to Poland and Hungary.[7]

*Statements* Statements are the vehicle by which ministers report to the House on the business of the European Council and the Council of Ministers. These include not only the twice-yearly meetings of heads of government but also the meetings of sectoral ministers. The Prime Minister reports on the summits with an oral statement, which is usually followed by an extended period of questions. Sectoral ministers may report with either an oral or a written statement (see Chapter 4 for further discussion of the arguments about the merits of oral rather than written statements). In the 1990–91 session the Prime Minister made statements in December (on the Rome European Council) and in July (on the Luxembourg European Council).[8] On 3 June 1991 the Minister of Agriculture made an oral statement on the outcome of the Agriculture Council.[9] In addition the Trade and Industry Secretary made an oral statement on 10 December 1990 on the break-down of the Uruguay Round/GATT negotiations (in which the European Commission negotiated on behalf of the governments of the Community).[10] On 13 June 1991 the Trade and Industry Secretary made an oral statement on special support for Cumbria, following substantial job losses at Vickers' Barrow shipyard, the measures involved having first been cleared with European Commission.[11]

However, the vast majority of ministerial statements during the session—55 in all—took the form of written answers to questions: for example, there were written statements in December 1990 and October 1991 on meetings of the Labour and Social Affairs Council;[12] in November 1990, April, June and October 1991 on meetings of the Transport Council;[13] in January, March, June and October 1991 on

---

[7] HC Deb 15 January 1991 c 492–3w.

[8] HC Deb 19 December 1990 cc 157–174; and 1 July 1991 cc 21–41.

[9] HC Deb 3 June 1991 cc 25–34.

[10] HC Deb 10 December 1990 cc 669–681.

[11] HC Deb 13 June 1991 cc 1054–63.

[12] HC Deb 20 December 1990 cc 312–3w; and 18 October 1991 cc 264–5w.

[13] HC Deb 13 November 1990 cc 97–8w; 24 April 1991 cc 448–9w; 26 June 1991 cc 461–2w and 473–4w; 16 October 1991 cc 163–4w.

meetings of the Environment Council;[14] and in November and December (twice) 1990 and April, June (twice) and July 1991 on meetings of Ecofin.[15] In addition, written statements were the means by which ministers reported to the House on such varied topics as: bathing water quality;[16] a directive on the inspection of foodstuffs (November 1990);[17] vehicle exhaust pollution (January 1991);[18] hot dry rock technology research;[19] shipbuilding aids;[20] the Commission's proposals for the social action programme (February 1991);[21] pharmaceutical patents (April 1991);[22] metrication;[23] duty free shopping;[24] and the proposed package travel directive (July 1991).[25]

*Euro-legislation* Since the passage of the European Communities Act 1972 the House has had to evolve special procedures to deal with legislation emanating from the Community. As explained in Chapter 4, these procedures were revised in the 1989–90 session, with new standing orders being approved just before the commencement of the session under review.[26] Under these arrangements, European Community documents recommended by the European Legislation Committee for further consideration are normally referred to a European Standing Committee and, after consideration there, any necessary motions are taken formally on the floor of the House. (The work of the European Legislation Committee and European Standing Committees is considered in detail below.) However, if the European Legislation Committee considers a

---

[14] HC Deb 15 January 1991 cc 455–6w and 453–4w; 20 March 1991 cc 129–30w; 18 June 1991 cc 131–2w and 142–4w; and 15 October 1991 cc 120–1w.

[15] HC Deb 23 November 1990 cc 232–3w; 3 December 1990 cc 213–4w; 20 December 1990 cc 303–4w; 16 April 1991 cc 140–1w; 7 June 1991 cc 371–3w; 25 June 1991 cc 422–4w and 434–6w; 10 July 1991 cc 367–70w.

[16] HC Deb 14 November 1990 cc 170–1w.

[17] HC Deb 26 November 1990 c 322w.

[18] HC Deb 14 January 1991 cc 399w and 401w.

[19] HC Deb 1 February 1991 cc 647w and 651w.

[20] HC Deb 5 February 1991 c 77w.

[21] HC Deb 15 February 1991 cc 627w and 629w.

[22] HC Deb 15 April 1991 cc 32–3w.

[23] HC Deb 2 July 1991 c 99w.

[24] HC Deb 24 July 1991 cc 603w and 605w.

[25] HC Deb 24 July 1991 cc 719–20w and 721w.

[26] HC Deb 24 October 1990 cc 375–401.

particular document to be especially important, it may recommend that it be considered on the floor of the House.

Such a recommendation is then considered by the Government's business managers, in consultation with the usual channels. Thus the majority of Euro-legislation is taken formally on the floor (even if opposed); only exceptional items are debated. In the 1990–91 Session, there were 24 motions which were taken formally. 21 motions required some form of debate on the floor: 11 of these motions were agreed to without a division after debate.[27] The debates on nine motions resulted in divisions: in three cases[28] the division was on the main question, in five cases[29] it was on an amendment, and in the remaining case[30] there was a division on an amendment and on the main question.

*Financial Procedures* The House's financial procedures have long been used as a vehicle for wider political debate. This was formerly especially true of consideration of Consolidated Fund Bills and the Estimates and is recognised with the designation of Opposition Days in place of the old Supply Days. In the 1990-91 session European business was raised in the Consolidated Fund debates in December (by Bill Cash on the Intergovernmental Conferences[31]) and March (by Bob Cryer on EC

---

[27] Co-operation on indirect taxation and harmonisation of excise duties, HC Deb 15 November 1990 cc 715–93; advertising of tobacco products, 18 November 1990 cc 971–89; research and development programme on information technology, 12 December 1990 cc 1079–84; research and development in human capital and mobility, 18 December 1990 cc 252–64; food aid to the Soviet Union and Eastern Europe, 4 March 1991 cc 82–110; compulsory use of seat belts, 27 March 1991 cc 1056–8; agricultural prices and the future of the CAP, 18 April 1991 cc 599–665; European energy charter, 20 May 1991 c 754; excise duty on mineral oils, 2 July 1991 c 290; supplementary protection certificates for medical products, 24 July 1991 cc 1266–70; aid to developing countries in Asia and Latin America, 21 October 1991 cc 747–68.

[28] Fishing conservation measures, HC Deb 15 November 1990 cc 752–97; aid for shipbuilding, 20 November 1990 cc 241–64; weapons controls, 29 November 1990 cc 1062–100.

[29] Draft Community Budget, HC Deb 4 December 1990 cc 200–28; non-standard (part-time) work, 12 December 1990 cc 1051–78; total allowable catches (fisheries), 13 December 1990 cc 1161–1226; annual report of the Court of Auditors, 13 March 1991 cc 1045–67; future of the European Coal and Steel Community, 15 October 1991 cc 257–83.

[30] Proposed establishment of European Works Councils, HC Deb 9 July 1991 cc 918–21.

[31] HC Deb 19 December 1990 cc 422–38.

costs[32]), in Estimates day debates on 3 July (unemployment[33]) and 4 July (on the steel industry, initiated by the Select Committee on Trade and Industry[34]) and on opposition days on 30 January (recession in industry, by Labour[35]) and 14 February (CAP reform and the fishing industry, both by the Liberal Democrats[36]). In addition, there was in April a short debate on a money bill in connection with the EC suckler cow scheme.[37]

*Delegated Legislation* A considerable quantity of delegated legislation is approved by Parliament each year. A significant proportion of it has European content. During the 1990-91 session 103 such statutory instruments were approved by Parliament. 90 of these were taken formally on the floor of the House of Commons. They covered a wide range of governmental activity, including such diverse matters as air navigation,[38] electrical equipment for explosive atmospheres,[39] grubbing up orchards,[40] recognising professional qualifications,[41] the pollution of bathing waters, intellectual property,[42] the classification of beef carcases,[43] and occupational pensions.[44] Of the thirteen instruments which required a resolution of the House, three were the subject of a debate, including one (on sea fishing conservation measures) which was an instance of a prayer against a statutory instrument.[45]

---

[32] HC Deb 14 March 1991 cc 1284–97.

[33] HC Deb 3 July 1991 cc 381–413.

[34] HC Deb 4 July 1991 cc 460–502.

[35] HC Deb 30 January 1991 cc 946–996.

[36] HC Deb 14 February 1991 cc 1012–53 and 1054–95.

[37] Agriculture and Forestry (Financial Provisions) Bill, HC Deb 22 April 1991 cc 874–6.

[38] Air Navigation (Amendment) Order 1990, laid 8 November 1990.

[39] Electrical Equipment for Explosive Atmospheres (Certification) Regulation 1990, laid 10 December 1990.

[40] Apple Orchard Grubbing Up Regulations 1991, laid 16 January 1991.

[41] European Communities (Recognition of Professional Qualifications) Regulations 1991, laid 27 March 1991.

[42] Design Right (Semiconductor Topographies) (Amendment) Regulations 1991, laid 9 October 1991.

[43] Beef Carcase (Classification) Regulations 1991, laid 10 October 1991.

[44] Occupational Pension Schemes (Miscellaneous Amendments) Regulations 1991, laid 14 October 1991.

[45] The three debated were: European Communities (Definition of Treaties) (Fourth ACP-EEC Convention of Lomé) Order 1991—HC Deb 26 February 1991 cc 932–952; Hill Livestock (Compensatory Allowances) (Amendment) Regulations 1991, 27

*Adjournment Debates* Adjournment debates are well recognised opportunities for backbenchers to raise issues. In the 1990–91 session one end-of-day adjournment debate had an explicitly European theme—on 12 March, concerning green labelling[46]—and European matters were also raised in the debates on the Christmas and Summer adjournments—on 19 December, concerning the ERM,[47] and on 22 July, concerning EC agricultural policies.[48] On Friday 14 December 1990 a debate on overseas development aid took place on a motion for the adjournment.[49]

*Early Day Motions* Early Day Motions (EDMs) are an opportunity for MPs to express an opinion on a particular issue and, by attracting the support of other MPs, to create a lobby on that issue. In the 1990-91 session 28 EDMs were tabled on issues connected with the EC, attracting 1,729 signatures from 405 MPs.[50] That tabled by Harry Greenway on the export of horses and ponies after 1992 obtained the most signatures (162—82 Labour; 57 Conservative; 11 Liberal Democrats; 7 Ulster Unionists; 3 Welsh and 1 Scottish Nationalist and 1 SDP) closely followed by one from William Clark on duty free shops (157—84 Conservative, 58 Labour, 9 Liberal Democrats, 4 Scottish and 1 Welsh Nationalist and 1 SDP). At the other end of the scale, Bill Cash's motion rejecting a federal European union and European central bank attracted only three signatures (all Conservatives) and Thomas Graham's motion supporting a proposed

---

1991, 5 March 1991 cc 233–257. The other ten were: Agricultural Fishery and Aquaculture Products (Improvement Grant) Regulations 1991, laid 1 February 1991; European Communities (Employment in the Civil Service) Order 1991, laid on 15 April 1991; Veterinary Surgeons Qualifications (EEC Recognition) (German Democratic Republic Qualifications) Order 1991, laid 25 April 1991; Farm Diversification Grant (Variation) (No 2) Scheme 1991, laid 10 June 1991; Farm & Conservation Grant Regulations 1991, laid 10 June 1991; Farm & Conservation Grant (Variation) Scheme 1991, laid 10 June 1991; Farm Woodland (Variation) Scheme 1991, laid 12 June 1991; Motor Vehicles (International Circulation) (Amendment) (No 2) Order 1991, laid 20 June 1991; Water & Sewerage Services (Amendment) (Northern Ireland) Order 1991, laid 9 July 1991; Companies Act 1985 (Bank Accounts) Regulations 1991, laid 16 October 1991; and the Bank Accounts Directive (Miscellaneous Banks) Regulations 1991, laid 16 October 1991.

[46] HC Deb 12 March 1991 cc 915–922.

[47] HC Deb 19 December 1990 cc 316–9, John Biffen MP.

[48] HC Deb 22 July 1991 cc 994–1006.

[49] HC Deb 14 December 1990 cc 1235–1299.

[50] See Appendix, below, pp 156–158. Information derived from POLIS listings on 'EC action' and 'EC law'.

Europol police agency attracted only 7 (all Labour)—this motion was tabled on 16 October, right at the end of the session.

The motions covered a wide range of topics (see Appendix, Table 6A.3), some more significant than others: alongside famine in Africa (Jim Lester—93 signatures: 38 Conservative, 36 Labour, 14 Liberal Democrat, 3 Ulster Unionist and 2 SDP), European contributions to the cost of the Gulf war (Bill Walker—14 signatures, all Conservatives), reform of the CAP (Paul Marland—54 signatures, all Conservatives) and the directive on data protection and the UK voluntary sector (Robert Maclennan—131 signatures: 73 Labour, 33 Conservative, 15 Liberal Democrat, 3 Scottish and 2 Welsh Nationalists, 3 Ulster Unionists, 1 SDP and 1 SDLP) stand the British custard tart (Alex Carlile—9 signatures: 7 Liberal Democrats, 1 Conservative and 1 Labour) and defence of the British sausage (Michael Colvin—34 signatures, 16 Conservative, 14 Labour, 2 Liberal Democrat and 2 Ulster Unionists).

Such motions commonly included a call for European Community or British government action. Thus, Mr Greenway's second motion read:

That this House takes notes of European Community Document No 7871/89 relating to the protection of animals during transport; and urges Her Majesty's Government to negotiate the adoption of acceptable regulations governing the standards of welfare, inspection and enforcement by members states after 1992, particularly those which would sustain the current arrangements relating to the export of live equines from the United Kingdom ...

And Malcolm Thornton's motion read:

That this House welcomes the European Community Commission proposal to restore intellectual property rights to the pharmaceutical industry by means of the Supplementary Protection Certificate; and urges Her Majesty's Government to give full support to this proposal.

EDMs are thus used as part of the process of creating a climate of opinion within which the government pursues its European policies. They provide an opportunity for MPs to express opinions which may, or may not, influence ministers. Such motions rarely engage directly with proceedings on the floor of the House (other than during business questions), though it is easy to see the relevance of those on CAP reform and banana policy to the House's debates on agricultural and aid policies.

Some MPs take advantage of EDMs more than others. Not surprisingly, opposition members do so more than government back-benchers (see Appendix, Tables 6A.1 and 6A.2). Of the 1,729 signatures 54% came from Labour members, 34% from Conservatives, 7% from Liberal Democrats, and 5% from the other parties. 53 MPs (38 Labour, 8 Conservative, 6 Liberal Democrats and 1 Ulster Unionist) were responsible for a third of the total signatures (585 out of 1,729) whereas 85 MPs (44 Conservative, 34 Labour, 2 Liberal Democrats, 2 Scottish Nationalist, 2 Ulster Unionist and 1 SDLP) signed only one motion during the session.

Top of the league (Appendix, Table 6A.2) of signatories was Alan Meale who signed 20 of the 28 motions; the next three, who each signed 15 motions, were also Labour members—Lawrence Cunliffe, Jimmy Dunnachie and Thomas Graham. The leading Conservative was David Mudd, who signed 13 motions, followed by David Knox and Tim Rathbone (11). Ronnie Fearn led the Liberal Democrats with 14 motions signed, followed by David Bellotti (12), James Wallace (11) and Russell Johnston (10). Conservatives 'antis' did not make a particularly strong showing in the lists: whereas Nicholas Winterton and Tim Janman were at the top end with 10 and 9 motions respectively, Bill Cash (6) and Teddy Taylor (5) were solidly in the middle and Richard Body signed only 2 and Nicholas Budgen 1. Similarly, prominent Labour 'antis' were not particularly salient: eg Nigel Spearing (3), Dennis Skinner (2), Peter Shore (1) and Ron Leighton (0).

Of the total of 28 EDMs just over half (15) could be classified as critical of EC action or proposals and a quarter (7) as broadly supportive (Appendix, Table 6A.4). About a third (9) could be considered genuinely cross-party, nearly a half (13) drew support from more than one party, but predominantly (more than two-thirds) from one, and just under a quarter (6) drew signatories exclusively from one party.

*Debates* In addition to the procedural opportunities described above, the House holds a debate in December and June on the White Paper on Developments in the European Community, which is an opportunity for a wide-ranging review.[51] And, finally, in the 1990–91 session the debate

---

[51] HC Deb 6 December 1990 cc 477–555; and 26 June 1991 cc 1011–96.

on the Queen's Speech, coming hard on the heels of Sir Geoffrey Howe's resignation, inevitably contained many references to European policy.[52]

Thus the opportunities for the consideration of European matters on the floor of the House were plentiful. In addition to questions, there were thirty debates of one kind or another on explicitly European themes (plus three on related issues) and four statements (plus the one on Cumbria). While some debates were short, several were full-day affairs (the two six-monthly debates on Developments, one on EMU in January[53] and one on agriculture in April[54]). But even together with the 40 hours the House spent on EC documents, the total time spent on European related business was not a large proportion of the 1,374 sitting hours of the 1990–91 session.[55]

*Committees* The above opportunities occur on the floor of the House. However, a substantial amount of European business is done by the House in its Committees—principally the Select Committee on European Legislation (the 'scrutiny committee'), the European Standing Committees and the departmentally-related select committees. These are dealt with below, pages 138–154.

## 3. Issues

Given all the opportunities which MPs have to raise matters European in the House, it is not surprising that many issues were referred to. There were, however, three which featured particularly strongly in the 1990–91 session: reform of the CAP; fisheries policy and the Intergovernmental Conferences. Reform of the CAP is dealt with separately in Chapter 8, so here we will consider only the latter two issues.

*Fisheries Policy* The 1990–91 session saw three major debates on fisheries policy as the 1991 settlement was negotiated and implemented. The Community's fisheries policy has to deal with the need to conserve stocks

---

[52] Eg speeches by Neil Kinnock, Paddy Ashdown, John Biffen, Roy Hughes, David Owen, David Knox, John Stokes, Anthony Meyer, Austin Mitchell, Alan Haselhurst, Douglas Hurd, Gerald Kaufman, HC Deb 7–8 November 1990 cc 10 *et seq*.
[53] HC Deb 24 January 1991 cc 470–551.
[54] HC Deb 18 April 1991 cc 599–665.
[55] *Sessional Returns 1990–91*, HC 271, 1991–92.

without sacrificing the livelihood of fishing communities in the member states, in the context of whatever agreements could be negotiated with nonmember states such as Norway. The first debate of the session took place, unhappily, the day after the loss of the fishing vessel *The Premier* off the Shetlands, which grimly underlined the hazardous nature of the industry and was frequently referred to in the debate. The government's motion sought the support of the House for its negotiating position in the Fisheries Council. This showed the tightness of the timetable: the Community's negotiations with Norway were completed on 7 December, the same day that the Commission released its main proposals on total allowable catches (TACs) and quotas. The debate took place on 13 December; the meeting of the Fisheries Council on 19 December. Between the announcement of the Commission's proposals and the debate in the House, on the 11 and 12 December, MAFF submitted to the House four explanatory memoranda in which the implications of the proposals were set out. As Mr Gummer stated in his opening speech, it was important to have the views of the House before the Fisheries Council met.[56]

The government's position, as set out by Mr Gummer at the start of the debate, was that it wished to have the Commission's proposals amended so that they would be both more effective as conservation measures and less damaging to fishing communities:

> Our key objective must be to obtain the highest level of quota compatible with scientific advice (on stock levels) and to maximise opportunities for United Kingdom fishermen. We must also aim to ensure parity of treatment through the Community where measures are taken to deal with particular stocks.[57]

That negotiating objective was uncontentious. Debate focussed upon the practicality and fairness of the measures proposed by the Commission —quota levels, a ten-day-per-month tie-up rule—and the relative merits of various net sizes and shapes. Whilst there was agreement that the Commission's proposals were unsatisfactory, there was considerable controversy both about what would be more effective than the Commission's proposals and whether a majority could be found for such alternatives in the Fisheries Council.

---

[56] HC Deb 13 December 1990 c 1166.

[57] Ibid, c 1176.

A major issue in the debate was the idea of a decommissioning scheme —a 'fisheries set-aside'. The minister firmly rejected this idea, arguing that it would not achieve the objective of reducing the total catch and pointing out that a previous decommissioning scheme had been heavily criticised by the Public Accounts Committee. The minister received little support for this line in the debate, even from his own backbenchers. Critics (who included Alick Buchanan-Smith, a former fisheries minister) pointed out that decommissioning schemes were in operation in other member states and were advocated by many in the industry. The inadequacies of a previous scheme should not prevent a better one being devised.

The opposition again found itself in the position of wanting to give general support to the government as the minister entered the negotiations (and so declined to divide the House[58]) but also to criticise the position he was adopting. As well as urging re-consideration of a decommissioning scheme, the opposition also pressed for adoption of 90mm square mesh panel nets, which the British fishing industry considered the most effective means of conserving stocks, but in an intervention in the debate the fisheries minister David Curry stated, although the government was itself sympathetic to that proposal, it was almost impossible to negotiate.[59]

Not surprisingly, MPs with fishing constituency interests featured prominently in the debate, particularly Scottish members. This was in part because SNP members moved an amendment critical both of the 'discriminatory and unworkable proposals' from the Commission and of the government's lack of vigour in the negotiations.[60] In the event this amendment was defeated by 76 votes to 22, with 10 Labour and 8 Liberal Democrat members voting against the Government.

The Liberal Democrats took the opportunity of their opposition day on 14 February to return to the subject. In a half-day debate[61] they argued vigorously against the 'compulsory tie-up scheme' proposed by the Commission, preferring (again) decommissioning and conservation through use of square-mesh panel nets. In the debate they were again supported by Labour, by SNP members and the Rev Ian Paisley. For the government David Curry repeated the arguments used in the December debate —decommissioning would not bring value for money; the tie-up scheme

---

[58] Ibid, c 1220.
[59] Ibid, c 1190.
[60] Ibid, cc 1194–95 (Alex Salmond).
[61] HC Deb 14 February 1991 cc 1054–95.

had its origin in the technical scientific advice given to the Commission, though the government had succeeded in negotiating a reduction in the number of days from 10 to 8. The government would continue to press the question of alternative gear.[62]

Once again the government's position received scant support in the debate. In a stinging attack on the ministerial line Alick Buchanan-Smith said:

> I regard the tie-up rule as patent nonsense … To neglect or dismiss structure, as Ministers often do, is like trying to fight for the industry with one hand tied behind one's back. We will not get effective conservation or build an efficient and effective British fishing industry if we do not show much more readiness to tackle structure.[63]

Robert Maclennan criticised the government for giving 'the impression that they are running before the wind of opinion in Europe' and supported the Commission's policy. He condemned the tie-up scheme as too rigid, not safe and likely seriously to erode fishermen's livelihoods; a highly dangerous precedent for regulation within the Community.[64]

In reply, the Minister of State at the Scottish Office, Michael Forsyth, could only repeat the government's objection to decommissioning as likely to lead to a more modernised fleet which would catch more fish, not less. But he did undertake to continue to press the case for alternative gear options.[65] The Liberal Democrats pressed their critical motion to a division but, notwithstanding support from some Labour, SNP and Ulster members, were defeated by 99 votes to 37.

The House returned to the subject for a third time in March when the opposition put down a prayer against a statutory instrument implementing a change to the fisheries regulations.[66] 13 members took part in the debate and once again the government's position received little support, even though ministers had obtained a further concession from Brussels—exemption for boats using 110mm mesh nets. Once again the government was heavily criticised for ignoring the industry's preference for a decommissioning scheme and the 8-day tie-up rule was criticised for being

---

[62] Ibid, cc 1060–67.
[63] Ibid, cc 1077–78.
[64] Ibid, cc 1087–88.
[65] Ibid, cc 1090–94.
[66] HC Deb 5 March 1991 cc 233–257.

inflexible and dangerous. Once again there was a strong attack on the government's position from Alick Buchanan-Smith, who indicated that he would not be able to support ministers in the division.[67] The Parliamentary Secretary repeated the government's case from previous debates, including the commitment to continue to try to persuade the Commission and the Fisheries Council to agree to other technical conservation measures. However, he stressed the difficulty ministers faced in obtaining agreement in Brussels:

> As I have said frankly in the past to fishermen, if they are merely offering a 90mm diamond mesh with an 80 mm square-mesh panel, we are unable to get that accepted in Brussels. We tried. I argued throughout a Fisheries Council for that, but it is not sufficient to be accepted in Brussels, and that is the fact of the matter ... it does not take us far enough. That is the political reality.[68]

The government won the division by 75 votes to 51, with Liberal Democrat, SNP and Ulster members again voting with Labour to record the highest of the three votes against the government.

These three debates illustrate well the problems the House faces in dealing with European business. The first debate was held against a very tight timetable; the third debate was held after the regulations had come into effect. The government was constrained in its ability to respond to opinion in the House (and in the industry) by the need to find support in Brussels—though critics of the government argued that it would have been easier to negotiate if the government had accepted a decommissioning scheme as other member states had done. Nevertheless, notwithstanding the frustrations of the context, the issues were thoroughly aired and the strength of parliamentary opinion was made known, even if it was not manifested in the division lobby. To what extent such vigorous parliamentary criticism assisted the government's negotiating position in Brussels one cannot at this stage judge.

*The Intergovernmental Conferences* The third issue to feature strongly in the House during the 1990–91 session was the progress of the inter-governmental negotiations on the revision of the Community treaties.

---

[67] Ibid, c 246.
[68] Ibid, c 254.

In this case there were the regular opportunities for debate provided by the six-monthly White Papers on *Developments in the European Community* as well as the extended periods of questions which followed the Prime Minister's statements on the outcome of the Rome and Luxembourg meetings of heads of government. In addition, Bill Cash raised the subject during the all-night on debate on the Consolidated Fund Bill in December taking the opportunity of an audience of five members (including the Chair and the whip) to denounce 'creeping federalism' and the proposals for a central bank which struck at the heart of democracy and consent, giving the Foreign Office Minister, Mark Lennox-Boyd, the opportunity in turn to reiterate the government's negotiating position that progress on monetary issues must run with the market, not against it.[69]

The first EC Developments debate took place a week before the Rome Council and ten days before the opening of the two Intergovernmental Conferences. It was therefore a good opportunity for the Foreign Secretary, Douglas Hurd, to outline the government's position—and for critics to make their voices heard. Mr Hurd stated that the government intended to resist proposals for an extension to the competence of the Commission, or for wholesale extension of qualified majority voting, or adding further to the legislative powers of the European Parliament. However, the government did wish to see the Community made more efficient and effective by improving compliance with ECJ rulings and the introduction of the principle of subsidiarity into the treaties; the European Parliament directing its energies towards the strengthening of financial accountability through the Budgetary Control Committee and the Court of Auditors; and the Community as a whole strengthening its position in the world through more co-ordination on foreign policy and security, though not defence, for which, in the government's view, the WEU was a more suitable mechanism.[70]

For the opposition Gerald Kaufman moved an amendment condemning the government for its neglect of British interests in the Community and its failure to produce a coherent policy for the IGCs. In his speech he concentrated on seeking to expose the ambiguities in the government's position, particularly on the single currency, and stated that Labour would propose the extension of qualified majority voting and an enhanced role

---

[69] HC Deb 19 December 1990 cc 422–438.
[70] HC Deb 6 December 1990 cc 483–86.

for the European Parliament. On monetary union Labour would argue for progress to be conditioned by the degree of on economic convergence.[71]

The debate took place the day after the Foreign Secretary had given evidence to the Foreign Affairs Select Committee on the same topics and a week after a conference of national parliaments in Rome (the Rome 'assize') which occasioned a good deal of controversy in this debate on the status of what was said. The backbench debate on 6 December featured pro's and anti's from both sides rehearsing their positions: Peter Shore, Ron Leighton, Bill Cash, Teddy Taylor for the Euro-critics; Ray Whitney, Kate Hoey, Tim Devlin, Giles Radice for the supporters. Russell Johnston for the Liberal Democrats advanced the lone Euro-federalist case. At the end of the debate the Labour amendment was defeated by 308 votes to 215, and the government's 'take note' motion approved without a division.

The Prime Minister made a statement on the outcome of the Rome European Council on 18 December. He then responded to 50 questions.[72] The IGC on political union was only one of the topics considered by the Council but it featured strongly in the questioning from MPs, though not as strongly as the proposals for a single currency and European central bank, which although not formally discussed at the European Council, were raised by eight MPs in questions, including the leaders of the Labour and Liberal parties.[73] John Major's 'new style' in Euro-negotiations was welcomed by several members, including in particular Sir Anthony Meyer. Jim Sillars and John Butterfill raised the question of the legal place of the principle of subsidiarity and Stuart Bell and Tim Devlin raised the question of the Community's role in defence matters. Peter Shore and Nigel Spearing sought assurances on reports back to the House during the negotiations. Other items were raised by individual MPs.[74] Generally the tone was supportive but probing, as Neil Kinnock's opening questions well illustrated.

In January the House held a full-scale debate on economic and monetary union (EMU) in the shadow of the outbreak of hostilities in the Gulf.[75] The debate took place on a motion for the adjournment of the

---

[71] Ibid, cc 487–98.

[72] HC Deb 18 December 1990 cc 157–174.

[73] The others were Giles Radice, William Cash, Ron Leighton, James Arbuthnot, Dennis Skinner and Nicholas Budgen.

[74] Hugh Dykes (the role of the European Parliament); Geoffrey Finsberg (the Rome assize); Andrew Rowe (other member states' failure to comply with EC decisions).

[75] HC Deb 24 January 1991 cc 470–551.

House, with the government laying before the House its own proposed treaty provisions for EMU and drawing attention to evidence taken by the Treasury Committee in July of the previous session.[76] As Peter Shore was quick to point out in an early intervention, however, the House did not have before it either the Commission's draft treaty on EMU or the draft statute for a European central bank which central bank governors had prepared for the Intergovernmental Conference.[77]

Opening the debate, Chancellor of the Exchequer Norman Lamont set out to explain the government's own proposals and why they found the Commission's plans defective. The government preferred the creation not of a single but of a common currency, one which 'would exist alongside or parallel with national currencies rather than replace them'. This so-called hard ecu 'could, over time, evolve towards a single currency. But that ... is a decision not for now but for the future, and one that would be debated fully in the House'. And, rather than a European central bank to manage a single currency, the government proposed instead a new institution, a European monetary fund, which would be responsible for issuing the new currency in exchange for national currencies and for operating in the money markets, setting hard ecu interest rates.[78] The government's objective, Mr Lamont explained, was 'to leave the realisation of monetary union, if it happens, to an evolutionary approach to be determined by markets, individuals and businesses. We are not prepared to sign up to move to single currency with a single central bank'. He added that the Delors report 'would mean that the House of Commons would no longer be sovereign on matters of taxation or public expenditure or both—a position we could not accept ... National governments can and should be left to make those decisions within the disciplines created by financial markets'.[79]

The Shadow Chancellor, John Smith, criticised the government's position as confused and failing to deal adequately with the issue. He agreed that a completely independent European central bank would not be acceptable as there had to be some form of political accountability—but argued that the government's proposed hard ecu would mean in practice total dependence on Bundesbank with the result that the question of

---

[76] Minutes of evidence taken before the Treasury and Civil Service Committee on 25 July 1990 on Economic and Monetary Union, 1989–90, HC 690.

[77] HC Deb 24 January 1991 c 470.

[78] Ibid, cc 471–2.

[79] Ibid, cc 475–6.

accountability would be almost academic. Labour's alternative, Mr Smith explained, was to build on a strengthened ECOFIN which would be 'given the task of providing strategic guidance to the process of monetary co-ordination. It would become, in effect, the political supervising body, with its own secretariat and permanent representatives'. It was also necessary, in the Opposition's view, for there to be 'a substantial degree of convergence in the economic and social performance of individual states' before further movements towards monetary union. A greatly expanded system of regional and structural funds at Community level would be necessary for this to be achieved. The Shadow Chancellor also stated that it was 'important to distinguish between monetary union and the far from precise notion of economic union, implying, as it might, the loss of fiscal and budgetary sovereignty. The principle of subsidiarity should ensure that progress towards monetary union does not require a common fiscal or budgetary policy for the Community as a whole'.[80]

In the ensuing debate (which concluded without a division) 10 of the 22 speakers were hostile to the Commission's proposals and suspicious of the government's alternative,[81] some seeing them as a prelude to federal type political union.[82] A similar number of speakers were supportive of the government's step-by-step approach[83] and some specifically endorsed the hard ecu proposal[84] but only Russell Johnston for the Liberal Democrats fully endorsed the EMU concept.

The House's review of EC Developments in June 1991 took place at the half-way point of the inter-governmental conferences and a few days before the heads of government meeting in Luxembourg. This produced a weighty debate[85] with contributions, in addition to frontbench spokesmen, from two former Prime Ministers,[86] five former Cabinet ministers[87] and three other former Ministers.[88] Inevitably at this

---

[80] Ibid, cc 479–89.

[81] Ian Stewart, Robert Sheldon, Christopher Gill, Peter Shore, Ron Leighton, Michael Spicer, Austin Mitchell, Peter Hordern, Bill Cash, Tony Favell.

[82] Peter Shore, Michael Spicer, Bill Cash, Tony Favell.

[83] Ray Whitney, Quentin Davies, Ian Taylor, John Butterfill, Nigel Forman, Alistair Burt, Anthony Meyer, Andrew Hargreaves, Patrick Ground.

[84] Ian Stewart, Quentin Davies, Ian Taylor, Patrick Ground.

[85] HC Deb 26 June 1991 cc 1097–1114.

[86] Margaret Thatcher and Edward Heath.

[87] Denis Healey, David Howell, Peter Shore, Nigel Lawson, David Owen.

[88] Robert Sheldon, Richard Luce, Terence Higgins.

half-way point a good deal was said about negotiating tactics and the implications of Britain being left out—'on the side-lines'—of important developments in the Community.

Opening the debate, Foreign Secretary Douglas Hurd began by restating the government's position that while it would 'not recommend to this Parliament acceptance of a commitment to a single currency', it was in favour of practical steps towards closer economic and monetary integration that would produce convergence on low inflation and sound public finance across the Community.[89] Mr Hurd then concentrated on the proposed treaty on political union and the government's view that it would be mistaken to concentrate all co-operation through the institutions of the Community, preferring rather inter-governmental cooperation in such areas as foreign and security policy and the work of Interior or Justice ministries —the 'separate pillars' approach.[90] The Foreign Secretary also repeated the case for the ECJ to be given powers to impose fines on member states who fail to comply with its judgements and for the European Parliament's powers over Community spending to be strengthened, as well as emphasizing the importance of establishing in the treaties the principle of subsidiarity.[91] Mr Hurd re-iterated the government's opposition to an extension of the Community's competence into social fields such as industrial relations[92] and, in response to an intervention from Tony Benn, stated his strong opposition to a referendum on the outcome of the conferences.[93]

In a much-interrupted speech, the Shadow Foreign Secretary Gerald Kaufmann argued that the government's handling of the negotiations had been incompetent as they had failed to work out a clear line and stick to it. Accordingly, the opposition had decided to vote against the government at the end of the debate—an unusual move on a motion for the adjournment. Mr Kaufman recognised that there were issues on which it was necessary to disagree strongly with the proposals being made by our Community partners—and instanced the proposed common defence policy. He argued, however, that our partners would listen to such disagreement with more respect if ministers took a more constructive line, as Labour proposed, on majority voting, extended powers for the European

---

[89] HC Deb 26 June 1991 c 1012.

[90] Ibid, c 1013.

[91] Ibid, cc 1015–6.

[92] Ibid, c 1017.

[93] Ibid, c 1019.

Parliament and the social charter and made practical proposals on regional policies, structural policies and policies to combat unemployment which would help to bring about the economic and social convergence which would be essential if there was to be a central bank and a single currency.[94]

The government's political difficulty in the debate was well illustrated when Mrs Thatcher and Mr Heath gave their support to the Prime Minister's position with totally contrasting speeches. Mrs Thatcher denounced the proposed 'massive extension of the Community's powers and competence' as 'the greatest abdication of national and Parliamentary sovereignty in our history' and fully supported the firm stand ministers had taken in their preference for inter-governmental co-operation as opposed to making any commitment to a federal Europe. She was opposed to the social charter and a single currency. Mr Heath, by contrast, argued that economic and monetary union must come as soon as possible because industry wanted it, and with it a single currency. Britain must not repeat the mistake made in 1950 and stand apart from future developments of political unity, foreign policy and defence policy. In his view sovereignty should be used for the benefit of the people, not the satisfaction of Governments or politicians: MPs were unnecessarily concerned about 'federalism'—a form of government we gave to many of our colonies when they became independent.[95]

In spite of Mr Heath's re-assurance, the question of federalism did occur frequently in the debate. Euro-sceptics in particular focussed upon the implications for the role of the Westminster Parliament of such a development[96] but there were also notable advocates of a more sympathetic approach to the concept.[97] A parallel issue frequently raised —particularly by former Treasury ministers—was the implication of EMU and a single currency for national democratic control and accountability.[98]

Although the opposition divided the House (and were defeated by 312 votes to 158), there was discernible agreement across the House in support of a sceptical position towards political integration combined with a general recognition of the need for wider European co-operation.

---

[94] Ibid, cc 1028-9.

[95] Ibid, cc 1040-1.

[96] Peter Shore, Jonathan Aitken, Bill Cash, Nigel Spearing, Teddy Taylor.

[97] Russell Johnston, David Howell, Giles Radice, Jim Sillars, Brian Sedgemore.

[98] Eg Nigel Lawson, Robert Sheldon, Nigel Spearing, Terence Higgins.

These issues were aired again a week later when the Prime Minister made a statement to the House on the outcome of the heads of government meeting at Luxembourg and was questioned by more than 50 members.[99] In his statement Mr Major made clear that the Council had been engaged in a stock-taking rather than decision-taking exercise on the inter-governmental conferences. He welcomed the structure of the draft treaty, which incorporated the 'three pillars' approach, although he acknowledged that some other member states were opposed and disagreed with it strongly. He made it clear that the government would continue to resist the inclusion of the word 'federal' in the treaty text because of its ambiguity and opposition to it in the British Parliament and explained again the government's reservations on EMU, a single currency and a central bank as well as the proposed extended role for the European Parliament.[100]

The Leader of the Opposition, Neil Kinnock, pressed the Prime Minister on the reasons for his opposition to the extension of qualified majority voting on environmental matters and the social charter and on what was meant by economic convergence in the context of EMU.[101] In the back-bench questioning, three themes were prominent: federalism,[102] EMU[103] and the social charter[104] but a large number of Conservative MPs took the opportunity to express their support for the positions adopted by the Prime Minister and his negotiating style.[105]

The inter-governmental conferences were not completed until the heads of government met at Maastricht. Chapter 10 continues the story into 1991 and Chapter 11 covers the process by which the British parliament dealt with the consequences of the Maastricht Treaty. But it was already clear in the 1990–91 session that MPs were closely scrutinising the progress of the negotiations and the conclusions which were emerging from them. The lines of argument—between and within the parties—which were to dominate the debate on the Maastricht Treaty were already well rehearsed

---

[99] HC Deb 1 July 1991 cc 21–41.

[100] Ibid, cc 21–2.

[101] Ibid, c 24.

[102] Peter Blaker, Wyn Griffiths, Harry Barnes, Michael Irvine, Toby Jessel.

[103] Anthony Nelson, Ian Taylor, John Butterfill, Nigel Spearing.

[104] Jack Ashley, Dale Campbell-Savours, Norman Godman, David Madel.

[105] Cranley Onslow, Fergus Montgomery, Alan Haselhurst, Anthony Meyer, Marion Roe, Robert Adley, Andrew Rowe, Ivor Stanbrook, Simon Burns, Quentin Davies, David Sumberg.

in the process of scrutinising the progress of the inter-governmental conferences.

## 4. The work of committees

Much of the work of the House in connection with routine EC business, particularly the scrutiny of legislation and the detailed examination of specific policy areas, is carried out away from the floor of the House in various committees. The Select Committee on European Legislation and the European Standing Committees have specific responsibilities in connection with the scrutiny of documents emanating from the EC, particularly those containing proposals for legislation. The departmental select committees do not have particular responsibilities in that area but can, and do, investigate aspects of EC policies, often as part of wider inquiries.

*The Select Committee on European Legislation* As described in Chapter 4, in October 1990 the government accepted minor changes in the terms of reference of the Select Committee on European Legislation, based on recommendations in the 1988–89 Procedure Committee report, which were implemented just before the start of the 1990–91 session. The immediate effect of these changes on the Committee's work in the 1990–91 session was not particularly noticeable, although there was some growth in the volume of non-legislative documents considered. Despite an almost unprecedented amount of EC business on the floor of the House, the Committee continued throughout that session (and the short one which followed) to operate much as before. The Committee's *modus operandi* is well-established: there is a more or less regular pattern of weekly reports when the House is sitting and the reports almost always follow the same general format, although they have become considerably more detailed than in the early years of EC membership.

The Committee produced thirty reports in 1990–91[106] (three fewer than in the previous session but close to the normal number) and fifteen in 1991–92[107] (a session of about half the normal length because of the 1992 general election). In 1990–91, there were three sittings where

---

[106] All the reports in 1990–91 were published as parts of HC 29.
[107] All the reports in 1991–92 were published as parts of HC 24.

evidence was taken from Ministers, once from the Minister of Agriculture, John Gummer (on 16 April 1991[108]), and twice from the Minister of State at the Foreign and Commonwealth Office, Tristan Garel-Jones.[109] In none of the reports in 1990–91 was there any protest by the Committee about a failure to ensure that a recommendation for further consideration of a particular document was not acted upon in time, although at the end of the session 19 documents were listed as awaiting further consideration by the House—a considerable reduction from the 39 awaiting consideration in March 1991.[110] Attendance was not conspicuously high (59.8% out of a committee of sixteen Members in 1990–91[111]) and was dominated by about ten regulars, almost all Conservatives and two (William Cash and Tony Marlow) well-known EC opponents.

In the 1990–91 session, the subject matter of the documents considered by the Committee covered a very wide range, considerably wider than in the earlier years of EC membership because of the extension of Community competence into new areas and the development of the Single Market. The documents covered Commission legislative proposals in such diverse areas as:

employment of pregnant women and recent mothers (Second and Twelfth Reports);

unfair terms in consumer contracts (Twelfth Report);

efficiency of hot water boilers (Thirteenth and Twenty-Sixth Reports);

oil supplies and stocks (Fifteenth Report);

protection of wildlife and natural habitats (Sixteenth Report);

milk quotas (Seventh and Seventeenth Reports);

tobacco labelling and advertising (Twentieth and Twenty-Ninth Reports, 1990–91 and again in the Fourteenth Report, 1991–92);

ecolabelling (Twenty-Fifth Report);

the movement of radioactive waste (Twenty-Fifth Report);

bird conservation (Twenty-Seventh Report);

---

[108] Published with the Sixteenth Report from the Select Committee on European Legislation, 1990–91, HC 29–xvi.

[109] On 25 March 1991, evidence published with Sixteenth Report from the Select Committee on European Legislation, 1990–91, HC 29–xvi; and on 23 July 1991, evidence published with Twenty-Ninth Report, 1990–91, HC 29–xxix.

[110] Thirteenth Report from the Select Committee on European Legislation, 1990–91, HC 29–xiii (published in March 1991); and Thirtieth Report, 1990–91, HC 29–xxx.

[111] House of Commons *Sessional Returns 1990–91*—1991–92, HC 271 p 97.

the European Company Statute (Twenty-Eighth Report);
harmonisation of indirect taxation (Twenty-Eighth Report, 1990–91,
and First Report, 1991–92).

They also covered topics of major political interest such as political union
and economic and monetary union (both in Second Report).

In 1990–91, the Committee considered fairly typical mixtures of new
draft legislation, which included three separate considerations of the
Commission's proposals for reforming the common agricultural policy
(CAP) (Twelfth, Twenty-Ninth and Thirtieth Reports) and the CAP annual
price proposals (Fifteenth Report), a range of Commission
Communications on regular business such as the annual review of the
Commission's Programme (Fourteenth Report), the EC Budget proposals
(First and Thirtieth Reports), and the Commission's 1990–91 Annual
Economic Report (Twelfth Report). A significant proportion of the
documents considered in 1990–91 was non-legislative and concerned with
such topics as the poverty programme (Seventeenth Report), food and its
scientific evaluation and life assurance (both in Twenty-First report). The
Committee also examined proposals for the landfill of waste at the same
time as the Environment Committee and the report (Twenty-Seventh
Report) referred specifically to the Environment Committee's inquiry.
Similarly, the Agriculture Committee conducted an inquiry into the
transport of animals which the European Legislation Committee had
previously considered (Third Report).

The 1991–92 session, which was cut short by the general election,
contained a similar mixture of reports, some of them returning to
documents considered in the previous session. The final one (Fifteenth
Report) contained a round-up of over twenty documents considered by the
Committee in an obvious effort to clear outstanding matters before the
impending election. It also included a cautious initial reaction—the
Committee 'should not at this stage offer any firm recommendations'—to
the Maastricht Treaty on European Union plus a long summary of the
Treaty itself by the Legal Adviser, published when the impenetrability of
the Treaty's text was a matter of widespread criticism and a masterly
analysis which was undoubtedly one of the best available at the time.

The Committee's sifting function is essentially practical and as almost
all its work is carried out in private deliberative sessions, it does not have
a high public profile. A great deal of its work does not feature in its
published reports, particularly its efforts to ensure that government
departments (and the EC Commission) keep parliament properly informed

about all aspects of EC activities. The reports do, however, reveal some of the Committee's preoccupations connected with the scrutiny process. In 1990–91, they contained constant reminders to the government about the need to keep the Committee informed about how particular proposals were developing, especially those where there was no recommendation for further consideration by a European Standing Committee. There was also continuing concern about the treaty base of some of the Commission's proposals and the related (and vexed) questions of Community competence and subsidiarity. The Committee has a responsibility to draw the attention of the House to unusual or unexpected use of powers under the Treaty and numerous reports contained comments by the Legal Adviser, or the Committee itself, on that specific aspect of individual proposals.

This concern emerged very noticeably in the 1991–92 session when a Commission proposal on sport, considered in the Twelfth Report,[112] generated a lengthy and strongly-worded note by the Legal Adviser who saw it as providing 'valuable material, and (affording) an excellent opportunity for an assessment of Community competence in relation to sport.' The note went on to discuss the Commission's approach to subsidiarity, described as 'a doctrine rooted in continental socio-philosophical thinking', but one which, in the context of the Commission's proposals, 'needed no philosophical underpinning.' That might have 'perhaps less palatable' consequences:

> the Commission may have to recognise, on occasion, that its involvement, for its own purposes as declared in the Communication, in various sporting activities will depend entirely on the goodwill of those responsible ... Hence ... what is entailed in following through the aim of enhancing Community awareness is essentially a political matter.

Similar concerns about Community competence were expressed, this time by the Committee itself, in the Thirteenth Report[113] of that session in connection with Commission proposals on asylum and immigration:

> On the competence issues, the Committee had hoped the EM would go further and indicate what specific aspects of asylum and immigration

---

[112] Twelfth Report from the Select Committee on European Legislation, 1991–92, HC 24–xii.

[113] Thirteenth Report from the Select Committee on European Legislation, 1991–92, HC 24–xiii.

fall inside or outside the Treaty provisions on free movement, but this will doubtless have to be explained in the course of further considerations of these Communications and the Treaty of Union. The Committee would not, in particular, regard it as safe to assume that mention of any matter as being of common interest in the new provisions on cooperation over justice and home affairs can be taken as recognising that they are now wholly outside Community competence.

Although the Committee does not concern itself with the merits of the documents it considers, in one or two cases in 1991–92 it went out of its way to draw attention to what it saw as the risks involved in Commission proposals. The most prominent of these was a draft on management and investment of pension funds, considered in the Eighth Report,[114] where considerable concern was expressed about the effects of the proposals in the context of the collapse of the late Robert Maxwell's empire:

> The Committee considers that because of the current concerns over the safety of pension funds there are bound to be reservations about proposals for Community legislation which would either entrench or extend the freedom of United Kingdom pension fund administrators, even when such measures are clearly within the objectives of a Single Market in financial services.

The Committee also wanted much more information from the government about such matters as the extent to which pension arrangements in individual member states would become subject to the provisions of the draft directive.

From the late 1970s, the Committee began to make more or less regular visits to Brussels to meet the EC Commission and other Community institutions as well as the UK Permanent Representation at the EC. There were also occasional visits to the European Parliament and to the parliaments of other member states, with a total of two or three visits of all kinds each session. From the mid-1980s onwards such visits became more frequent and a pattern emerged of two regular visits each year to the parliament of the country about to hold the EC presidency, plus an annual visit to Brussels. From 1989 the chairman, sometimes accompanied by one other member, also attended the formal six-monthly conferences of

---

[114] Eighth Report from the Select Committee on European Legislation, 1991–92, HC 24–viii.

European Affairs Committees, hosted by the parliament of the member state holding the European Presidency. In 1990–91 there was a total of three visits by the Committee (one each to Luxembourg and Brussels and a combined one to The Hague and Strasbourg) and one by the chairman to the Fourth Inter-Parliamentary Conference of European Affairs Committees.[115]

The value of these visits was highlighted in the Committee's First Special Report in 1991–92[116] which appeared in March 1992, shortly before Parliament was dissolved. The Committee had been invited to the sixth Conference of European Affairs Committees which was scheduled to be held in Lisbon in May when it was known that parliament would be dissolved, so the Committee would technically not exist. The report said:

> The Committee believes that previous conferences have provided valuable opportunities for improving links both with other national parliaments and with the European Parliament. It is keen that Members of the House of Commons should continue to play as full a part as possible in these conferences including the role as a member of the Troika. It would therefore obviously have accepted the invitation it has received. The Committee recommends that, as in the event it will not be possible for it to participate, other arrangements might be made to permit Members of this House to attend the Lisbon Conference.

The Committee also made a Special Report in November 1990 which contained the text of a working document which it had been invited by the Presidency to submit to the forthcoming Conference of the Parliaments of the European Community (the 'Rome assize') on 'The future of the Community: the implications for the European Community and the Member States of the proposals concering economic and monetary union and political union, with particular reference to the role of the national parliaments and the European Parliament.'[117] That document urged a flexible approach to cooperation between national parliaments and that 'the opportunity should be taken to ensure that, whatever arrangements emerge,

---

[115] House of Commons *Sessional Returns, 1990–91*, 1991–92, HC 271.

[116] First Special Report from the Select Committee on European Legislation, 1991–92, HC 352, para 2.

[117] First Special Report from the Select Committee on European Leislation, 1990–91, HC 30: *The Conference of the Parliaments of the European Community*.

there is effective oversight by parliamentarians of the actions of all executive and legislative organs of the Community.'

*The European Standing Committees* The two European Standing Committees were first set up at the end of January 1991, part-way through the 1990–91 session. Their genesis in the Procedure Committee's 1988–89 report and the initial difficulties over setting them up are described in Chapter 4. Their creation was widely seen as a major innovation but, as so often, the new committees were essentially a development of an existing system which complicates any assessment of their impact. As evidence to the 1988–89 Procedure Committee showed, since October 1980, when the standing orders had been amended, the practice became mainly to refer the more technical European Community proposals to a standing committee and the pattern of referral varied from session to session. The number of documents so considered was a significant proportion of the total recommended for debate by the European Legislation Committee: an average of 22 European documents (or groups of related documents) was considered in each of the five sessions before the Procedure Committee's 1988–89 report. These gave rise to an average of ten standing committee debates per session.[118] In 1988–89, there were 22 documents considered at 13 sittings but in 1989–90 there were 43 documents considered at a total of 23 sittings. In 1990–91, European Standing Committee A considered a total of 21 documents at 16 meetings, while European Standing Committee B considered a total of 22 documents at 17 meetings.[119]

The table reproduced below from the Procedure Committee's 1991–92 *Review of European Standing Committees*[120] gives the total numbers of European Community documents considered and the number of debates both on the floor of the House and in the old and new standing committees in 1990–91 and the two preceding sessions:

---

[118] Fourth Report from the Select Committee on Procedure, 1988–89, HC 622–I, *The Scrutiny of European Legislation* para 55.

[119] House of Commons *Sessional Returns 1988–89*, 1989–90, HC 110; *Sessional Returns 1989–90*, 1990–91, HC 218; and First Report from the Select Committee on Procedure, 1991–92, HC 31: *Review of European Standing Committees*, Appendix 16.

[120] First Report from the Select Committee on Procedure, 1991–92, HC 31: *Review of European Standing Committees*, Appendix 16.

## Table 6.5
## Debates on European Community Documents

|  | 1988–89 | 1989–90 | 1990–91 |
|---|---|---|---|
| Debates in the House ... ... ... (Total number of ECDs considered) | 38 (82) | 22 (39) | 20 (47) |
| Meetings of Standing Committees (Total number of ECDs considered) | 13 (22) | 23 (43) | 33 (43) |
| TOTALS | 51 (104) | 45 (82) | 53 (90) |

*Source*: 1991–92, HC 31, Appendix 16

The 1988–89 session was clearly unusual in the large numbers of documents considered and debates on the floor of the House rather than in standing committees. Contrary to what may appear to have been happening, and allowing for the fact that the European Standing Committees were not set up until the end of January 1991, the table shows that the committees' existence did not substantially reduce the numbers of documents considered or debates held on the floor of the House in the 1990–91 session. Nor did they achieve the government's stated objective of shifting the balance so that about two-thirds of debates took place in standing committee rather than on the floor of the House, as Sir Geoffrey Howe had said in the debate on the Procedure Committee's report on 28 June 1990.[121] That is undoubtedly at least partly a reflection of events in Europe at the time. The tables reproduced below[122] show that a major immediate consequence of the existence of the European Standing Committees was to change the *timing* of debates on the floor of the House, particularly the amount of time spent after 10.00 pm:

[121] HC Deb 28 June 1990 cc 529–30.
[122] First Report from the Select Committee on Procedure, 1991–92, HC 31: *Review of European Standing Committees*, Appendix 16.

### Table 6.6
### Timing of Debates on the Floor of the House

|  | 1988–89 | 1989–90 | 1990–91 |
|---|:---:|:---:|:---:|
| (A) Number of Debates commencing: | | | |
| (1) Before 7 pm | 4 | 7 | 5 |
| (2) At/or after 7 pm and before 10 pm | 4 | 4 | 4 |
| (3) At/or after 10 pm | 28 | 8 | 8 |
| TOTALS | 36 | 19 | 17 |
| (B) Time spent after 10 pm on dates on ECDs: Total number of hours/minutes | 40.58 | 17.03 | 13.34 |

*Source*: 1991–92, HC 31, Appendix 16

The *Sessional Returns* confirm this general picture and show that in 1989–90, a total of 40.20 hours was spent on government motions on European Community documents, of which 17.03 hours were after 10.00 pm, compared with a total in 1990–91 of 40.18 hours of which 13.34 hours were after 10.00 pm.

Thus the Procedure Committee's aim, endorsed by the government in the debate on 28 June 1990, of meeting Members' desire to reduce the number of debates on European documents which took place late at night was initially largely met, but in 1990–91 that led neither to any reduction in the total amount of time which the House spent debating European documents nor to the complete disappearance of such debates after 10.00 pm. There was, however, a significant increase in the number of European Standing Committee debates compared with the former standing committees. The majority of those debates lasted appreciably longer, as well as being devoted to relatively more important topics and held in what might be described as high-quality time. The average length of sitting of standing committees considering European documents in 1989–90 was just under one hour and no sitting lasted the permitted two and a half hours. In 1990–91, European Standing Committee A sat for an average of 1 hour and 33 minutes (excluding one sitting cut short because of procedural arguments), while European Standing Committee B sat for an average of 1 hour and 54 minutes (excluding one sitting abandoned for procedural reasons) and on five occasions sat for two and a half hours. Attendance at the European Standing Committees was generally marginally higher (an average of 12 Members attended both Committees compared with an average of ten at the former committees). Many of the Members who gave evidence to the Procedure Committee during the review in 1991–92 commented favourably on the benefits of holding debates in the morning rather than late at night, as well as welcoming the opportunity to question Ministers before the start of the debate itself.

The Procedure Committee's *Review of European Standing Committees* concluded that, despite the problems associated with setting them up, the Committees had been a success and were there to stay:

> apart from a very few unavoidable teething problems, they have functioned remarkably well ... There is general agreement that the Committees have provided a more efficient forum both for sustained questioning and subsequent debate. Similarly, it is widely accepted that the marked shift away from sterile late night debates in the Chamber represents a much more productive use of the House's time. Against this generally favourable background, therefore, we have not been persuaded of the need for far-reaching changes to a system which is fundamentally sound.[123]

The publicity which surrounded the creation of the European Standing Committees at least initially gave their sittings a much higher profile than was enjoyed either by the previous late night debates on the floor of the House or by the former standing committee debates. The Committees' main impact has obviously been to provide more time for debates on important European draft legislation away from the floor of the House and not late at night. As the then Leader of the House acknowledged in response to a PQ on 25 November 1991:

> One recent improvement (in the hours of sitting of the House) has been that, since they were set up in January, the European Standing Committees have made a significant contribution to reducing the burden

---

[123] 1991–92, HC 31, para 52.

of late night debates on the Floor. Some 20 or so of their debates would probably have been held on the Floor after 10 pm under the previous arrangements.[124]

That change did not lead initially to much reduction in the total number of hours for which the House sat, but it has increased significantly the amount of time which is available for consideration of European draft legislation. Quality of debate is always difficult to judge, but the opportunities for detailed questioning of ministers which the procedures allow was undoubtedly challenging and time-consuming for ministers. This appears to have been generally welcomed and to have improved Members' (and others') understanding of the issues involved. This point was strongly emphasised by witnesses, including the Leader of the House, to the Procedure Committee in its *Review of European Standing Committees*.[125] In response to another PQ on 25 November 1991, Mr John MacGregor also said:

> Experience so far shows that the two European Standing Committees are working well and have made a real contribution to the improved scrutiny of European legislation.[126]

## Departmentally-related select committees

In its 1988–89 report on *The Scrutiny of European Legislation*,[127] the Procedure Committee observed that the terms of reference of the departmentally-related select committees undoubtedly included 'both European legislation and more general European issues which impinge on domestic departmental responsibilities.' The Procedure Committee started from the premise that the departmental select committees 'had a distinct part to play, complementary to the functions of Special Standing Committees, rather than as an alternative' in the scrutiny of EC legislation.[128] The Procedure Committee found widely varying attitudes

---

[124] HC Deb 25 November 1991 c 415w.

[125] 1991–92, HC 31, paras 7 and 34.

[126] HC Deb 25 November 1991 c 415w.

[127] Fourth Report from the Select Committee on Procedure, 1988–89, HC 622 I–II: *The Scrutiny of European Legislation*.

[128] Ibid, para 75.

on the part of the chairmen of select committees towards the importance of scrutinising EC legislation and commented:

> Even allowing for the fact that some Committees are monitoring Departments with little or no workload of European documents, the total amount of time and resources devoted to this subject does not appear to be very great. No Committees claimed to conduct anything approaching systematic scrutiny of European legislation.[129]

Some committees had indicated that 'whilst individual European documents were rarely, if ever, the subject of specific enquiries, they often formed a central part of wider investigations of policy issues.' Nevertheless, '(t)he great majority of Committees saw little practical prospect of devoting significantly more effort to the consideration of European legislation and several were not convinced in any case that this would be desirable.'[130] Despite the evident reluctance on the part of select committees to become more closely involved in the scrutiny of European legislation, the Procedure Committee saw some scope for the committees to expand their activities in that area. It rejected the idea that the House should seek formally to direct select committees about their priorities in order to achieve that—a recommendation which the government subsequently endorsed[131]—but made

> no apology for having drawn attention to the ways in which the House would benefit from an increased contribution by Select Committees to the scrutiny process. If the House approves the main thrust of our Report, it will send a strong signal to Select Committees that it wishes to see them adopt a higher profile in this area.[132]

On neither occasion when the Procedure Committee report was debated (on 28 June and 24 October 1990) was there any discussion of the possibility of enhancing the role of the departmentally-related select committees in scrutinising European legislation.

---

[129] Ibid, para 86.
[130] Ibid.
[131] *Fourth Report from the House of Commons Select Committee on Procedure Session 1988–89: The Scrutiny of European Legislation—Government Response*—Cm 1081; May 1990.
[132] 1988–89, HC 622–I, para 103.

All the speakers in those debates, including those from the government front bench, were clearly mainly concerned with matters other than the potential role of select committees in scrutinising European legislation. It would therefore be mistaken to draw conclusions from the absence of any specific endorsement of that particular aspect of the Procedure Committee's report, or to suggest that any subsequent trends in the work of the select committees have necessarily arisen as a direct result of the Committee's 'strong signal' about adopting a higher profile in that area. Analysis of their work in the 1990–91 and (short) 1991–92 sessions does, however, show that although in some respects the committees continued much on the lines described by the Procedure Committee two or more years earlier, there were some detectable changes. There are few government departments on which European legislation does not now impinge to a greater or lesser extent, while what may be described as the European dimension has become almost all-pervasive, and those developments began to be reflected in the pattern of work of the departmentally-related select committees.

Categorising select committee activity is not entirely straightforward, but the Procedure Committee made a useful distinction between routine scrutiny of European legislation and the examination of what it termed 'individual European documents' as part of wider investigations of policy issues. In the 1990–91 and 1991–92 sessions the departmentally-related committees did not attempt for the most part to conduct any systematic scrutiny of European legislation within their own areas, although the European dimension continued to form part of wider investigations of policy issues in an increasing number of cases. Three reports stand out in that category: in 1990–91, the Education, Science and Arts Committee reported on *Science Policy and the European Dimension*[133] and examined United Kingdom science policy in the context of the European Community's role in European science; and the Employment Committee reported on *The European Community Social Charter*;[134] in 1991–92 the newly established Health Committee reported on *The European Community and Health Policy*[135] and examined the Community's post-Maastricht competence in health matters as well as specific aspects of existing Community policy which had an impact on health. Other reports with a

---

[133] First Report, 1990–91, HC 127.
[134] Fourth Report, 1990–91, HC 509.
[135] Third Report, 1991–92, HC 180.

significant EC dimension were the Environment Committee's inquiries into *Environmental Issues in Northern Ireland*[136] and into *Eco-labelling*,[137] while both the Agriculture Committee's 1991–92 inquiries were concerned with topics (*Commodity Markets in the 1990s—Cereals* and *The Trade Gap in Food and Drink*) with a high European content,[138] as was the Trade and Industry Committee's inquiry into *Takeovers and Mergers*.[139] The Home Affairs Committee also started, but did not complete, an inquiry in 1991–92 into *Migration and the External Frontiers of the European Community*.[140]

The Foreign Affairs Committee might be expected to have a general interest in European matters but has tended to leave the scrutiny of routine European Community matters to other parliamentary bodies and to conduct only occasional inquiries into major EC policy issues. Thus in 1989–90 it published a report on the *Operation of the Single European Act*[141] and in 1990–91 there were two sessions of evidence before the European Council meetings in Rome and Luxembourg[142] but none of its reports in 1990–91 was specifically concerned with European matters. In the brief 1991–92 session, however, it published a two-page report (truncated by the impending general election) on *Europe after Maastricht*[143] and started an inquiry (also halted by the general election) into the future financing of the European Community. The *Europe after Maastricht* inquiry was subsequently completed in April 1993.[144]

The Treasury and Civil Service Committee has been an exception to select committees' general reluctance to undertake routine monitoring and its regular reports each session on the Budget and Autumn Statement have often referred to the economic and financial impact of European Community membership. During the 1987–92 Parliament, the Committee also published reports on a range of European financial and fiscal issues such as *The European Commission's Proposals on the Approximation of*

---

[136] First Report, 1990–91, HC 39.

[137] Eighth Report, 1990–91, HC 474.

[138] First Report, 1991–92, HC 98; and Second Report, 1991–92, HC 112.

[139] First Report, 1991–92, HC 90.

[140] Evidence published as 1991–92, HC 215.

[141] Second Report, 1989–90, HC 82.

[142] Published as 1990–91, HC 77-i and ii respectively.

[143] Second Report, 1991–92, HC 223 I–II.

[144] Second Report, 1992–93, HC 642.

*Indirect Taxation*,[145] *European Community Finance*,[146] and *The Delors Report*.[147] In the 1990–91 session, the Committee took evidence twice (in January and July) but published no report on *Plans for Economic and Monetary Union*.[148] In 1991–92, it published a Special Report in advance of the general election which reproduced a Treasury Memorandum on *European Community Finances*[149] as well as taking evidence from the Chancellor of the Exchequer on *Economic and Monetary Union* on the outcome of the December 1991 Maastricht Summit.[150] Almost all this work reflected the Committee's well-established preoccupation with major issues of economic and financial policy. It also involved politically sensitive areas with a high profile where there have often been major policy differences both within and between the parties.

An increasing number of select committee inquiries conducted in the 1990–91 (and subsequent) sessions was concerned with specific EC legislative proposals, a noticeable change from earlier years. The Agriculture Committee's 1990–91 inquiry into *Animals in Transit*[151] was explicitly a 'direct response' to draft European legislation, as well as reflecting widespread public concern about the issue. As the report said, 'The prospect of replacing a tried and tested body of British law with a Community Directive of uncertain content has excited considerable alarm and suspicion in this country.'[152] That Committee's first report in 1991–92 on *Commodity Markets in the 1990s—Cereals*[153] also examined one of the most important and problematic sectors of the agricultural industry in the Community and considered in some detail the effect of legislative proposals for CAP reform on that sector.

The Environment Committee conducted a specific inquiry into *The EC Draft Directive on the Landfill of Waste*[154] which the Committee saw as

---

[145] Third Report, 1987–88, HC 248.
[146] Fifth Report, 1987–88, HC 358.
[147] Fourth Report, 1988–89, HC 341.
[148] Evidence published as 1990–91, HC 195–i and ii.
[149] Fourth Special Report, 1991–92, HC 334.
[150] Evidence published as 1991–92, HC 285.
[151] Third Report, 1990–91, HC 45.
[152] Ibid, para 7.
[153] First Report, 1991–92, HC 98.
[154] Seventh Report, 1990–91, HC 263.

(bringing) together our several years' interest in both landfill and the growing importance of the European Commission's role in the formulation of environmental protection policy. We hope that our critique of the Directive and its implications for landfill operations is well timed to make a constructive contribution to further discussions on the draft.[155]

The Employment Committee's report on *The European Community Social Charter*[156] went somewhat wider than the Charter itself and the directives made under it and examined 'the general progress of the implementation of the ideas contained in the Charter, and at the differing positions of Member States.'[157] The Transport Committee took a rather different approach in its inquiry into *Developments in European Community Air Transport Policy*[158] when it examined mainly the impact of the Community's general policies as they had evolved in a series of earlier measures but also considered some draft proposals for further measures.

Attempting to quantify the content of select committees' work is full of well-known pitfalls, but an examination of the subjects of inquiry during the 1987–92 Parliament (as listed in the *Sessional Returns*) does suggest that the European element grew significantly even in that relatively short period. The committees are gradually integrating 'Europe' into their normal pattern of work, although it is still a long way from dominating, let alone dictating, their agendas—the Procedure Committee notwithstanding. It is not altogether surprising that the departmentally-related committees have tended to be reluctant to become involved in routine scrutiny of EC legislative proposals and have continued to concentrate mainly on essentially domestic issues. Committees anyway prefer to choose their own agendas and not to have their work disrupted by the need to respond in a hurry to the unpredictable demands imposed by the vagaries of the timetables of EC draft legislation. In the two cases where committees did examine draft legislation—*Animals in Transit* and *Landfill of Waste*—it was known in advance that there would be long delays before the drafts were considered by the Council so that inquiries could be completed in time to be incorporated into the consultation

---

[155] Ibid, para 1.
[156] Fourth Report, 1990–91, HC 509.
[157] Ibid, para 2.
[158] First Report, 1991–92, HC 147.

process. The Transport Committee, on the other hand, was unable to examine the final group of proposals on air transport policy because they appeared too late. As the Treasury and Civil Service Committee has also found, too much routine scrutiny can be very time-consuming and inhibit committees from undertaking other, often more rewarding, work.

The total amount of time and resources which the departmentally related select committees devote to European matters has continued to grow but is still not substantial, nor have the committees explicitly responded to the Procedure Committee's exhortations to do more in that area. Their interest in European matters also remains patchy, although there are some obvious reasons for the variations in select committee involvement. It is no coincidence that the work of the Defence and Social Services Committees, for example, has had little or no significant European content. On the other hand, in some cases where there was a potential European dimension, such as the Agriculture Committee's inquiry into *Disposal of Fallen Livestock*,[159] no reference was made to it. The committees are, however, gradually responding to the growing European dimension which has followed the Single European Act and the post-Maastricht extension of Community competence into new policy areas. There are nevertheless some odd gaps—for example, the Trade and Industry Committee conducted only one inquiry into any aspect of the Single European Market during the 1987–92 Parliament—but inquiries such as those by the Health Committee and Employment Committee which have looked at the implementation of EC policies in particular areas and in other member states are possible pointers to the direction in which the departmentally-related committees will go. Such a development would be a natural evolution of both the established working patterns of the committees and the changing nature of the post-Maastricht Community.

## 5. The work of the session

From this account of the work of the 1990–91 session, it will be evident that MPs were carrying out a number of different functions in using procedural opportunities to discuss European matters. Primarily they were carrying out the basic constitutional function of parliamentary scrutiny—in this case scrutiny both of the decisions of Her Majesty's Government and

---

[159] Fourth Report, 1990–91, HC 493.

also, through the scrutiny of ministers, of some aspects of the activities of the European Community. This was apparent in the questioning of ministers, particularly when they made statements on European Council business and in the debates on fisheries policy.

It was evident also that MPs were performing a representative role—representing the interests of their constituencies (in the fisheries debates) and a variety of other interests affected by EC decisions (as in the EDMs and use of questions). In debate it was more evident that MPs were acting as political and partisan advocates—representing particular points of view on economic and social issues (eg the social charter and the CAP) as well as on the development of the Community and the United Kingdom's relationship to it (eg the Euro-sceptics). The House of Commons provided a forum in which these interests and issues could be articulated—and challenged.

Finally, to a small degree the House was legislating—directly, as in the consideration of statutory instruments implementing EC directives, and indirectly as in the consideration of EC proposals about to be debated in the Council of Ministers.

Scrutiny, representation and legislation are classic parliamentary roles. How effectively they were performed is a question to be considered in our final chapter. But it is already noteworthy that these parliamentary activities also served wider political purposes for the parties involved. For the government intensive parliamentary scrutiny could serve a wider purpose—the strengthening of its negotiating position in Brussels. This was made explicit on a number of occasions, particularly when the House was considering reform of the CAP (see Chapter 8). For a minister who could be confident of winning the vote (an important qualification, as the Maastricht debates were to show), pressure in the House was a welcome addition to the store of ammunition for the long nights of negotiating with Community partners and the Commission. Equally, the European debates provided an opportunity for the opposition parties to attempt to exploit the divisions within the governing Conservative party on this topic, particularly on EMU and political union, and to mark out their own distinctive positions for the approaching general election. As we noted at the beginning of this chapter, the political context of these debates is crucial to understanding and interpreting what was taking place.

# Appendix

### Table 6A.1
### Signatories and Signatures to EDMs by Party

| Party | Signatories | Signatures |
|-------|-------------|------------|
| Conservative | 182 | 591 |
| Labour | 182 | 926 |
| Liberal Democrat | 20 | 124 |
| Ulster Unionist | 9 | 39 |
| Scottish Nationalist | 5 | 13 |
| Plaid Cymru | 3 | 17 |
| SDP | 2 | 16 |
| SDLP | 2 | 3 |
| | | |
| Total | 405 | 1,729 |

### Table 6A.2
### Most Active Signatories by Party

| Conservative | | Labour | |
|--------------|-----|--------|-----|
| Mudd, D | 13 | Meale, A | 20 |
| Knox, D | 11 | Cunliffe, L | 15 |
| Rathbone, T | 11 | Dunnachie, J | 15 |
| Greenway, H | 10 | Graham, T | 15 |
| Winterton, A | 10 | Cummings, J | 14 |
| Winterton, N | 10 | Hardy, P | 14 |
| | | Illsley, E | 14 |
| **Liberal Democrat** | | **Other** | |
| Fearn, R | 14 | Beggs, R (UUP) | 9 |
| Bellotti, D | 12 | Barnes, R (SDP) | 8 |
| Wallace, J | 11 | Cartwright, J (SDP) | 8 |
| Johnston, R | 10 | Wigley, D (PC) | 8 |
| Howells, G | 9 | Kilfedder, J (UPUP) | 7 |
| | | Ewing, M (SNP) | 6 |

## Table 6A.3
## EC-related Early Day Motions

| Date | Sponsor | Short Title | Number of Signatures |
|------|---------|-------------|----------------------|
| 07 Nov | Harry Greenway | Export of horses and ponies after 1992 . | 162 |
| 07 Nov | Harry Greenway | Export of horses and ponies after 1992 (no 2) . . . . . . . . . . . . . . . . . . . . . | 150 |
| 08 Nov | Richard Livsey | Family farms in Britain . . . . . . . . . . | 17 |
| 13 Nov | Nicholas Bonsor | EC Birds directive—pest species . . . . . | 86 |
| 20 Dec | Alex Carlile | British custard tart . . . . . . . . . . . . . . | 9 |
| 10 Dec | William Cash | Federal European Union and the European Central Bank . . . . . . . . . . . | 3 |
| 12 Dec | Roger Gale | Transport of live animals . . . . . . . . . . | 78 |
| 18 Dec | Simon Hughes | Arms exports . . . . . . . . . . . . . . . . | 52 |
| 15 Jan | Richard Caborn | Apartheid . . . . . . . . . . . . . . . . . . | 78 |
| 24 Jan | Bill Walker | Gulf War and European contributions towards its cost . . . . . . . . . . . . . . . | 14 |
| 11 Mar | Jim Lester | Famine in Africa . . . . . . . . . . . . . . | 93 |
| 14 Mar | William Clark | Duty free shops . . . . . . . . . . . . . . . | 157 |
| 25 Apr | Keith Vaz | Genetic patenting . . . . . . . . . . . . . . | 44 |
| 30 Apr | Gordon McMaster | British crisp industry . . . . . . . . . . . | 20 |
| 09 May | Alan Meal | European VAT rates—thoroughbred breeding industry . . . . . . . . . . . . . | 20 |
| 21 May | Jimmy Wray | European Community money for Israel . | 27 |
| 23 May | Michael Colvin | Defence of the British sausage . . . . . . | 34 |
| 11 Jun | Malcolm Thornton | Pharmaceutical industry and intellectual property rights . . . . . . . . . . . . . . . . | 106 |
| 11 Jun | Jack Ashley | British sign language . . . . . . . . . . . . | 76 |
| 12 Jun | Robert Maclennan | EC directive and data protection and the UK voluntary sector . . . . . . . . . . | 131 |
| 24 Jun | Jim Lester | Co-ordination of famine relief . . . . . . | 59 |
| 10 Jul | Simon Coombes | Open skies policy . . . . . . . . . . . . . | 11 |
| 10 Jul | Terry Lewis | Doctors for tobacco law and cigarette advertising . . . . . . . . . . . . . . . . . | 36 |
| 11 Jul | Bowen Wells | European banana policy . . . . . . . . . . | 53 |
| 16 Jul | Paul Marland | CAP reform . . . . . . . . . . . . . . . . . | 54 |
| 17 Jul | Ron Davies | Veal production . . . . . . . . . . . . . . . | 63 |
| 23 Jul | Ted Garrett | Tobacco Products Labelling (Safety) Regulations 1991 . . . . . . . . . . . . . | 26 |
| 16 Oct | Thomas Graham | Europol policy agency . . . . . . . . . . . | 7 |

**Table 6A.4**
**Classification of EDMs by Partisanship and EC Stance**

| Short Title | Partisanship | EC Stance |
|---|---|---|
| Export of horses and ponies after 1992 | Cross-party | C |
| Export of horses and ponies after 1992 (no 2) | Cross-part | C |
| Family farms in Britain | 13/17 Lib Dem | — |
| EC birds directive—pest species | 81/86 Con | C |
| British custard tart | 7/9 Lib Dem | C |
| Federal European Union and Central Bank | All 3 Cons | C |
| Transport and live animals | 55/78 Lab | C |
| Arms exports | 37/52 Lab | — |
| Apartheid | All 78 Lab | C |
| Gulf war and European contributions to costs | All 14 Con | — |
| Famine in Africa | Cross-party | S |
| Duty free shops | Cross-party | C |
| Genetic patenting | Cross-party | C |
| British crisp industry | 61/83 Lab | C |
| European VAT rates—thoroughbred breeding | 18/20 Lab | S |
| EC money for Israel | All 27 Lab | C |
| Defence of the British sausage | Cross-party | C |
| Pharmaceutical industry & intellectual property rights | Cross-party | S |
| British sign language | 60/76 Lab | S |
| EC directive on data protection | Cross-party | C |
| Co-ordination of famine relief | 40/59 Lab | S |
| Open skies policy | 10/11 Con | S |
| Doctors for tobacco law & cigarette advertising | 31/36 lab | S |
| European banana policy | 37/53 Lab | C |
| CAP reform | All 54 Con | C |
| Veal production | 56/63 lab | — |
| Effect of Tobacco Products Labelling (Safety) Regulations 1991 | Cross-party | — |
| Europol policy agency | All 7 Lab | S |

*Key*: C=Critical  S=Supportive

# 7

# The House of Lords
# and the European Community 1990–91

## *Donald Shell*

This chapter examines the activity of the House of Lords in relation to
European Community matters during the 1990–91 session, with a few
selected references to the short subsequent session of 1991–92. As already
indicated in this volume these were somewhat turbulent years in respect
of Britain's relations with other Community members. The consequences
of that turbulence were most keenly felt within the ruling Conservative
party. As Chapter 5 has argued, the contemporary House of Lords stands
on the side-lines of the struggle for political power and its members are
essentially spectators rather than players when it comes to decisions on key
policy questions. Nevertheless, as Chapter 5 makes clear, the House of
Lords has maintained an active role in relation to the examination of
significant developments within the European Community and the making
of detailed Community policy. The major method by which the House
scrutinises Community matters has been through its Select Committee on
the European Communities (ECC).

The bulk of this chapter therefore examines the work of this Committee
in the 1990–91 session. In doing this reference is made to other
proceedings of the House in which reports from the Select Committee
were taken up, most notably debates specifically on reports. But before
doing that the chapter begins by examining the floor of the House
proceedings concerned with European Community matters.

## Floor of the House

The House of Lords is very much a chamber of influence, not of power.
Its influence partly derives from its membership, containing as it does
many experienced and knowledgeable men and women, a significant
proportion of whom are old hands in the Westminster and Whitehall
political game. But its members do not simply talk to each other; they also

have the opportunity to talk to the Government. Ministers must answer debates and questions in the House, and this at least opens up the possibility that somewhere within Westminster or Whitehall, as the proceedings of the House are monitored and ministerial contributions drafted, views expressed in the House percolate through to decision-makers. Like the Commons the House of Lords affords to its members opportunities to address specific questions to the Government, and to initiate or participate in debates on any issue for which government carries some kind of responsibility. But though superficially similar, the proceedings of the two Houses are in practice very different in character.

*Questions* Oral questions in the Lords are limited to four per day, with each question typically generating a short string of supplementaries, which may sometimes continue for up to ten minutes.[1] An analysis of oral questions asked during the 1990–91 session indicates that approximately one in ten were directly concerned with European Community matters, the questioner referring to the Community in some way in the question itself, while at least another one in ten drew in some reference to the Community during supplementary exchanges. The 51 oral questions (out of 531 in the session) directly relating to the Community were asked by 23 different peers. The subject matter of these questions was very varied; some were quite specific, others wide in scope; some were clearly hostile in intent towards Community policy, others apparently simply seeking information.

For example, Baroness Burton of Coventry asked five questions all concerned with consumer issues in relation to Community matters; this doughty 86 year old champion of consumer rights continually sought to keep the interests and needs of consumers in the forefront of ministers and officials minds.[2] Lord Boyd-Carpenter, the senior Tory peer, former MP and sometime Treasury minister, asked seven EC related questions; these dealt with various topics, including the costs of Community subsidies to tobacco growers;[3] the contributions other Community countries had made to the costs of the Gulf War;[4] and on 22 July 1991: 'What is the length of the appointment of Mr Jacques Delors with the European Commission,

---

[1] Donald Shell, 'Questions in the House of Lords', Mark Franklin and Philip Norton (eds) *Parliamentary Questions*, Clarendon Press, Oxford, 1993.

[2] HL Deb 6 December 1990 cc 267–68; 13 December 1990 cc 575–76; 17 January 1991 cc 1249–50; 24 January 1991 c 327; 6 February 1991 c 1155.

[3] HL Deb 5 December 1991 cc 1063–65; 19 July 1991 cc 364–67.

[4] HL Deb 12 March 1991 cc 65–66; 25 March 1991 c 844.

and when that period is due to expire?'[5] His fellow Conservative, Lord Campbell of Croy (formerly Gordon Campbell MP and Secretary of State for Scotland in the Heath Government), asked a larger number of the EC-related questions than any other peer; his eight were on the whole probing questions, seeking to establish what progress had been made with this or that, for example the prevention of money laundering or the removal of obstacles to electricity transfer between member countries.[6] The former leader of the House, Baroness Young, asked a question following up an earlier report from the ECC on progress being made in securing the appointment of more British nationals to posts in Community institutions.[7] Lord Ezra, the Liberal Democrat peer asked two questions, one about monetary union, and the other on the meaning of the term 'federalism'.[8]

On the Labour side Lord Clinton-Davis (formerly Stanley Clinton Davis, a Labour MP) asked about matters he had dealt with in his time as a Community Commissioner;[9] the former trade union leader Baroness Turner of Camden asked about occupational pensions.[10] Some Euro-sceptics were also active questioners, notably Lord Bruce of Donington, Lord Stoddart of Swindon (formerly David Stoddart MP), and Lord Jay (formerly Douglas Jay MP, and President of the Board of Trade in Wilson's first Government). Questions about the costs of the Common Agricultural Policy[11] and the effects of the Exchange Rate Mechanism were prominent.[12] Lord Bruce asked a question demanding that a senior Treasury minister accompany the Minister of Agriculture to meetings of the Agriculture Council.[13] Later in the session the same peer asked about accountability for views expressed by the President of the Commission, whom he described as 'a paid international civil servant', a remark which drew forth a stinging rebuke from another former Commissioner in the

---

[5] HL Deb 22 July 1991 c 457.

[6] HL Deb 8 July 1991 c 1203 and 18 June 1991 cc 40–42. See also 26 February 1991 cc 863–64; 1 May 1991 cc 745–47; 10 May 1991 cc 1276–77; 13 May 1991 c 1353; 24 June 1991 cc 420–22; and 5 November 1991 cc 146–47.

[7] HL Deb 28 February 1991 cc 1102–03.

[8] HL Deb 6 June 1991 cc 737–39; 27 June 1991 cc 576–77.

[9] HL Deb 19 March 1991 c 525; 10 May 1991 c 1280; 9 July 1991 c 1312.

[10] HL Deb 28 November 1991 c 963.

[11] HL Deb 14 June 1991 cc 1279–80; 27 June 1991 cc 701–02.

[12] HL Deb 13 February 1991 c 107; 25 June 1991 cc 490–91.

[13] HL Deb 25 February 1991 cc 763–65.

House, Lord Cockfield.[14] Interventions in the form of supplementaries
from peers such as Lord Cockfield, or Baroness Elles (a former vice-
president of the European Parliament) were a regular feature of
proceedings on starred questions; such peers at times almost took the role
of spokesmen in the House for the Community.[15]

*Questions for Written Answer* Similarly a significant proportion of the
1300 or so questions for written answer in the House during the session
concerned the Community. Many of these appeared to be questions
'planted' by the government, seeking statements on recently concluded
meetings of the Council of Ministers.[16] Most questions for written answer
were primarily concerned with seeking information, often of a quite
specific statistical kind. For example, Lord Wade of Chorlton, a prominent
Conservative farmer and cheese-maker, asked three questions about the
relative position of milk producers in specified Community countries and
the value of trade in certain dairy products between states.[17] Some
questions were clearly designed to prompt government into doing
something it had hitherto failed to do, such as to reply to a select
committee report; for example, Lord Middleton, former chairman of the
ECC sub-committee dealing with agriculture asked the government for its
response to the Committee's report on non-food uses of agricultural
products.[18] Some appeared aimed at exposing the government's failure
to take advantage of some Community provision; for example Lord
O'Hagan (a Conservative MEP) asked five simultaneous questions about
the use being made within Britain of the European Social Fund.[19] The
same peer also asked written questions about the scrutiny of Community
proposals by national parliaments, and about the attitude of the
Government to the prospect of greater powers being granted to the
European Parliament.[20]

---

[14] HL Deb 24 July 1991 cc 774–76.

[15] See for example HL Deb 13 May 1991 c 1354; 27 June 1991 c 703; 14 June 1991
c 1282; 2 July 1991 c 897.

[16] For example written questions concerning the outcome of successive meetings of the
Transport Council were asked by Baroness Cox on 13 November 1990 cc 5–6w; Lord
Lindsey and Abingdon on 26 June 1991 cc 41–42w; Lord Brougham and Vaux on 16
October 1991 cc 105–06w.

[17] HL Deb 3 June 1991 cc 27–32w.

[18] HL Deb 11 November 1991 c 22w.

[19] HL Deb 14 February 1991 cc 16–17w.

[20] HL Deb 13 December 1990 c 38w: 18 December 1990 c 45w.

*Debate on Motions* Major debates related to the preparations for the Maastricht Treaty are dealt with separately in the next section. Debates on ECC reports are also discussed later in this chapter. Other than these, two motions specifically referring to the Community were debated during the 1990–91 session. The first of these was a motion moved by Lord Benson, a prominent accountant, 'calling attention to the volume of fraud which continues to take place in the conduct of affairs in the EC and the case for specific programmes of reform in a number of areas if fraud is to be curtailed'.[21] This was a subject upon which an ad hoc sub-committee of the ECC had reported in 1989; it was a matter the House had then debated and returned to on several occasions subsequently.[22] Pressure from the House had probably strengthened the government's resolve to tackle the issues involved. The other debate was initiated by the cross-bench peer Lord Annan 'calling attention to the case for improving relations between member states within the Community, especially Germany'.[23]

*Unstarred Questions* Debate takes place on unstarred questions as well as motions in the Lords. Unstarred questions are usually the last business of the day, like adjournment debates in the Commons, but unlike the Commons such debates have no formal time limit, and in consequence these sometimes run on for two or three hours. Four of the 42 unstarred questions during the session related directly to EC issues. Two of these were introduced by Lord Hacking, a lawyer with special interests in European law. One concerned voting rights in local elections for EC nationals in the country of their residence; this was a subject upon which an ECC report had been made in 1990, but the report had not otherwise been debated.[24] His other question concerned patent protection for medicinal products, and this too was a subject where a relevant ECC report had been made. Lord Hacking expressed some strong criticism of

---

[21] HL Deb 28 November 1990 cc 968–994.

[22] Fifth Report from the Select Committee on the European Communities 1988–89, *Fraud Against the Community*, HL 27; See HL Deb 13 April 1989; also questions on 14 February 1989, 23 June 1989, and 13 July 1989.

[23] HL Deb 8 May 1991 cc 1093–1120.

[24] HL Deb 18 December 1990 cc 801–21; Sixth Report from the Select Committee on the European Communities, 1989–90, HL 25, February 1990.

the government for its hesitancy in responding to a proposal from the Commission to extend patent protection.[25]

*Statements* Oral Statements made by the Prime Minister following the six-monthly meetings of the European Council are always repeated in the Lords.[26] Other Statements occasionally draw forth references to Community concerns; for example in responding from the Opposition front-bench to a Statement on education and training for 16 to 19 year olds, Baroness Turner of Camden criticised the government for adopting a policy that ran counter to the recommendations made by an ECC report on Vocational Training and Re-Training.[27]

### Table 7.1
### Major Lords Debates on European Union 1990–92

| | |
|---|---|
| **22 Nov 1990:** | take note of report on economic and monetary and political union, *Lord Aldington*, 34 speeches, 7hr 48min |
| **21 Oct 1991:** | take note of report on political Union, *Lord Oliver of Aylmerton*, 14 speeches, 3hr 49min |
| **25 Nov 1991:** | take note of forthcoming negotiations at the European Council at Maastricht, *Lord Waddington*, 36 speeches, 8hr 14min. |
| **18 Dec 1991:** | to resolve that this House warmly endorses the agreement secured at Maastricht, and congratulates the PM on securing all HMG's negotiating objectives, *Lord Waddington*, 42 speeches, 6hr 0min |

*Major Debates on the Future of the Community* The 1990–91 session together with the subsequent session running up to the 1992 general

---

[25] HL Deb 15 April 1991 cc 1322–1338; see also 17 April 1991 cc 87–88w, and for earlier debate 25 April 1990, cc 637–58.

[26] HL Deb 18 December 1990 cc 742–51; 1 July 1991 cc 788–98.

[27] HL Deb 20 May 1991 cc 51–52.

election were marked by intense debate on the future of the Community associated with the intergovernmental conferences which led up to the Maastricht Treaty. In the Lords as in the Commons there were four such debates which may be highlighted, which are listed in Table 7.1.

In addition to these the second day of the Queen's Speech debate on 4 November 1991 was devoted to Foreign Affairs and Defence, and dealt largely, but by no means exclusively, with European Community developments.

The first two debates listed in Table 7.1 were on ECC reports. The first was a report made by a 20 strong ad hoc sub-committee chaired by Lord Aldington (formerly Sir Toby Low, a Conservative MP from 1945 to 1962, and chairman of the Select Committee on Nationalised Industries from 1957 to 1961). This report drew not only on deliberations and evidence taken at the 21 sessions the ECC sub-committee held, but also on the accumulated wisdom derived from many of the 500 or so enquiries conducted by the select committee since its inception. The report was undoubtedly a most lucid analysis of the arguments swirling around on the highly charged subjects being debated at the inter-governmental conference.[28] By a strange irony the debate took place on the day Mrs Thatcher resigned as prime minister, in his 37 minute opening speech Lord Aldington spoke of the 'distractions along the corridor and in another place'. Peers were restrained in their references to these events, but it was possible to discern a note of quiet satisfaction in the speeches of several committed Europeans. Media attention was, however, very firmly fixed elsewhere than the House of Lords! The debate on 21 October arose from a report made by the Law and Institutions sub-committee of the ECC.[29] This had examined the draft Treaty of Union published by the Luxembourg presidency. The report sought to clarify the proposals being made, indicate their possible consequences, and highlight areas of obscurity or conflict of interest. The debate was an opportunity to carry this process further.

---

[28] Twenty-seventh Report from the Select Committee on the European Communities 1989–90, *Economic and Monetary Union and Political Union*, HL 88, October 1990; HL Deb 22 November 1990 cc 778–892.

[29] Seventeenth Report from the Select Committee on the European Communities, 1990–91 *Political Union: Law Making Powers and Procedures*, HL 80, HL Deb 21 October 1991 cc 1343–96.

Both these reports were frequently referred to when the House debated the Maastricht Council. The debate on 25 November was held a few days after a similar debate in the Commons; this was on a government take note motion with no vote occurring. Some four weeks later the House debated the outcome of the Maastricht Summit, but this time on the same day as the Commons debated an identical motion. On this latter occasion the Government had decided to seek the specific endorsement of the House. Both major Opposition parties in the Lords put down amendments to the government motion, and both were handsomely defeated.[30]

*Conclusion* It is far from clear how to assess such proceedings. In terms of the participants their combined knowledge and experience was truly impressive. Speeches came from numerous ex-ministers and senior diplomats. The debates listed in Table 7.1 included speeches from three former governors of the Bank of England, five MEPs or former MEPs, three former European Community Commissioners, and many others with relevant very senior experience (though surprisingly the House did not hear from a single Bishop in any of these debates). The general tone was supportive of the Community, but the Euro-sceptics though in a clear minority were also vigorously represented. In terms of the content of the debates, speeches were undoubtedly very well informed and carefully argued. The few exceptions to this generalisation stand out.

In terms of style speeches were usually made without interruption, though that should not be taken to imply that sharp disagreements were not expressed; they certainly were. Occasionally a lordly style intervention was provoked, as for example when Lord Aldington was moved to comment during Lord Stoddart of Swindon's castigation of the Community: 'My Lords, that really is rubbish, if I may say so'.[31] Party politics was manifestly subdued though a little gentle mischief-making did creep into the debates, for example some Conservatives teased Labour peers about their party's change of mind on Europe. But clearly the contrast with the Commons is very marked. Peers prepare their speeches for an attentive, interested, informed and basically friendly audience. Speeches read well as peers are able to develop their arguments in an untroubled manner. Judged by the standards of the Commons some would

---

[30] Labour's by 184 to 86; the Liberal Democrats by 185 to 81, with most of the 27 Liberal Democrats and 60 Labour peers who voted supporting both amendments, and only one Labour peer supporting the Government in one division.

[31] HL Deb 22 November 1990 c 872.

argue this was not real debate, rather a succession of speeches. But peers do seek to answer each other's arguments, if in a sequential rather than an interrogatory style. Before offering further conclusions on the role of the House in relation to Community issues in this period, we turn to an examination of the work of the Select Committee on the European Communities.

### The European Communities Committee

In the 1990–91 session the ECC consisted of 24 members, 19 of whom also served on one or other of the six sub-committees. A further 55 peers served during the session as co-opted members of sub-committees. As explained in Chapter 5 the actual process of scrutiny involving the taking of evidence and the drawing up of reports is conducted by these subject based sub-committees. Each sub-committee as well as having between two and five members of the main committee had between five and twelve other peers as co-opted members. Each sub-committee was served by a clerk, but the clerks concerned all had other responsibilities which they were required concurrently to fulfil. Sub-committees were and remain free to appoint specialist advisers, and this has become their normal but not invariable practice.[32] Members of the Committee and sub-committees, as well as clerks assisting the Committee, travel in the course of their enquiries; in 1990–91 the total cost of such travel was £28,835.[33] A legal adviser assists the chairman of the main committee. The sub-committee structure as it was in 1990–91 is shown in Table 7.2 (overleaf).

---

[32] Baroness Serota spoke of the increasing difficulties the sub-committees were experiencing in finding at short notice suitable people to accept the role of advisers; see evidence to Select Committee on the Committee Work of the House, HL 35–ii, 1991–2, p 28, para 50.

[33] See evidence to Select Committee on the Committee Work of the House, HL 35–ii, 1991–92, p 30, para 64.

**Table 7.2**
**Sub-Committee Structure 1990–91**

| |
|---|
| **A: Finance, Trade and Industry, and External Relations**<br>*Chairman*: Lord Aldington, Conservative; created hereditary peer; former Conservative MP and minister in 1950s; former chairman Sun Alliance Insurance Company, and other companies. |
| **B: Energy, Transport and Technology**<br>*Chairman*: Lord Ezra, Liberal Democrat; life peer; former chairman of the National Coal Board. |
| **C: Social and Consumer Affairs**<br>*Chairman*: Baroness Lockwood, Labour; life peer; former chairman Equal Opportunities Commission. |
| **D: Agriculture and Food.**<br>*Chairman*: Lord Middleton, Conservative; hereditary peer; former president Country Landowners' Association |
| **E: Law and Institutions.**<br>*Chairman*: Lord Oliver of Aylmerton, Cross-bencher; life peer; Lord of Appeal in Ordinary |
| **F: Environment.**<br>*Chairman*: Lord Nathan, Cross-bencher; hereditary peer; solicitor. |

The main committee was presided over by Baroness Serota, chairman since 1986. She was a Labour life peer who had held ministerial office in the Wilson Government of the late 1960s. She retired from the post of chairman in 1992, having reached her 73rd year. She was succeeded by Lord Boston of Faversham, the seventh peer to hold this office and the sixth former Labour minister to do so. This indicates the relative indifference to party affiliations which characterises select committee membership in the upper House. Given the political balance in the House as a whole, and the large number of non-party peers, no specific formula exists to determine the composition of investigatory select committees. The membership of the ECC in the 1990–91 session is analysed by type of peerage and party affiliation in Table 7.3.

**Table 7.3**

**Composition of the European Communities Committee and Sub-Committees 1990–91 by Peerage and Party Affiliation**

| Peerage | Hereditary | Life | Total |
|---|---|---|---|
| Cons | 18 | 12 | 30 |
| Lab | 1 | 15 | 16 |
| Dem | 3 | 6 | 9 |
| Cross Bench | 12 | 12 | 24 |
| Total | 34 | 45 | 79 |

In terms of party balance the figures are roughly proportionate to the House as a whole, except for the relatively high number of cross bench peers. The balance between created and hereditary peers is roughly similar to that among active peers in the total membership of the House. Within some of the sub-committees the party balance is more disproportionate. Sub-committee A dealing with Finance, Trade and Industry and External Relations, had only two Labour members among fifteen; of its total membership no less than eleven had very substantial city experience, mostly as chairmen of banks or insurance companies. Sub-committee D which covered Agriculture consisted predominantly of farmers or landowners.

The main Committee, generally speaking, keeps a low profile. It usually meets fortnightly when the House is sitting but met nineteen times during the 1990–91 session. At these regular meetings the Committee considers and approves draft reports from sub-committees, and also ratifies the decisions made by its chairman concerning the allocation of documents to sub-committees for scrutiny. The main Committee watches over the sub-committees and does what it can to ensure their effectiveness. For example, at the beginning of the 1990–91 session it agreed to appoint a working group of six members to 'undertake an analysis of the Committee's working methods', and subsequently this group represented the interests of the Committee to the Procedure Committee, the newly established Liaison Committee and indeed the House as a whole.

The main committee has also sought to keep itself informed about more general Community developments. For example, increasingly in recent years it has met with prominent overseas visitors for informal private discussion. Sometimes the purpose of such visits is to allow parliamentarians from elsewhere in the Community to learn how the Committee operates. Sometimes the Committee meets ministers; for example, a series of informal meetings were held with Foreign Office ministers in the Summer and Autumn of 1991 prior to the Maastricht summit. In addition a small group from the Committee attended two meetings of the European Community's Conference of Committees specialising in European Affairs, the body which since 1989 has brought together members of scrutiny committees in the parliaments of Community countries for meetings once every six months.

As explained in Chapter 5, a principal task for the chairman is deciding which documents should be referred to which sub-committees. It is then for the sub-committees to decide which documents they will select for actual enquiry. Sub-committee chairmen in interview indicated that these decisions were not generally difficult; 'subjects tend to choose themselves' was a typical comment.[34] Over a period of time sub-committees cover a range of topics within their subject area; having examined one such topic, maybe in some depth in one session, they may return to that topic to make a much shorter enquiry a year or two later, or they may draw on their earlier inquiry to respond to some new document, not with a further enquiry and report, but with a letter to the relevant minister. In deciding what to enquire into, sub-committees may receive advice from various quarters. Some sub-committee chairmen talk to government ministers or their senior officials; sub-committee clerks regularly attend sessions of the European Parliament and keep in close touch with committees there. The ECC as a whole clearly tries to develop good intelligence about the subject matter and likely time scale of Community developments and policy proposals. Sometimes sub-committees deliberately move 'up-stream' a bit in the policy process, perhaps examining a broad-based green paper issued by the Commission. But the danger is that such enquiries become too diffuse and lack clear focus. Most sub-committees seem happier to be dealing with clearly defined quite specific proposals, even if they also place some emphasis on the need to examine the wider context within which proposals are formulated. Sub-committees generally avoid enquiring into something chosen by a Commons departmental select committee, but the reason for this is the practical question of avoiding duplication rather

---

[34] For the purposes of this research interviews were conducted with the chairman of the main committee and four of the six sub-committee chairmen.

than any feeling that in principle the Lords ought to avoid subjects currently being examined by the Commons.[35]

Having decided on a topic for enquiry a sub-committee may well hold an informal seminar with representatives from the government department most concerned; as one sub-committee chairman said in interview: 'this possibly points us in certain directions; it may reveal more than we had appreciated about the politics behind some proposals, for example differences of view between ministers'. Such seminars are private, though the sub-committee concerned keeps a note of what is said—and all take pride in the fact that this never leaks. A sub-committee then issues a general invitation to interested parties to submit evidence. Alongside this, however, a list of specific invitations to those from whom the sub-committee specifically wishes to hear evidence will be drawn up, with the clerk and, if appointed, the specialist adviser assisting with this choice. Usually at least some of these are invited to give oral evidence, though some enquiries are completed on the basis of written evidence only.

Sub-committee chairmen emphasised the importance of this process of setting up an enquiry; evidence must be seen as broadly representative in terms of those from whom it is taken. Invariably for a major enquiry this means that witnesses from the most relevant Whitehall department are called, at least one Member of the European Parliament and someone from the relevant section of the EC Commission. Beyond this representatives from interest groups, academic experts and others may be summoned. Given that the Committee is seeking to influence opinion its choice of witnesses has a further importance; those who give evidence on a particular subject themselves take notice of the committee's report on that subject, and as one sub-committee chairman put it: 'they then go and talk about it with their friends, who are often the very kind of people we want to get to read our report'. Witnesses are thus in part chosen with an eye to their value in disseminating the work of the Committee. Another sub-committee chairman emphasised that the activity of taking oral evidence was also helpful to the dynamics of a committee.

The length and scope of enquiries and reports varies a good deal. (A full list of reports made during the session is given as an appendix to this chapter). The report on the future of the *Development and Future of the Common Agricultural Policy* ran to 223 paragraphs and drew on extensive evidence presented to the sub-committee and published with its report; ten

---

[35] Select Committee on the Committee Work of the House, HL 35–ii, February 1992, p 25 para 30.

days were spent taking oral evidence, which ran to 640 questions, and a further 180 pages of written evidence were published. The report on *Municipal Waste Water Treatment* was likewise a very substantial document. Other reports were relatively brief, such as that on *Working Time*, or *Money Laundering*, both of which were some 50 to 60 paragraphs in length and based on one day of oral evidence taking.

While enquiries by sub-committees usually focus on some Community document, the idea that it is possible sharply to separate an examination of so-called 'European issues' from domestic issues is outdated. The way in which Community policy as it develops meshes with the pattern of policy that has evolved within the UK necessarily requires examination of the latter. In attempting to offer viable policy recommendations in complex areas it can well be argued that thorough enquiries drawing out a wide range and depth of evidence are advantageous. If this approach were not adopted then it would be all too easy to criticise a select committee for the superficiality of its work.

In a formal sense the main target of committee reports is the House itself. Reports may be made for the information of the House or be recommended for debate. As the appendix shows, most reports in the 1990–91 session were recommended for debate. Where this is the case a debate is usually arranged relatively quickly. A debate helps to bring a report to the attention of other peers. It also ensures that front-bench spokesmen clarify their attitude to a report. While the government will always now publish a written reply to a report, a debate can still be useful in drawing a government spokesman out somewhat further than a written reply has done. Specific points can be put to ministers, and given the fast-moving nature of developments on many of the issues about which reports are made, a debate provides opportunity for some updating on the part of all concerned—both government spokesmen and committee members. A debate also gives members of the sub-committee which has produced a report themselves the chance to indicate something of the variety of views represented within their sub-committee where this has not come out in the report itself. Speeches from other members of the House, who have not themselves served on the sub-committee concerned, can add context to a report, perhaps reinforcing its recommendations or in places seeking to qualify them. Sometimes such speeches from non-committee members attract additional publicity.[36]

But the value of debate on committee reports can easily be exaggerated. The fact that the House devotes so much of its collective effort to the ECC, and something over one-quarter of its clerk power, yet less than one twentieth of its debating time may seem puzzling. Almost half the speeches in such debates are made by members of the sub-committees concerned. Rarely is much added to what has already been well expressed in a report. As in the Commons a debate on the floor of the House is more likely to be evidence of the fact that attention is being given to a select committee report than it is likely to be the cause of such attention.

Reference may be made to any reports (whether recommended for debate or not) in other proceedings of the House and indeed this frequently occurs. As already indicated a good many questions in the House are about Community matters, sometimes directly on the content of a select committee report. Debates on unstarred questions also sometimes deal with subjects covered in reports, as do proceedings on some orders and on some bills. In these ways the work of the Select Committee may be said to add depth and quality to other activities of the House.

## Reports during the 1990–91 Session

Altogether fourteen reports emanating from enquiries conducted by sub-committees were published during the session. In this section we look briefly at each of these reports.

*Sub-Committee A: Finance, Trade and Industry and External Relations.* This sub-committee spent much of the session enquiring into a communication from the Commission concerning Association Agreements with countries of Central and Eastern Europe. This was not therefore an enquiry focused on draft legislation. It was a good example of the select committee making use of its wide terms of reference to enquire into and report on a major area of potential development for the Community. The enquiry was wide-ranging in effect taking stock of the condition of former

---

[36] In July 1992 two new peers (the former Sir Geoffrey Howe and Denis Healey) chose to make their maiden speeches in the House on the Tenth Report from the Select Committee on the European Communities 1991–92, *The Enlargement of the Community*, HL 55, March 1992; see HL Deb 14 July 1992 cc 149–52 and cc 155–58.

Warsaw Pact countries which 'had decided to change their political systems from communist states into democracies and their economic systems from command economies to market economies', as the report boldly stated at its outset.[37] As well as its published evidence from the Department for Trade and Industry, the Foreign and Commonwealth Office, two MEPs, officials from the Commission, and academics, the sub-committee held private discussions with diplomats from eastern Europe and met various political figures when it visited Prague. In a fast changing situation the sub-committee were able to benefit from the emergence of more information while their enquiry was proceeding. The sub-committee's report appeared at the end of March, a time considered helpful by civil servants from the DTI.[38] It spoke eloquently of the immensity of the task facing such countries as Poland, Hungary and the Czech and Slovak Federal Republic. The need for massive change was emphasised, and the evidence presented with the report constituted a survey helpful to anyone seeking to understand the process of change required. When the report was debated in the House among those who spoke was the former diplomat, Lord Bridges, who suggested that the report was a 'shade too dispassionate'.[39] Certainly the language of the report was restrained and its tone appeared detached—given the scale of the problems it described. It concluded with a summary of the opinion of the sub-committee rather than with recommendations, a summary the flavour of which can be given from the following quotations: 'all three countries need urgently to attract private investment'; 'trade is as important as aid'; and 'there are good potential markets for British exports'.

The sub-committee next examined directives designed to facilitate the creation of a single market in insurance. Its concern here was to ensure that a 'level' playing field existed; this required giving attention, first, to some complex questions concerned with the tax treatment of reserves, and, secondly to mandatory provisions in contracts specifying the jurisdiction within which any disputes of a cross-border kind would be resolved. Most of what the sub-committee recommended was agreed through the Council

---

[37] Eighth Report from the Select Committee on the European Communities, 1990–91, HL 35, March 1991, para 7.

[38] Ibid, Q 531–32.

[39] HL Deb 3 June 1991 c 480.

of Ministers shortly after the report was published.[40] The sub-committee then embarked on an enquiry into regional development policy, upon which it published a report in January 1992.[41] Its next enquiry concerned the enlargement of the Community;[42] the tone of its report on this topic was a good deal less dispassionate than had been the report on relations with the Central and Eastern European countries.

*Sub-Committee B: Energy, Transport and Technology* Sub-committee B had begun taking evidence on railways in July 1990; its report on this topic, entitled *A New Structure for Community Railways*, was published in late 1990, and debated by the House in March 1991.[43] The need to harmonise developments in the structure of railways in order to take advantage of the single market had prompted wide-ranging recommendations from the Commission. This was not the only reason why 1991 was 'a time of opportunity for railways';[44] greater awareness of the environmental benefits of increased rail transport and the problems associated with congestion on roads and in the air were further factors underlying the renaissance in railways. The report concentrated on the managerial and financial autonomy of the railway system; high speed trains; and combined transport. While accepting the case put by the Commission for separating responsibility for infrastructure from responsibility for operations, the sub-committee argued that the former should remain the responsibility of the State. The sub-committee had moved with the times. Such a separation was accepted in this report, but this was a principle not even mentioned in a report on traffic infrastructure made by the sub-committee two years earlier, a point emphasised by Lord Underhill when the House debated this report.[45]

The sub-committee then launched into a five month enquiry entitled *Energy and the Environment*. Four documents were under scrutiny; a

---

[40] Twelfth Report from the Select Committee on the European Communities, 1990–91, *Single Insurance Market*, HL 59, June 1991.

[41] Fourth Report from the Select Committee on the European Communities, 1991–92, *EEC Regional Development Policy*, HL 20, January 1992.

[42] First Report from the Select Committee on the European Communities, 1992–93 *Enlargement of the Community*, HL 5, June 1992.

[43] Third Report from the Select Committee on the European Communities, 1990–91, HL 11, December 1990; HL Deb 4 March 1991 cc 1201–47.

[44] A phrase used by Lord Tordoff when the report was debated, see HL Deb 4 March 1991 c 1231.

[45] Ibid, c 1238.

Commission discussion paper, a proposal for a SAVE programme (Specific Actions for Vigorous Energy Efficiency), a directive on energy requirements for hot water boilers and another directive concerned with the labelling of household appliances to show their energy consumption. The report was dated June 1991, but dealt primarily with a communication from the Commission of 1989; on 7 November an answer to a written question from the chairman of the committee, Lord Ezra, revealed that the Government had only that day placed a reply to the report in the Library of the House. Four days later, on 11 November, the House debated the report.[46] Apart from five members of the sub-committee, and two front-bench speakers, only one other peer took part in the debate. That was the former European Community Commissioner, Lord Cockfield, whose main concern was to urge the sub-committee to enquire immediately into a new proposal from the Commission for an energy tax. In another debate a fortnight later, on a motion introduced by Lord Campbell of Croy concerned with pollution and energy, frequent further mention was made of this report.[47] The so-called 'carbon tax' was an issue to which the sub-committee did almost immediately turn its attention, producing a further report in March 1992.[48]

*Sub-Committee C: Social and Consumer Affairs* This sub-committee began the session by working on three draft directives concerned with part-time and temporary working. These arose from the Community Social Charter, which had become an area of considerable sensitivity following the refusal of the UK Government to accept the Charter in late 1989. Resistance to proposals flowing from it was to be expected. As regards these draft directives there seemed initially to be a sense of urgency because the Commission had requested the Council to reach decisions on one, and adopt its common position on the other two, by the end of 1990. The sub-committee's report was completed by December, but in the event at a Council meeting in November objections were raised to the Treaty base chosen by the Commission for one of the related directives, and this led to the postponement of decisions. This allowed the House the opportunity to hold a timely debate on the report.[49] The sub-committee had attempted

---

[46] HL Deb 11 November 1991 cc 409–436.

[47] HL Deb 27 November 1991 cc 1321–48.

[48] Eight Report from the Select Committee on the European Communities, 1991–92, *Carbon/Energy Tax*, HL 52, March 1992.

[49] HL Deb 26 February 1991 cc 908–935.

to show that government concern over the possible loss of jobs consequent on the adoption of directives giving more rights to temporary and part-time workers was misplaced. However, a fundamental conflict of view about this persisted and was still clearly evident when the House debated the report. Excluding three front-bench contributions, six of the seven speakers in that debate had been members of the sub-committee responsible for the report; one of these, the cross-bencher, Lord Northbourne, expressed quite sharply his disagreement with the report, while two other Conservative members of the sub-committee did not attend any of the evidence taking sessions. This illustrates how, even when a sub-committee has not formally voted, a report may mask sharply conflicting views. The report could be criticised as having been produced by a group of like-minded and virtually self-selected peers.

The sub-committee conducted a short enquiry into a draft directive on working time, recommending a number of modifications to the draft directive which accorded with the general approach being adopted by the UK government. The sub-committee then turned to make a lengthy enquiry directed at the needs of young people, occasioned by a Commission Communication, looking 'generally at Community activities devoted exclusively to young people'.[50] The fact that some 130 million of the Community's 340 million people were under the age of 25 gave the Committee plenty of scope for its enquiry! The report returned to the themes of several earlier reports, for example on language training. The sub-committee clearly experienced problems in focusing this enquiry, illustrating the difficulty involved in taking a discussion document as its starting point rather than a clear statement of policy or draft legislation.[51] The report read like a browse through a wide ranging and ill defined field; the sub-committee met to take evidence on nine separate occasions, and for this enquiry attendance by peers, including Conservative members, was high. Perhaps keeping together peers from every point across the political spectrum accounted for the remarkable blandness found in the report's recommendations, most of which drew attention to this or that. It seems unlikely that sub-committee members believed that a 48 page report

---

[50] Fourteenth Report from the Select Committee on the European Communities 1990–91, *Young People in the European Community*, HL 63, para 3.

[51] According to the chairman of the select committee (Baroness Serota) this report showed that 'it can be hard to structure an enquiry early in the Community consultative process'. See evidence to the Select Committee on the Committee Work of the House, HL 35–ii, 1991–92, February 1992, p 27, para 43.

costing £9-80 (or the version with evidence at £22-00) was really likely to popularise some causes otherwise passing unnoticed. The desirability of greater co-operation between government departments concerned with youth programmes was one of the more tangible recommendations. The sub-committee's principal finding was 'that many young people in the Community face multiple problems'; the report continued: 'The Committee concludes that there exists in many Member States a small but significant group of especially disadvantaged young people who form an isolated or 'marginalised' element of society living in very deprived conditions ...'[52] The sub-committee members presumably felt better for being able to deliver themselves of such weighty verdicts. As a document containing some interesting source material for social analysis the report may have had some value. When the report was debated attention focused chiefly on disadvantaged young people; half the speakers in the debate were committee members.[53] A week after the debate a parliamentary written question from Baroness Lockwood, the sub-committee chairman, suggested that she had not noticed the government's response to the report which had apparently been made early in the previous month.[54]

*Sub-Committee D: Agriculture and Food* For the first part of the session this sub-committee was chaired by Lord Middleton, a former president of the Country Landowners' Association, but he was replaced during the year by the Earl of Selborne, a Hampshire farmer who had been prominent in agricultural circles for many years. Its first enquiry occupied the committee from October to February and concerned non-food uses of agricultural products. This lengthy and diligent report probed the possible consequences of increased emphasis being given to the production of fuels and chemicals from plants.[55] Six months after the report was published the government placed its response in the Library of the House; in answer to a written question from Lord Middleton this was summarised by Baroness Trumpington: 'The Government supported the committee's

---

[52] Fourteenth Report from the Select Committee on the European Communities, 1990–91, HL 63, June 1991, para 110.

[53] HL Deb 11 November 1991 cc 436–472. See also reference to the Report in a debate on Youth Training initiated by Lord Beaumont of Whitley, HL Deb 27 November 1991 cc 1357–80.

[54] HL Deb 18 November 1991 cc 55–6w.

[55] Seventh Report from the Select Committee on the European Communities, 1990–91, *Non Food Uses of Agricultural Products*, HL 26, February 1991.

overall conclusion that non-food uses are not, at present, a large economic alternative to traditional outlets for agricultural products'.[56] The report appeared to do little more than string together a number of ideas.

However the sub-committee then turned to a subject of major significance, the reform of the Common Agricultural Policy. (See also Chapter 8.) Back in 1985 the Commission had published a green paper *Perspectives for the Common Agricultural Policy* which had placed the argument for reform beyond doubt. The ECC had reported on that document emphasising the necessity for reform.[57] But for six more years no such reform had taken place. By 1991 the GATT negotiations, upon which so many hopes of world economic recovery had been pinned, were stalled because of the failure of the EC to adopt an effective policy for the reduction of surplus food production. Then in February 1991 the MacSharry proposals were put forward. The sub-committee immediately launched into its enquiry, which was also able to take account of further proposals from Commissioner MacSharry in July, though the enquiry went much wider than these. The report was published in late August and debated in the House in October a few days before a crucial meeting of the European Council.[58]

For several reasons the MacSharry proposals were viewed with anxiety from both within the agricultural community in the UK as well as beyond that community. For a start they espoused the principle of 'modulation' under which aid was concentrated on smaller holdings. Furthermore cuts in quotas were to be concentrated on larger producers. Both these principles adversely affected UK farmers, because the average farm size in Britain was so much larger than the average in the Community (69 hectares as opposed to 16.5 hectares). MacSharry also adopted the principle of 'cross-compliance' stressing the need to support farmers as a means to improve environmental protection and conservation, rather than 'de-coupling' agricultural from environmental support, as had been the basis of British policy. A final cause of concern was that the MacSharry

---

[56] HL Deb 11 November 1991 c 22w. Earlier Baroness Trumpington had referred to the report in support of the decision not to allow 'set-aside' land to be used for non-food products; see HL Deb 11 July 1991 c 100w.

[57] Seventeenth Report from the Select Committee on the European Communities 1984–85, *Reform of the Common Agricultural Policy*, HL 23, July 1985.

[58] Sixteenth Report from the Select Committee on the European Communities 1990–91, *Development and Future of the Common Agricultural Policy*, HL 79, July 1991; HL Deb 17 October 1991 cc 1224–1290.

proposals envisaged increases rather than decreases in the costs of the Common Agricultural Policy, and appeared to be aimed not so much at phasing out financial support for farmers but accepting its indefinite continuation.

The sub-committee took evidence from all the 'good and the great' in the world of agriculture as well as prominent bodies concerned with environmental matters, though not the Commissioner himself: 'we were disappointed that Mr MacSharry was unable to meet us' said the sub-committee chairman when the report was debated in the House. The report was a very substantial and comprehensive document, which was indeed the committee's aim. It was also outspoken: 'We do not believe the proposals as they stand are an acceptable basis for reform ... We consider the Commission is altogether too conservative in its outlook'.[59] This report was published at a time when a vigorous debate was taking place and it was followed by a flurry of other documents. According to Lord Selborne the six months following its publication 'saw a growing acceptance of the ideas it contained', with several other bodies, including the Royal Agricultural Society, making use of the Lords' Committee report. Perhaps more significant was the reaction from farmers and the National Farmers' Union; by accepting the need for fundamental reform the committee, composed as it was by so many prominent agriculturalists, was sending a strong message to the farming community. To farmers this report, publicised in articles in the farming press (for example Anthony Rosen in *Farming News*), had a blunt unpalatable message; the effect of a House of Lords select committee saying these things was quite different from the Minister doing so. It helped to bring a new realism into the thinking of the NFU and other similarly placed bodies. This note of realism was evident too when 23 peers contributed to the five hour debate on the report.

*Sub-Committee E: Law and Institutions* As explained in Chapter 5 this sub-committee differs from the others in having quite specific terms of reference directing it to examine legal issues. This sub-committee has almost always had a law lord as chairman, Lord Oliver of Aylmerton in the 1990–91 session, and its membership was heavy with legal expertise. The four reports made in the 1990–91 session illustrate well the range of its work. The first concerned a draft directive on money laundering; the second dealt with a proposal for a directive coordinating rules on public

---

[59] Ibid, paras 138 and 143.

procurement in the utilities sector; the third focused on procedure for making agreements concerning commercial aviation relations between the member states of the Community and third countries; while the fourth dealt with an aspect of political union, namely law making powers and procedures within the Community. It can readily be seen that the sub-committee probes some highly difficult and complex questions. Sometimes these are, or at least appear, relatively arcane, such as the mechanisms which might be put in place to prevent the laundering of funds acquired by illicit means. But in tackling the law-making powers of the Community the sub-committee was walking into a mine-field of controversy at a time when the inter-governmental conferences on political union and monetary union leading up to the Maastricht Treaty were producing draft proposals.[60]

A high proportion of the letters sent to ministers on behalf of the ECC emanate from this sub-committee; a particular concern has been the treaty base which the Commission has used for particular directives. When Lord Oliver retired from the Committee at the end of the session he was replaced by Baroness Elles, a lawyer and a former MEP and vice-president of the European Parliament. She was in effect a stop gap before Lord Slynn of Hadley, formerly a UK appointed judge at the European Court of Justice, was ready to take over. Having a Lord of Appeal in Ordinary sign the letters sent to ministers, as well as having responsibility for the reports of this sub-committee, probably induces a degree of care on the part of ministers and civil servants in framing their responses.[61]

*Sub-Committee F: Environment* This sub-committee spent most of the session conducting an enquiry based on a directive dealing with sewage treatment. This was another sub-committee producing a very comprehensive report. Lord Nathan took the view that it was necessary to publish substantial quantities of evidence to show people that a sub-committee really had followed up all relevant aspects of a topic thoroughly, and to ensure that people who read the evidence could see why the committee had arrived at its view. When the report was debated

---

[60] See too the debate on this report HL Deb 21 October 1991 cc 1343–1396.

[61] Such was the view of a former Chairman of the European Communities Committee in interview. But note the impatience of the sub-committee chairman when on 16 July 1991 he asked the question ('When will the Government reply to the letter of the Lord Oliver of Aylmerton of 21 March 1991 ...'). A reply was apparently sent the day the question was published; see HL Deb 16 July 1991 c 10w.

Lord Nathan said: 'The report is a long and heavy one. The directive is extensive in its provisions and its implications; the costs in resources and money are enormous. It represents a major contribution to environmental protection'.[62] Lord Nugent of Guildford, an acknowledged authority on the subject of water, said the report was undoubtedly 'the best review of the problems of waste water disposal and the solutions to those problems that I have ever seen'.[63] But six months into the enquiry, and three months ahead of the report being made, the Council had adopted the directive. This understandably caused some annoyance among committee members, but in the debate on the report, over six months after the directive had been adopted, the Minister in response said: 'many points made by witnesses were of use to us in the negotiations in Brussels, and of course having agreed a text does not mean the job is finished. The directive leaves a number of issues to member states and here, in particular, the report will be helpful'.[64]

This illustrated both the extent to which the subject matter of sub-committee enquiries inevitably bring together what may be thought of as domestic politics and Community politics, and the relatively relaxed and flexible view taken by sub-committees about what is appropriate for their enquiries. The Select Committee and its sub-committees do not in practice feel themselves tied closely to directives. They explore surrounding issues, many of which are matters of domestic politics and national decision making.

*Conclusion* Most peers clearly think highly of the work of their select committee on the European Communities. In its defence it can certainly be argued that at little public expense the Committee has mobilised the peculiar membership of the House of Lords to do a useful job. Primarily this has involved probing policy proposals with a view to exposing weaknesses and seeking to exert influence. The Committee has not sought to provide comprehensive scrutiny of all directives; rather it has been unashamedly selective. Nor has it confined itself to specific examination of formal proposals being made to the Council for decision. Rather it has felt free to examine the broad context within which such proposals are made. Sometimes this has taken it upstream of draft directives to look at

---

[62] HL Deb 22 October 1991 c 1427.

[63] Ibid, c 1428.

[64] Ibid, c 1445.

issues which are just beginning to appear on policy agendas. Sometimes the Committee has clearly sought itself to be pro-active rather than simply reactive. Its occasional ad hoc sub-committees perhaps provide the best example of this. It clearly attempts to exert influence, upon Parliament and Government and upon other institutions throughout the European Community. How well does it succeed?

Beyond the House of Lords itself the most obvious target for reports is the government. At ministerial level it is probably fair to say there is generally little more than an awareness of the existence of the ECC and its work. A junior minister in the Commons whose departmental work overwhelmingly consisted of Community business claimed in interview that he had never read a single one of the Committee's reports. However, a sub-committee chairman in the Lords said that he regularly talked to the senior minister in that same department about the work of the sub-committee. But his conversations were directed more at ascertaining what the minister concerned thought and what he perceived to be the most pressing problems rather than at seeking to influence him. Nor did this sub-committee chairman feel that the cabinet minister concerned was trying to steer the sub-committee in relation to the subjects it chose to investigate.

If it is true that ministers frequently read the papers relevant to a Council meeting only on the plane as they travel,[65] then it is not surprising that they do not spend time reading select committee reports. But the more relevant question concerns their civil servants. A sub-committee chairman emphasised in interview the importance of this point. Within a department reports must be digested by civil servants if only to ensure that they are aware of matters about which their minister may need to be warned. And the preparation of a reply to a report must be undertaken by civil servants. But once having prepared a reply civil servants may quickly forget about a report. When a Lords' Minister answered a starred question about money laundering in July 1991 it was not surprising that he was asked about a select committee report which had dealt with this very topic two years earlier. But he was quite unable to respond to a supplementary question about the report because his briefing contained no reference to it, suggesting that the civil servants responsible for his briefing had also forgotten about the report's existence.[66]

---

[65] See for example remarks made by Lord Bruce of Donington, HL Deb 9 July 1992, cc 1278–9.

[66] See HL Deb 8 July 1991, c 1204.

Committee reports, like House of Lords debates, receive very little public attention domestically, even in the 'quality' press. But some are mentioned. For example, the report on *Municipal Waste Water Treatment* published in May 1991 drew media attention for its suggestion that water bills would have to rise by 25 per cent in real terms over the next few years in order to pay for the higher standards demanded by the draft directive under consideration.[67] The report on *Young People in the European Community* received publicity particularly for its call for a government minister for youth to be appointed.[68] The report on *Energy and the Environment* was written up prominently in the *Observer* which described its conclusions as 'stinging' and spoke of it as having condemned the government for relying on the market to protect the environment. The same report featured in a report in a specialist magazine *Building Design*, which took up the recommendations about insulation.[69] The report on *Compliance with Public Procurement Rules in the Utilities Sector* was the subject of a lengthy report in the *Electrical Review*, clearly aimed at informing its readers about the changing legal situation in this area, doubtless of potential importance to many of them.[70] Such magazines probably find the summary and elucidation of evidence typically contained in a select committee report a convenient source upon which to build articles. In alerting a specialised readership they may be contributing to an influence significantly greater than that available through a much more widely read newspaper. This creates a potential for influence upon ministers, officials and MPs by those alerted to the possible impact of Community proposals, a potential arising from the work of the select committee. Reports from Lords' select committees are certainly used by some MPs, and some—for example the above mentioned report entitled *Fraud Against the Community*—are the subject of a good many references in Commons debates. House of Commons library staff in preparing research papers for MPs make frequent use of reports from the ECC, and this provides another indirect means by which the influence of the Committee's reports can be spread.

Further targets for reports are found within the institutions of the Community. Indeed in many cases such bodies may be the most important

---

[67] See *Financial Times* 'Water Bills may rise 25 per cent' and *Guardian* 'Water bills rise fear' both 25 May 1991.

[68] See *Independent* 14 August 1991 and *Times Educational Supplement* 23 August 1991.

[69] See *Observer* 8 September 1991; *Building Design* 2 August 1991.

[70] *Electrical Review* 2 May 1991.

targets. As the ECC recently expressed itself: 'Unlike other Select Committees which act in dialogue with the Government, we have one voice in a much wider debate at Community level'.[71] Copies of reports are always sent to the relevant section of the European Commission, as well as to the Council Secretariat, the current Presidency, the European Parliament, and to all the scrutiny committees of parliaments of member states.[72] One insider spoke of the frequency with which he found House of Lords reports in the hands of desk officers in the Commission; one reason for this lay in the fact that reports typically included such useful and comprehensive collections of relevant evidence.[73]

Reports also go to selected members of the European Parliament and to the clerk to the counterpart European Parliament Committee where, according to Sir Christopher Prout, then Chairman of the European Democratic Group, they have earned a high reputation. In evidence to the Select Committee on the Committee Work of the House he spoke of his own experience as rapporteur to a European Parliament committee and the help which a report from the House of Lords' Select Committee had given him. In that particular case he doubted if the Lords sub-committee report had any direct influence on the Commission, but it certainly had influenced the relevant Committee of the European Parliament, and 'the legislation which finally emerged from the European Council was almost a carbon copy of what the European Parliament, influenced by you, recommended'. A former European Commissioner observed to the same committee that 'the House of Lords reports do better in Europe than they do in their own country'.[74]

When the Select Committee on the Committee Work of the House examined the role of the ECC during 1991, it was ready to pay tribute to the Committee. But a careful reading of the evidence given to the committee enquiring into committee work indicated areas of concern. When Baroness Serota appeared as chairman of the ECC she was in effect asked to justify the commitment the House made to the ECC in terms of its impact on Government decision-making. A question from Lord Bancroft, the former head of the home civil service, is worth quoting:

---

[71] See evidence to the Select Committee on the Committee Work of the House, 1991–92, HL 35-ii, p 30 para 61.
[72] See evidence to the Select Committee on the Committee Work of the House, 1991–92, HL 35-ii, p 23 para 13.
[73] Ibid, Q 475.
[74] Ibid, Qs 502–506.

We know of the extremely high reputation of the work of the Committee and its powerful influence on Brussels. We know that in terms of other European countries that are members of the Community the work of the Committee is outstanding. Equally, we devote to the Committee a very large proportion of Lords' time and over one quarter of the clerk power of the House ... The paradox I find very baffling is that on the one hand we have the way in which the Committee by its own efficiency has levered itself into a position of very great influence and repute and yet on the other hand the amount of time devoted to debating its labours on the floor of the House and the effect it has on our own Ministers and Government seems much smaller than would correspond to the amount of resources devoted to it and the influence which it has outside this country.

Baroness Serota took Lord Bancroft's point. It was ultimately a matter for the House to decide, and questions about the lack of impact upon government should, she suggested, be put to ministers. Influence elsewhere in Europe was hard to assess, but she did produce as a supplement to her evidence a paper giving a range of examples of where the Committee had perhaps had some influence on government.[75]

But is some sort of cost-benefit analysis the right way to justify the activities of select committees? Or should they be seen as an intrinsic part of parliament's scrutiny role, and justified in such terms? The work of the ECC has certainly contributed to that role. What has caused questions to be raised about the scale of its work has not been doubt about its value, but a growing awareness of its opportunity cost in an increasingly hard pressed House. It is not surprising that some peers have felt that directing the resources of the House into select committees examining quite different subjects might show a better return, at least in terms of tangible impact on the British Government and changes in public policy.

## Conclusion

It is clear that the House of Lords has given considerable attention to European Community concerns, especially through its Select Committee on the European Communities. To some degree the House has probably

---

[75] See evidence to the Select Committee on the Committee Work of the House 1991–92, HL 35–ii, Q 55; Supplementary Memorandum pp 48–58.

felt this whole area has deserved priority consideration from the second chamber, precisely because for so much of the time since British accession to the European Community the House of Commons has approached the work of scrutiny in an inhibited manner. But who listens to the House of Lords? Certainly the media give very little on-going attention to what the upper House is doing. For example, the debate and vote in the Lords on 18 December 1991 on the outcome of the Maastricht summit received virtually no mention even in the serious press; all eyes were turned on the debate going on the same day in the Commons. The earlier debate on 25 November, in advance of the European Council meeting, did not coincide with the Commons debate on the same subject, which had been held the previous week and had to some extent alerted public interest. Against that background the Lords' debate did attract a good deal more publicity. The debate a year earlier on the ECC report on Economic and Monetary Union and Political Union passed virtually unnoticed amidst the excitement of Thatcher's departure, but the report on which it was based did receive some explicit press attention. Perhaps indirectly its influence was greater. Those in the media or elsewhere, for example in academic institutions, who had to elucidate what was going on, found in that report a ready and helpful range of material.

Government cannot entirely ignore the House of Lords, if only because ministers must reply to debates there. But how much attention is given to the upper House is problematic. Replying to the debate on 25 November 1991 the Earl of Caithness, Minister of State at the Foreign Office, assured peers that the Prime Minister, the Foreign Secretary and the Chancellor of the Exchequer would read the debate with great interest.[76] During the November 1990 debate several peers expressed the hope that the new Prime Minister and his colleagues, whoever they might be, would study the Lords debate and its select committee report with care prior to the imminent Rome summit. Maybe.

These debates in the Lords are probably best thought of as providing a bit of ballast to the on-going national debate. The wider debate developed very strident tones. The Commons with its addiction to competitive political advocacy is ill-equipped to curb the shrillness and the distortions characteristic of the media. The Lords can act as a steadying and calming influence. In the run up to the Maastricht Treaty, and before the arrival of the new crop of post-1992 election peers, this is probably

---

[76] HL Deb 25 November 1991 c 1258.

what the House contributed to public debate. Attention naturally focuses on the front of stage battle as it is played out in the Commons; but down the corridor, in 'another place', not quite backstage but certainly in the shadows well away from the footlights, contest is also joined. Occasionally something happens there that momentarily attracts public attention. But essentially it is a supportive role. Ideas and arguments developed there may be picked up elsewhere. Fatherly advice from the elderly who have more or less retired from active play in the Westminster theatre may be considered worth listening to. Those whose experience and public recognition derives from some other theatre altogether may prove useful sources of informed views.

In short the progress of ideas and the development of opinion in a complex modern society is difficult to chart precisely. But the different style and the different perspective brought to bear by the second chamber is certainly not without its influence. And those who argue the contribution made by that House should be more widely acknowledged may be surprised to find in how many different ways that contribution has percolated through to public opinion.

# Appendix

## Table 7A.1
## Report from the European Communities Committee 1990–91

**Sub-Committee A Finance, Trade and Industry, External Relations**

8th Report (HL 35) *European Agreements with Poland, Hungary and the Czech and Slovak Federal Republic.* 13 March 1991; debated 3 June 1991.
12th Report (HL 59) *Single Insurance Market*, 25 June 1991; for information only

**Sub-Committee B Energy, Transport and Technology**

3rd Report (HL 11) *A New Structure for Community Railways*,
18 December 1990; debated 4 March 1991
13th Report (HL 62) *Energy and the Environment*, 25 June 1991; debated
11 November 1991

**Sub-Committee C Social and Consumer Affairs**

2nd Report (HL 7) *Part Time and Temporary Employment*, 4 December
1990; debated 26 February 1991
4th Report (HL 12) *Working Time* 18 December 1990; for information
only
14th Report (HL 63) *Young People in the European Community*, 25 June
1991; debated 11 November 1991

**Sub-Committee D Agriculture and Food**

7th Report (HL 26) *Non-Food Uses of Agricultural Products,* 9 February
1991; for information only
16th Report (HL 79) *Development and Future of the Common Agricultural
Policy* 23 July 1991; debated 17 October 1991

**Sub-Committee E Law and Institutions**

1st Report (HL 6) *Money Laundering* 4 December 1990; for information
only
9th Report (HL 39) *Conduct of the Community's External Aviation
Relations*, 23 April 1991; for information only
11th Report (HL 51) *Compliance with Public Procurement Rules in the
Utilities Sector*; for information only
17th Report (HL 80) *Political Union: Law-Making Powers and Procedures*
23 July 1991; debated 21 October 1991

**Sub-Committee F Environment**

10th Report (HL 50) *Municipal Waste Water Treatment*, 14 May 1991; debated 22 October 1991

**Reports made by the Main Committee**

5th Report (HL 20) *Conference of Parliaments of the European Community*
6th Report (HL 21) *Correspondence with Ministers*
15th Report (HL 66) *Correspondence with Ministers*

# 8

# Parliament and the Common Agricultural Policy, 1990–92

*Priscilla Baines*[1]

## Introduction

Britain's accession to the European Economic Community in 1973 brought not only a virtually fully-fledged common agricultural policy (CAP) but also fundamental changes in the system of agricultural support and the institutional agricultural policy-making framework. Although the transitional arrangements in the Treaty of Accession allowed five years for the CAP to be applied in full within the United Kingdom, the focus of agricultural policy-making moved immediately from Whitehall and Westminster to Brussels and the Community's decision-making and legislative machinery. That was not a complete novelty: during the negotiation of Britain's entry to the Community, many of those involved, including ministers, officials and pressure groups, had become familiar with Community procedures and working methods, while some aspects of agricultural support systems had already been amended in anticipation of EC membership. Nevertheless, entry meant that many long-established national procedures, most notably the annual price review, either disappeared or were conducted in a completely different context. For parliament, it meant the virtual disappearance of new primary legislation and its replacement by Community measures although some secondary legislation was still required to implement directives.

From the Community's inception, a common agricultural policy was seen as essential to its existence. Throughout the 1970s the CAP was the cornerstone of Community activity and, more importantly, by far the biggest element of Community expenditure. As in other member states, it was (and remains) the sector of the British economy where the

---

[1] I am grateful to Philip Giddings for his substantial contribution to the work which forms the basis of this chapter, including parts of the introduction and conclusion and the detailed analysis of debates on the floor of the House.

consequences of EC membership have been most pervasive. By the 1990s there was a growing emphasis on other areas of activity but only a relatively limited decline in expenditure on the CAP as a proportion of total Community expenditure.

For parliament, which had been had been largely by-passed in British pre-EC agricultural policy-making, the introduction of the CAP represented both an opportunity and a challenge. The application of the Community's legislative procedures for the first time allowed parliamentary involvement in agricultural policy-making at a formative stage. Throughout United Kingdom membership of the EC, the CAP has been sufficiently important to provide a litmus test of the effectiveness of parliament's procedures for scrutinising EC legislative and other proposals. This applies *a fortiori* to the negotiations about reforming the CAP which dominated the 1990–91 and 1991–92 sessions.

## Agricultural policy-making in Britain and the effects of the EC

Agricultural policy-making in Britain has traditionally had its peculiarities and has often been seen as a largely self-contained area which could be left to the specialists. It has also been characterised for much of the period since the second world war by a relatively unusual degree of bi-partisanship, probably encouraged by the dwindling significance of the agricultural vote—a noticeable difference from the position in some other member states. One commentator has described the British pre-EC agricultural policy community as unusually tightly closed, a state of affairs which the participants had gone to considerable lengths to preserve[2] and which may be partly attributable to the lack of major differences between the parties. Smith also claimed that despite, or possibly even because of, EC membership, by the end of the 1980s the British agricultural policy community had managed largely to preserve its exclusive nature, although there had been some radical changes compared with the early years of British EC membership. The consensual, mainly producer-dominated policy community which had almost exclusively determined agricultural policy since the early 1950s had not disappeared, but new elements had

---

[2] Martin J Smith 'The Agricultural Policy Community-Maintaining a Closed Relationship' in David Marsh and R A W Rhodes (eds) *Policy Networks in British Government* Oxford: Clarendon Press, 1992 p 34.

entered the debate and assumed steadily increasing significance within both Britain and the EC.

The CAP had always had its British (and other) critics but during the early years of Community membership it was mostly perceived, at least by those outside farming, as the price which the United Kingdom would have to pay for the other advantages to be gained from Community membership. Farming interests were initially more ambivalent but steadily rising incomes in almost all sectors of the industry throughout the 1970s led most of those interests to become for a time enthusiastic advocates for the CAP. By the mid-1980s, however, not only had the general public's perceptions of farming become distinctly hostile, particularly towards the environmental and food safety consequences of intensive husbandry practices, but the CAP itself, its high cost and seemingly unavoidable surpluses had attracted a host of increasingly vociferous critics. Those critics included consumer groups and environmentalists as well as farmers themselves and, most notably, the British government which throughout the 1980s was in the forefront of efforts to persuade the Community of the need for CAP reform.

The Conservative Party has traditionally been seen as pro-farmer but the seemingly unstoppable rise in the cost of the CAP and its impact on the Community budget led Mrs Thatcher's government to campaign initially for a ceiling on CAP expenditure, then for more radical reform of the CAP as a whole. In 1988, agreement was reached on budgetary limits on CAP expenditure but that was seen, particularly by Britain, as at best an interim measure pending more fundamental reforms. By the end of the 1980s, even the CAP's foremost advocates in the Community, who had previously hardly questioned its merits, had begun to accept the need for reform. In Britain, and elsewhere, the case for reform began to be actively encouraged by a somewhat disparate range of interests, many from outside the traditional policy-making consensus, and including environmentalists and consumers as well as the governments of some other member states.

The case for CAP reform was given considerable impetus by the Community's involvement in the Uruguay Round of negotiations under the General Agreement on Tariffs and Trade (GATT) which had started in 1986. From an early stage in the negotiations, there was widespread agreement, particularly among some agricultural exporting countries such as Australia which formed the so-called Cairns Group, that the level of agricultural support in countries such as the United States, the EC and Japan needed to be substantially reduced because of its distorting effects on world trade and markets in agricultural products. They argued that the EC would have to reduce its support levels if agreement were to be reached with the United States, on the one hand, and the Cairns Group on the other. The Community initially insisted that there was no direct linkage between the GATT negotiations and the internal discussions on CAP reform and delayed making its initial offer in the negotiations, which included reducing agricultural support by 30 per cent from a 1986 base, until November 1990, by which time proposals for CAP reform were already under active internal discussion.

The offer raised considerable alarm within the Community, although it was well below the 75 per cent cut in overall support levels and 90 per cent reduction in export subsidies sought by the United States and the Cairns Group. It was immediately rejected by the other major parties involved. The ensuing deadlock was only partially resolved by the Blair House agreement between the EC and the United States, reached in autumn 1992 after the Community had concluded its discussions on CAP reform in May 1992 (the GATT negotiations were finally concluded only in December 1993). The importance of achieving a satisfactory outcome to the protracted GATT negotiations undoubtedly introduced an additional element of urgency into some of the discussions on CAP reform, particularly as it was understood (although sometimes denied) that the results of the two sets of discussions would ultimately have to be reconciled with each other.

## Parliament and the CAP: the 1990–92 sessions

As far as parliamentary consideration of the CAP was concerned, both the 1990–91 and the short 1991–92 sessions were unusual. They were dominated initially by the GATT negotiations and then by the proposals for CAP reform published in February 1991 by the Irish Agriculture Commissioner, Ray MacSharry, and known as the MacSharry plan. A further set of MacSharry proposals was published in July 1991. After the deadlock in the GATT negotiations in December 1990, the talks were reactivated at official level in March 1991 and the two sets of negotiations continued in parallel. Agricultural topics therefore had a higher profile than usual and there were more full-scale debates on the floor of the House of Commons. This did not mean, however, that more routine CAP matters were ignored. In the course of any normal session, the volume of legislation involved means that a variable but substantial share of the time devoted to EC matters is spent on the CAP, although this share has gradually diminished (and is continuing to diminish) with the growth in Community activity in other areas. Inevitably, a substantial share of the time devoted to agricultural business is concerned with the CAP. The 1990–91 and 1991–92 sessions were generally typical in this respect.

The Minister of Agriculture normally answers oral questions for 45 minutes every four sitting weeks, when the usual practice is for 10 to 15 of the questions tabled to be answered. The three territorial Secretaries of State (for Scotland, Wales and Northern Ireland) also answer questions on agricultural topics within their own areas. Agriculture is not a department which attracts very large numbers of written questions, but during both sessions there was a steady flow of between six and 12 written questions, or sometimes groups of questions on a related topic, answered each sitting day, with rather larger numbers (often as many as 20) answered on the days when oral questions were taken. Throughout both sessions there were frequent references by both backbenchers and frontbenchers to various aspects of the CAP, including the problems faced by particular sectors of the industry, although not to the exclusion of other issues of purely national concern. The need for CAP reform was raised very regularly by Members from both sides and on several occasions dominated question time.[3] Ministers often used replies to oral questions to state or re-state the government's approach to the negotiations both in the GATT round and in the EC Council. The CAP figured much less in written questions, which tend to be more concerned with eliciting factual information. Between 10 and 20 per cent usually had some CAP content, and it was (and remains) normal practice for the outcome of all but the most important Agriculture Council meetings to be reported to the House in the form of a written answer.

As described in Chapter 6, there are several occasions throughout the parliamentary year when EC business is regularly debated on the floor of the House. A few committed EC opponents such as Teddy Taylor, Ian Paisley (also an MEP), Christopher Gill, and William Cash lost few such opportunities to voice their dislike of the Community in general and of the CAP in particular, as exemplifying the Community's worst features. In 1990–91 and 1991–92, these occasions included the annual three-hour debates on the floor of the House on the Community budget proposals. The CAP achieved some prominence in the budget debate on 4 December

---

[3] See, for example, oral questions on 24 January 1991—HC Deb c 439 et seq.

1990 when its relationship with the GATT round was referred to in the opening speech by the Treasury Minister, Francis Maude. The CAP was subsequently strongly criticised by Teddy Taylor and Ian Paisley, among others, while Jonathan Aitken, another Conservative Euro-sceptic, tabled an amendment to the government's motion expressing his 'deep concern at the agricultural spending element in the European Community budget'. Winding up the debate, Francis Maude remarked that 'the common agricultural policy has not found many friends in the House today.'[4] The corresponding debate the following year (on 27 November 1991) similarly attracted criticism of the CAP from Teddy Taylor, as well as from the opposition front bench spokesman, Chris Smith.[5]

Dr Paisley also used a debate on 11 March 1991 on the Northern Ireland Appropriation Order to attack the CAP and how in his view politics was being played with agriculture in Europe.[6] With others, including Jonathan Aitken, William Cash and Christopher Gill, he returned to the attack only two days later, on 13 March 1991, in a debate on a Court of Auditors report which had dealt specifically with fraud in connection with the CAP. Dr Paisley reminded the House that the Council was to blame for the problems, not the Commission, while Jonathan Aitken described the Commission's financial accounting methods for agriculture as being 'roughly those of Polly Peck or Bernie Cornfeld's Investors Overseas Services.'[7]

It is noticeable that almost the only backbenchers to exploit such occasions were committed EC opponents. By contrast, there were no more than passing references (almost invariably unfavourable ones) to the CAP in the debates on the six-monthly White Papers on *Developments in the European Community*. The CAP also scarcely figured, and then only to be pilloried, in the more general debates on the EC such as a debate on economic and monetary union on 24 January 1991 and the two-day debate on the inter-governmental conferences on 20 and 21 November 1991.[8] Conversely, the wider issues about the future of the Community which

---

[4] HC Deb 4 December 1990 cc 202–224.

[5] HC Deb 27 November 1991 cc 1026–1034.

[6] HC Deb 11 March 1991 c 735.

[7] HC Deb 13 March 1991 cc 1045–1064.

[8] See, for example, the speeches on 24 January 1991 by Christopher Gill and Sir Peter Hordern—HC Deb c 497 and 519 respectively; and on 20 and 21 November 1991 by Cranley Onslow and (again) Christopher Gill—c 323 and 366 respectively.

were being intensively debated throughout both sessions were almost totally ignored in the debates on the CAP.

Away from the floor of the House, a substantial proportion of the work of the Select Committee on European Legislation was spent considering policy documents and draft legislation on a very wide range of agricultural and related topics. About a quarter of the documents considered by the Committee were within the area of responsibility of the Ministry of Agriculture, although by no means all those were concerned with the CAP and they included documents on such diverse topics as fisheries, food composition, hygiene and labelling, and plant and animal health. As described later in this chapter, the Committee considered documents concerned with CAP reform in five of the 45 reports of the two sessions and with one exception they were all recommended for further consideration on the floor of the House rather than in European Standing Committee A. In 1990–91, six of the 17 sittings of European Standing Committee A were devoted to agricultural documents and two of the five sittings in 1991–92.

The Agriculture Committee also devoted a significant amount of effort to Community topics. One of its two reports in 1990–91—*Animals in Transit*[9]—was produced in direct response to draft Community legislation (see Chapter 9), while the first in 1991–92—*Commodity Markets in the 1990s—Cereals*[10]—dealt with one of the largest and most problematic sectors of the industry, and considered in detail the MacSharry proposals for that particular sector.

The annual agricultural price proposals are an integral part of the CAP and illustrate how both Houses have adapted their procedures to match the Community's timetable. The proposals are normally published in about January each year and should be agreed by the Council by the end of March, although that is rarely achieved. The timing of the Agriculture Council meetings at which the proposals are considered is known in advance but their outcome is often unpredictable and the negotiations can last until May or early June. The usual pattern for the Commons European Legislation Committee is to give preliminary consideration to the proposals soon after they are published and invite relevant interests to submit written evidence. The proposals are recommended for debate on the floor of the House and there is a session of oral evidence from the Minister of

---

[9] Third Report from the Agriculture Committee, 1990–91, HC 45.
[10] First Report from the Agriculture Committee, 1991–92, HC 98.

Agriculture timed for shortly before the debate is scheduled. The report and evidence are published before the debate. Specific aspects of the proposals are also sometimes recommended for debate in European Standing Committee A.

In 1990–91, consideration of the 1991–92 price proposals was largely subsumed by that of the MacSharry proposals. The Committee reported twice on the price proposals, the second time at some length with summaries of the written evidence received and the Minister's oral evidence[11] but the debate on 18 April 1991 was based on both the price proposals and the MacSharry plan. Much of it was concerned with CAP reform, with only a few references to the price proposals, which was to be expected as the price proposals were intended to take account of the general principles of the MacSharry plan. Consideration by the Committee of the 1992–93 proposals was prevented by the general election. The Agriculture Council's deliberations that year were also much delayed but they were debated, with the results of the second stage of negotiations on the detailed MacSharry proposals, on the floor of the House on 12 June 1992.

Until the late 1980s, the House of Lords European Communities Committee also took evidence and reported regularly on the price proposals. The reports were much longer than those of the Commons Committee and contained both oral and written evidence, usually in greater detail than that submitted to the Commons. The reports often severely criticised both the proposals themselves and what the Committee saw as the Commission's unwillingness to tackle the CAP's mounting problems. The reports were almost always debated. By the late 1980s, the price proposals were no longer being routinely considered as the Committee began to concentrate more on other areas of Community activity. As described in Chapter 7, in 1990–91, Sub-Committee D produced a magisterial report on the MacSharry plan, as well as a shorter one on non-food crops, but only the former was debated. The price proposals were not considered and there were no reports on any agricultural topic in the short 1991–92 session.

---

[11] Sixteenth Report from the Select Committee on European Legislation, 1990–91, HC 29–xvi.

## The GATT negotiations and CAP reform: consideration by the House of Commons

The beginning of the 1990–91 session coincided with a long-awaited announcement (in the form of a draft Council decision) of the Community's overall position in the GATT negotiations, including confirmation of earlier proposals for reducing agricultural support levels. This was announced to the House by the Minister of Agriculture in a short written answer on 8 November 1990.[12] In its first report of that session,[13] the Select Committee on European Legislation recommended further consideration of the draft on the floor of the House, rather than in European Standing Committee B, together with an earlier draft decision on agricultural issues.

The full day's debate which took place on 23 November 1990—a Friday —was technically on an adjournment motion, but was accepted by the European Legislation Committee as having fulfilled the recommendation for a debate.[14] Opening the debate, the Minister of Agriculture, John Gummer, remarked that the agricultural elements of the draft decision were 'burnt on my heart because we have sat longer and argued to a greater tedium on that than on almost any topic I can remember.'[15] He emphasised several aspects of the government's position which were to become recurring themes throughout the subsequent debates on CAP reform—the importance for the preservation of the countryside and of rural communities of a 'healthy agriculture', the need to reduce the level (and hence the cost) of agricultural support world-wide but progressively so that farmers could adjust to the change, and the need for agricultural support methods which would protect the environment. He also stated that neither Britain nor the Community could accept some of the more extreme proposals for subsidy reduction which other countries, especially the United States, had made and that he attached particular importance to the inclusion, at Britain's insistence, of the word 'non-discriminatory' in both the GATT negotiations and any measures introduced by the Community following the GATT round. He ended a long (46-minute) speech by

---

[12] HC Deb 8 November 1990 c 8w.

[13] Published on 14 November 1990—First Report from the Select Committee on European Legislation, 1990–91, HC 29-i.

[14] Ninth Report from the Select Committee on European Legislation, 1990–91, HC 29–ix.

[15] HC Deb 23 November 1990 c 531.

pledging that the Community, supported by the United Kingdom, would negotiate for a fair deal in the world for Community farmers, and the United Kingdom's 'utter determination' to ensure a fair deal within the Community for British farmers. That could be achieved only if changes in support systems and the CAP were made 'on the basis of equality and non-discrimination and aim at preserving competitive agriculture.'[16]

The speech by the official opposition spokesman, Dr David Clark, illustrated the tactical difficulties of an opposition which generally agreed with the government about the objectives of both the GATT round and CAP reform and understood the difficulties which British ministers faced in Community negotiations. Dr Clark supported the government (and the Community) in the GATT negotiations and acknowledged the importance of achieving a successful outcome of the Uruguay Round. However, he criticised the slow pace of CAP reform, the failure of the 1988 budgetary guidelines to control agricultural expenditure, the high cost of the CAP to consumers and the government's refusal to make alternative proposals for reform to those put forward by the Commission (an approach which was supported, both then and later, by others in his own party as well as the Liberal Democrats). He also criticised ministers for failing to grasp the significance of the linkage between the opportunity offered by the GATT round and the need for CAP reform. He advocated a switch by the Community to deficiency payments, but Mr Gummer intervened to point out that that was not acceptable to other EC member states.[17]

Dr Clark was followed by the Chairman of the Agriculture Committee, Jerry Wiggin, who argued that, given the chronic decline in agricultural profitability, support for the industry would have to continue. Others among the 13 backbench speakers referred frequently to the depressed state of farming incomes and farmers' anxieties about the prospect of cuts in support levels. They also insisted that British farmers should not be discriminated against in any reforms of the CAP. There was general recognition that it might be easy to criticise the CAP but much more difficult to suggest alternatives which would be acceptable to the rest of the Community. There was also universal agreement about the importance of achieving a GATT settlement in order to avoid a slide into protectionism and trade wars—a point strongly underlined by the Secretary

---

[16] Ibid, c 537.
[17] Ibid, c 542.

of State for Trade and Industry, Peter Lilley, when he wound up the debate.

Two weeks later, the GATT negotiations reached deadlock in Brussels and the talks were suspended. In a statement to the House on 10 December 1990, Mr Lilley said that the main reason for the deadlock was that 'serious negotiations on the crucial issue of agriculture' had started too late in the week to enable the process to be completed, although he emphasised that the blame could not be laid at the door of any one participant: 'All needed to move. They started too late, and moved too little.'[18] In subsequent questioning of Mr Lilley, the opposition spokeswoman, Joyce Quin, and more than half the 22 other questioners blamed the CAP for the breakdown in the talks and pressed the case for CAP reform if further progress were to be made. One questioner, Roger Knapman, expressed a widely held view that British taxpayers' money should not be used to shore up 'part-time peasant and inefficient farmers' in other countries.[19]

On 18 December 1990, the Prime Minister, John Major, made a statement following an EC Council meeting in Rome when he initially played down the significance of the CAP, saying that it was not directly related to the GATT discussions, although he later acknowledged that the successful conclusion of the GATT talks was the key to CAP reform.[20] That approach was later supported by Mr Gummer when he gave evidence to the Commons European Legislation Committee on 16 April 1991.[21]

Mr MacSharry's 'oral presentation' of his proposals for CAP reform at a Council meeting on 21 and 22 January 1991 caused Mr Gummer considerable concern, particularly over the probable cost of the proposals, but further consideration had had to be postponed, as was reported in a written answer on 23 January.[22] The 'MacSharry plan' was published on 1 February 1991 as a Commission Communication ('a reflections paper') on 'the development and future of the CAP'.[23] The proposals were considered very briefly by the Agriculture Council on 4 and 5 February.

---

[18] HC Deb 10 December 1990 c 667.
[19] Ibid, c 674.
[20] HC Deb 18 December 1990 cc 159–168.
[21] Sixteenth Report from the European Legislation Committee, 1990–91, HC 29–xvi Q 530.
[22] HC Deb 23 January 1991 c 247w.
[23] COM(91)100.

As they had already been widely leaked,[24] they contained few surprises and no firm proposals. For the British, their most controversial elements were the suggestion that support should be concentrated on smaller-scale producers and the initially substantially higher budgetary costs.

The Agriculture Council's initial response to the MacSharry proposals was reported to the House in a written answer on 6 February. Mr Gummer had 'welcomed the Commission's willingness to contemplate radical reform' of the CAP but had expressed considerable reservations about the likely cost, the way in which the proposals would probably place the more efficient and competitive Community producers at a disadvantage compared with their international competitors, and the unacceptable discrimination between member states—a veiled reference to the adverse effects on Britain with its larger than average farm size. Several other ministers had expressed 'similar hesitations' and it was not clear what the Commission would do next.[25]

The first opportunity for the MacSharry plan to be considered in detail in the Commons came on 14 February, when the Liberal Democrats used half an opposition day for a debate on agriculture during which CAP reform was the predominant topic. The debate was opened by the Liberal Democrats' spokesman, Geraint Howells (himself a farmer in Wales), who argued that, while the MacSharry plan undoubtedly discriminated against the United Kingdom with its relatively large farms, the CAP was not wholly to blame for farming's economic problems: the government was guilty of short-termism and the industry urgently needed a ten-year plan. 'The future of the European family farm should not be sacrificed in any attempt to bring the GATT negotiations to a conclusion' and the support system should be used both to sustain local farming communities and to encourage environmentally friendly farming.[26]

For the government, Mr Gummer reminded the House of the crucial importance of the CAP to the agricultural industry: more than 80 per cent of agricultural spending in Britain originated in Brussels. He recognised that he faced difficulties in the forthcoming negotiations but comprehensively denounced the MacSharry proposals: 'We hate them. We condemn them.'[27] The CAP had to be fundamentally reformed: farmers

---

[24] See Ministry of Agriculture evidence to the House of Lords European Communities Select Committee on 6 March 1991—1990–91, HL Paper 79–II, p 1.
[25] HC Deb 6 February 1991 cc 201–2w.
[26] HC Deb 14 February 1991 cc 1014–1019.
[27] Ibid, c 1021.

had to be brought closer to the market and helped to care for the countryside. He hoped that the Community would move in the right environmental directions, but the MacSharry proposals would not achieve that and would have to be got rid of. For Labour, Elliot Morley endorsed the urgency of CAP reform and a successful conclusion to the GATT round, but did not totally condemn the MacSharry proposals: in other member states, smaller farms had been more favourable for the environment because their production had been much less intensive than on Britain's larger farms. Small farms might not be economically efficient but the debate was also about keeping people on the land and helping rural communities.

Other speakers agreed that agriculture was in a serious crisis. Adequate income levels were essential if farmers were not to leave the land and to continue to care for the countryside. There were several references to the effects on farmers of uncertainty about the outcome of the CAP and GATT negotiations although a Conservative, Dame Elaine Kellett-Bowman, remarked that the MacSharry proposals might be disastrous for Britain, but at least other member states had finally supported the Conservatives' efforts to achieve CAP reform. Several Labour speakers condemned the MacSharry proposals but, like Dr Clark in the previous debate, criticised the government for failing to suggest alternatives, while Ian Paisley thought the CAP ought to be scrapped, more particularly as Community voting procedures did not allow the proposals to be defeated. Like Mr Gummer, Sir Russell Johnston, a Liberal Democrat and former MEP, reminded the House that the CAP had solved Europe's post-war problems of food shortages and that it was the Council, not the Commission, which should be blamed for the failure to deal with current surpluses.

Winding up for the government, the junior agriculture minister, David Curry, argued strongly that the CAP had to become more market-oriented. He responded robustly to the argument that the level of subsidies needed to be maintained because the level of farm incomes had fallen so dramatically: 'It is not the policy of this government or any hypothetical government to allow farmers to become the recipients of perennial social security payments merely because they are farmers.' The debate had been useful in strengthening the government's negotiating position in the Community: 'It helps us to know that the House is united in its opposition to the proposals. We need that influence and certainty in Brussels in arguing why we think that MacSharry's proposals are unfriendly to the United Kingdom.' He also described how the government had to:

work to find allies in the Council ... we realised from the start that coalition building is the name of the game ... (in the earlier stages) We were at the heart of the successful opposition to the MacSharry proposals because we managed to persuade others to come to our side.

Under pressure from both Labour and Liberal Democrat speakers for the government to state its own policies, he also summarised the government's strategy towards the CAP:

We think it important to operate closer to the market place. We see a role for specific aid for farmers—well tested and well costed—when there is a countryside function for them to perform. We see a role for certain restraints on output, which we may well find ourselves obliged to observe under the GATT. That is an important element for our farmers as well as all the others; the alternative is an horrendous trade war.

A few days later (on 19 February 1991), Mr Gummer gave a short session of oral evidence (there was no subsequent report) to the Commons Agriculture Committee on the government's views on the MacSharry plan. That occasion illustrated the effect on ministers of a less confrontational, environment with well-briefed members. Mr Gummer obviously welcomed the opportunity to state the government's position in detail and without the element of inter-party conflict of the previous week's debate. Always a fluent and voluble speaker, he was more measured than in the debate and in replying to the chairman's initial questions went out of his way to try to put the MacSharry proposals into a wider Community context, as well as to explain how they related to the GATT negotiations. He also emphasised that he saw the need for CAP reform in European terms and that the solutions must be acceptable to all the member states—including the removal from the MacSharry proposals of those parts which discriminated against the United Kingdom.[28]

On 27 February 1991, William Cash used a short debate on the partly EC-funded hill livestock compensatory allowances to attack the MacSharry plan's whole approach. The real problem was the significance of the agricultural vote in France, Germany and Italy. Until that was dealt with, the GATT negotiations could not be resolved, so the government had to

---

[28] Evidence printed as: 1990–91, HC 240.

appeal to its friends and colleagues in Europe in order to address the issue of helping British farmers:

> The problem will not be solved by reducing it to an argument about technicalities. It is a political problem and one that must be resolved by Community policies directed at the Community, not at the specific interests of individual countries. It will not be resolved until the Community and the Commission are prepared to grapple with the problem, and Mr MacSharry is prepared to consider the interests of the Community as a whole, not just his own Irish farmers.[29]

On the same day (27 February), the European Legislation Committee published the first of three reports in the 1990–91 session which included consideration of the MacSharry proposals.[30] The Committee at that stage recommended initial consideration by European Standing Committee A. However, in its Fifteenth Report, published on 20 March, it recommended (as usual) that the 1991–92 price proposals should be further considered on the floor of the House[31] and on 16 April, just before that debate took place, Mr Gummer made the Minister of Agriculture's annual appearance before the Committee to give evidence about both the CAP in general and the price fixing in particular. As when he appeared before the Agriculture Committee, he seemed to welcome another opportunity to expound the government's position in considerable detail to a well-briefed audience, and admitted as much towards the end of the meeting.[32]

Much of the questioning was concerned with details of the price proposals but in reply to a question by the chairman, Nigel Spearing, Mr Gummer agreed that at least the MacSharry proposals faced up to the serious effects of the CAP. Later, in response to questions from William Cash, Mr Gummer described at length both the government's views on how the CAP should be reformed and Britain's negotiating position as a member of the Community. He admitted that he saw the more likely outcome as further incremental changes rather than radical reform. In an exchange initiated by the chairman, who asked where else the government's approach to CAP reform had been set out as clearly as in

[29] HC Deb 27 February 1991 c 1079.

[30] Twelfth Report from the European Legislation Committee, 1990–91, HC 29–xii.

[31] Fifteenth Report from the European Legislation Committee, 1990–91, HC 29–xv, para 6.

[32] Evidence printed with the Committee's Sixteenth Report, 1990–91, HC 29–xvi Q 64.

the Minister's replies to the Committee, Mr Gummer said that he had made the government's position very clear in the Agriculture Council, as well as to his own party and in public speeches, including one to the National Farmers' Union, 'and of course we add flesh to it as the opportunities arise', as was then being done on the environmental elements which arose from the MacSharry proposals. He did not, however, mention his earlier appearance before the Agriculture Committee or the debate which had already taken place in the House.

The debate on 18 April was on a 'take note' motion which referred to a series of EC documents recommended for debate by the European Legislation Committee including the price proposals, the MacSharry proposals, and a Court of Auditors' Special Report on export refunds; other EC documents and the evidence to European Legislation Committee were also tagged. In another long speech (42 minutes), Mr Gummer covered very similar ground to that in the February debate and in his two sessions of evidence to select committees. He responded to pressure from the opposition to spell out the government's objectives for the CAP but again refused to suggest alternatives to the MacSharry proposals, arguing, as he had told the European Legislation Committee, that it was for the Commission to make proposals for legislation, not member states. Farm incomes were under pressure throughout the Community, even though CAP expenditure was likely to be about 30 per cent more in 1991 than in 1990. Community policies, including the price fixing, therefore had to be changed, and CAP reform could not be put off.

For the opposition, Dr Clark supported the ministerial line on the EC budget and the MacSharry proposals but criticised the government's tactics, including its neglect of the interests of consumers and environmentalists. He insisted that, notwithstanding the pressures to increase Community expenditure to meet the cost of German unification, the budgetary guidelines agreed in 1988 should not be breached. He assured the government that, in view of the 'truly alarming' growth in the cost of the CAP, the opposition would back the use of the veto in Brussels on that point. He again urged the government to table alternatives to the MacSharry proposals which would achieve a fundamental reform of the CAP. Geraint Howells, for the Liberal Democrats, argued that, rather than opposing MacSharry on every occasion, the government should work with him to get better proposals agreed.

The other speakers in the debate almost all agreed with the need for CAP reform and opposed the MacSharry proposals but there was much less consensus about how reform should be achieved. Few went as far as

Christopher Gill who saw the CAP as fundamentally flawed because conditions in Europe were so varied that it was impossible to achieve convergence, a view shared by Nigel Spearing who questioned whether the CAP's general objectives could ever be achieved. Mr Gill also referred to the report from the Court of Auditors which had been tagged for the debate—'a catalogue of management failures, fraud, deficiencies and uncontrolled expenditure'—to support his case for fundamental reform, preferably by 'repatriating' the CAP so that responsibility for agricultural policy reverted to member states, an approach which was supported by a few other speakers. Ian Paisley opposed the MacSharry proposals but argued that the minister could not be blamed for all the industry's problems as he had no real control:

> ... the House has ... learnt that its powers have been seriously eroded. It is not right to charge the Minister of Agriculture, Fisheries and Food with responsibility for all our ills. Let this House know it: his powers have been greatly reduced and are entirely different from those of previous Ministers. In the old days Agriculture Ministers had to persuade the Cabinet. Today, the Minister has to go and fight in Europe and, at the end of the day, he may be overruled.

Winding up for the opposition, Ron Davies followed a similar line to Dr Clark—the main difference between the two sides was over means rather than ends and over how orderly change in the CAP could be achieved. He too castigated the government for its poor record towards the industry but 'With one or two exceptions the House believes that the Minister is following the right course and we wish him well in defending those budgetary limits.' Mr Gummer firmly rejected any suggestion that repatriation of the CAP was politically feasible and ended by reminding the House that almost all the initiatives for CAP reform had been of British origin.

The outcome of the negotiations on the price proposals was reported to the House on 3 June 1991 when Mr Gummer, having announced what he considered a satisfactory conclusion to the negotiations, admitted in reply to a supplementary question that the future of agriculture 'depends centrally on the decisions that we shall make over the next six months' (on the MacSharry proposals) as well as on achieving agreement in the GATT negotiations.[33] The detailed measures to implement the MacSharry proposals were announced on 9 July 1991 and included Commission estimates of their financial effects.[34] The Commission had made some concessions to the criticisms of the earlier paper but had not totally abandoned the much-disliked concept of 'modulation', while the proposed measures covered only about 75 per cent of agricultural products.

The second MacSharry Communication was considered in detail by the European Legislation Committee in a report published on 23 July[35] and was recommended for debate on the floor of the House, after the Committee had reported further on the written evidence it was seeking from relevant interests. The report summarised the proposals and the government's initial response, including its very considerable reservations about the proposals. At oral questions in the House on 18 July 1991, Mr Gummer expressed his continuing fierce opposition to the proposals which were being used not to achieve reform but to put forward Mr MacSharry's personal views.[36]

Just before the summer recess, on 22 July, there was a short Consolidated Fund debate on the EC's agricultural policies in which William Hague, a Conservative, argued that the new proposals should be strongly opposed because they discriminated against large, efficient farms. He was supported by speakers from both sides of the House. The Parliamentary Secretary to the Ministry of Agriculture, David Maclean, agreed that the latest version of MacSharry would devastate the rural economy and also cost more. Sensible reform was needed, with progressive reductions in support at a pace which would enable efficient farmers to adjust, reforms which would bear equally on all producers and keep within the budgetary guidelines.[37]

The European Legislation Committee's third consideration in the 1990–91 session of the proposals for CAP reform was published in mid-October.[38] That report contained full summaries of the written evidence

---

[33] HC Deb 3 June 1991 c 30.

[34] *Commission Communication on the Development and Future of the Common Agricultural Policy* COM(91)258.

[35] Twenty-Ninth Report from the European Legislation Committee, 1990–91, HC 29–xxix.

[36] HC Deb 18 July 1991 c 484.

[37] HC Deb 22 July 1991 cc 994–1006.

[38] Thirtieth Report from the Select Committee on European Legislation, 1990–91, HC 29–xxx para 1.

which the Committee had received—from a total of fourteen organisations including the farmers' unions, food processors and distributors, environmentalists and consumer bodies—as well as a shorter commentary which summarised the main themes of the evidence. The Committee confirmed its earlier recommendation that the second stage of the MacSharry proposals should be debated on the floor of the House. In late November, the Agriculture Committee also published its report on *Commodity Markets in the 1990s—Cereals*[39] which examined the MacSharry proposals for the cereals sector and how they would affect British producers.

The full day's debate on 4 December 1991 was in government time, extended by an hour and a half, and even then with a ten-minute limit on speeches between 7.00 pm and 9.00 pm, a measure of the level of interest in the subject. It was on a motion to take note of a series of EC documents recommended for further consideration by the European Legislation Committee, including the July MacSharry proposals (the Agriculture Committee's very recent report was not tagged). There was a total of 21 speakers, plus Mr Gummer and Dr Clark, who opened, and Ron Davies and David Curry, who wound up.

As Christopher Gill remarked, the debate had a strong sense of 'déjà vu'. There were, however, some changes of emphasis since the April debate, especially among the front bench speakers. Mr Gummer opened with another long speech and claimed growing support for his approach to the MacSharry proposals from some other member states, particularly over the need to protect commercial farms as the key to a viable agricultural industry. He criticised the continuing efforts to persuade him to put forward his own proposals for CAP reform—'I am the only Minister negotiating on the basis that the Opposition are demanding constantly that I do something different'—but ended, somewhat unusually for him, by counselling caution about the possible outcome of the negotiations: they would take time to complete and the results would not necessarily be perfect for the United Kingdom.

Dr Clark argued that while the Labour Party disagreed with MacSharry it nevertheless thought that the proposals were likely to be accepted—a possible outcome which Mr Gummer had explicitly rejected. Dr Clark also argued that after thirteen years in office the government could not escape responsibility for the CAP's present problems. The opposition was

---

[39] First Report from the Agriculture Committee, 1991–92, HC 98.

sceptical about the government's negotiating position: its record gave cause for doubt about its ability to deliver—a charge described by Mr Gummer in an intervention as undermining the government's position. It would help if the opposition would support the government's arguments and they were the only opposition party in the Community not to do that. Dr Clark retorted that the MacSharry proposals were revision, not reform, and would be disastrous for the United Kingdom. Like other Labour speakers, he argued that the government should put forward its own alternative proposals as the French had recently done.

For the Liberal Democrats, Geraint Howells again emphasised the need to restore farmers' confidence about the future, a comment repeated by several other speakers. There was some support from all sides for the minister's general approach in the negotiations while several speakers referred to the need for British producers to gain a larger share of the United Kingdom market and reduce the trade deficit in food and drink—the subject-matter of the Agriculture Committee's current inquiry and a growing pre-occupation for the industry. Winding up for the opposition, Ron Davies underlined the numerous uncertainties facing the industry. The government had lost the confidence of farmers and had failed farming 'by any objective test' but he accepted that both ministers would negotiate to the best of their abilities in Brussels. For the government, David Curry ended by reminding the House that the debate was not about repatriating the CAP: if the United Kingdom wanted to be at the heart of the debate it must not espouse ideas which put it at the margins.

Subsequent detailed consideration of CAP reform by the House was curtailed by the 1992 general election. In the run-up to the election, Mr Gummer and his fellow Ministers continued at question time to argue the government's case over the MacSharry proposals while in a series of answers to written questions, Mr Gummer chronicled slow progress at successive Council meetings. On 13 December 1991, the Council was 'still some way from agreement' and several Ministers thought that final decisions could not be taken until the outcome of the GATT round was known.[40] The same point was made more strongly on 30 January when Mr Gummer also described the position he had taken over the most recent GATT Secretariat paper.[41] On 13 February, the Portuguese presidency

---

[40] HC Deb 13 December 1991 c 593w.
[41] HC Deb 30 January 1991 c 665w.

had 'presented a new compromise paper which may have moved matters forward by a small amount, but major divergences of view remain.' 'I maintained the United Kingdom position on the lines I have explained to the House on several occasions.'[42] In a statement on 4 March, the last before parliament was dissolved, 'The presidency presented a new compromise document which was, however, seriously questioned by most delegations, among them the United Kingdom. After the initial table round the President concluded that a satisfactory basis for continuing negotiations at this meeting did not exist.' There was, however, an informal joint meeting with trade ministers which considered draft schedules on agricultural support and protection, drawn up by the Commission for submission as a Community contribution to the GATT negotiations.[43]

Draft legal texts to implement the detailed MacSharry proposals were published by the Commission in the autumn of 1991, well ahead of agreement in principle being reached on the proposals as a whole. The European Legislation Committee considered the draft texts in four reports in the 1991–92 session, but its recommendations for further consideration were largely overtaken by the dissolution and general election. In the Committee's Second Report,[44] eight draft regulations on particular sectors and on proposals for set-aside were considered. The Report noted that the Committee had already reported twice on the second round of MacSharry proposals but the second report had not yet been considered by the House. As it was known that further draft legal texts were on the way, the Committee recommended that all the drafts should be considered together on the floor of the House.

The Committee's 3rd Report considered nine further draft regulations and repeated the recommendation that all the proposals should be further considered on the floor of the House, together with those already recommended for such consideration.[45] The Tenth Report considered a further draft regulation on compensatory aid for small producers and said that evidence would be sought about its effects on farmers and landowners, after which the Committee would look at it again.[46] In the Fourteenth

---

[42] HC Deb 13 February 1991 c 618w.

[43] HC Deb 4 March 1991 cc 187–188w.

[44] Second Report from the Select Committee on European Legislation, 1991–92, HC 24–ii para 5.

[45] Third Report from the Select Committee on European Legislation, 1991–92, HC 24–iii paras 6 and 7.

[46] Tenth Report from the Select Committee on European Legislation, 1991–92, HC–x.

Report, that evidence was summarised and reviewed. No further consideration was recommended.[47]

The final outcome of the Council's consideration of the MacSharry proposals was announced to the House by Mr Gummer (reappointed as agriculture minister) on 22 May 1992, very soon after the start of the new parliament. In a relatively short statement, he sounded a near-triumphal note about the government's achievements as he described the main features of the agreement reached the day before: a 30 per cent reduction in cereal prices (which would also help in the GATT negotiations); removal of the various provisions which would have discriminated against Britain; more support to be directed towards farmers in hill areas; environmental issues 'brought closer to the heart of the CAP'; and the costs of the reformed CAP to be met within the existing agricultural expenditure guideline. 'In all these areas, we have fundamentally altered the Commission's proposals and confounded those who said we should give in.'[48] Dr Clark, also reappointed as opposition spokesman, urged a full day's debate but attributed the minister's euphoria to lack of sleep: the deal was wanting and the reforms inadequate if they were to lead to progress in the GATT negotiations. They were the start rather than the end of a long path to reform. The CAP remained a nonsense and the reforms, like their predecessors, were unlikely to work. They should be the first step towards the abolition of the CAP. 15 other Members questioned the minister, with Conservatives uniting in congratulating him and several Members joining Dr Clark in seeking more details as well as pressing him on how far the reduction in prices would benefit consumers.

There was a full day's debate in government time on 12 June 1992—a Friday—on both the outcome of the negotiations on the MacSharry proposals and the 1992–93 price proposals. There were sufficient speakers for a ten-minute time limit on speeches for part of the time. As usual, Mr Gummer opened with a lengthy (55 much-interrupted minutes) exposition of the results of the negotiations in the Council. He emphasised his achievements and how much more difficult the process would have been had he followed the tactics advocated by the opposition and put forward his own alternative proposals. He listed the new provisions for the major sectors of the industry, and the resulting savings, particularly for consumers. There would be a shift from a system of support which had

---

[47] Fourteenth Report from the Select Committee on European Legislation, 1991–92, HC–xiv.

[48] HC Deb 22 May 1992 c 629.

led to surpluses to one which did not increase production and of which a larger share was borne by the taxpayer rather than the consumer. The radical nature of the changes and their impact on member states should not be underestimated and the agreement had fundamentally changed the nature of farm support. It had also met the government's main objectives and safeguarded the future of farming in both the United Kingdom and Europe as a whole.[49]

Not surprisingly, Dr Clark was considerably less enthusiastic about what had been achieved: the agreement and its reforms were not what the minister claimed and would not work. They would lead to higher consumer prices, no significant benefits for farming incomes and higher contributions from the taxpayer. He particularly criticised one of the cornerstones of the agreement, the dependence on set-aside (taking a proportion of arable land out of production) as a means of reducing cereal production, which would create a bureaucratic nightmare. Other speakers shared Dr Clark's doubts about set-aside, as well as about the minister's claims for the scale of the reforms. They also expressed anxieties about the effect of the agreement on their farming constituents and about whether it would meet the requirements of the GATT round. Winding up for the government, David Curry regretted the absence of information about the detailed regulations to implement the Council's decisions but pointed out that the move towards CAP reform, particularly the price cuts in the cereal sector, had brought the Community to a stage where it could 'meet the reasonable requirements and hopes of the United States in the volume of exports'. He ended by injecting a note of caution about the future: a good deal had been achieved, including a degree of much-sought stability, but there would have to be further reforms.


## CAP reform and the House of Lords

Early in the 1990–91 session (on 15 November 1990), the House of Lords debated two recent reports, one from the European Communities Committee in the previous session on *The Future of Rural Society*[50] and the other from the Church of England on *Faith in the Countryside*.[51] The

---

[49] HC Deb 12 June 1992 cc 554–568.

[50] 1989–90, HL Paper 80.

[51] Report of the Archbishops' Commission on Rural Areas, Churchman Publishing, Worthing, 1990.

timing of the debate and the subject of the two reports meant that the GATT negotiations and CAP reform were major topics of discussion. The Chairman of Sub-Committee D, Lord Middleton, opened the debate and reminded the House that Mr MacSharry had expressed his support for the proposals in the original Commission document on which the Sub-Committee had reported. He acknowledged the link between agriculture and rural society, particularly for some member states which saw the CAP primarily as an instrument of social policy, but thought that the Commission tended to over-emphasise the relative importance of agriculture in most rural communities. He emphasised the Sub-Committee's strong views on the importance of the CAP's market support mechanisms being neutral as between regions and farmers: his Sub-Committee thought that the issue of small farms and small farmers in Less Favoured Areas was primarily social and should not be distorted by being supported by the CAP.[52]

For the government, Baroness Blatch said it would be wrong to introduce into the CAP, in the name of rural development, measures which were primarily social in character but it was government policy to integrate environmental objectives into agricultural support measures. The government was in the forefront of attempts to shift the emphasis of the CAP towards improving the environment. Many of the other speakers in the debate were members of the Sub-Committee or had farming interests and several referred to the need for progress in the GATT negotiations and for CAP reform, as well as to the problems currently faced by farmers and the importance of agriculture for the prosperity of rural areas. Winding up for the government, the junior agriculture minister, Baroness Trumpington, said that farmers both produced food and looked after the countryside but had become too good at food production, hence their unpopularity, and a new balance had to be struck. The outcome of the GATT round was not clear but if the Community had not been able to agree a negotiating position on agriculture, the whole of the GATT would have been at risk. There was no question, as some speakers had suggested, of dismantling the CAP but the government would continue to press the environmental case.

On 6 February 1991, a short debate was initiated by a backbench peer and farmer, Lord Stanley of Alderley, on the over-production of farm commodities in which, predictably, there were many references to the

---

[52] HL Deb 15 November 1990 cc 452–460.

recently-published MacSharry proposals. Lord Stanley himself saw the proposals as damaging both to United Kingdom agriculture and to the prospects for the GATT round. Efficient United Kingdom agriculture should not, he said, be sacrificed on the altar of the EC's inefficient and high-cost peasant system.[53] Lord Middleton said that his Sub-Committee's conclusions about the CAP's deficiencies had been consistent: it opposed supply controls but recognised that for economic and social reasons agricultural support could not be abandoned. The EC's budgetary problems were, however, intractable and the GATT negotiations were bedevilled by the friction caused by agricultural subsidies. The MacSharry proposals had called for fundamental reform of the CAP and his Sub-Committee would look at them in detail. Other speakers recognised the need for CAP reform but expressed varying degrees of unease about the MacSharry proposals. For the opposition, Lord Carter said that both the MacSharry proposals and a free market would be disastrous for British agriculture but it was too soon to respond in detail to MacSharry. For the government, Baroness Trumpington argued that over-production was a Community problem which the Community had to solve. It was in the United Kingdom's to achieve a satisfactory solution to the GATT round but CAP reform was vital in its own right, although the MacSharry approach was fundamentally flawed.

As described in Chapter 7, the second inquiry in 1990–91 by Sub-Committee D of the Lords Select Committee on the European Communities was devoted specifically to CAP reform. For the Sub-Committee, that was not new ground since it had reported at length in 1985 on the previous EC Commission green paper, *Perspectives for the Common Agricultural Policy*[54] and had agreed then with the Commission about the urgent need for CAP reform. Subsequent reports by the Committee, particularly those on the annual price proposals, had also emphasised the CAP's underlying problems and the Committee had always been an outspoken critic of what it saw as the Commission's failures to address those problems sufficiently radically. The inquiry into the first stage of the MacSharry proposals (the 'Reflections' paper) started as soon as the proposals were published and was concluded late the following July. The second stage of the proposals was published just in time for the Sub-

---

[53] HL Deb 6 February 1991 c 1200.

[54] Seventeenth Report, 1984–85, HL Paper 237.

Committee to describe them in the report, but too late for them to be covered by any of the evidence.

The Sub-Committee took evidence from a wide range of interests and held seventeen sessions of oral evidence, beginning with one from Ministry of Agriculture officials and concluding with one from the minister, Mr Gummer. Other witnesses, nearly all of whom also submitted written evidence, included three academic agricultural economists, the farmers' unions, the Country Landowners' Association, representatives of the food processors and distributors, consumer groups, environmental groups, the Australian and New Zealand High Commissions and the American Embassy in London, and a member of the European Court of Auditors. Written evidence alone was received from forty-one further individuals and organisations. The Ministry of Agriculture's opening session of written and oral evidence on 6 March 1991 was essentially a scene-setting exercise and included the earliest detailed statement of the government's initial reactions to the MacSharry proposals and its general approach to CAP reform. The oral evidence described at length how far the negotiations on the MacSharry proposals had reached, as well as how they were affected by consideration of the price proposals and the recently reactivated GATT negotiations.

Other witnesses brought a wide variety of approaches and, predictably, some special pleading. There was almost universal acceptance of the need for reform but much scepticism about the MacSharry proposals. In the final session of oral evidence on 5 June 1991 (just after the conclusion of the price fixing), Mr Gummer urged caution about what might be achieved: 'we should not automatically make the assumption that we shall come up at the end of 6 or 9 months with the kind of overwhelming reform which we know to be necessary ... there is a very great deal between now and reform'.[55]

The Report was long (193 paragraphs plus 30 paragraphs of summary and conclusions), thorough and measured. It examined the CAP's socio-economic and environmental objectives and possible mechanisms of reform, including making some suggestions of its own, based mainly on those made by witnesses. The Committee's opinion (in the final chapter of the report) was robust and uncompromising. The Commission might at long last have accepted the need for reform but the proposals as they stood were not an acceptable basis for reform and the Commission was too

---

[55] Sixteenth Report from the European Communities Committee, 1990–91, HL Paper 791-II: *Development and Future of the Common Agricultural Policy*, vol II, Q 589.

conservative in its outlook.[56] The CAP in its present form was indefensible but the chief obstacle to reform was undoubtedly political:

> It has been the politicisation of agricultural policy in the Council of Ministers to accommodate vested interests in the Member States which has led to the creation of the economically perverse and socially regressive system now in place ... We were disappointed, but not surprised, to hear the Minister report that in his view his colleagues in the Agriculture Council were unlikely to contemplate the possibility of a fundamental reform. This implies that the system will remain largely unscathed, and that a series of *ad hoc* measures will be introduced in order to alleviate the pressure on the budget. We would deplore such an outcome. Governments in the Member States must recognise that perpetuation of protectionism in agriculture as practised under the CAP is neither in the interests of society as a whole nor of the taxpayers and consumers who fund the CAP ... It is now up to the Council to exhibit the political leadership so badly lacking in the past, and to grasp the nettle of reform.'[57]

The timing of the Report (shortly after publication of the second stage of the MacSharry proposals and before the Council started considering them in detail) and its uncompromising message from an essentially neutral but well-informed source meant that, as recorded in Chapter 7, it had some influence in the ensuing policy debate outside the House. The Report was also the subject of a full day's debate in the House on 17 October 1991, just before an important European Council meeting. It was opened by Lord Middleton and most of the other 21 backbench speakers were farmers, members of the Sub-Committee or both, many of whom drew heavily on the report. Lord Middleton underlined the Sub-Committee's insistence that CAP reform was essential and its concern that the MacSharry proposals would impede rather than encourage efficient production, as well as discriminating against the United Kingdom. Other speakers, like their Commons counterparts and including one of the opposition spokesmen, Lord Carter, urged the government to produce alternative proposals while several, particularly the farmers, acknowledged that, essential though it was, CAP reform was bound to hurt. Lord Carter,

---

[56] Ibid, paras 137–8 and 143.
[57] Ibid, paras 135 and 193.

winding up for the opposition, argued that agricultural policy should be repatriated and replaced by free trade in agricultural products within the Community. Baroness Trumpington, for the government, welcomed the Report's conclusions including the finding that the MacSharry proposals were an unsuitable basis for CAP reform. She also welcomed the clarity of the Sub-Committee's assessment of the Commission's proposals.

## Conclusions

Before trying to draw conclusions about the effectiveness (or otherwise) of parliament's procedures for scrutinising the CAP, it is worth speculating, if only briefly, on what parliament's position would be had agriculture remained a policy area where there was no EC involvement. This is not to argue the case for 'repatriating' the CAP or to guess what might have happened to British agricultural policy in the absence of the CAP, but simply to look at the direct impact on parliament of Community involvement in this particular policy area. The size of the agricultural sector and the extent of government intervention in post-war agricultural policy have meant that agriculture has always received a certain amount of parliamentary attention. There has also always been a good deal of agricultural legislation, both primary and secondary, and the existence of the CAP has to a large extent meant the replacement of national measures by Community ones, rather than legislation where there was none before. For parliament, the main effect of the existence of the CAP has therefore been to shift the business concerned with agricultural matters to the EC scrutiny machinery, although there is also a substantial amount of secondary legislation which is subject to the normal scrutiny procedures for that type of legislation.

The unusual amount of time devoted to agricultural matters in general and the CAP in particular in the two sessions examined in this chapter reflected the importance of the issues being addressed. The problems which the CAP had created for the Community, both internally and externally, were on such a scale and so far-reaching that it could justifiably be argued that both Houses would have been guilty of a significant dereliction of their duty had they not devoted substantial amounts of time to consideration of a topic of such major importance. As the earlier parts of this chapter show, the major issues connected with CAP reform were frequently and thoroughly aired in some depth and in a variety of fora in both Houses, from the non-judgmental and generally factual approach of the Commons European Legislation Committee, through the inquisitorial and analytical process of other select committees, most notably the Lords European Communities Committee, to the adversarial approach in questions and debates, especially in the Commons.

For any parliamentarian and, indeed, any member of the public with a serious interest in the subject, the proceedings in the two European select committees in particular provided a great deal of information, often very detailed, about the CAP and the proposals for its reform. The way in which both committees gathered and published the evidence which they received from a wide range of relevant interests also meant that they provided a useful platform for those interests to place their views on the public record. For the Minister of Agriculture, and sometimes for his officials, giving oral evidence to the committees provided opportunities for more balanced and extended dialogue than was possible either at question time or in debates in the Chamber of the Commons. With such a wide-ranging topic as CAP reform, there was inevitably a certain amount of duplication between the two committees and some of the evidence which they both received was fairly repetitive. Nevertheless, even for specialist students of the subject, the House of Lords Committee report stands out as a measured, thorough and detailed examination of a major policy issue and appears to have had significant influence as well as raising the quality of the debate outside parliament.

Where more routine agricultural business is concerned, the committees' methods of operation appear in practice to be complementary, especially since the Lords Committee has reduced the amount of time it spends on agricultural topics. Familiarity with the Community's ways of doing business has enabled the Commons Committee to handle the vagaries of the timetabling of Community legislation, particularly legislation which recurs regularly each year to a relatively predictable schedule such as the price proposals. The need to avoid overlaps with both the Lords and Commons European committees, as well as select committees' general reluctance to undertake routine monitoring, probably explain why the Commons Agriculture Committee has never examined the price proposals and has tended to concentrate on more specific topics. Two of that Committee's four reports in 1990–91 and 1991–92 were, however, specifically concerned with topics which were under active consideration within both the EC and Britain at the time. They were clearly intended to have some impact on the government's approach to the issues.

Proceedings on the floor of the Commons have a very different quality and tend to serve rather different purposes from those in select committees, with much more emphasis on an adversarial, partisan approach. As noted in the introduction to this chapter, agriculture is seen as an insider's subject and this is illustrated by the relatively limited number of speakers who dominated almost all the debates and agricultural question time. Given the limitations of the parliamentary timetable, it is a measure of the importance which the government attached to the GATT negotiations and CAP reform that so much government time, some of it admittedly on Fridays, was allowed for the topics to be debated on the floor of the House, quite apart from the occasions when opposition parties and backbenchers used their own time for debates on those topics. In a normal session, at least a half-day debate would anyway have been allocated to consideration of the price proposals, but the extra time provided allowed a very thorough airing of most of the issues, even if relatively few Members other than the regulars took part and the debates were often somewhat parochial. The domination of debates by the regulars probably meant, however, that some of the issues of wider public concern, particularly environmental ones, did not achieve as much prominence as they might have done.

Repetitive though they were, the debates served several interests. For the government, they showed a substantial measure of agreement between the parties and among backbenchers about the need for CAP reform, while the consistent and near-universal expressions of hostility to the MacSharry proposals strengthened the hands of ministers negotiating in the Community. For backbench Members, they provided opportunities to articulate the concerns being expressed particularly, but not only, in agricultural constituencies about the depressed condition of the industry and the potential effects of the MacSharry proposals on British farmers. For the Euro-sceptics, they provided opportunities to draw attention to the costs and anomalies of the CAP and to use it as an illustration of the damaging consequences of Community membership. For the opposition, the position was more ambiguous. They shared the government's views about the need for CAP reform and the unacceptability of the MacSharry proposals, and admitted as much, but differed about how reform should be achieved. They were left with little choice but to attack the government's negotiating tactics, in the knowledge that by doing so they risked undermining the government's negotiating position in the Community—as government ministers were not slow to point out.

It is not easy to assess how much, if anything, either the committees' scrutiny process or the numerous debates and questions on the floor of the House achieved, partly because it is impossible to know what other outcome there might have been to the negotiations. At a very negative level, the fact that the government largely achieved its major objectives in relation to the MacSharry proposals suggests that parliamentary scrutiny did no harm to the government's cause, and may well have done it some good by demonstrating the strength of feeling on the issues, particularly as there were no major differences between the parties. The scrutiny procedures of the committees of the two Houses also had their advantages. By contrast with other consultation processes which are almost invariably conducted in private (including those on agricultural policy-making in the years prior to EC membership), they gave outside interests opportunities to make a public input on the published record and allowed detailed parliamentary consideration while the proposals were still in draft form. That opportunity was of particular importance in relation to such major policy initiatives and provided at least some of the information necessary for more informed debate and understanding of the issues.

# 9

# The Welfare of Farm Animals

## *Priscilla Baines*

Animal welfare in its widest sense has always been a matter of major public concern in Britain and two particular aspects of the welfare of farm animals, the transport of live animals and intensive livestock husbandry methods, have for many years aroused strong feelings on the part of the public. This level of concern means that such issues have an unexpectedly high, but generally non-party, political and parliamentary profile. It is well known that few topics figure more regularly in MPs' postbags (and agriculture ministers' correspondence) and the animal welfare lobby is both active and well-organised. There is also a widespread and often explicit assumption in Britain that cruelty to animals begins (or ends) at Calais and a concomitant view that British standards of animal welfare are higher and more rigorously enforced than those in other member states. As the government itself has had to acknowledge,[1] increasing Community involvement in this area, especially in the context of the Single Market initiative, has created particular difficulties, especially as other member states mostly do not share the British preoccupation with animal welfare. As one Member (Edwina Currie) has described one particularly prominent manifestation of this preoccupation, 'Britain regards horses as honorary human beings, whereas the rest of Europe regards them as dinner.'[2]

Much of the rest of Europe is genuinely puzzled by British attitudes to animal welfare and therefore tends to be unsympathetic towards what are often perceived as British efforts to impose unwanted higher standards on the rest of the Community. These difficulties are not unique to this particular issue: they illustrate a common problem for member states where they are in a minority and where national powers of initiative are inhibited by the existence of Community legislation or by the Treaties

---

[1] See, for example, a letter of 10 April 1991 from the Parliamentary Secretary to the Ministry of Agriculture to the Parliamentary Liaison Officer of the Royal Society for the Prevention of Cruelty to Animals—MAFF press notice, 16 April 1991.

[2] In a debate in European Standing Committee A—SC Deb 27 March 1991 c 10.

themselves. In this case, however, no British agriculture minister could afford not to be seen to be taking on the rest of the Community and doing his best for British cows, sheep and pigs and, most of all, horses which may no longer be classified as agricultural animals in Britain but are subject to much of the same welfare legislation.

In a written statement on 7 February 1990, the Minister of Agriculture, John Gummer, went so far as to express his determination that:

> the special concern which the United Kingdom has shown towards animal welfare is carried across to our partners in the European Community. The protection of farm animals is now inevitably a European issue and Britain will have to play an active part in getting higher standards of animal welfare throughout the Community.

Animal welfare was, he said, an issue which transcended national boundaries and 'The way forward ... is to seek the fullest degree of harmonisation so that all countries of the Community operate to the same high standards.' Mr Gummer went on to list the various areas in which the government would press for action in the Community, including the transit of animals, the protection of horses, the welfare of pigs and calves and the welfare of poultry, as well as the need for common standards of slaughter and enforcement.[3] Modest though these objectives may appear, the government's difficulties in achieving them were well summarised by the Commons Agriculture Committee in its 1991 report on *Animals in Transit*:

> The prospect of replacing a tried and trusted body of British law with a Community Directive of uncertain content has excited considerable alarm and suspicion in this country. It would not be an exaggeration to say the people's fears of surrendering national sovereignty to an unsympathetic Brussels bureaucracy have been quickened by this issue more than any other ... The basis of people's fears can be simply explained. Existing UK safeguards for animals in transit are very much more stringent that those prevailing in the Community ... The Community also has a record of heel-dragging and procrastination on this issue which does not bode well for the future ... Those who claim the high moral ground in politics tend to do so at their peril ... but if there is one area of Community law in which the UK can plausibly set

---

[3] HC Deb 7 February 1990 c 712w; see also PQ answered by David Maclean, 25 July 1990 c 251w.

out to raise European standards to its own, and should resist degrading its standards to European ones, this must be it ... (The Minister) has a tough time ahead of him.[4]

## Transport of farm animals

Since the introduction of two directives in 1977 and 1981 to apply within the EC the provisions of the 1968 (Council of Europe) *European Convention for the Protection of Animals during International Transport*, Britain had had a mixture of Community and national legislation on the transport of animals, as had other member states. Much of the British legislation pre-dated both the European Convention and the Community directives and relatively few amendments were needed to apply the directives within the United Kingdom. That legislation had two notable features, both of which survived the application of the directives. First, since the late 1950s there had been specific controls on the destinations, in some cases including countries within the Community, to which live farm animals could be exported from the United Kingdom for immediate slaughter or further fattening. Secondly, there was a system of minimum values for horses exported from the United Kingdom which was deliberately devised to prevent the export of horses and ponies to other European countries for immediate slaughter (and consumption as meat).

Throughout the 1970s and 1980s, the latter provision had in practice more or less completely prevented any legal or illegal trade in live horses and ponies for slaughter. It was widely regarded as a success and the animal welfare organisations saw it as an essential safeguard. That did not apply to the provisions about farm animals. From the mid-1960s onwards, there had been concern among animal welfare interests about conditions in the export trade in farm animals. In 1973, very shortly after Britain joined the Community, the trade was suspended altogether during an independent official inquiry, chaired by Lord O'Brien of Lothbury, and resumed only after the inquiry found that a permanent ban on the export of animals for slaughter was not justified on either economic or welfare grounds. The inquiry also suggested that common European welfare regulations were the most effective means of safeguarding the trade in live

---

[4] Third Report from the Agriculture Committee, 1990–91, HC 45–I: *Animals in Transit*, paras 7–11.

animals within the EEC.[5] A further official inquiry was initiated in 1977, following fresh allegations that the controls were not being observed. That inquiry reported in 1978 and for the first time raised serious legal doubts about whether the United Kingdom could impose a unilateral ban on the export of live animals to other member states. It concluded that there would be difficulty in justifying such a ban, even on the grounds of animal welfare,[6] a conclusion which the then Minister of Agriculture (John Silkin) did not dispute, even though he was a known opponent of the EC and made no secret of his own preference for a carcase rather than a live animal trade.

Throughout the 1980s, following the introduction of the Community directives, there was a steady stream of complaints from animal welfare organisations that other member states did not enforce their provisions. Successive British Ministers of Agriculture continued to reject suggestions that the trade should be banned, arguing that, whatever the welfare arguments in favour of a carcase-only trade, such a ban would contravene the EC treaties. It was also pointed out that there was a demand in other member states for home-killed meat and if supplies from Britain were banned, importers would simply go elsewhere for their supplies. As one minister put it, 'There is no point in our ceasing to supply a market with our higher welfare standards only for that market to be flooded by animals from other countries which might have lower standards.'[7]

Given this background, it is not surprising that proposals for new EC legislation in this area were greeted extremely warily in Britain. In 1989, as part of the Single Market initiative, the Commission introduced a draft regulation on the transport of animals which would, it was envisaged, replace existing national and Community provisions. The original draft was first considered by the European Legislation Committee in October 1989, when it was recommended that it should be debated by a Standing Committee on European Community Documents. The Committee sounded a warning note when it pointed out in its report that the Ministry of Agriculture's explanatory memorandum had emphasised that the proposal as it stood would require significant changes in the United Kingdom's

---

[5] Report of the Committee on the Export of Animals for Slaughter (the O'Brien Report): Cmnd 5566, March 1974.

[6] Report by the Agriculture Departments on *The Export Trade in Live Animals for Slaughter or Further Fattening*, March 1978.

[7] Speech by David Maclean in reply to an adjournment debate, HC Deb 6 December 1989 c 456.

current arrangements to protect the welfare of animals during transit and also stated that: 'The Government welcomes moves to introduce common standards for animal welfare in the Community, but will seek to ensure during negotiations that any welfare standards agreed are fully adequate.'[8]

The two-hour debate took place in the Second Standing Committee on European Community Documents on 11 January 1990 and was opened by the Parliamentary Secretary to the Ministry of Agriculture, David Curry. He explained that the government had already sought the views of interested parties on the draft regulations and received many responses. Negotiations in the Community were still at an early stage and 'realistically we should not expect agreement before the end of 1990.' There were several faults in the proposals and he was well aware of public concern about the possible renewal of the export trade in horses for slaughter, where the government accepted the need for special safeguards for the United Kingdom, including the minimum values system, which the government would do its best to retain. He anticipated difficulties in doing that because the proposals were subject to majority voting: 'If I said that we should insist upon minimum values to defend the system, I should be saying something that I could not guarantee to deliver.' If the government failed to defend the system, a different method would be tried, such as a derogation. In other areas, the government would seek to make the proposals as comprehensive as possible and ensure that the best of British laws were maintained rather than swept away by European measures. The government strongly supported rigorous enforcement of welfare controls by other member states 'but our writ runs to Dover, not beyond Calais' and the government was not responsible for enforcement measures beyond the United Kingdom.

For the opposition, Ron Davies, who had earlier intervened to say that the opposition would support the government over retaining the minimum values system for horses, argued that in making the proposals the Community was asserting that encouraging the free market was more important than animal welfare. He nevertheless supported the government's efforts to get the best British practices adopted, although he questioned whether British standards in relation to welfare practices were invariably among the highest in Europe and whether British enforcement of the rules was always as rigorous as was claimed. He accepted that the negotiations were at an early stage and ended by urging the Minister to

---

[8] Thirty-Fourth Report from the Select Committee on European Legislation, 1988–89, HC 15–xxxiv, para 3.

ensure that the Community's veterinary committee was fully aware of the welfare lobby's views and of political opinion in Britain on welfare matters.

There were only four backbench speakers in the debate, three of them Euro-sceptics and two of whom used it partly as an opportunity to air more general reservations about the Community's legislative procedures and their application in the United Kingdom. One Conservative, Roger Moate, regretted what he saw as the strong possibility that the debate could be the last opportunity for the House of Commons to exercise any influence over the matter under debate and, because of majority voting, the likelihood that the minister would have to accept a 'poor compromise' which would mean Europe-wide lower standards than the existing British ones. The then chairman of the European Legislation Committee, Nigel Spearing, spoke at some length about the deficiencies of the Commission's proposals, the lack of any information about the consultations with member states before the proposals were made, and the inadequacies of the Ministry of Agriculture's explanatory memorandum. When he wound up the debate, David Curry emphasised again that he would be 'robust' in the negotiations but acknowledged that he had no power of veto and could not bring the negotiations to a halt, although he would do his utmost to achieve the desired results.

In April 1990, following an opinion from the European Parliament, an amended version of the proposals was published and considered by the European Legislation Committee in July 1990.[9] In that report, the Committee invited evidence from relevant interests on two particular aspects of the new draft regulation—the need for different journey limits for different species and the scope for evasion of the proposed rules—as well as seeking a view from the Ministry of Agriculture about a possible conflict to which the proposal might give rise between the elimination of barriers to trade and animal welfare considerations.

By December 1990, when the Committee made its Third Report in the 1990–91 session, there had been some slippage in the expected timetable for the proposals to reach the Council, mainly because it had become evident that the Commission was having difficulty in devising workable and enforceable standards which would be acceptable to all member states. In its report, the Committee summarised the evidence which it had received from a range of farming, veterinary, haulage and animal welfare

---

[9] Thirty-First Report from the Select Committee on European Legislation, 1989–90, HC 11–xxxi para 7.

interests on the two aspects of the draft legislation. It also reported the Ministry of Agriculture's view that there was likely to be 'some tension' between the two Community objectives of eliminating barriers to trade and improving animal welfare:

> The Department considers that, ultimately, the question of the extent to which trade in live animals should be affected by welfare considerations will need to be determined by a political decision in the Council rather than by general principles relating to the Single Market.[10]

The Committee said that, in the light of the evidence it had received, it was clear that the new draft raised new and politically sensitive issues and recommended that it should be further considered by European Standing Committee A. That debate took place on 27 March 1991, just after Community negotiations had re-started on the Commission's proposals and a few weeks after a short Lords debate on 22 January 1991, initiated by Lord Houghton of Sowerby, a well-known animal welfare campaigner, in which Baroness Trumpington had reminded the House of the government's determination not to allow an export trade in live horses and ponies for slaughter to resume.[11]

Unusually, the European Standing Committee debate took almost the full two and a half hours available, a reflection of the level of interest in the subject. It was obviously seen by the junior agriculture minister, David Maclean, as an occasion for demonstrating to the members of the Committee the strength of the government's commitment to achieving its objectives, although he did not hesitate to underline the difficulties he faced in persuading other member states to support the British stance. In the opening question and answer session, he stated that in the negotiations the government would take full account of British attitudes to animal welfare and was fully aware of the specially strong public anxiety about the possibility of a resumption in the export trade in horses for slaughter. It would press for provisions which would allow the existing ban on such exports to be maintained. 'The Government have made it clear on several occasions that we intend to win. We do not intend to concede the issue, nor are we preparing a fall-back position.'[12] He also stated several times

---

[10] Third Report from the Select Committee on European Legislation, 1990–91, HC 29-iii, para 1.

[11] HL Deb 22 January 1991 c 217.

[12] European Standing Committee A SC Deb 27 March 1991 cc 3–4.

the government's view that animal welfare was the most important consideration and should prevail in any case where there was a conflict with the requirements of the single market. 'Our great problem is to get across to the Commission and other countries that we obtain no market advantage from our attitude ... That is not the case.'[13]

Much of the questioning of Mr Maclean was concerned with detailed aspects of the proposed regulations but the questioners and speakers in the debate showed very clearly their desire to strengthen the minister's negotiating hand (see, for example, the speech by Harry Barnes when he moved an amendment to strengthen the government's motion[14]), although one (David Harris) pointed out that the real target of any lobbying should be the Commission and other member states. Lobbying the British government was preaching to the converted.[15] Another speaker (Gwyneth Dunwoody) warned the Committee that the British were in danger of overkill in their attitude towards other European countries on that particular issue[16] but otherwise there was general support for the Minister's robust line and the government accepted Mr Barnes's amendment to the original motion which emphasised the need to ensure that any Community legislation met the standards of the existing British provisions.

Mr Maclean and other speakers referred several times to the Agriculture Committee's concurrent inquiry into *Animals in Transit,* an inquiry which had been undertaken in direct response to the Community's original proposal for new regulations on the transport of farm animals. Like the consideration in European Standing Committee A, the Committee's report, published in June 1991, was essentially little more that an exercise in ministerial spine-stiffening: 'Our Report is both a commentary on the implications for the United Kingdom of the draft legislation and an open letter to the Minister of Agriculture, offering him our considered advice on how best to pursue the UK interest as the legislation is finalised.'[17] Mr Gummer's attempts in evidence to the Committee to inject a note of what he clearly saw as realism into the government's approach to the negotiations were rejected out of hand:

---

[13] Ibid, c 7.

[14] Ibid, cc 15–19.

[15] Ibid, cc 22–23.

[16] Ibid, c 24.

[17] Third Report from the Agriculture Committee, 1990–91, HC 45–I, para 1.

... we would see merit in principle in insisting that UK safeguards would not be lifted until the UK government was satisfied that the EC Directive replacing those safeguards offered broadly comparable guarantees of animal welfare ... But for there to be imposed on the UK a body of law which offered inherently weaker safeguards than existing domestic provisions would be politically intolerable, and the Minister should say so loud and clear.[18]

On the particular question of the export trade in live horses, the Committee took a high moral tone: the British revulsion towards eating horsemeat was fundamentally a cultural difference from other member states, 'Yet it is precisely the kind of cultural difference which the Community must accommodate if it is not to become the overbearing superstate which some people fear.'[19] It was nevertheless recognised that the Minister was going to have an uphill struggle—'In throwing down a challenge of this sort to the Commission, the Minister would obviously need to tread carefully'[20]—and Part XIV of the report was devoted to providing him with some additional arguments to support his case.

The government's response to the Committee's report in October 1991 was (predictably) phrased in more measured language and, as in Mr Gummer's appearance before the Committee, clearly showed a desire to negotiate on a realistic basis, although it referred to the 'areas where there is rightly deep concern about the welfare of animals.' The Report was seen as timely because the Netherlands Presidency hoped to complete negotiations before the end of the year on at least a general framework directive. The government still intended to stand firm against any proposals which would weaken domestic legislative safeguards, but it had to be accepted that under the Community arrangements the safeguards would 'be set out in a different form and it is not realistic to assume that every detailed provision of existing law will remain unchanged.' On the vexed question of the export of horses:

... the Government agrees that this is a trade which should not resume. The Government recognise the great depth of feeling on this issue and this concern will continue to be reflected in the Government's approach

---

[18] Ibid, para 17.
[19] Ibid, para 72.
[20] Ibid, para 7.

in the negotiations. The Government is also pressing other Member States to recognise that the potential welfare problems with the transport of horses exist throughtout the Community. The Government is therefore pressing for the highest standards of welfare for all categories of horses during transport throughout the Community.[21]

Apart from their detailed consideration by various committees, from the moment the Commission's proposals were first published there was a steady stream of questions about them, particularly about the export of horses, as well as a series of early day motions, several of them all-party ones, which attracted numerous signatures.[22] Ministers' replies to the questions were inevitably somewhat repetitive, particularly as progress in the negotiations was very slow with long gaps between periods of apparently desultory activity. In view of the obvious strength of feeling on the issue in the House (as well as among the public), it is perhaps remarkable that the almost entirely successful outcome (for the British) of the negotiations in the Council on the Commission's proposals was reported to the House only as a short written statement, made the day the House prorogued at the end of the session. It was announced on 22 October 1991 that the Council had agreed that the draft regulations should become a directive[23] and that the national rules on the transport of horses should remain applicable. That meant that the existing controls on exports to other member states could be retained. The Council would, however, return to the issue at a later stage 'with a view to setting additional welfare safeguards for all transport of horses in the Community.'[24] At Prime Minister's questions on the same day, the Leader of the House, John MacGregor, who was standing in for the Prime Minister, took the opportunity of a reply to a supplementary question to congratulate Mr Gummer on the successful outcome of the negotiations,[25] but that can only be seen as an anti-climax after all the earlier hyperbole and colourful language, not least that in the Agriculture Committee's report.

Moreover, the issue remained far from closed. In his statement on 22 October 1991, Mr Gummer said that before the directive came into force

---

[21] Third Special Report from the Agriculture Committee, 1990–91, HC 678.

[22] In the course of the 1990–91 session, there were 70 written questions, 16 oral supplementaries and eight early day motions on the export of animals.

[23] Directive 91/628/EEC.

[24] HC Deb 22 October 1991 cc 510–511w.

[25] HC Deb 22 October 1991 c 793.

(in January 1993) the Council would 'address the issue of an overall limitation of journeys' for all livestock, which would be of particular relevance to the transport of animals for slaughter. Article 13(1) of the directive also required the Commission to report before 1 July 1992 on additional detailed rules, on the basis of advice from the Scientific Veterinary Committee. In addition, the Council had agreed to return to the issue of the transport of horses at a later stage 'with a view to setting additional welfare safeguards for all transport of horses in the Community.' It was later made clear that there was no specific timetable for the additional rules, but there was also no time limit on the continuation of the national arrangements for the transport of horses.[26]

There was then a great deal of delay in publishing the Commission's report and associated proposals on journey limitations, which did not appear until July 1993, six months after the directive had come into force and one year late—a measure of the difficulty which the Commission had faced in drafting the proposals. That meant that national rules on journey times had to remain in force, to the accompaniment of continuing British allegations that other member states were not applying or enforcing the rules. The British also had to introduce new secondary legislation to extend the operation of the existing provisions.

The proposals' subsequent slow progress—they had still not been agreed in November 1994—revealed once more the differences between Britain and other member states in this area and the consequent difficulties in reaching a workable conclusion to the negotiations.

## Intensive livestock husbandry

The welfare of farm animals kept in intensive systems is another long-running British concern where feelings run high. In this case, too, there was a substantial amount of British legislation, much of it dating from the late 1960s and early 1970s, as well as a series of Community measures which were generally seen in the United Kingdom as being less than satisfactory. The Community measures were partly based on the provisions of the 1978 (Council of Europe) *European Convention on the Protection of Animals kept for Farming Purposes*. The welfare of pigs, calves and poultry were three of the specific areas listed by Mr Gummer in his

---

[26] HC Deb 21 November 1991 c 406 and 295w.

statement on 7 February 1990 where the government sought to raise minimum welfare standards throughout the Community, while in a later statement the Parliamentary Secretary at the Ministry of Agriculture, David Maclean, confirmed that one of the government's objectives in negotiations in the EC Council on animal welfare standards was the phasing out of 'unacceptable husbandry systems'.[27] In all three cases, by the end of the 1980s the Community had taken initiatives which severely limited the room for independent manoeuvre by member states.

In the case of poultry, in March 1986 the EC had adopted a directive on minimum cage sizes for battery hens which was to come into effect two years after its adoption for new cages (ie at the beginning of 1988).[28] The British government made it clear at the time of its original adoption that it was unhappy about the directive's provisions, which were thought not to go far enough, and were below the minimum space allowance sought by the United Kingdom. The British government also subsequently challenged the directive in the European Court on the grounds of procedural irregularities and the directive had to be re-adopted in 1988.

The directive required the Commission to submit a review and scientific report by 1 January 1993 and there was a seven-year period of grace (to 1 January 1995) for existing cages to conform with the new requirements. In November 1989, in the light of new scientific evidence about minimum space requirements, the (British) Farm Animal Welfare Council tried unsuccessfully to persuade the Commission to bring forward its review. In February 1992, Mr Gummer listed improved conditions for battery hens among the government's priorities for international action on animal welfare during the United Kingdom's forthcoming presidency in the second half of that year,[29] but the Commission's review failed to appear on time. By late 1994, the review had still not appeared—again, a measure of the difficulties which the Commission faced in this area—and, more surprisingly in the light of the level of earlier public concern on the subject, from about 1990 onwards parliamentary interest in the topic faded almost completely away.

Specific aspects of the welfare of both calves and pigs had been the subject of national initiatives within the United Kingdom in the late 1980s, following widespread criticisms of the system of using crates for rearing

---

[27] HC Deb 25 July 1990 c 251w.

[28] Directive 86/113/EEC, subsequently readopted as Directive 88/166/EC.

[29] Ministry of Agriculture press notice 27 February 1992.

veal calves and the practice of confining dry (ie non-lactating but pregnant) sows in stalls. Regulations had been introduced in 1987 to ban the use of crates for the rearing of veal calves with effect from January 1990, while in March 1988 the Farm Animal Welfare Council had reported on pig production systems, including the use of stalls for housing dry sows in close confinement which, it was recommended, should be banned. The government's response in March 1989[30] to that report took specific account of the fact that, following a European Parliament Resolution in 1987, the Commission was known to be preparing proposals on the welfare of intensively kept pigs and calves. The response stated that the government's position on the forthcoming EC proposal on pigs would be that no new sow stall units should be built throughout the EC and that existing sow stall systems should be phased out as soon as possible.

In July 1989, the Commission published its proposals for the welfare of calves and pigs in two draft regulations which dealt with more wide-ranging welfare matters than the two aspects of particular concern to the British, although both were included. For the United Kingdom, the Commission's proposals could be seen as essentially a catching-up exercise in that most of the measures were already in existence in the United Kingdom, a point which was noted by the European Legislation Committee in its 30th Report of that session. The Committee recommended that, in view of the long-standing political sensitivity of the proposals, they should be further considered by the House.[31]

Both drafts were debated by the Second Standing Committee on European Community Documents on 8 November 1989, when the Parliamentary Secretary to the Ministry of Agriculture (David Curry) emphasised that the United Kingdom's existing provisions on veal calves, although not yet in force, were more stringent than the Commission's proposals. The government had no intention of reverting to less stringent rules simply in order to comply with Commission measures. Most of the other provisions were, however, broadly acceptable with the exception of those on sow stalls and tethers which did not go far enough and would take too long to introduce. The government's aim in the negotiations would therefore be to secure the Farm Animal Welfare Council's recommendations on sow stalls and tethers on a Community basis and, more generally, to achieve uniformity throughout the Community, an

---

[30] Ministry of Agriculture press notice 13 March 1989.

[31] Thirtieth Report from the Select Committee on European Legislation, 1988–89, HC 15-xxx.

approach which was supported, but with considerable reservations, by the opposition spokesman, Ron Davies, who argued that both the government and the Commission were too lax about animal welfare. He urged the minister to ensure that the Commission knew about the strong feelings, not only among politicians but also among the general public, that 'we are lagging behind in animal welfare'; the government should be prepared to act unilaterally if necessary to maintain British standards. The Commission's proposals for veal crates fell short of those standards and the minister should press for the complete abolition of veal crates. Other speakers in the debate endorsed the minister's approach, although two Conservatives were concerned about the cost of implementing the higher standards while several speakers from both sides raised the question of ensuring proper enforcement throughout the Community and expressed doubts about the availability of adequate resources to achieve that.

The Commission's proposals thereafter made slow progress and were not finally agreed by the Council until October 1991. In the meantime, Sir Richard Body (a very long-standing EC opponent as well as a pig breeder and former chairman of the Agriculture Committee) had introduced a Pig Husbandry Bill in 1990–91 which sought to ban the use of stalls and tethers for breeding sows. Although the measure was explicitly intended to be applied only to British pig producers, the second reading debate on 25 January 1991 provided some interesting illustrations of backbenchers' perspectives on Community issues, particularly one where there was a great deal of public concern. When he opened the debate, Sir Richard reminded the House that there was what he termed a European dimension in that such a ban might put British farmers at a disadvantage compared with their counterparts elsewhere in the Community. He had concluded that for various reasons it would not, partly because the systems which the bill sought to ban were not commonly used in other member states.[32]

Several other speakers took a rather different line: they felt that there should be EC-wide higher standards on farm animal welfare and that the United Kingdom should take a lead in introducing such provisions, rather than waiting for Community initiatives (little heed seems to have been given to Sir Richard's point that the systems covered by his bill were not widely used elsewhere). A Labour Member, Peter Hardy, argued that if the bill were rejected, the rest of the EC would say that the United Kingdom was not prepared either to take a lead or to insist on decent and

---

[32] HC Deb 25 January 1991 c 567–568.

humane standards. 'Opposing the bill would be damaging not only to Britain but to its reputation throughout Europe,'[33] a view shared by a Liberal Democrat, Malcolm Bruce. Peter Bottomley, a Conservative, on the other hand, thought that, while both Britain and Europe should have higher animal welfare standards, Sir Richard needed to explain why Britain should lead Europe on this particular issue. William Hague, another Conservative, did not support the bill because of its probable effect on pig producers' costs but pointed out that progress on animal welfare matters in the EC was very slow. A Labour Member, Harry Cohen, cited the United Kingdom's ban on the use of crates for rearing veal calves even though crates were permitted (and used) elsewhere in the EC as an example of how the United Kingdom could act unilaterally. The minister who replied to the debate, David Maclean, pointed out that such a ban was problematic in that imports of veal were still allowed from countries where crates were used. He nevertheless went on to announce that the government would be pre-empting the bill's provisions by introducing its own regulations to ban sow stalls and tethers, although he accepted that it was difficult to know when the rest of the EC would follow the United Kingdom's lead.[34]

Sir Richard subsequently withdrew his bill after its Commons third reading, and the government introduced the promised regulations in May 1991. In a short debate in the Fourth Standing Committee on Statutory Instruments on 19 June 1991, the minister (David Maclean) reminded the committee of the need for the rest of the Community to follow the United Kingdom's lead as soon as possible:

> We will press for our standards to be adopted on a Community basis and we know that we will have the support of the Commission. We also know that some other Member States share our aims and are interested in our actions. The Committee has my assurance that the Government will do all that it can to bring about a Community phase-out of these systems from the earliest possible date ... we know ... that we lead (the Community) on welfare.[35]

---

[33] Ibid, c 575.
[34] Ibid, cc 615–619.
[35] Fourth Standing Committee on Statutory Instruments SC Deb 19 June 1991 c 4.

A Conservative backbench speaker, Donald Thompson, strongly supported the minister and went so far as to claim:

> Nowhere in Europe is animal welfare regarded one-fifth as highly as it is in this country. Other countries may have green parties, but they have peculiar ideas about animal welfare ... Take no lessons whatsoever, Mr Minister, from anything people tell you about animal welfare in Europe ... Examples of good practice in Europe are often the exception. In this country, examples of bad practice are the exception.[36]

When the regulations were debated in the Lords on 20 June 1991, the Minister of State at the Ministry of Agriculture, Baroness Trumpington, reminded the House of the long delays in getting agreement on the Community's proposals on pig welfare, although the incoming Dutch Presidency had made them a priority in its work programme.[37]

In the event, the outcome of the negotiations about the Commission's proposals could only be regarded as somewhat unsatisfactory. They were considered at the same Council as the proposals on the transport of animals in October 1991 and two directives were agreed but Mr Gummer's statement on 22 October 1991 referred only to the agreement on animal transport. There was no reference to the fate of the proposals on the welfare of pigs and calves and, thanks to parliament's being prorogued, it emerged in stages, at least as far as parliament was concerned, that the government had failed to achieve Mr Maclean's stated objectives in relation to either pigs or calves. In reply to a question on 21 November 1991, Mr Maclean said that the government would 'continue to strive for adoption of United Kingdom standards, including calf and pig farming, throughout the EC.'[38] He also admitted in reply to a question on 19 December 1991 that the United Kingdom had voted against the proposals on veal crates, which the directive did not properly tackle, but British standards for veal production would not be reduced. He went on:

---

[36] Ibid, c 7.
[37] HL Deb 20 June 1991 c 290 and c 300.
[38] HC Deb 21 November 1991 c 293w.

We held out strongly in the EC to have our standards implemented widely throughout the Community and when it was clear that other nations were not of a similar mind, we voted against the directive.[39]

## Conclusion

Lord Bethell, a former MEP and member of the European Parliament's human rights sub-committee, remarked in October 1989 that in that capacity he was sometimes written to about man's beastliness to man but ten times more often about man's inhumanity to animals.[40] Since then, public interest in the subject in Britain has grown rather than diminished, to the point where agriculture ministers were reported in May 1994 as receiving over 30,000 letters a month on animal welfare issues, an indication that animal rights could have become the most popular issue in British politics.[41] The events of 1994, when several cross-Channel ferry undertakings were forced to give in to public pressure and stop carrying lorries containing live farm animals, are proof of the strength and impact of public feeling on only one aspect of the subject.

It has already been remarked that no Minister of Agriculture could be seen not to be doing his best in Brussels for British farm animals and there can be no doubt that parliament more than adequately reflects the high level of public concern on the subject. This is not the occasion to analyse the causes of that concern nor, irrational though it may often appear to be especially when compared with the relative lack of interest in what might justifiably be seen as some of the great issues of the day, to question its legitimacy. There is equally no reason why Members of Parliament should not use every opportunity available to them to raise a matter of legitimate concern to their constituents, especially when that concern is so strongly felt and widely articulated. It could, indeed, be argued that Members might well be seen as failing in their duties if they did not respond to an issue of such public concern. As a moral or ethical issue, animal welfare also raises few difficulties for politicians: some (possibly many) of them may not be particularly interested in it, but it is generally and genuinely

---

[39] HC Deb 19 December 1991 cc 441–2.
[40] *The House Magazine* 30 October 1989.
[41] *Scotsman* 21 May 1994.

non-partisan and it is impossible politically not to support efforts to improve the welfare of animals.

The question which does, however, arise is whether parliament's interventions over the Community's efforts to introduce common animal welfare standards had any significant effect on the negotiations and whether they helped to achieve the government's objectives. Here the picture is much more ambiguous. Parliament may well reflect accurately public concerns on the issue but over the transport of animals the evidence suggests that because ministers were forced, not least by parliament, to take a completely uncompromising stance in the negotiations, the outcome was overall less favourable towards British interests than it might otherwise have been, notwithstanding the success over exports of horses.

Furthermore, British intransigence, aided and abetted by parliament, undoubtedly contributed towards the long delays in reaching agreement in the Community, largely because it precluded the building of alliances with other member states which would have speeded progress towards reaching agreement. To that extent, it could be seen as acting *against* the welfare of animals throughout the Community, including British ones being transported in other member states. During the five years from 1989 when animal welfare matters were relatively high on the Community's agenda, the United Kingdom admittedly gained some allies among the more northern member states (Denmark, Germany and the Netherlands in particular), especially in relation to the provisions on transport of animals, but that did not help significantly in reaching rapid agreement on Community-wide measures. It is not altogether surprising that in 1993 the Commission started to change its approach and to suggest that the Community should proceed on the basis of a mixture of the various Council of Europe Conventions on animal welfare (to which all member states were already signatories), supplemented by Community measures.[42]

---

[42] See Thirty-Eighth Report from the Select Committee on European Legislation, 1992–93, HC 79–xxxviii; and Twenty-Fifth Report, 1993–94, HC 48–xxv.

# 10

## The Road to Maastricht: Parliament and the Intergovernmental Conferences of 1991

### Richard Ware

### Introduction

The British Parliament has developed two modes for dealing with the European Community: one for the routine business of scrutinising the proposals for legislation which emerge from the Community, for monitoring other 'one-off' documents such as the reports of the Court of Auditors and draft Community budgets, and, more occasionally, for keeping a check on its external relations and foreign policy initiatives; and quite another for the periodic bouts of intense negotiation which take place when the Community decides to reform itself. In the first case the normal procedure is for the Select Committee on European Legislation to draw the attention of the House to a particular proposal or document and then for the House to debate it, either in committee or on the floor of the chamber. These procedures are described in detail elsewhere in this book.[1]

In the second, 'constitutional' mode, the attention of the British Parliament is necessarily engaged more intensively, usually over a longer period, and more often on the floor of the House. The present chapter is concerned with the second of these modes, as illustrated by the negotiations of 1991 concerning amendments to the Treaty of Rome to bring about a political union, and economic and monetary union. It covers the conclusion of the agreement at Maastricht on 11 December 1991 and the immediate parliamentary reaction, but not the process of amending the European Communities Act in order to ratify the treaty which is the subject of the next chapter.

The negotiations in the intergovernmental conferences of 1991 were about the achievement of Economic and Monetary Union (EMU) in three stages and about progress towards a European Political Union (EPU). Proposals to this end included the extension of majority voting to new

---

[1] Chapter 4.

areas of Community activity, provisions on cooperation in the field of home affairs and judiciary matters and a new set of treaty arrangements for foreign affairs and defence. Issues were raised in the negotiations about the future size and shape of the Community, about the inter-relationship of its institutions and about the nature of democratic accountability in the Community. At the heart of the debate was the question of power in the Community, its distribution to different levels and its allocation as between 'federal' institutions, such as the Commission and European Parliament, and governmental institutions, meaning primarily the Councils of Ministers, but also ministerial meetings outside the Treaty of Rome framework. One of the key concepts introduced into the discussions at an early stage was 'subsidiarity', an approach to determining the most appropriate level for decision-making in different matters. The majority of the governments involved in the negotiations wanted to make a qualitative leap towards a federal constitution, in which the relationship between the centre and the member states would be as clearly defined as in an avowedly federal state, like the Federal Republic of Germany. For the British government, and for the British Parliament, this turned the issue into a debate about sovereignty, its loss and transfer away from the United Kingdom, replaying the arguments of the 1970s and with many of the same participants.

This perception of the significance of the negotiations persuaded the House of Commons and the House of Lords to devote more time to the consideration of the EMU and EPU proposals than to any European matter since the passage of the European Communities Bill in 1972 and far more than had been devoted to the negotiation of the Single European Act in 1985. Despite the amount of parliamentary time expended on the treaty negotiations in 1991, it was frequently alleged later, when the ratification process ran into difficulty, that the British Parliament had not fully come to terms with the text adopted at Maastricht and that some of those who had approved the government's negotiating stance had suppressed serious doubts about the treaty's contents. Similar allegations have been made subsequently in the course of controversies about qualified majority voting following enlargement and also about the implementation of the 1992 Edinburgh Agreement on own resources.

The mechanism which the Community has adopted for its own institutional review and reform process under Article 236 of the Treaty of Rome is the 'conference of representatives of the Governments of the Member States' or Inter-governmental Conference (IGC). In January 1991 two parallel IGCs began work, one for EMU and one for EPU. The IGCs work like the Council of Ministers, with the successive presidencies in the chair, but are kept formally separate from the continuing routine business of the Council of Ministers. The EMU IGC was entrusted to EC Finance Ministers and the EPU IGC to Foreign Ministers, in both cases supported by their deputies and officials. Since under Article 236 amendments to the Treaty are to be determined 'by common accord' there was no majority voting in the IGCs. In practice, as in any complex multilateral negotiation there had to be a great deal of informal bargaining outside the formal sessions in order to produce an acceptable consensus.[2]

The bargaining continued in public and in private throughout 1991 and it was not certain until the last moment that an agreement would be reached at the Maastricht Summit in December of that year. In the end an agreement was reached only by accepting a certain amount of 'variable geometry' whereby the UK was to opt out of an agreement based on the Social Charter and to reserve its position on EMU while the special national interests of some other member states were safeguarded in protocols attached to the Maastricht Treaty.

For each government there was a dual aspect to the negotiations. Sitting at the IGC table the minister responsible had to bargain with his ministerial counterparts. Returning home he had to bargain with his ministerial colleagues (who in more than half of the member states could be representatives of different political parties working together in coalition) and with other domestic forces. Some ministers had to take direct account of public opinion because of commitments to submit the agreement to a referendum, while others had to take account of forthcoming national elections or of the possibility that an agreement might be rejected by their national parliament.

The metaphor of the two tables, international and domestic, at which each ministerial team has to bargain, gaining a 'ratification' at the domestic table for any initiative or concession made at the international table, is a plausible one.[3] The essential point, that any participant in an

---

[2] A systematic account of the IGCs may be found, along with documentation, in R Corbett, *The Treaty of Maastricht. From Conception to Ratification: A Comprehensive Reference Guide*, Longman, 1993.

[3] Such a model was proposed by R D Putnam: 'Neither of the two games can be ignored by central decision-makers, so long as their countries remain interdependent, yet sovereign. Each national political leader appears at both game boards. Across the international table sit his foreign counterparts ... Around the domestic table behind him sit party and parliamentary figures, spokespersons for domestic agencies, representatives of key interest groups, and the leader's own political advisers.'—R D Putnam,

international negotiation is constrained by what can be 'sold' back home to those who invest responsibility in the negotiator, merely states an obvious feature of negotiation and diplomacy. The question explored in this chapter is therefore: to what extent does parliament serve as the domestic negotiating table for the UK? Clearly it is not the only forum which matters: the cabinet, the back-bench caucus, the annual conference and local associations of the governing political party, the amorphous fraternity of newspaper, magazine and TV pundits, the anonymous opinion formers of 'the City' are also players in the drama and the electorate in the next general election may have the final word. In theory parliament should be capable of representing and synthesising all significant national points of view on a matter such as the European Union negotiations. To what extent did parliament actually succeed in playing this role over Maastricht?

## Debates and Participation

Judging by the priority which it gave to the IGC negotiations and by the number of individual parliamentarians who took part in the discussions, parliament took the matter very seriously.

The first of three Commons debates took place on 26 June 1991 by which time the negotiations were already well under way.[4] It occupied almost six hours of government time and gave 24 Members, including two ministers, the opportunity to make formal speeches and a number of others to make interventions. This debate preceded the meeting of the European Council at Luxembourg. After the meeting the Prime Minister, John Major, made a statement to the House of Commons on its outcome and on progress in the IGCs and 53 Members asked him questions.[5]

The second debate, also in government time, occupied approximately 13 hours spread over 20–21 November 1991, by which time the Maastricht European Council, intended to finalise the Treaty, was looming. The first day of the debate had been extended from the usual finishing time of 10 pm to midnight in order to accommodate more of the exceptionally large number of back-bench members who had indicated to

---

'Diplomacy and domestic politics: the logic of two-level games', *International Organization*, vol 43, Summer 1988, p 434.

[4] HC Deb 26 June 1991 cc 1007–1091.

[5] HC Deb 1 July 1991 cc 21–41.

the Speaker that they wished to take part. On the second day the Speaker told the House that 82 Members had notified him of this wish. In the end there was time for 56 speeches, four of them from ministers.

On 11 December 1991 the Prime Minister reported back from Maastricht. This time 45 Members questioned Mr Major and some were left uncalled and disappointed when the Speaker decided to move on to other business.[6] However, the government had promised a full debate on the outcome of Maastricht and this took place on 18–19 December 1991. The first day of debate was allowed to run until 2.00 am and by the end of the second day 61 Members had been called to speak.

Thus, a total of some 141 speeches by 99 different Members (from the total of 650) had been devoted to the IGCs along with more than 200 questions and interventions in speeches. Seven MPs spoke in all three debates (three ministers, four backbenchers); 24 spoke in two of the three debates. Each of these stages in the negotiations was also debated in the House of Lords.[7]

Committees played a relatively unimportant part. The Commons Treasury and Civil Service Committee had reported on the Delors Report, precursor of the EMU IGC in June 1989[8] and took further evidence in July 1991 and February 1992,[9] but did not deliver a further report. The Lords Committee on the European Communities had also reported on the Delors Report in 1989.[10] It reported on *Political Union: Law-making powers and procedures* in July 1991.[11] The Commons Committee on European Legislation, members of which played a prominent part in the debates on the floor of the House, had taken evidence from ministers twice on the priorities of the two EC presidencies of 1991 (25 March and 23 July 1991) and the Commons Foreign Affairs Committee had taken

---

[6] HC Deb 11 December 1991 c 879.

[7] Details are given in Chapter 7.

[8] Fourth Report from the Treasury and Civil Service Committee 1988–89, *The Delors Report*, HC 341, July 1989.

[9] Plans for economic and monetary union. Minutes of evidence, HC 195 1990/91; Minutes of Evidence, HC 285 1991–92.

[10] Third Report from the European Communities Select Committee (HL), 1989–90, *The Delors Committee Report*, HL 3, December 1989.

[11] Seventeenth Report of the European Communities Select Committee (HL), 1990–91, *Political Union: Law-making powers and procedures*, HL 80, July 1991; see also Chapter 7.

evidence from the Foreign Secretary on 12 June and 19 November 1991. It was to report on the outcome of Maastricht in March 1992.[12]

## Availability of Information

The key documents on which Parliament had to base its scrutiny of the negotiations were the successive draft treaties which emerged from April 1991 onwards. The information provided by ministers in the course of their speeches and in reply to questions could be no substitute for the texts, if only because it came too late for most MPs to analyse and draw upon for their own contributions to the debates.

One of the difficulties which dogged the parliamentary consideration of the IGCs was the late provision of documents. This problem arose from the nature of the IGCs, which were supposed to be confidential inter-governmental dialogues. The British government was reluctant to break the rule of confidentiality of drafts to which all of the governments had agreed and was placed in an awkward position when drafts did in fact enter the public domain, either through journalistic enterprise in Brussels, or as a result of a technical breach by one of the other governments. The first draft to emerge was the 'non-paper' of April 1991, so-called because it was prepared by the Luxembourg presidency as an aid to the negotiating process, but was not officially tabled.[13] This was the only text available to most interested MPs until 26 June, the day of the debate on the approaching Luxembourg European Council, but by then it had, in fact, been superseded. The new draft, prepared by the Luxembourg presidency for that meeting, became known through press reports, but was received in the Library of the House of Commons, in one copy of 134 pages, only three hours before the debate was due to start. This was unsatisfactory, as the Speaker made clear in response to points of order from four Members at the beginning of the debate.[14] Several others protested in the course of

---

[12] Second Report from the Foreign Affairs Select Committee, 1991–92, *Europe after Maastricht*, HC 223, March 1992.

[13] Non-paper by the Luxembourg Presidency concerning draft articles 2 to 4 Bis of 102A to 104A of the Treaty, amended with a view to creation of economic & monetary union, Agence Europe Document 1693; Draft treaty article with a view to achieving political union. Non-paper submitted by Luxembourg Presidency of EC to Intergovernmental Conference on Political Union issued on 12 April 1991, Agence Europe Doc 1709/1710. The text is also in Corbett, pp 267–288.

[14] HC Deb 26 June 1991 c 1009.

the debate, including Mrs Margaret Thatcher, the former Prime Minister: 'I have not seen the full documents, because they came too late, and I share the views of those who protested that they were not available'.[15]

During the Netherlands presidency, which presided over the IGCs from July to December, the attempt to keep significant new drafts confidential was abandoned and the availability of texts did not present a problem during the debate of 20–21 November.[16] After the Maastricht summit, which saw the text finalised in all but a few details, the British government was released from its inhibitions and placed the full bundle of documents in the Library and Vote Office.

Being able to obtain and read the documents was a vital, but not a sufficient, condition for serious debate. The Maastricht Treaty, even in its final version, was a highly confusing document.[17] Some of its provisions were drafted as new free-standing agreements on co-operation in various areas, but others were drafted in the form of amendments to existing articles of the Treaty of Rome. The whole bundle was tied up with an over-arching agreement to create a European Union with objectives which had to be read alongside the detail of the new agreements. A series of detailed protocols and declarations had been tagged on at the end and, in order to understand the arrangements for a common foreign and security policy, it was necessary to take account of two further agreements which did not form part of the Treaty at all, one adopted by the European Council outside the IGC framework, and the other adopted by nine of the ministers only, wearing their Western European Union hats.

Few of the complexities and technicalities of the texts came over in the summaries and analysis which appeared in the press and broadcast media. MPs had access to analytical papers on the treaties and their significance prepared by the research service of the House of Commons Library, but these also suffered in the early stages from the non-availability, or late availability, of the documents and could not overcome the central problem, which was that in order to satisfy conflicting interests the Luxembourg and Netherlands presidencies and the other negotiating parties had larded the drafts with a great deal of detail and with many subtleties designed to

---

[15] HC Deb 26 June 1991 c 1031.

[16] Draft Union treaty. Dutch Presidency's working document prepared for the conclave of Foreign Ministers on 12–13 November 1991, *Agence Europe* Document 1746/1747. Text also in Corbett, pp 346–374.

[17] Treaty on European Union including the Protocols and Final Act with Declarations, Cm 1934, reprinted in the Treaty Series after ratification as Cm 2485.

create balances between the powers of different Community institutions. This was particularly true of the 'non-paper', which would have created an entirely new and additional category of European Community law and was described by critics as 'baroque' and 'a jungle',[18] but was true also of the carefully crafted compromise which finally secured agreement at Maastricht.

The debates on the drafts in the House of Commons reveal that many parliamentarians had read the documents closely. Some, like Norman Tebbit, prided themselves on this and made a point of quizzing their colleagues on the small print.[19] Others admitted frankly that they were unqualified to analyse the small print.[20] Disagreements about the meaning of clauses in the documents were relatively scarce, but the front bench speakers during the debate of 18–19 December engaged in a number of acrimonious disputes of this nature.[21] Perhaps the greater problem for MPs was how to explain the new treaty to their constituents and to take soundings about the public reaction to it. One Labour sceptic described the texts as 'these complicated treaties which our electorates will not see'.[22] This difficulty would arise for politicians throughout the twelve member states when they embarked on ratification procedures the following year and would set the scene for the rejection of the treaty by a narrow majority of the Danish electorate in the first referendum of 2 June 1992.

## The Range of Views

How did the House of Commons encompass and express the many different points of view on the IGC negotiations and their outcome at Maastricht?

The most striking feature of parliamentary debates about Britain's relationship with the European Community since the 1950s has been their propensity to cross party political lines. The debates of 1991 were no exception to this, though there was a perceptible closing of party ranks, particularly on the Conservative side, as the prospect of a general election

---

[18] *Agence Europe*, Nos 5472 and 5473, 15–16, 17 April 1991.

[19] HC Deb 18 December 1991, c 326.

[20] Ibid, c 344.

[21] See, for example, Neil Kinnock's arguments with Norman Lamont and Michael Howard, ibid, cc 291–4.

[22] Gwyneth Dunwoody, HC Deb 18 December 1991, c 357.

approached. The earlier debates constantly gave rise to sharp disagreements between members of the same party and ad hoc alliances between party political opponents such as Norman Tebbit and Tony Benn. Denis Healey, speaking in the debate of 26 June, noted that 'these are not necessarily party issues, but, inevitably, party politics sometimes become mixed up with them'.[23] The admixture of party politics increased as the year wore on, raised by the efforts of the ministers and shadow ministers to rally their party supporters and prepare the ground for the general election. In the November and December debates the front benchers repeatedly presented the real issue as being which of the rival teams was more competent and able to negotiate the best deal for Britain. Thus Tristan Garel-Jones, the Minister of State responsible for the detailed negotiations on Political Union, claimed at the close of debate on 18 December: 'My political point is this: Hurd—Kaufman, Kinnock—Major. That point is understood on both sides of the House'.[24]

Many different shades of opinion were expressed, often very eloquently. The nuances became rather more pronounced as the year progressed, with different groups expressing different desiderata for the negotiations and reacting to the outcome in different ways. Inevitably there were shifts in the loose coalitions of opinion and the following summary tends to simplify.

## (i)   The Negotiators

This group consisted of the ministers directly involved in the negotiations and their loyal supporters on the back benches. Their motto (in the words of Norman Lamont, then the Chancellor of the Exchequer, on 21 November 1991) was 'constructive but cautious'. In order to maximise support at home and add to their muscle in the IGCs, the ministers made much of their opposition to the 'federalist' orientation of the successive drafts and how they would fight for the right outcome for Britain. In the light of the fact that all the debates on the IGCs had exposed deep disagreements within and beyond the Conservative Party on the possibility of Britain eventually entering into a single European currency system and given that the question of how to manage the sterling exchange rate was still one of the most sensitive in internal Conservative politics, the

---

[23] Ibid, c 1044.
[24] Ibid, c 425.

ministerial group had decided at an early stage that this particular issue could not be finally agreed at Maastricht and that, if the other 11 states wanted to commit themselves in advance to a single currency later in the decade, Britain must negotiate a right to decide later. By leaving options open on the single currency, and by returning from Maastricht with an explicit article reserving Britain's position, the Prime Minister was able to avoid a schism in his own party.

The ministerial team was also very anxious to steer European co-operation onto the road of 'inter-governmentalism', ie direct negotiation between ministers without the intervention of the Commission, the European Parliament and the European Court of Justice, all institutions regarded with suspicion by many Conservative MPs at Westminster. For this reason the negotiators were keen to prevent all new areas of co-operation going into the structures of the Treaty of Rome and set their sights on separate 'pillars' of inter-governmentalism under the new treaty.

The British negotiators were also anxious to excise from the treaty text any direct reference to federalism and therefore presented as a considerable victory at Maastricht the replacement of the reference to Europe having a 'vocation fédérale' ('federal goal'), which appeared in the earlier drafts, by the call to 'ever closer union' which had appeared in the preamble to the original Treaty of Rome.

Finally, the government set much store on the principle of 'subsidiarity', which had already been adopted in the Single European Act for environmental matters, as a device to limit Community 'interference' in national matters and as a reassurance to those who feared that Britain was being dragged inexorably towards mere provincial status in a European super-state.[25]

Among those on the back benches who were supportive of the ministerial line at each stage were David Howell (chairman of the Foreign Affairs Committee), Sir Norman Fowler (newly elected on 13 November 1991 to be the chairman of the Conservative back bench committee on Europe), Jonathan Aitken (a long-standing doubter on Europe) and Terence Higgins, chairman of the Treasury Committee. More unexpected support for the Major-Hurd-Lamont axis came from Dr David Owen, the former leader of the SDP.

---

[25] See Chapter 2.

## (ii) The Official Opposition

The opposition front bench found itself frequently in an uncomfortable position during the negotiations, agreeing with the government on a wide range of points, but nonetheless trying to carve out a distinctive and constructive line of criticism. Both Neil Kinnock and his shadow foreign secretary Gerald Kaufman had been opponents of British entry into the European Community in the past, whereas the shadow Chancellor, John Smith, and the European spokesman, George Robertson, had been enthusiastic supporters. The Labour Party had officially adopted a pro-European Community stance in the 1980s. The Labour leadership based its change of mind partly on pragmatism, but also on the strong perception that the Community had changed and that the efforts of politicians like Jacques Delors to create a social dimension to the Community had made it much more compatible with Labour's economic and social goals. The strongest criticism of the government was therefore that it opposed this expanded social dimension and, at Maastricht, insisted on 'opting out' from an agreement on workers' rights and related matters which the other eleven agreed upon. On the question of the single currency the opposition found it more difficult to distinguish its position clearly from that of the government, not least because a vocal minority of Labour MPs, including former ministers Peter Shore and Denzil Davies, were firmly opposed to the single currency on political and economic grounds.

## (iii) The 'Federalists'

A third strand of opinion was represented by those who would have gone further towards European Union at Maastricht. In the Commons this group crossed all party lines, bringing together Conservatives like the former Prime Minister Edward Heath, the chairman of the European Movement, Hugh Dykes, and Sir Antony Meyer, who had launched a personal challenge to Mrs Thatcher on European issues in 1989, most of the Liberal Democrat Party, and some enthusiastic recruits to the European cause from the Labour left, such as Brian Sedgemore and Tony Banks.

## (iv) The Bruges Group and its allies

This group came overwhelmingly from the Conservative Party, and indeed largely from the right wing of the Conservative Party, but was joined in the main planks of its campaign by individuals from the Labour Party who were not necessarily veterans of old anti-common market campaigns, but felt that Maastricht was 'a treaty too far'. The Bruges tendency, drawing its inspiration from Mrs Thatcher's speech at Bruges on 20 September 1988, was actually a coalition of those, like Teddy (latterly Sir Teddy) Taylor, who had long campaigned against most features of the European Community from the back benches, and those, like Mrs Thatcher herself, and her former cabinet colleagues, Norman Tebbit and Nicholas Ridley, who had been instrumental in committing Britain to the Single European Act in 1986, but were dismayed by subsequent developments in Europe, enraged by all the words and deeds of Jacques Delors and deeply suspicious of the intentions of the Euro-federalists (including those believed to lurk in the Foreign and Commonwealth Office). The main strategy of this group was to use the parliamentary platform to lay down guidelines for those negotiating at the IGCs with the implicit threat that, unless these guidelines were broadly followed, the MPs of the Bruges tendency would be unable to support the government. Indeed Mrs Thatcher, while praising her successor, set down in her speeches of 26 June and 20 November a list of such conditions.[26] Although some of their number became renowned for their mastery of tedious detail, the 'Eurosceptics' also produced some of the most witty, memorable and impassioned speeches on Europe in the debates studied here. Those of Norman Tebbit and Michael Spicer in the debate of 21 November were classics of this genre.[27]

## (v)   The Labour anti-marketeers

While the Conservative Party under Mrs Thatcher's leadership had become increasingly disillusioned with the European Community, the Labour Party under Neil Kinnock had moved in the opposite direction. Consequently, the resistance on the Labour benches to a further round of European integration came mainly from veterans of the anti-Common Market campaign of the 1970s: Peter Shore, Austin Mitchell, Ron Leighton, Nigel Spearing, Denzil Davies and others.

---

[26] HC Deb 26 June 1991, cc 1026–1031 and 20 November 1991 cc 290–298.
[27] HC Deb 21 November 1991, cc 480–483 and 502–504.

## (vi) The nationalists and regionalists

One of the features of recent UK debates on Europe and federalism has been the new-found enthusiasm for the Community on the part of Scottish and Welsh politicians, chafing against the rule of London. For these groups federalism and subsidiarity are promising and positive slogans. In the European debates of 1991 this line was uniformly taken by the SNP and Plaid Cymru and also by the SDLP leader John Hume and by some enthusiastic Labour Scottish devolutionists like John Home Robertson.[28] A similar line was taken by the Liberal Democrats, many of whose MPs represent constituencies in Scotland, Wales and peripheral regions of England.

## (vii) The pro-Referendum case

This argument was put at various times by protagonists from several of the groups described above, including Margaret Thatcher and Norman Tebbit, and the leader of the Liberal Democrats, Paddy Ashdown. Its most consistent champion, singing as often before a solo line without noticeable choral support from his own side of the House, was Tony Benn.[29]

## Did Parliament Speak?

We have seen that many different strands of opinion were expressed in the course of the debates and statements. Indeed, given the large number of participants and the loose party discipline, we can be fairly confident that every point of view with any significant public support was heard in parliament. But did one particular point of view prevail? If parliament spoke, what exactly did it say? And did it reflect or somehow absorb and translate public opinion?

In all three debates the Speaker ensured that, in addition to the usual alternation of contributions from the government and opposition sides of the chamber, the different points of view on each side of the argument were also balanced against each other. In the first debate, on 26 June, only 24 MPs were called and almost all of them had views on the European

---

[28] Ibid, c 488.

[29] HC Debate 20 November 1991, cc 333–4: 'I recognise that, when the members of the three front benches agree, I am in a minority'.

Community which were already well known to the House. There was the usual complaint about the precedence traditionally given to Privy Counsellors, most of whom were ex-ministers.[30] In the November and December debates much larger numbers of Members were called to speak (56 and 61 respectively), because of the extra time allowed, and the spread of views was probably more representative of the House of Commons as a whole. Moreover there were many contributions from Members who did not habitually take part in European or foreign affairs debates.

Neither the June nor the November debate delivered a clear message in the form of a motion. The June debate was on a formal motion for the adjournment of the House and the voting at the end followed party lines except that the Liberal Democrat spokesman joined the Conservatives in the 'no' lobby. The November debate was on a substantive motion in the name of John Major, to which Neil Kinnock, as Leader of the Opposition, had tabled an amendment, but the two texts, both running to 200 words, were contrived to highlight the differences between the Conservative and Labour front benches. Many speakers commented on the fact that the motion and the amendment did not address the real divisions in the House. Broadly speaking the voting did follow party lines, but the Labour anti-marketeers abstained on the Labour amendment and a few Bruges Group members abstained on the main question.

The December debate gave the House of Commons the opportunity to pronounce upon the outcome of the Maastricht summit. A general election now had to be held within six months (it was actually to follow in less than four months) and the vote became a test of confidence in the Prime Minister who had returned from Maastricht claiming to have won 'game, set and match'. The Conservative critics of Maastricht were naturally somewhat subdued. The Prime Minister was interrupted only from the Labour side and, apart from one or two minor interventions, one of them provoked by the federalist Hugh Dykes, the first Conservative critic to break cover was Norman Tebbit, more than three hours into the debate. The next of the critics to speak, Sir Teddy Taylor, announced that he would support the government in the vote. Of the other 'Euro-sceptics' to speak in the debate only Richard Shepherd indicated that he would vote against the government; Toby Jessel and Gerald Howarth both said that they would abstain. Thus the Conservative 'sceptics' divided three ways on the vote; Mrs Thatcher herself was present for the first day of the

---

[30] HC Deb 26 June 1991, c 1088.

debate, but absent for the vote on the second day. At the end of the debate the Liberal Democrat amendment (none had been tabled by the Labour Party) was defeated by 364 to 18 and the main motion, a short text this time which congratulated the Prime Minister and endorsed the Maastricht agreement, was carried by 339 to 253.

Looking behind these figures to the arguments deployed in the final debate, it was clear that there was a good deal of common ground between the mainstream of the Conservative and Labour parties. The European enthusiasts like Hugh Dykes and Brian Sedgemore knew that they were in the minority. Most wanted something of what was on offer at Maastricht, but were relieved to find that there was no great extension of Community competence or majority voting. Most disliked the Common Agricultural Policy and wanted to reform it. The division of opinion over the single currency issue ran deep among the economic specialists and the proposal to postpone a British decision was probably the only one that could have commanded a majority in the House. The Social Charter argument produced an almost straight Conservative/Labour split and was close to the agenda of domestic politics, but though it provided a convenient rallying point for the supporters of both parties, few speakers presented this as the crunch issue for the future of Europe.

If the Conservative critics of Maastricht did not in the end make a big impact it was partly because John Major had turned his handling of the negotiations into an issue of confidence and an election was looming. Conservative hostility to Maastricht would revive following the Danish electorate's rejection of the Treaty in June 1992 and some would claim that this event opened the way for a renegotiation of aspects of the Treaty with which they had never been happy.

While the Prime Minister's pragmatic view of the European Community prevailed in December, there was an undercurrent to all the European debates which revealed an uneasiness about the state of public opinion. The November debate was dominated by the question of whether or not there should be a referendum in Britain on the new European Treaty, as there would be in Denmark and Ireland and and as there had been over British membership of the Community in 1975.[31] A strange alliance of Margaret Thatcher, Tony Benn and Paddy Ashdown argued strongly for the referendum, but they were opposed by both the Conservative and Labour front benches. It was Tony Benn who declared on 20 November,

---

[31] As it turned out there would also be a referendum in France, though this was not a constitutional requirement.

'We have had a marvellous debate about Europe, but none of us has discussed our relationship with the people who sent us here'.[32] The referendum issue also produced an electric clash on 21 November between the two former Conservative Prime Ministers, Sir Edward Heath and Margaret Thatcher. Sir Edward quoted Mrs Thatcher's own words from 1975 to the effect that a referendum 'would bind and fetter parliamentary sovereignty'. She retorted that she had loyally upheld a policy inherited from Sir Edward and asked 'how people can make their views known when all the parties take the same view but each is divided?', to which Sir Edward replied that 'this is an occasion which constantly occurs in parliamentary history'.[33]

Some MPs claimed that government policy on the European Community did reflect the views of their constituents (Sir Michael Marshall on 21 November, Sir Norman Fowler and Sir Antony Durant on 11 December), but others were equally certain that there was no popular mandate for Maastricht (Ian Paisley on 21 November, Gwyneth Dunwoody on 18 December). The truth was, perhaps, that Parliament could not adequately reflect the views of the public, because few members of the public had really had occasion to turn their minds to the matter. After the treaty was concluded in December 1991 copies were made available free of charge to members of the public pending the publication of the Command Paper edition on 7 May 1992, but only some 100 copies were sent out.[34] Despite their high profile in Parliament, the negotiations on political, economic and monetary union had not set people talking in pubs and clubs. Parliament could have decided to hold a referendum, but it would then have been faced with the problem of explaining to the general public a complex and obscure agreement to amend an existing, but also complex and obscure treaty. And yet without such a test of opinion MPs could only guess at what their constituents might make of it all. The question of the appropriateness of the referendum as an instrument to legitimate future moves towards European integration would return to haunt ministers in coming years.

---

[32] HC Deb 20 November 1991, c 334.
[33] HC Deb 21 November 1991, cc 464–5.
[34] HC Deb 9 June 1992, vol 209, c 86w.

## Influencing the Government

Did Parliament have any impact on the government's negotiating stance at Maastricht? An answer can only be provisional—the public record does not reveal the tactics and motives of ministers and the different factors in their minds. Certainly there was no doubt that Conservative ministers were aware that at the end of the day they would have to justify their decisions to the House of Commons and obtain votes of approval, both for the general outcome of Maastricht and for the legislation to amend the European Communities Act which would have to be passed before Britain could ratify the new Treaty. Given the psychological gulf between the main parties after a long spell of Conservative Party government, it is unlikely that they ever contemplated relying on Labour or Liberal Democrat MPs to achieve a majority, so their strategy had to be to secure the solid support of the great majority of Conservative MPs.

At the beginning of the June debate Douglas Hurd, the Foreign Secretary, outlined what he regarded as a consensual UK negotiating stance which could command majority support in the House of Commons. The significance of the subsequent debates was that they gave the House the opportunity to decide whether the Government had stuck sufficiently closely to its opening position in the course of the negotiations. Those MPs who were most anxious to keep the government on course, or, in Mrs Thatcher's terminology, to prevent it from going 'wobbly', strove hard to define the lines beyond which their personal support would be uncertain. Responding to this challenge, Mr Hurd and Mr Major worked equally hard to reassure the House that the battle against federalism had been fought and won in the IGC on 30 September 1991 (the rejection of the first Netherlands presidency draft which put everything into the Treaty of Rome) and that in December *all* the British objectives set out in the November debate had been met. To an impartial observer it might have appeared that the Government had given some ground in the lead in to Maastricht, for example over modest extensions of Community competence, but these 'concessions' were turned around and presented as useful redefinitions.

It does appear, without the knowledge which the publication of confidential papers and candid memoirs may eventually bring, that the government's room for manoeuvre was significantly curtailed by what was happening in parliament, and in particular by the fact that following the replacement of Margaret Thatcher by John Major as Conservative Prime Minister in November 1990, there was an unusually large number of senior Conservative ex-cabinet ministers on the back benches, forming a kind of informal senate to which the new Prime Minister had to show some deference as a matter of internal party politics. Perhaps it is always true in British parliamentary practice that ministers are more concerned with the criticisms coming from their own side of the House than with those coming from the opposition. On the European issues this was particularly apparent and attracted frequent comment from the Labour side.[35]

On the other hand the existence of this ex-ministerial group was well known to the other member state governments—Margaret Thatcher's speeches and her clashes with Sir Edward Heath were headline news in several EC states—and may have served to strengthen the hands of British ministers in arguing for a line which they hoped to follow anyway. On 20 November John Major, though speaking to the House of Commons, addressed himself to the other eleven governments, warning them not to expect the UK to back down at the last moment: 'I urge them not to make that misjudgment'.[36] Certainly the other governments, particularly those of France and Germany, seem to have concluded that there was no point in trying to steamroller British ministers into concessions which they would be unable to defend in the House of Commons. In his speech on 26 June Sir Edward Heath, who as Prime Minister had negotiated British entry to the European Community, recalled the incredulity of other European ministers at the British habit, or constitutional requirement, of subjecting ministers to interrogation at each stage of a negotiation and expecting them to give solemn undertakings about it.[37] On this occasion, as in the past, ministers seem to have exploited what might have been a liability and turned it into an advantage.

---

[35] Eg from Gerald Kaufman, HC Deb 21 November 1991, c 1021.

[36] HC Deb 20 November 1991 c 270. F W Mayer has observed, 'Having one's hands tied can be quite useful in extracting concessions from an opponent in negotiation. US negotiators, for example, have long used the threat of congressional rejection as a device for leveraging concessions at the bargaining table'—F W Mayer, 'Managing domestic differences in international negotiations: the strategic use of internal side-payments', *International Organization*, vol 46, Autumn 1992, p 796.

[37] HC Deb 26 June 1991, c 1040.

## Conclusions

It is difficult to draw firm conclusions about the role of Parliament on the road to Maastricht. The conventional wisdom at the end of 1991 was that Britain had disposed of the national and parliamentary debate over the next stage of European Community development at the negotiation stage, whereas other countries would have to face the same challenges and convince their parliaments of the wisdom of the agreement at the ratification stage. Indeed John Major alluded to this in his speech of 18 December, noting that the debate was only just beginning in other countries. Several other speakers referred to growing doubts in Germany about the wisdom of exchanging the deutschmark for a common European currency. At the time it appeared to many that the ratification process in the UK would present few problems: if the Labour Party were to win the coming election, it would probably offer to opt back in to the Social Affairs Agreement, and possibly also to embrace EMU, whereas if the Conservatives won they would use a whipped majority to overcome the resistance of the remaining unconverted 'sceptics', whose ranks would in any case be thinned by the retirement of Margaret Thatcher, Norman Tebbit and Nicholas Ridley from the Commons.

In the event the surprise outcome of the Danish referendum would temporarily halt the ratification process and fuel doubts about the treaty in several countries, including the UK and the passage of the implementing legislation would prove extremely difficult. The new Parliament elected in April 1992 would turn out to be more and not less troubled and divided over Maastricht than its predecessor.

This was not because of any particular flaw in the parliamentary monitoring of the negotiating phase. As has been demonstrated in this chapter, the EPU and EMU negotiations were debated thoroughly and at some considerable length in the House of Commons and also in the House of Lords before and after the Maastricht summit and many different views and criticisms were aired. The debate was generally well-informed and lively, despite the difficulties which the House sometimes had in obtaining, digesting and understanding the documents. Party political pressures and the imminence of the general election tended to squeeze the debate into a partisan mode to which it was not entirely suited, but the pressures were not so strong as to silence minority points of view in either party. Indeed, though the whips may have exerted some influence behind the scenes, especially ahead of the December debate, no serious attempt appears to have been made to restrain the critics. This may have been because they included senior figures on both sides of the House who felt very strongly on the issue and would have resisted pleas not to rock the boat. This was particularly true on the Conservative side where a whole generation of senior ex-cabinet ministers were actively engaged in the debate and intended to retire from Parliament at the coming election.

On the whole it seems likely that the approach of the British government to the negotiations was affected by their perception of what could be 'sold' to Parliament and that, in the absence of a referendum or other solid indications of public opinion, Parliament did represent and articulate the interests of the electorate. The provisional verdict was in favour of accepting the changes to the treaties and the creation of the European Union, but this did not mean that British parliamentary or public opinion was united on this issue, or that the process of implementing the treaty, followed by the accession of new member states and the preparation of yet further institutional changes would run smoothly thereafter.

# 11

# Legislation and Ratification: the Passage of the European Communities (Amendment) Act 1993

*Richard Ware*

## Introduction

While in normal times parliamentary business connected with the European Community has consisted of a multitude of separate items, most of which have been dealt with by a relatively small group of members in committee or late at night, the 1992/93 parliamentary session was dominated by 'Europe' to an extraordinary degree. There were two main reasons for this. One was simply the run of new and unexpected events affecting the ratification of the Maastricht Treaty—the first Danish referendum of June 1992, the exchange rate mechanism crisis of 16 September 1992 and the French referendum in its aftermath, the Edinburgh summit of December 1992, the second Danish referendum of May 1993. The other was the sheer complexity and time-consuming nature of the parliamentary method of validating and implementing EC treaties as it has emerged in the UK. Both the unexpected turns of events and the procedural complexities were fully exploited by those British MPs who opposed the treaty.

The previous chapter examined the ways in which parliament monitored the events leading up to the adoption of the Maastricht Treaty on European Union. The present one seeks to describe and analyze the passage of the subsequent implementing legislation through parliament, to raise questions about the nature of the parliamentary process and its rationality, and to test the accusation often made in the media at the time that the obscurity of the process, added to the obscurity of the Maastricht Treaty itself, had created a gulf of misunderstanding between legislature and electorate.

An account of the constitutional and legal difficulties which had to be overcome is followed by a brief description of the mechanics of the parliamentary process and the nature of participation in it by MPs. This is followed by an exploration of the confusion surrounding the proceedings and how it arose. From the myriad of topics covered within the ambit of the Maastricht Treaty, special attention is paid to two topics which generated particular heat and on which the legislation was amended in ways which did not prevent ratification: the Committee of the Regions and the Social Protocol. A final section asks whether different parliamentary rules and procedures would have worked better, whether parliament can be seen ultimately to have served a rational purpose and whether there might be lessons in all of this for the future, given that there seems to be every likelihood that the EC member states, already committed by Article N.2 of the Maastricht Treaty to a further review in 1996, will want to make further changes to the basic treaties at least once within the next decade.

## Maastricht and the British Constitution

Following the adoption of the Maastricht Treaty on European Union on 10 December 1991 John Major returned to the House of Commons to announce a victory 'game, set and match' for the British negotiating position and, a few days later, secured a vote approving the treaty (see previous chapter). A British general election was now imminent and this made it virtually impossible to depart from the partisan line which had prevailed during earlier debates on the draft treaties. On paper the Conservative government still had a majority of 88 over all other parties combined in the House of Commons and, although six Conservative MPs voted against the government at the end of the debate on 19 December[1] and 20 were absent or abstained, there was no difficulty in carrying the day and no need to look for bipartisan support of the kind which had been vital in 1972 to secure the passage of the original European Communities Act.

The general election of 9 April 1992 changed the parliamentary arithmetic, reducing the Conservative majority over all other parties to 21, fewer than the number of Conservative MPs unhappy and prepared to rebel over the Maastricht Treaty (22 on Second Reading, 27 on the 'paving' motion, 41 on third reading). By the time of the final Maastricht votes the Conservative majority over all other parties had been reduced to 18 by the loss of one by-election and the death of another sitting member. These facts were to colour the events of the next 15 months as the

---

[1] John Biffen, John Browne, Nicholas Budgen, Richard Shepherd, Norman Tebbit and Bill Walker—HC Deb 19 December 1991, cc 553-5.

European Communities (Amendment) Bill wound its way tortuously through both Houses of Parliament.

The precise connection between the legislation and the Maastricht Treaty was to be a matter of confusion to many during this period. The Treaty of Rome established a procedure for its own amendment in Article 236 which lays down that, following the adoption of amendments, by common accord (ie unanimity) at a conference of representatives of the member state governments, these amendments 'shall enter into force after being ratified by all the Member States *in accordance with their respective constitutional requirements'* (emphasis added).

In the other member states the procedures were generally much clearer, although not free of their own difficulties. In most of them the constitutional requirements involved the approval of the text of the treaty by parliament or parliament and referendum and in some there was also a requirement for amendments to be made to the constitution. In Britain, in the absence of a written constitution, the constitutional requirement for amending Treaty of Rome obligations rests on a body of rules and practices which were developed at the time of accession to the EC, and subsequently, to meet the peculiar characteristics of the EC treaties and their legal consequences.

Ratification is the expression by a state of its consent to be bound by a treaty. The formal process is usually carried out by a letter of notification addressed to the state (in this case Italy, the original depositary of the Treaty of Rome) which is acting as the depositary for the treaty instruments. British governments formally ratify treaties by a letter of notification and by symbolically attaching the Great Seal to a facsimile of the treaty concerned.

In the United Kingdom ratification of treaties is still done under prerogative powers. The term 'prerogative' or 'royal prerogative' denotes the residual power of the British monarch to act, through ministers of the Crown, without the express authority of parliament. Many international agreements are signed using prerogative powers and enter into force immediately on signature, giving no opportunity for parliamentary approval, but these are usually agreements of a technical or commercial nature. Agreements on larger and more permanent issues, particularly where these require domestic legislation, are usually negotiated on the responsibility of ministers and are signed by ministers, but provide for a ratification process before the United Kingdom is finally bound by the treaty.

The British parliament does not ratify treaties. Even in countries where parliaments are directly involved in the ratification process their deliberations form the internal constitutional prerequisite for ratification, but not the act of ratification itself. Oppenheim notes in a footnote that 'the expression, "Parliament has ratified" a certain treaty, though occasionally met with, is objectionable when used of a British treaty. Parliament, if invited by the Government to do so, may authorise the government to ratify a treaty, but it is the Crown, upon the advice of ministers responsible, which ratifies a treaty. Legislation may be necessary to give effect to the treaty, but that is not ratification'.[2]

The British parliament's role in respect of treaties which do not require specific parliamentary approval or legislation is governed by what is known as the Ponsonby Rule and by subsequent practice. The rule states that all treaties which require ratification are laid before parliament for at least 21 days before they are ratified.[3] The Ponsonby Rule belongs to the category of conventions rather than laws. It has no statutory basis and was first introduced as a voluntary undertaking by a Labour government in April 1924, but has been observed and upheld by all governments since 1935.

Ambiguity about the implications of the rule is reflected in the editors' commentary on the Ponsonby Rule which appeared in the 1924 edition of the *British Year Book of International Law*. The editors quote Arthur Ponsonby's announcement and then add:

No machinery is introduced which renders a formal expression of Parliamentary concurrence necessary; neither a resolution approving the treaty, still less an Act of Parliament, will be required. It is the absence of disapproval which will be taken as the sanction of the legislators assembled in Parliament. It is publicity and opportunity for discussion and criticism which the new system is intended to ensure.

Technically publicity is not the same as Parliamentary control. From the point of view of the constitutional expert they are radically different, but publicity, coupled with assurance of opportunity of

---

[2] R Jennings & A Watts (eds), *Oppenheim's International Law*, ninth edition, Longman, Harlow, 1992, vol 1, 1227. The issue is treated in a broader constitutional context in Chapter 2.

[3] C J Boulton (ed), Erskine May's *Treatise on the Law, Privileges, Proceedings and Usages of Parliament*, 21st edition, Butterworths, London, 1989, p 215.

Parliamentary discussion if called for, achieves the same purpose as Parliamentary control and achieves it in a much more elastic form, as no Parliamentary action will be called for in the case of a treaty which provokes no serious criticism.[4]

Despite the formal distinction which has always been maintained between the act of ratification in the sense in which it is understood in international law and any parliamentary proceedings, the fact that parliament has usually been asked to approve important treaties (and, in the pre-war period, to approve *their ratification*), has reinforced the assumption that the real purpose of the Ponsonby Rule was not simply 'publicity', but to obtain the approval of parliament for important treaties. The assumption is reinforced by the pragmatic consideration that it is lack of information and lack of time which normally makes parliamentary control of the executive imperfect and the Ponsonby Rule was designed to ensure that in the case of treaties requiring ratification parliament would be guaranteed both.

Speaking on the European Parliamentary Elections Bill in 1978 the then Foreign Secretary, Dr Owen, gave the House of Commons an interpretation of the significance of the Ponsonby Rule:

In Britain confusion often arises because the outward form of our constitutional procedures disguises the underlying reality of parliamentary control. The prerogative to negotiate and ratify treaties belongs to the Crown and has not hitherto been fettered by statute ...

Treaties are laid before Parliament for 21 days under the so-called Ponsonby Rule before they are ratified, and if Parliament were to express objection during this time the Crown would not proceed to ratification ...

The reality of parliamentary control therefore already exists beneath the Royal Prerogative.[5]

The existence of the Ponsonby Rule and the body of parliamentary practice which has accumulated around it was a major source of the

---

[4] *British Year Book of International Law* 1924, p 191.

[5] HC Deb 2 February 1978 c 801.

confusion surrounding the British parliamentary proceedings on the Maastricht Treaty. Strictly speaking, the Ponsonby Rule was only of relevance to the parts of the Treaty which did *not* require UK legislation since those which did were unambiguously subject to parliamentary approval via the legislation itself. The fact that significant parts of the Treaty were not covered by the legislation, however, encouraged both the outright opponents of the Treaty and those who wanted to force the government to adopt the Social Policy agreement to create new opportunities for debate and voting on the treaty as a whole and to assert that passage of the legislation was a necessary, but not sufficient, part of the ratification process. This was to be the background both to the so-called 'paving debate' between second reading and the committee stage and to the final debates in both Houses on the question of the Social Protocol. The Social Protocol is the instrument by which the UK consented to the other 11 member states' using the EC institutions for the purpose of the Social Policy agreement, the UK having insisted on the non-applicability of this agreement to itself.[6]

The requirement for legislation for some parts of the treaty arose from the dualist approach towards international law which British courts have long adopted, that is to say, the refusal to apply international law directly in the UK unless it has been the subject of legislation by parliament. A classic statement of this position was made by Lord Atkin for the Privy Council in 1939:

> so far ... as the courts of this country are concerned, international law has no validity save in so far as its principles are accepted and adopted by our own domestic law.[7]

Since the Treaty of Rome bound the UK not just to a set of international obligations, but also to a system of law, accession to the EC in 1973 followed the passage of UK primary legislation (the European Communities Act 1972) to 'import' EC law into the UK. Abiding by the dualist approach meant that the European Communities Act 1972 was a necessary precursor to the ratification of the Accession Treaties by the United Kingdom.

---

[6] *Treaty on European Union including the Protocols and Final Act*, Cm 2485, p 117 (protocol), pp 118–120 (annexed agreement).
[7] Chung Chi Cheung v R [1939] AC 160, at 167–8.

Some constitutional lawyers have argued that accession to the EC in itself changed the British dualist approach to international law and brought Britain closer to the 'monist' approach of most continental European states, but the majority view, and that upheld by the government, has been that EC law is still only directly applicable in the UK by virtue of the European Communities Act and therefore that any changes to the Treaty of Rome must be mirrored by changes to the European Communities Act 1972. This was the reason for passing the European Communities (Amendment) Act of 1986 to cover the changes introduced by the Single European Act.[8]

The European Communities (Amendment) Bill of 1992/93 was drafted so as to legislate for those parts of the Maastricht Treaty which gave rise to Community rights and obligations under the treaties. The other sections of the Maastricht Treaty dealing with inter-governmental co-operation in home affairs, judicial matters, and foreign and security policy did not require changes in UK legislation and were therefore not covered by the Bill.

Neither the text of the European Communities (Amendment) Bill nor the explanatory memorandum which accompanied it referred to 'ratification' as such. The formal purpose of the Bill was 'to make provision consequential on the Treaty on European Union signed at Maastricht on 7th February 1992'. Therefore as with any other primary legislation the Bill could be amended by parliament and the chair was not bound to consider whether or not any particular amendment might make it impossible for the government to ratify.[9] The omission of overt references in the Bill to ratification followed previous British practice, respecting the distinction between the roles of parliament and the Crown, and had the incidental effect of making it more difficult (although not in the end impossible) for the critics of the treaty to table amendments which might have tied the government's hands, one way or the other, over final ratification.

---

[8] A discussion of the constitutional and legal significance of the European Communities Act 1972 may be found in J D B Mitchell, 'The Sovereignty of Parliament and Community Law: the Stumbling Block that isn't there', *International Affairs*, January 1979, 33–46. See also Chapter 2 *ante*.

[9] During proceedings on the Ottawa Agreements Bill in 1932 the Chairman of Ways and Means ruled: 'If Parliament refuses to pass legislation which would enable the Executive Government to give effect to the Agreements which have been entered into, that would raise a situation which it is not for me to deal with at this moment', HC Deb 28 October 1932, c 1334.

Had any amendment been adopted which left the European Communities Act 1972 incompatible with the obligations assumed under the Maastricht Treaty then the British government would have been unable to ratify the treaty (it would have been consenting to be bound by obligations which were in conflict with UK law). In this sense parliament was free to amend the Bill, but not the treaty: had it decided to exclude from the Bill any part of the treaty which definitely gave rise to Community rights and obligations, it would have rendered ratification of the treaty impossible because the British government would have been incapable of ensuring that its international obligations would be upheld by British courts. This point would also be a source of much argument and confusion during the proceedings.

Not all amendments to the Bill would necessarily have this effect. In the event a number of amendments were to be adopted, but none of them, in the government's view, produced an obstacle to ratification. The treaty was finally ratified by the UK on 2 August 1993 following the failure of the attempt by Lord Rees-Mogg to challenge its validity in the courts.[10]

## The parliamentary process and involvement of MPs

The parliamentary stages of the European Communities (Amendment) Bill commenced with its publication and introduction in the House of Commons on 7 May 1992. There followed a two-day second reading debate on 20–21 May 1992. The Commons committee stage was deferred following the rejection of the treaty by a narrow majority in the Danish referendum of 4 June 1992. This event placed the future of the treaty in grave jeopardy and encouraged its opponents in the British Conservative Party. The events of September 1992, culminating in the unplanned departure of sterling from the European Exchange Rate Mechanism (ERM), had a similar effect and the government was persuaded that it was necessary to hold a further general debate on the principle of persevering with the treaty before beginning the committee stage. This led to the 'paving' debate of 4 November 1992, so called after the complex preparatory legislation of the 1980s which had 'paved the way' for the abolition of the Greater London Council and for various privatisations.

---

[10] For a full account of which see R Rawlings, 'Legal Politics: The United Kingdom and Ratification of the Treaty on European Union (Part Two), *Public Law*, Autumn 1994, pp 367–391.

The result of this debate was a very narrow victory for the government (319:316), obtained only by virtue of the decision of the Liberal Democrats to vote with the government for the Bill to proceed.[11]

The Commons committee stage was taken on the floor of the House, in accordance with established practice for legislation of a constitutional nature. It began on 1 December 1992 and ended on 22 April 1993 having occupied 23 parliamentary days and a total of 162 hours and 45 minutes, a total which includes time taken up by points of order, but not the debate of 21 April concerning a controversial ruling by the Chairman of Ways and Means (ie the Deputy Speaker, Michael Morris, who chaired the committee stage).[12]

The report stage occupied a further two parliamentary days (4–5 May 1993) and the third reading another (20 May). In the interval between these the Danish electorate had, on 18 May, reversed its previous rejection of the Treaty in the light of the assurances gained at the Edinburgh summit. The Bill then went to the House of Lords where it received a second reading after two days of debate on 7–8 June 1993, a committee stage of 6 days (22–30 June) and report stage of 3 days (12–14 July). The House of Lords gave the Bill a third reading on 20 July and it received Royal Assent later on the same day.

Finally, both Houses debated the principle of the adoption of the Social Protocol again on 22 July, as required under a new clause added to the Bill during the Commons committee stage. The Lords approved the government motion, but the Commons failed to reach a resolution at 10pm on 22 July, whereupon the government tabled a new motion turning the issue into one of confidence and threatening its own dissident backbenchers with a snap general election should they persist in their rebellion. At the second attempt on 23 July the government received the backing it needed for the Act to come into force.

Given the prolonged opportunities for debate and the wide range of policy topics covered by the Maastricht Treaty, it is not surprising to find that a very large number of MPs—310 out of 651—made contributions to the debates. Perhaps it is more surprising that the other 341, although obliged to attend and vote at frequent intervals, remained silent. The total

---

[11] For an account see D Baker, A Gamble and S Ludlam, 'Whips or Scorpions? The Maastricht Vote and the Conservative Party', *Parliamentary Affairs*, vol 46, April 1993, pp 151–166.

[12] According to a convention which goes back to the origins of committees in the House of Commons, the Speaker never chairs committee proceedings.

of 310, which is derived from the computerised records of POLIS, (the Parliamentary On-Line Information System created by the House of Commons Library), includes 114 who contributed on only one day, in some cases with only the briefest of interventions in another's speech. Many took part on only a handful of days in debates on a particular subject such as monetary policy, culture or the regions. Even when these members are taken out of the totals, the number of regular contributors to the Maastricht debates is still high: 68 MPs have eight or more entries in the POLIS records.

The entries record contributions on a single day, except that contributions before and after 10.30 pm count twice (because the late debates are printed separately with the next day's proceedings in the daily and weekly editions of Hansard) and points of order are counted as additional to other interventions. Some MPs have high scores in the POLIS count mainly because of frequent brief interventions and points of order (for example Tony Marlow with 51 entries), while others, such as Sir Teddy Taylor and Bill Cash (37 and 36 entries respectively) also made numerous set-piece speeches. Other high scorers, such as Nigel Spearing (38), Bill Walker (28), Peter Shore and Nicholas Budgen (both 27) made many speeches and interventions. The principal front-bench spokesmen Tristan Garel-Jones (the FCO Minister of State), Sir Russell Johnston (both 29) and George Robertson (24) were also frequent speakers. The Chairman of Ways and Means kept a detailed log of the length of speeches during the committee stage and this reveals that Bill Cash was on his feet for longer than any other MP—indeed for 583 minutes of speeches and 29 minutes of points of order.[13]

It emerges from an analysis of the 68 most regular contributors that a clear majority were opponents of the Treaty, 16 of them belonging to the Labour party. Of the 31 Conservative backbenchers on the list, 19 voted against the third reading of the Bill and one other (Sir Ivan Lawrence) voted against the treaty on other occasions. The list also contains two Ulster unionist critics of the treaty: Ian Paisley and David Trimble. Thus, of the 68, 38, including most of the highest scorers, were opponents. This merely confirms that it was the opponents of the treaty who were mainly responsible for prolonging the proceedings. By doing so they forced the government to pay a high price for the treaty in terms of parliamentary time and kept alive their hope that the government would finally be forced

---

[13] Copies of the log are held by the House of Commons Library.

to abandon ratification. Until the second Danish referendum on 18 May 1993 the opponents of the treaty also hoped that their campaign would encourage Danish doubters. As John Biffen, himself an eminent 'sceptic', wrote in *The Guardian*, 'The Westminster campaign against the Maastricht Bill was substantially designed to prolong the committee stage of the Bill and thereby demonstrate the intensity and success of British scepticism. It was hoped this would influence the Danes again to vote "no" in the second referendum'.[14]

The list of regular contributors also includes groups of backbenchers on both sides who were energetic in supporting their respective front benches —with full support for the treaty as negotiated on the Conservative side and support for the treaty with the Social Agreement on the Labour side. The Conservative 'loyalists' included Mrs Edwina Currie (one of only three female MPs among the 68), Stephen Milligan, Andrew Rowe, Ian Taylor and Ray Whitney, plus the arch Euro-enthusiast Hugh Dykes. On the Labour side the 'loyalists' included Geoff Hoon (also, usefully, an MEP and constitutional lawyer), Calum Macdonald, Peter Mandelson, Giles Radice and Stuart Randall.

## Confusion: the fog of war?

'The British Parliament has been ridiculed. The public is baffled ... This week saw the nadir of confusion', announced *The Economist* on 8 May 1993.

'Politicians have been playing procedural games that have harmed the reputation of Parliament and damaged the standing of Britain's legislative democracy' declared *The Independent*, while the *Daily Telegraph* began its editorial: 'To the vast majority of electors, the manoeuvres by the Government in the House of Commons over the Maastricht Treaty's Social Chapter will be well-nigh incomprehensible'. *The Financial Times* weighed in with 'it is becoming increasingly difficult to resist the feeling that the parliamentary procedures which have been on display are unbecoming to Parliament and profoundly ill-adapted to the ratification of this kind of international agreement'.[15]

---

[14] 28 July 1993.
[15] Apart from *The Economist*, all the quotations are from the editions of 6 May 1993.

These were reactions to the announcement by the Foreign Secretary, Douglas Hurd, on 5 May that the government would acquiesce on report stage amendment 2, excluding the Social Protocol which was attached to the Maastricht Treaty from the coverage of the European Communities (Amendment) Bill, ie accepting it without a vote. The announcement followed logically from his statement almost three months earlier, on 15 February 1993, in respect of the similarly worded amendment 27 that, although undesirable, such an amendment would not prevent ratification. On the earlier occasion the government had been temporarily saved from further embarrassment by the decision of the Chairman of Ways and Means not to allow a vote on amendment 27, but at report stage the Speaker had taken a different view of amendment 2. Consequently the Foreign Secretary now had to tell the House of Commons that, despite the amendment being undesirable, he would not call on the government's supporters to vote against it; as for ratification, the outcome of the vote would be irrelevant. By contrast, on 20 January the minister of state, Tristan Garel-Jones, on the strength of legal advice which was now regarded as wrong, had said that, 'under the terms of the amendment, United Kingdom law would not conform to the Treaty's provisions, so it would be impossible for the United Kingdom to ratify the Treaty'.[16]

On 15 February 1993 the Foreign Secretary made a statement to the House of Commons in which he referred back to this statement by the minister of state and regretted that it had been incorrect. He said that the law officers had been consulted on the point and had concluded that the passing of the amendment would not after all prevent ratification of the treaty by the United Kingdom:

> In summary, the Law Officers consider that, while incorporation of the Protocol in domestic law is desirable, it is not necessary for ratification or implementation of the Maastricht Treaty. In other words, there would be no impediment to ratification if the amendment were carried because acts adopted under the Protocol would still not apply to the United Kingdom.[17]

In his responses to questions Mr Hurd explained that the government now regarded the inclusion of the Social Protocol in the list of texts

---

[16] HC Deb 20 January 1993 c 403.
[17] HC Deb 15 February 1993 c 27.

covered by the European Communities Act as desirable 'for the sake of completeness and tidiness', but no longer essential. In response to Mr Hoon's question about possible action in the Court of Justice on behalf of UK citizens he accepted that the possibility of a conflict of law was indeed the consideration which made the inclusion of the Social Protocol desirable, but the question was now whether or not this consideration 'implies or constitutes necessity'. The advice of the law officers was that it did not.[18]

The government's change of mind about the necessity of bringing the Social Protocol within the scope of the European Communities Act 1972 earned it much derision within the Commons chamber and in the media and undermined confidence in ministerial presentation of all the legal issues surrounding the treaty. At first glance the fuss may seem puzzling because the government itself had made so much of the fact that the Social Policy agreement reached by the other 11 states would *not* apply to the United Kingdom. Its omission from the British legislation might have seemed to be merely a logical reflection of this position. However, the Social Policy Agreement was contained in the Maastricht Treaty merely as an annex to the Social Protocol, whereas the Social Protocol itself, a treaty text to which all twelve signatories were parties, encapsulated Britain's 'opt-out' and gave Britain's consent to the others using the EC institutions for the Social Agreement. It had originally been the view of the FCO lawyers that it was necessary to give the Protocol the legal authority of the European Communities Act 1972 in order to protect the non-application of the agreement to the UK from possible legal challenges, for example, from trade unions claiming discrimination against British workers. Moreover the dualist approach to the problem of reconciling UK and EC law had in the past always led government lawyers to draft amendments to the European Communities Act in such a way as to avoid any possible conflict between the two systems. So it had been with the Single European Act (via the European Communities (Amendment) Act 1986) and with the initial version presented to parliament of the European Communities (Amendment) Bill of 1992/93.

When the committee stage resumed after this volte-face on 22 February the opposition successfully obtained an unscheduled debate on its implications when the Chairman of Ways and Means allowed the arguments to be pursued for four and a half hours on the technical motion

---

[18] Ibid, cc 30, 33.

that, 'the Chairman do report progress and ask leave to sit again'. He was later to describe this as a case of awarding injury time because of the government's 'muck up' of its legal advice.[19] The Attorney General came to the House to lend the weight of his office to the government's new stance on the legal position and at the end the government reluctantly accepted the motion without a vote, meaning that a whole day's committee proceedings had been lost.

The fact that the government was now prepared to do without a plank of its legislation which it had previously declared to be vital gave rise to speculation in the media that the government might, if frustrated over the Bill as a whole, bypass parliament altogether and ratify the treaty using prerogative powers alone. Legal sources were quoted in the newspapers to the effect that this would be perfectly possible because 'Parliament does not ratify treaties'.[20] This was a misunderstanding of the constitutional position. While there was room for argument about the Social Protocol there was no doubt that the government needed to legislate for those parts of the treaty which gave rise directly to obligations in the United Kingdom. Moreover, there was, to say the least, a strong constitutional presumption that the Crown would not ratify treaties in direct defiance of parliament and a specific statutory obligation on the government under the European Parliamentary Elections Act 1978 to gain parliamentary approval by Act of Parliament for any treaty extending the powers of the European Parliament, as the Maastricht Treaty clearly did.

If the prospect of ratification by ministerial fiat against the will of parliament was never more than a misunderstanding dressed up as a threat, the final drama of the sequence, the playing out of the consequences of New Clause 74 (adopted in committee on 22 April 1993) was surrounded by genuine constitutional and legal doubt. The New Clause, which became section 7 of the European Communities (Amendment) Act, prevented the Act from entering into force until such time as both Houses of Parliament had arrived at resolutions on the subject of the Social Protocol. As long as both Houses arrived at resolutions and the House of Commons, as the elected chamber, resolved in favour of the government's approach, the

---

[19] Transcript from *Westminster Live*, BBC, 14 April 1993.

[20] According to Baker, Gamble and Ludlam the rumours were fuelled by comments made by the Home Secretary, Kenneth Clarke, in a TV interview during the weekend of 13/14 February—'The Parliamentary Siege of Maastricht', *Parliamentary Affairs* Vol.47 No.1, January 1994, p 41; a misleading article in the *Guardian* on 12 February may also have played a part—Rawlings, p 264.

government could ratify without difficulty. It was also apparent that if there were no resolution at all the Act would not be in force and the government could not ratify. Doubt surrounded the third possibility, namely that the House of Commons might adopt an opposition wording for the resolution which called upon the government not to ratify until it had committed itself to the Social Policy Agreement by reversing the opt-out in the Social Protocol.

There could have been endless argument, and indeed there was much speculation in advance, about the extent to which such a resolution would have been binding and how the government could have extricated itself from the political and diplomatic difficulties which would have arisen. The opposition claimed consistently that the other member states would cooperate readily to overcome the legal problems involved in re-writing the Protocol at this late stage (it having been ratified already in its present form by all but Germany and Britain), but this pre-supposed that the Conservative government was able and willing to swallow its consistent rejection of the Social Policy agreement as a pernicious threat to employment. In the event the opposition wording was rejected, but at the first attempt the government failed to win its own version of the resolution. Only at a second attempt, by threatening a dissolution, did it eventually win the day. The procedural saga of the Social Protocol is discussed in more detail below.

It is not surprising that little of this was fully understood outside Westminster and that even at Westminster there was much confusion. However, it was the seemingly endless duration of the debates, and the apparent irrelevance to life outside in the streets of Britain of so much that was said, which gave the Maastricht proceedings such a bad name with political journalists and, indirectly, with the public at large. Perhaps parliamentary tactics designed to prolong debate, in order to win concessions, will never win their proponents awards for oratory and will never be fully appreciated outside parliament.[21] Few parliaments allow opposition parties and backbenchers as much scope as does the British one to harry governments with the weapon of parliamentary time in circumstances where a guillotine motion cannot be passed for political or constitutional reasons. However, it should be remembered that British

---

[21] These tactics were frequently described as 'trench warfare', a further confirmation of Paul Fussell's thesis (developed in *The Great War and Modern Memory*) that the imagery of the trenches has left a profound and lasting imprint on all areas of British life.

governments do have ways of blunting this weapon by letting debates run on into the night and moving for the closure of debate at regular intervals. The government's difficulty during the Maastricht debates was that it did not command a reliable majority even on the technical votes required to manage the timetable and often preferred to adjourn having made slight progress, rather than face defeat, even on a purely procedural motion. It was probably handicapped by the suspicion of the government whips that there were many more potential dissidents on its own benches than was apparent in the voting lobbies and more heavy-handed whipping tactics might have been counter-productive.

This vulnerability in turn reflected a distinct lack of enthusiasm for the Maastricht Treaty among Conservative Party activists and, most probably, although the proposition was never properly tested, among the electorate at large. After all, the Prime Minister's long-serving Conservative predecessor, now Baroness Thatcher, was herself a passionate opponent of Maastricht and would soon urge the House of Lords to reject it. Anti-Maastricht backbenchers in both the Labour and Conservative parties were constantly urging their leaders to capitalise on the perceived unpopularity of the treaty by using the many adverse events since its adoption as an excuse for a change of mind. It was in order to reconcile the tensions in its own ranks and to argue that the treaty could have been to the advantage of ordinary working people, that the Labour Party in Parliament seized on the deliberate exemption of the United Kingdom from the Social Policy agreement as the central point of its case against the Conservative government's handling of the treaty.

Given this political background, it is easier perhaps to understand why the parliamentary proceedings appeared to be such a mess. Had the Bill passed through parliament in a more tidy fashion and at a faster tempo this would hardly have reflected the mixed feelings towards it of parliamentarians and public alike. The referendum campaigns in Denmark and France had exposed similar anxieties and hesitations in those countries; even in Germany, widely regarded as the country whose needs and aspirations had been most influential on the drafting of the Maastricht Treaty, opinion polls would soon begin to indicate deep divisions.

## Representing the Regions[22]

The treaty provides in Article 198A that a Committee of the Regions with advisory status should be established, using the staff and facilities of the Economic and Social Committee in Brussels, to give opinions to the Commission and the Council of Ministers on matters defined by the treaty as including education and training, culture, public health, trans-European networks, cohesion, the Structural Funds and the Regional Fund. The committee also has the power to provide opinions for the Council and Commission on its own initiative.

The creation of such a committee in itself roused few passions in the House of Commons, but there was controversy about the composition and distribution of the members representing the United Kingdom. Article 198A specifies only that these members should be 'representatives of regional and local bodies'.

The Labour, Liberal Democrat, Scottish and Welsh Nationalist, and Ulster Unionist parties all tabled amendments at committee stage which sought to provide that the UK representatives should be appointed from among councillors elected to local authorities (amendments 28, 273) or, more radically, that they should be directly elected by a college of local authority councillors (amendments 106, 107, 431, 432, new clauses 63 and 64). Other amendments and new clauses sought to secure maximum representation of Scotland and Wales (amendment 438, new clauses 26, 41, 63). Other proposals were that Scotland should be represented by its eight MEPs (amendment 111), and that the Scottish and Welsh members of the Committee should reflect proportionately the votes cast for political parties at the 1989 European elections (new clause 41).

Debate on the lead amendment tabled by the Labour opposition (no 13) was opened on 4 February 1993.[23] The shadow Foreign Secretary Dr Jack Cunningham emphasised that both Europe-wide and UK local authority associations were 'almost unanimous' in accepting the principle of amendment 28.[24] He also pointed out that local authorities were responsible for implementing much the greater part of European Community (EC) law.

---

[22] The author is grateful to David Millar for the analysis used in this section.
[23] HC Deb 4 February 1993 c 503.
[24] Ibid, c 509.

Replying for the government, the Minister of State, Foreign and Commonwealth Office, Tristan Garel-Jones, stated that 'There are a range of national, regional and cultural interests of some importance and consequence that would not necessarily be adequately represented ...' if amendment 28 was agreed to. The minister made some play with the fact that the governments of Greece and Netherlands had already stated that they would nominate both elected and non-elected representatives of local authorities. He went on to state that he was 'not prepared to commit HMG to a guarantee that the 24 [titular UK] members appointed to the Committee of Regions will be elected local government councillors' and pointed out that committee business could claim two days' work each week from its members and that many elected councillors could not devote this amount of time to it.[25]

The Ulster Unionist MP, John D Taylor, thought that members of the Committee of the Regions should be elected councillors and he asked for two to represent Northern Ireland, as did Peter Hain (Labour) for Wales.[26]

The Liberal Democrat spokesman, Sir Russell Johnston, did not exclude the possibility of a mixed system, comprising both councillors and non-elected representatives of regional and local bodies. Turning to the distribution of committee members, he argued that, although on a population basis England should have 20, Scotland 2, and Wales and Northern Ireland one each, Scotland and Wales required stronger representation than this to take account of geographical factors and of the four-party system there.[27]

A Conservative backbencher, Michael Alison, accepted that some UK representatives to the committee could be elected councillors, but pointed out that the periods of appointment of the committee and of local government mandates in the UK were not synchronised, and that a committee member, by losing his or her seat in the UK, could cause disruption in the committee's work.[28] After five hours the debate was adjourned, this being one of the occasions when the government business managers decided not to prolong discussion after 10.00 pm. Geoff Hoon, who was speaking at the time, was to resume his speech only after an interval of three weeks.

---

[25] HC Deb 4 February 1993 cc 515, 517, 527.

[26] Ibid, c 530.

[27] Ibid, c 568.

[28] Ibid, c 571.

In the resumed debate on 25 February 1993, many points were repeated, but the distribution of Committee members was raised by Mrs Margaret Ewing (Scottish Nationalist), who called for a minimum of eight seats for Scotland, to be filled by direct election by local councillors or, failing that, in proportion to the votes cast for parties in Scotland at the last European election.[29] Speaking for Plaid Cymru, Ieuan Wyn Jones called for four members for Wales on grounds of geographical and political representation; he accepted that they need not all be elected councillors.[30]

Summing up for the Labour opposition, Joyce Quin, a former MEP, argued that business interests were already represented in the EC's Economic and Social Committee and in other bodies; and that the UK members of the Committee should be nominated in accordance with the political complexion of each English region and of Scotland, Wales and Northern Ireland. Like many other MPs, she believed that the Committee of the Regions would come to play a substantial role in the EC.[31]

For the government, Mr Garel-Jones said that he valued the views of MPs on the composition and distribution of the Committee of the Regions and that the government had come to no decisions on this.[32] The inclusion of elected councillors was not ruled out; consultations would be carried out; and Conservatives would not be unduly favoured. After three hours, the debate was closed by a government majority of 29 and the government went on to win easily a vote defeating the probing lead amendment because most opposition members abstained.

However, the division on the key amendment, no 28, which sought simply to ensure that committee members should be drawn from elected local government representatives, did not take place until 8 March when it was carried by 314 votes to 292. This, the first amendment to be carried in committee, ensured that the Bill would have to be given a report stage on the floor of the House, a fact which was of some significance both to the official opposition, because of its campaign in favour of the Social Protocol and to the anti-treaty Conservatives who hoped for another opportunity to defeat the legislation. On 8 March 26 Conservatives voted with Labour, the Liberal Democrats and the Ulster Unionists in favour of

---

[29] HC Deb 25 February 1993 cc 1038–39.
[30] Ibid, c 1046.
[31] Ibid, cc 1053–54.
[32] Ibid, c 1062.

the amendment; the Scottish and Welsh Nationalists voted with the government against it.[33]

After this vote, Labour accused the Nationalists of trying to make deals with the government in order to secure more places for their party on the Committee of the Regions, and extracts from correspondence between the Secretary of State for Scotland and Mrs Ewing, were published in Scottish newspapers.[34] The Scottish Secretary later denied that any 'deal' had been struck with Mrs Ewing but the incident caused major repercussions within her party.[35]

At the report stage of the Bill ministers were faced with the options of asking the House to reverse amendment 28, or to accept that only elected councillors should be appointed to the Committee of the Regions. Bearing in mind, perhaps, that the Ulster Unionists had voted for the amendment and that their support might be crucial to the further progress of the Bill, the government accepted the decision of the committee of the whole House.

On 4 May Mr Garel-Jones therefore moved a new clause giving effect to the principle of amendment 28, but in different words:

A person may be proposed as a member or alternate member for the UK of the Committee of the Regions ... only if, at the time of the proposal, he is an elected member of a local authority.

The minister stated that the government had always envisaged some— indeed even a large majority—of the members of the committee being elected councillors, and would have preferred sufficient flexibility to have permitted the appointment of representatives of business.[36]

Mrs Ewing emphasised that the Scottish Nationalist party had sought plurality and consultation in the nomination of Scottish members of the committee. For the Ulster Unionists, John D Taylor reminded the House of his party's vote in favour of elected councillors, and sought a fair representation in numbers for Northern Ireland.[37]

---

[33] HC Deb 8 March 1993 cc 715–718.

[34] *The Scotsman*, 9 March 1993.

[35] A detailed account of this incident and its aftermath by Peter Jones of *The Scotsman* was published as 'Playing the Westminster Numbers Game' *Scottish Affairs*, no 5, Autumn 1993, pp 26–40.

[36] HC Deb 4 May 1993, c 61.

[37] Ibid, cc 49, 56.

Only after the Bill had received the Royal Assent did the government announce that five seats had been allocated to Scotland, three to Wales, two to Northern Ireland and 14 to England. When the Scottish names were announced, they consisted of two Labour, one Conservative, one Independent and one Scottish Nationalist as the titular members of the Committee, and of two Labour, one Conservative, one Independent and one Liberal Democrat as the alternate members. Thus the Scottish Secretary had been successful in securing, as he had undertaken to do, a strong representation for Scotland; and room was created for a Scottish Nationalist member of the committee. The Scottish Liberal Democrats complained that their single alternate member under-represented their strength.[38]

The majority of members of the new Committee of the Regions from all member states would in fact be elected councillors, at regional, municipal or local level. The nomination of non-elected officials (Queen's Commissioners in the Netherlands and Nomarchs in Greece) was justified by their unique role in the respective systems of provincial and local government in these countries.

In Britain this apparently minor issue had taken on a particular significance, partly because it connected with a wider debate about the nature of democratic accountability in the new European Union and partly because it was symbolically important to the nationalist and unionist parties which, although they had only 24 MPs altogether at Westminster, now represented a crucial element in the parliamentary arithmetic of the Maastricht Bill. The final key ingredient in the argument was that the outcome did not affect the Government's ability to ratify the treaty.

## The Social Protocol: in or out?

The question of the Social Protocol opt-out had been central to the partisan debate across the House of Commons when the treaty was first brought back to the House in December 1991 and was the principal bone of contention between the two front benches in all the subsequent general debates, including those on second reading and on the motion to proceed (the 'paving debate'), so it was no surprise that this should also provide

---

[38] More remarkable, however, was the fact that the huge South of Scotland Euro-constituency, stretching from Ayr and Stranraer in the West to the North Sea coast and South to the Border, was not represented at all. HC Deb 8 July 1994 c 363w.

the recurrent theme of the detailed consideration in committee and on report.

The committee debates were organised around clusters of amendments which had a thematic unity, although they might relate to different parts of the Bill. The order of debates was determined by the position of the lead amendment in each cluster according to the usual rules for committee stages of bills. Other amendments selected for debate with a particular subject cluster would not necessarily be voted on at all, unless the chairman so decided, but if selected for voting, the vote would take place at the appropriate point in the consideration of the Bill, which might be long after the amendment had been debated.

Debate on the 'social policy' cluster of amendments began on 20 January and continued on 27 January 1993. There were six amendments selected in this group, but the one with the greatest political impact, amendment 27, fell last in the group and was therefore not due to be voted on immediately, if at all. It added the words 'with the exception of the Protocol on Social Policy' as a qualification to the phrase 'Protocols adopted at Maastricht on that date and annexed to the Treaty' in the list of items to be inserted in section 1(2) of the European Communities Act 1972. In practice virtually all the debate focused on amendment 27 to the exclusion of the other amendments in the group.

There were many cross-currents to the debate. A group of Conservative sceptics, including Iain Duncan Smith, Lord Tebbit's successor as the Member for Chingford, who made a much-quoted speech, had argued vigorously that the opt-out was worthless because objectionable legislation in the social field could be imposed on the United Kingdom by future judgments of the European Court of Justice, building on provisions in the Single European Act and the main text of the Maastricht Treaty. For these Conservatives this was an additional reason to reject the whole treaty. For others the Social Protocol opt-out was the ultimate confirmation of the Government's wisdom and the fact that made Maastricht acceptable. While rejecting once again the Labour frontbench argument and tactics, the Minister of State, Tristan Garel-Jones, was at even greater pains to refute the legal arguments of his honourable friend, Iain Duncan Smith, in the face of a barrage of questions and observations from the Conservative Euro-sceptics.[39] These revealed the depths of suspicion and distaste on the Conservative benches for the European Court and its method of

---

[39] HC Deb 27 January 1993, c 1053.

interpreting European Community law.[40] While his critics dwelt on the iniquities of the Court, Mr Garel-Jones preferred to emphasize the strength of Britain's position in the Council and to underline that Britain had never been outvoted on an occasion when qualified majority voting was possible. While acknowledging that criticism of the court had sometimes been justified in the past, he emphasized that it was now 'less inventive in its interpretation of Community law' and more tolerant of exceptions and derogations.[41]

A similar view, also from the Conservative side, was that the Social Policy Agreement was greatly over-rated and would turn out to be a non-event.[42] This was a minority view, but it helped some Conservative 'sceptics' to justify voting with the opposition in the attempt to prevent ratification. On the opposition side the Labour critics of Maastricht were delighted to be able to support their own front bench in the belief that amendment 27 would prevent ratification.[43]

Throughout the debate of 20 and 27 January it was assumed by all the participants that sooner or later there would be a separate vote on amendment 27. Indeed it was in anticipation of such a vote that on 15 February the Foreign Secretary announced the change of view about the legal consequences of the amendment referred to above. On 22 February George Robertson put it to the committee that, in the light of the changed legal advice, the amendment ought to be re-debated. The Chairman of Ways and Means was not at liberty to re-run the debate on the amendments, but he agreed, as we have seen above, to allow a debate on the dilatory motion (ie that the chairman do report progress etc) strictly confined to the implications of the Foreign Secretary's statement. This was the debate in which the Attorney General enlarged on the legal position and other Members, lawyers and non-lawyers alike, made the most of the government's obvious embarrassment. Donald Anderson, a Labour lawyer, for example, claimed:

> With the best will in the world, the Committee is not at its best when it tries to come to a conclusion on what may be a narrow technical and legal point. There is a whole host of witnesses—'a cloud of witnesses', as the old book would say, and the word 'cloud' may be relevant in the

---

[40] Eg Michael Spicer, c 1054, Sir Teddy Taylor, c 1058, Michael Lord, c 1068.
[41] Ibid, cc 1056–7.
[42] Eg Sir Teddy Taylor, c 1063.
[43] Eg Ron Leighton, c 1072.

context. Sir Anthony Lester has said one thing and the gentleman who writes research notes for the Library has said another. Mr Alan Watkins, the lawyer manqué of *The Observer*, has written a third thing. Everyone gives us the benefit of his views. What is the correct view?[44]

Bill Cash also reflected the mood of the day by quoting Humpty Dumpty on the meaning of words.[45]

At this stage it was still generally anticipated that amendment 27 would be the subject of a vote. It was therefore with some surprise that on 30 March the House received the Chairman of Ways and Means's decision, for which he was not required to give reasons, that there would be no separate vote on amendment 27, although there would be an opportunity to debate the newly-tabled new clause 75. The decision was upheld, after many representations had been made in public and in private, on 15 April.[46] The announcement was badly received by the opposition front bench, by the opponents of the treaty in all parts of the House, and by many commentators in the press who could not understand why the single issue which had most deeply divided the political parties in their assessment of the treaty could not, for procedural reasons, be the subject of a separate vote at this stage. The Chairman of Ways and Means had hinted at his reasoning in a BBC interview on 14 April in which he explained that new clause 75 was 'more workable' than amendment 27. In his original announcement of 30 March he had described the decision on amendment 27 as 'a corollary' of the decision on new clause 75.[47] In the TV interview he noted that the Bill had received substantial backing on second reading, which meant that the House wanted the Bill to go through. In the Chairman of Ways and Means's eyes new clause 75 was preferable 'because what it really says is that, yes, the Bill can go through, but the House shall have to have a vote after the Royal Assent on whether it now ... wants the Social Chapter in there'.[48]

---

[44] HC Deb 22 February 1993 c 712. Rawlings comments on the parliamentary battles: 'legal discourse has loomed uncommonly large in the conflict', 'Legal Politics: The United Kingdom and Ratification of the Treaty on European Union' (Part One), *Public Law*, Summer 1994, p 255.

[45] Ibid, c 716.

[46] HC Deb 15 April 1993 c 961.

[47] HC Deb 30 March 1993 c 16.

[48] BBC transcript of *Westminster Live*, 14 April 1993.

On the floor of the chamber the Chairman of Ways and Means came under sustained pressure, including implied criticism of his comments on TV. Eventually he decided to allow a short debate again on the motion to report progress in order to let the situation be discussed in a more orderly fashion. The shadow Foreign Secretary, Dr Jack Cunningham, used this opportunity to insist that a vote on new clause 75 would not be acceptable as a substitute for one on amendment 27. He cited media stories, allegedly based on official briefing, claiming that the government felt able to ignore the outcome of a vote on new clause 75, whereas they could not escape from a defeat on amendment 27.[49] This charge was emphatically denied by Tristan Garel-Jones. Later in the debate Sir Peter Emery, chairman of the Select Committee on Procedure, voiced his disquiet at the fact that the debate on the motion to report progress seemed to be turning into a series of challenges to the authority of the chair.[50] The debate ended at 6.45 pm with a 556–9 vote in favour of the closure and the committee rose again without having made any progress with the Bill.

At this point a group of MPs led by Tony Benn (who had campaigned for a referendum on the Maastricht Treaty) decided to invoke the rarely used official procedure for questioning a decision by the chair. A formal motion regretting the Chairman of Ways and Means's ruling on amendment 27 was tabled and time was allocated for it be debated on 21 April, this time with Speaker Boothroyd presiding. The debate ran until 7.00 pm (ie for 3 hrs 16 minutes) and ended with a substantial vote for the closure, followed by a heavy defeat (450–81) for Mr Benn's motion. As usual on occasions of this kind the government was represented in the debate by the Leader of the House, Tony Newton, and the shadow Leader, Mrs Margaret Beckett, spoke from the opposition front bench. Once again many different views were expressed on the procedural issues and many precedents were dusted off.

Wholehearted support for the authority of the chair was urged by Sir Peter Emery, who quoted a precedent from 1957 in which a clear distinction was made from the chair between selection for debate and selection for vote.[51] Other MPs felt that the present occasion was distinguished by the fact that the amendment on which a vote had been denied had stood in the name of the Leader of the Opposition. Tam

---

[49] HC Deb 15 April 1993 c 973–4.
[50] Ibid, cc 978, 989–990.
[51] HC Deb 21 April 1993 c 349.

Dalyell was among those who was swayed by the incomprehension of those outside the House:

> I was greatly influenced by the comments I heard in my constituency over the weekend. I do not suggest for a moment that all our constituents understand the finer points of *Erskine May*, but somehow the fact had percolated through that the House of Commons was not acting quite properly—that there was something unfair going on. In schoolboy slang, there was a general feeling that there had been a bit of a swizz ... (...) Constituents ask what the House of Commons is for if it cannot make up its mind on the question of the social chapter. They ask whether we cannot think of a way of bringing the matter to a decision.[52]

In the final vote a combination of Labour left-wingers and anti-marketeers, and Ulster unionists, supported Mr Benn's motion, as did two Conservatives (Nicholas Winterton and Anne Winterton), but a large number of Labour members, including the front bench, joined the great majority of Conservatives and Liberals in upholding the authority of the chair. Some anti-Maastricht Conservatives abstained. The House then proceeded to debate the new clauses which would have made the entry into force of the legislation dependent on a referendum. These were rejected.

It was on the next afternoon (22 April) that the committee turned to the two new clauses (new clause 74 had now joined 75 in the Chairman of Ways and Means's selection) which would create a further opportunity for debate and resolution on the Social Protocol once the Bill had received Royal Assent. This was another chance for a general debate on the merits or otherwise of the Social Protocol, but many members alluded also to the tactical considerations which might persuade Conservative opponents of Maastricht to vote with Labour and Liberal members. George Robertson, one of the originators of the amendment, described it again as a ticking time bomb because in the debate which would result from the new clauses the Leader of the Opposition would link parliamentary permission to ratify the treaty to government action on the Social Protocol. New clause 74 was duly added to the Bill when the government conceded it without a vote. In its original form it referred only to the House of Commons, but at report

---

[52] Ibid, c 372.

stage the House accepted a government amendment which required resolutions to be reached by both Houses.

Had the Bill emerged unamended from committee of the whole House it would not have been the subject of a report stage, but the Bill had now been amended considerably. Consequently there was a new opportunity to revive amendment 27, now recast as report stage amendment 2 and to petition the Speaker, rather than the Chairman of Ways and Means, for its selection. Madam Speaker selected the amendment and this led to the whole battle of the Social Protocol being fought yet again on 5 May. The Foreign Secretary described it as 'a situation comedy that runs and runs, episode by episode' and declined to enter into the issues of substance again in his speech, except in the briefest summary. There was still a good deal of legalistic fog, but the government stuck to its earlier position that the acceptance of the amendment, and hence the removal of the Social Protocol from the coverage of the Bill, although undesirable in principle, would not prevent ratification because it constituted a double negative, ie the excision from the legislation of something which was by its very nature an exemption from the treaty. Mr Hurd made much play of the 'alliance of opposites' supporting the amendment, and said that the government would acquiesce on the amendment to deprive these combined opposites of an 'entirely synthetic victory'.[53]

Once new clause 74 had been accepted the stage was set for a final climactic debate and vote after Royal Assent, but this did not prevent the Social Protocol from rearing its head once more in the Commons debate on third reading on 20 May. After this the Bill went to the House of Lords and received Royal Assent immediately after completing its Lords stages on 20 July. The debates in both Houses required by new clause 74 (now section 7 of the Act) were fixed for 22 July. There is no need to describe the first Commons debate in detail. All the old arguments were rehearsed once more, this time by the Prime Minister and Leader of the Opposition as well as by many of the Maastricht regulars. The greatest interest was created by hints from potential Conservative dissidents as to their intentions at the end of the debate. When the first vote came on the opposition amendment to the motion, the result was announced as a tie (317–317) and Speaker Boothroyd used her casting vote, in accordance

---

[53] HC Deb 5 May 1993 cc 200–201, 207.

with precedent, to defeat the amendment.[54] Later it turned out that there had been an error in the counting of the votes and the amendment had actually been defeated 318–317 without the casting vote. At this point the opposition attempt to bind the government to accede to the Social Policy agreement of the other eleven member states was definitely foiled, but the House had still to arrive at a resolution, as required by the Act.

In the second vote, this time on the Prime Minister's motion, the government was defeated 324–316 because 23 Conservative rebels had voted with the opposition and 1 had abstained, outweighing the effect of the Ulster Unionists, whose support had been assiduously courted by ministers for several weeks, who voted with the government. This result meant that there was no resolution and that therefore the European Communities (Amendment) Act had still not been brought into force and ratification could not take place. The Prime Minister rose in his seat and told the House:

> We must resolve this issue; it cannot be allowed to fester any longer. I therefore give notice that the government will invite the House to come to a resolution tomorrow in support of the Government's policy on the social chapter by tabling a motion of confidence in the following terms: That the House has confidence in the policy of Her Majesty's Government on the adoption of the Protocol on Social Policy.[55]

The Leader of the Opposition, John Smith, rose to say that he would once again seek to amend the motion, giving the House an opportunity to vote positively for the social chapter. He accused Mr Major of being 'driven to use the confidence factor because he cannot win the vote on any other terms', while Sir Russell Johnston, speaking for the Liberal Democrats and alluding to the price allegedly paid for Ulster Unionist support, said that the government 'have been willing to strengthen sectarian politics in Northern Ireland to deny workers' rights in the United Kingdom as a whole'.[56]

---

[54] By convention the chair votes for the status quo in the event of a tie. Thus the chair will vote against a second reading of a bill which will change the law and, in committee or other proceedings, against any amendment, including, as in this case, an amendment to a motion.

[55] HC Deb 22 July 1993 c 613.

[56] Ibid, c 613.

On Friday 23 July the House met again to debate the Prime Minister's new motion, knowing that during the night the Prime Minister had let it be known that he would seek a dissolution of parliament if defeated again. After a further 6 hrs 30 minutes of debate during which, inevitably, little new could be said, the opposition amendment was decisively defeated (339–301) and the Government motion carried (339–299). Only one Conservative MP, Rupert Allason, continued to defy the party whip by being absent for the vote, an action which was to lead to his suspension from the parliamentary party for a year. The House of Lords had already endorsed the government motion on the previous day, so the Commons vote finally brought the Act into force.

For all practical purposes this seemed to be the end of the story, but it is worth noting that one eminent authority was unconvinced by the procedure used and put forward the argument in *Public Law*, Autumn 1993, that the resolution adopted on 23 July did not literally comply with section 7 of the Act, from which the conclusion is drawn that 'the Act was not brought into force on July 23 and the Government did not have the parliamentary authority for ratification required by section 6 of the European Assembly Elections Act'.[57] The point was taken up on the floor of the House of Commons when it returned from the summer recess by Bill Walker, who obtained from the Speaker the promise that she would make a statement *if the need arises*.[58]

## A better way?

The handling of the Maastricht legislation by parliament was widely criticised and some aspects of it met with incredulity and even derision in the media. Pressed by Archy Kirkwood (Liberal Democrat) to consider a statement or a debate 'to get a bit of rational sanity into the way in which the House works' even the Leader of the House admitted at business questions on 20 May 1993 that 'it is not only those outside who have been bemused by some of the procedures of the House'.[59]

In fact some innovations had been introduced during the Maastricht proceedings in order to bring some greater clarity to them. For example,

---

[57] G Marshall, 'The Maastricht proceedings', *Public Law*, Autumn 1993, pp 406–7.
[58] HC Debates, 18 October 1993, cc 25–6  Rawlings endorses the Speaker's evident view that the requirement had been met—Rawlings, op cit, part one, pp 277–8 and n56.
[59] HC Deb 20 May 1993, c 372.

the addition of subject headings to the clusters of amendments and new clauses selected for debate was new and in the course of the committee stage the chair agreed to the further refinement of adding an asterisk to any amendment or new clause which appeared on the selection list for the first time. Taken together these changes meant that in addition to the lists of marshalled amendments on the order paper, which are difficult to use because they present the material in the order in which it falls on the Bill, rather than in the order it is to be debated, MPs were able to obtain on the morning of each day of debate a list of the outstanding clusters of selected amendments which served as an approximate subject 'menu' of what was to come.

The Chairman of Ways and Means had also invited representatives of all the various points of view on the treaty to meet him before the committee stage began in an effort to agree on a sensible approach. This may have reduced the amount of time devoted to points of order on the floor of the chamber, although this was still substantial.

Some of the confusion (and much of the legal argument) arose from the difference between the treaty and the Bill. It was often pointed out that the treaty was very long, while the Bill was very short and the connection between the two was often not understood. The Bill was short because its principal purpose was to define those parts of the treaty laid before the House as Command Paper (Cm) 1934 which were to be brought within the scope of the European Communities Act 1972. A second, but essential purpose was to satisfy the requirement of the European Parliamentary Elections Act 1978 in respect of Maastricht. These purposes could be served in very few words, but of course they related to the much larger body of words in Cm 1934 which effectively became an annex to the legislation.

Under constitutional arrangements in most other Community states the parliamentary prelude to ratification was the passage of a Bill which simply approved and gave legal force to the whole of the treaty. This was effectively the situation for Britain in 1972: the distinction between Treaty of Rome pillars and inter-governmental pillars was introduced by the Single European Act and extended by the Maastricht Treaty. Would a reversion to this approach, coupled with the innovation of a statutory role for parliament in advance of ratification be more appropriate for any future EC treaties? The case for such a role in future has been put by, among others, P J Cullen, who argues that an explicit general parliamentary right of approval or rejection would be a first step in keeping with the constitutional practice of most other states.[60]

The result of such changes would be that treaties amending the EC basic treaties would require to be approved in their entirety by Act of Parliament, in the same way that treaties extending the powers of the European Parliament must already be so approved, in that specific respect, under the European Parliamentary Elections Act 1978. This would represent a further limitation of prerogative powers, but the progressive reduction of prerogative power has been a feature of British constitutional development over several centuries and the 1978 Act already provides a framework and precedent. In the case of EC treaties the combination of political sensitivity with the convention of the Ponsonby Rule already means that the freedom of action conferred on ministers by the exercise of prerogative powers is more theoretical than real and to extinguish the prerogative in this instance would make no practical difference. The timing of the formal act of ratification would, as now, be a matter for ministerial decision.

In the European Communities (Amendment) Bill of 1992/93 the amendment of the European Communities Act 1972 and the requirement of the European Parliamentary Elections Act 1978 were dealt with in separate clauses. In order to avoid the confusion between the different pillars of the treaty and their respective legislative implementation it might be necessary not only to have the whole treaty subject to parliamentary approval, but also to have the whole of it inserted in the European Communities Act.

The institutional distinction between Treaty of Rome pillars and inter-governmental pillars would be unchanged, but both would then be equally enforceable in the United Kingdom under the European Communities Act in so far as their articles give rise to legal obligations. In theory it would be possible to extend the same approach to all British treaties under an 'International Agreements Act', but in order to avoid encumbering parliament with a mass of uncontroversial treaty work it would also be quite possible to limit the new statutory requirement to European Community treaties under Article 236 of the Treaty of Rome (or in future Article N of the Maastricht Treaty).

The practical effects of such a change are difficult to predict. Had it been unambiguously necessary to legislate for the whole of the Maastricht

---

[60] P J Cullen, *The United Kingdom and the Ratification of the Maastricht Treaty: the Constitutional Position*, University of Edinburgh Europa Institute, July 1993, 11.

Treaty in 1992/93 it is possible that the Labour and Liberal Democrat parties might have succeeded in combining with the Conservative opponents of Maastricht to defeat the Maastricht Bill by voting against the Social Protocol. In April-May 1993 they sought to do this, but were frustrated by the decision of the government that the Social Protocol did not, after all, require to be in the Bill. However, in the event, this merely postponed the moment of truth for the Government. Had the escape route from amendment 27 and report stage amendment 2 not been available it is entirely possible that the government might have used the strong-arm tactics which it finally employed over the Social Protocol resolution to prevent defeat at an earlier stage. The organisation of the proceedings would otherwise have been much as it was, but perhaps a little clearer, and the prolonged legal and procedural argument over amendment 27 and report stage amendment 2 would have been avoided.

Moving on to other possible criticisms of the procedures used, it is arguable that the detailed scrutiny of the treaty by subject area was superfluous, given that the treaty itself could not be amended by any national parliament acting alone. In 1972 the chair had taken a more restrictive view of this problem and this resulted in a much shorter committee stage on the original European Communities Bill, but there had been long debates on the principle of entry before the legislation was introduced. In practice it was possible during the committee stage of the Maastricht Bill to debate all the contents of the treaty, whether they were to be covered by the European Communities Act or not.[61] Many of the days of committee debate were formally triggered by 'probing amendments' which purported to propose technical amendments to the Bill, but actually facilitated the thematic approach. Only a relatively small portion of the committee stage was devoted to matters on which the legislation could be amended without wrecking its main purpose. These included the membership of the Committee of the Regions and the arrangements for entry into force, with or without a referendum.

Does the committee stage of a European Communities (Amendment) Bill necessarily need to be taken in committee of the whole House? The

---

[61] Baker, Gamble and Ludlam state incorrectly that 'Parliament was denied the opportunity to debate those major 'pillars' of the treaty, including the agreements on Justice and Home Affairs ... and on Common Foreign and Security Policy ... that did not amend the Treaty of Rome and did not require direct legislative recognition in Parliament'—D Baker, A Gamble and S Ludlam, 'The Parliamentary Siege of Maastricht', *Parliamentary Affairs,* vol 47, January 1994, p 49.

convention applies to all 'first class' constitutional measures and it would be difficult to argue that any matter concerning powers under the Treaty of Rome is not 'first class constitutional' for the UK.[62] Most written constitutions are entrenched by setting up hurdles for their own amendment which are more difficult to overcome than those facing routine legislation and the convention which involves all British MPs in voting on the details of constitutional legislation might be seen as a British equivalent of this. In some other Member States, including France and Ireland, the Maastricht Treaty did require formal amendment of the constitution. The fact that such a large proportion of the membership of the House of Commons took an active part in the Maastricht proceedings also seems to confirm that it would have been wrong to shunt the detailed scrutiny into a committee upstairs.

One additional complication which might be reviewed in connection with proceedings taken in committee of the whole House was the problem of the 10 o'clock rule, requiring the government to obtain the permission of the House to continue after that time each day. The rule was introduced in the 1880s as a means of regulating the hours of the House following a run of very late sittings.[63] For the government's opponents this was an obvious opportunity to cause further delay and on a number of occasions the government whips decided not to take the risk of being defeated. Even when they won, sometimes with Liberal Democrat support, it was at the cost of a further 15 minute division which did little to illuminate the scrutiny of the Maastricht Treaty. However, this was a relatively minor matter and it is in any case arguable that rational discussion of the treaty should have been possible without debates late at night.

Perhaps the single most problematic and least comprehensible aspect of the Maastricht proceedings was that no one could predict whether and when there would be a separate vote on the issue of the Social Protocol. The Chairman of Ways and Means frequently described the future progress of the committee and his selection of amendments as a 'moving target'. Would it have been better if the job of selecting amendments and organising the debate had been done at the beginning, making the whole process more predictable? The 'moving target' caused problems, but with most legislation it is unavoidable, because of the unpredictable effect of

---

[62] C J Boulton (ed), Erskine May's *Treatise on the Law, Privileges, Proceedings and Usages of Parliament*, 21st edition, Butterworths, London, 1989, p 479.
[63] The history of this arrangement was set out in a recent written answer: HC Deb 29 June 1994, c 628w.

votes on amendments. A fully predictable timetable would only have been possible if coupled with a bar on tabling amendments once the committee stage had begun and this would assume that all necessary consequential amendments had been anticipated at the outset. The result would be a loss of flexibility and of opportunity to improve legislation. The procedural rules applied to the Maastricht Treaty, although they often seemed arbitrary, were based on a logic which has evolved with the House of Commons in order to facilitate orderly debate of legislation.[64]

The question of the British opt-out from the Social Protocol had been debated at length immediately after the adoption of the treaty, on second reading of the Bill and on the 'paving motion', but none of the votes on these occasions had decisively settled the issue in the eyes of the official opposition or the Maastricht rebels. It is arguable that in terms of orderly and logical debate the best, and perhaps the only, time to settle the issue once and for all was at the very end, when all other outstanding matters had been settled, because a 'final' vote on the issue at any earlier point would not have been universally accepted as final. This in fact was what happened, as a result of new clause 74. This reasoning may have informed the Chairman of Ways and Means's decision to prefer new clauses 74 and 75 to amendment 27 as vehicles for such a decision, but it happened only after the issue had already been ventilated exhaustively and the damage to the public image of parliament had already been done. Only the government could have attempted to forestall this problem by including something like new clause 74 in the Bill at the outset, but this would have been tantamount to handing a murder weapon to the government's opponents, whom Douglas Hurd reasonably described as an 'alliance of opposites'.[65]

The whole Maastricht process in parliament was a cat and mouse game between the government and its various opponents and in situations of this kind it is unrealistic to expect any of the participants to plan every move and skirmish in advance. Again we are forced to conclude that the Maastricht mayhem was not the result of defective or obscure procedural rules, but of a particular matrix of political forces, combined with the

---

[64] Rawlings argues that the application of the procedural rules involves the Chair, and hence the House of Commons Clerks, in a quasi-judicial role and notes that, from a strictly legalistic point of view the tolerance shown towards 'probing amendments' might be regarded as inconsistent with the strict attitude taken towards 'unworkable' amendments. Rawlings, op cit, part one, p 270–2, part two p 390.

[65] HC Deb 15 April 1993 c 973–4.

peculiarities inherent in the way in which the British constitution has so far been adapted to deal with European Community membership.

## Conclusions

The British parliamentary proceedings concerned with the Maastricht Treaty were wreathed in complexities which did little to improve the standing with the British public of either parliament or the treaty. While all the indications are that the public perception of the treaty was one of either hostility or only grudging acceptance, parliament did little to clarify the arguments. At a time when there was evidence across Europe of mounting disillusionment with political parties and political dialogue, the abstruse legal and political debate about the treaty in the British Parliament did nothing to bridge the gulf.[66]

It would be wrong to present this as a failure of parliamentary procedure. The fault, if such it was, lay partly in the nature of the treaty itself—a text singularly ill-suited to either stirring rhetoric or rational argument—and partly in the condition of British party politics following the 1992 general election. There were also occasions when the media coverage of the proceedings was misleading.

If there is to be another round of amendments to the basic EC treaties, ie the 'constitution' of the EC in the mid-1990s, this analysis suggests certain conclusions about how it might be handled to avoid some of the negative aspects of the Maastricht experience. The content of such a treaty would be for the politicians of the member states to decide and each national parliament would have to reach a judgment of its political merits, but it is to be hoped that, whatever changes are agreed, the treaty document will be a great deal simpler and clearer than the one adopted at Maastricht.[67] This, above all, would facilitate rational public and parliamentary debate.

---

[66] Rawlings concludes that 'the process of legalisation may be said to have contributed to the democratic deficit, in the sense of distance between Parliament and the people', op cit, part two, p 391.

[67] Helen Wallace describes the Maastricht Treaty as 'a document negotiated in a room without windows, into which public opinion had subsequently bulldozed its unwelcome and critical presence', H Wallace, 'European Governance in Turbulent Times', *Journal of Common Market Studies*, vol 31, no 3, p 296.

Secondly, it would be helpful to clarify the British constitutional position ahead of any new treaty. This would probably entail an Act of Parliament to establish that the whole of any new EC treaty should be subject to parliamentary approval—ie an extension of the European Parliamentary Elections Act 1978 which at present only applies to treaties which extend the powers of the European Parliament. Ideally it would ease confusion if it were also established by statute or declaration that in future all EC treaties would be subject to the European Communities Act 1972 in their entirety, but since the present parliament has decided not to apply this principle to the whole of the Maastricht Treaty it may be unlikely to agree to reform in this direction.

Finally, there are detailed aspects of the procedural rules, particularly those governing committees of the whole House, which could usefully be reviewed in the light of the Maastricht experience.

The House of Commons was scolded by the *Financial Times* on 6 May 1993 for using procedures which 'had the effect of avoiding the main issues, while fuelling a phoney trench war between parliamentary factions on endless technicalities'. The accusation, as this chapter has suggested, is not an entirely fair one. The 'war' was real and the technicalities were sometimes the chosen weapons. The conclusion drawn by the *Financial Times* may not, however, be out of place:

> The mother of parliaments is going to have to work out a more effective relationship with the EC if it is to have any hope of representing its citizens' concerns effectively.

# PART III

## Conclusions

# 12

## Scrutiny without power?
## The Impact of the European Community on the Westminster Parliament[1]

### *Philip Giddings and Gavin Drewry*

Most Community legislation does not fit into the binary conception of politics dominant at Westminster; it departs from the normal pattern of a series of measures to which the government is committed and which it has an interest in defending. Community legislation, therefore, is bound to impose a strain upon the House of Commons as it struggles to assimilate an entirely different legislative process into its traditional procedures.[2]

Is it not true that we can scrutinise until we are blue in the face but the point is that power is being taken away from this parliament?[3]

### Europe and Westminster—Challenge, Threat or Opportunity?

To any neutral reader of this book it will be apparent that British membership of the European Community has, from the beginning, presented parliament with a unique constitutional **challenge**. However, in the real world, and particularly in the politically charged world of parliament itself, this is not a subject that lends itself to neutrality. From a Euro-sceptic standpoint, joining Europe has been seen as posing a **threat** to parliamentary government—requiring an unacceptable sacrifice of parliamentary sovereignty and the subordination of Westminster to the EC juggernaut in Brussels. Conversely, from the pro-European perspective,

---

[1] This chapter is based on a paper delivered to a workshop of parliamentary scholars and parliaments in Berlin in August 1994.

[2] V Bogdanor, 'Britain and the European Community', in J Jowell and D Oliver, eds, *The Changing Constitution*, 3rd edition, Oxford, Clarendon Press, 1994, p 8.

[3] Ron Leighton, HC Deb 28 June 1990, c 526.

EC membership is seen as having presented the Westminster parliament with an **opportunity** to extend its influence by becoming involved in both the continuing development and the day to day business of an increasingly integrated and prosperous Europe.

The fact that parliamentarians have been so divided, across party lines, in their perceptions of the constitutional significance of EC membership for the institution of parliament in which they work is apparent on almost every page of this book. And such a diversity of views has coloured the way in which parliament itself has responded, procedurally and behaviourally, to EC membership, and to the ever-growing volume of European business that appears on its order papers.

Controversy about the development of the European Community, now the European Union, has been at or near the top of the political agenda of British politics for more than twenty years. In the 1970s it threatened to split the Labour Party (and eventually did so, with the Social Democrat schism of the early 1980s, which was essentially a delayed reaction from Labour pro-Europeans who had defied their party by supporting Edward Heath's initiative ten years earlier). In the 1990s, it has deeply divided the Conservative Party—as was made starkly apparent in the stormy debates surrounding the Maastricht Treaty, described in Chapters 10 and 11.

This book does not address directly the burning political controversies about the future development of Europe. Rather, our authors have sought to analyse, in an objective and scholarly manner, the narrower but important issue of how the Westminster Parliament has responded to EC membership. Nevertheless, such analysis cannot be divorced from its controversial political context, nor have our authors sought to do that. The result, we believe, is that this volume casts useful light on the issues underlying the controversy but without engaging in it.

The main purpose of this concluding chapter is to draw together the evidence about the impact of EC membership on the Westminister Parliament, and arrive at an assessment of that parliament's role in the handling of Community business. Whether or not parliament's role has been enhanced or diminished in consequence of European membership depends on the answers to broader questions about its influence and significance—none of which is amenable to precise measurement.

More than a century after A V Dicey—a man who, incidentally, was not known for his sympathy towards European legal and political practices—first wrote about parliamentary sovereignty, there has been much recourse in recent debates to rhetoric about 'loss of sovereignty'. Such rhetoric has raised, and often begged, crucial questions about what parliamentary sovereignty really means in a modern world of economically interdependent nation states, and in a United Kingdom in which the sovereign parliament is normally controlled by the executive.[4]

In order to address these issues we need first to look at the constitutional context of Westminster's engagement with Europe.

## The Constitutional Context

There seems to be a certain reluctance among British ministers to concede that policy issues can have a constitutional dimension. However, the unique and manifest constitutional implications of Britain's membership of the Community have from the outset been acknowledged by the fact that the primary legislation ratifying the treaties—the European Communities Bill 1971–72; the European Communities (Amendment) Bill 1985–86 (ratifying the Single European Act); and the European Communities (Amendment) Bill 1992–93 (ratifying the Maastricht Treaty)—have all had their committee stages on the floor of the House of Commons, the procedure normally chosen for constitutional measures.[5] As governments are reluctant to use up valuable time on the floor of the House with detailed and potentially risky scrutiny of controversial legislation, the decisions to treat these bills in this way was a significant admission of their constitutional significance.

Traditionally, as Alan Page observes in Chapter 3, government in Britain has depended upon the approval of parliament for the making of laws, the raising of taxes and the spending of public money.[6] Parliament's power within the British political system has rested upon its constitutional monopoly in these areas. However, accession to the Community Treaties also gave to Community institutions the power to make law, raise revenue and spend money.

Moreover, as demonstrated by recent decisions of the European Court of Justice, national courts are obliged to give precedence to Community law over national law. As Alan Page explains in Chapter 3, the European Communities Act 1972 'does not attempt to deny Parliament the power to enact legislation which is in conflict with Community law ... Instead, it

---

[4] See D Judge, *The Parliamentary State*, London, Sage, 1993, pp 179–93.

[5] See J A G Griffith and M Ryle, *Parliament: Functions, Practice and Procedure*, London, Sweet & Maxwell, 1989, p 315.

[6] p 32 and 37, *ante*.

seeks to deny effect to such legislation by controlling the way in which the courts construe and give effect to it.' [7]

Thus from the start of British membership of the Community in 1973 the position of the Westminster Parliament changed from one in which it exercised the formal power of final approval over all legislation, taxation and public expenditure to one in which, in the areas covered by the treaties, it was able only to scrutinise the way in which those powers were exercised by other, European, institutions and to influence the United Kingdom's representatives in the Council of Ministers. As Alan Page says, parliament's legislative role has shrunk as the boundaries of the Community's competence have expanded, particularly as a result of the Single European Act and the Maastricht Treaty on European Union and, 'to the extent that Parliament's role in the constitution depends on its legislative role ... it is difficult to avoid the conclusion that its importance has been diminished.' [8]

Traditionally, the Westminster parliament has based its procedures upon the constitutional doctrine of ministerial responsibility. The advent of legislation originating with the European Commission and Council rather than Ministers of the Crown required a change in those procedures. In the case of draft directives, the Commission and not UK ministers are the authors of the proposals. And the Commission is neither represented in nor answerable to national parliaments. Moreover, leaving aside the complications of majority voting, UK ministers are just one voice out of fifteen in the Council of Ministers, which has the final word (subject in some cases also to the views of the European Parliament) on ratification; and any impact that Westminster might have on ministers is masked by the secrecy of Council deliberations. Here the national legislature does have a role to play, but it is clearly a subordinate one, relating to the form and method of implementation rather than to the substantive policy outcome.

In the case of Regulations, emanating from a separate European legislative process in which national legislatures play no formal part, parliament's role is even more limited.

Thus, from the moment that Britain joined the Community, in the areas covered by the Treaties Westminster ceased to be the sovereign legislature in the Diceyan sense: its role became, like other national parliaments in the Community (discussed in an Appendix to this book), one of **influence**

---

[7] p 44, *ante.*
[8] p 37, *ante.*

upon a process in which the final **power** of decision lay elsewhere, beyond its reach. This was clearly a constitutional change of the first order and one which was bound to have a major impact upon the procedures and culture of the Westminster Parliament.

In the first phase of British membership the reality of this change could be to some extent masked by appeal to the veto power held by national ministers in the Council. It could be argued that, whilst individual ministers, who were themselves accountable to their national parliaments, held the power of veto there was a route for national parliaments to exert their power, albeit only negatively. States for whom parliamentary sensibilities were important, such as Denmark and Britain, could therefore employ devices such as the 'parliamentary reserve' (see Chapters 4 and 5) to retain at least the appearance of involvement of their national parliaments in the Community's decision making process.

The credibility of this doctrine rested on the requirement for unanimity in the Council of Ministers, drawing heavily on the Luxembourg Compromise of 1966. However, as British ministers themselves discovered over milk prices in May 1982, it was one thing to claim to invoke the compromise on the grounds that an issue was a vital national interest, and quite another for that claim to be recognised by the rest of the Community. Moreover, as majority voting was extended, particularly by the SEA in 1986, and the Maastricht TEU in 1992, and the requirement for unanimity correspondingly reduced, the fragility of any doctrine resting on a supposed national ministerial veto became more and more exposed.

For the bulk of decisions, particularly legislative and financial decisions, national ministers had to obtain, and retain, the support of other national ministers if they were to create either a majority or a blocking minority and thus exert any significant influence upon the outcome of the process. And as the powers of the European Parliament were extended, so it became similarly necessary to obtain the support of the requisite majorities in that assembly. Formally, constitutionally, power had shifted from the national to the European level. And that fact could not be ignored by national parliaments, even if it was unpalatable for some of their members.

It is worth noting, in passing, that in the British case parliament had already long accepted that law-making powers could be delegated (to ministers). An inevitable consequence of such delegation was the sacrifice of its ability to determine the detail of the resulting statutory instruments. This severely limits the effectiveness of parliamentary scrutiny of such legislation, the volume of which far exceeds that of primary legislation—and has been augmented by the large number of statutory instruments that give effect to European directives.

Whilst such subordinate legislation remains, positively or negatively, subject to parliamentary approval, that approval has to be given to the legislative package as a whole; Westminster's procedures do not permit parliament formally to propose amendments, though it is possible for an instrument to be withdrawn, amended to meet points made, and then re-submitted. To that extent, parliament had already accepted the principle of another legislative authority, albeit one subject in theory to its veto. But in the case of instruments implementing EC directives, any exercise of this parliamentary veto would cause a constitutional crisis by placing the United Kingdom in default of its legal obligations to the Community.

Although accession to the Community gave Community legislation the force of law in the United Kingdom (by virtue of section 2(1) of the European Communities Act 1972), it did not formally impose any restriction on parliament's legislative competence. (This would have in any case have been problematic given the view that no parliament can bind its successors). Rather, the view was taken that all that was necessary was that British governments should refrain from proposing legislation which would be inconsistent with UK obligations as a member of the Community. However, what has been, and continues to be, necessary is that in pursuit of those obligations changes have to be made to UK domestic law, particularly in implementing directives, initially, and misleadingly, described as European 'secondary' legislation. In most cases these obligations are implemented by subordinate legislation but in a few cases primary legislation has to be used. One observer has described the role of the Westminster parliament in considering such legislation like this:

> [Parliament can play] only a limited and automatic role. It is cut out of any real choice as to substance ... and is confined, at most, to a technical role more appropriate to a parliamentary draftsman.[9]

As the directive is binding, parliament can do no more than consider whether the proposed legislation is technically efficient in giving it domestic legal effect. One consequence of this is in fact to increase the legislative freedom of the executive in Britain, since, as the Foster Committee put it:

---

[9] J D B Mitchell, 'British Law and British Membership', *Europarecht*, vol 6, April 1971, p 97.

... the Executive itself by agreeing with the other member governments to a proposal for legislation makes the law, ie has assumed the constitutional function and power of Parliament ...[10]

The extent of that increased Executive freedom is demonstrated by the use of the delegated law-making power under the 1972 Act to implement Community obligations. In practice, where subordinate legislation is used, the scope for parliamentary discussion is at the discretion of the government. Under the Act the 'negative resolution' procedure, whereby the legislation comes into effect automatically after forty days unless within that period either House of Parliament resolves to the contrary, applies unless the government positively chooses to ask each House to approve an instrument in draft. Given the constraints upon parliamentary time, this has led to criticism that substantial changes in the law have been made without parliamentary debate. Given that the obligations are binding, however, it is not clear what purpose could be served by more extensive debate.

**The Responses of the Two Chambers**

In this changed constitutional situation the Westminster parliament had to develop new procedures to deal with this new category of business. Until Britain joined the Community, legislation largely arose from domestic pressures which stimulated the political parties and government to develop particular policy responses. Parliamentary discussion of legislation therefore normally took place within a known policy context, one in which ministers certainly, and the opposition usually, had taken up a prepared position.

Community legislation, however, is as often as not the result of domestic pressures in other member states and thus finds something of a policy void in that national politicians have no immediate reference point by which to assess it and determine its political significance. Thus an important element in the process of considering European legislation at national level is a system for determining the significance of what is proposed. The government itself attaches to all draft Community

---

[10] Second Report from the Select Committee on European Community Secondary Legislation, 1972–73, HC 463, para 34.

legislation an explanatory memorandum (EM) giving its own assessment of the domestic policy significance of the measure concerned.

As has been explained in Chapters 4 and 5, after British accession to the Treaty of Rome both Houses of Parliament set up select committees to address their new role. As might have been predicted, these two committees both recommended the introduction of committees to facilitate the handling of EC business. The evidence to the Lords' committee, chaired by a former Speaker of the House of Commons, Lord Maybray-King,[11] initially favoured the setting up of a joint scrutiny committee of both houses. When this failed to win sufficient support, the two houses established their own separate committees. The remarks that follow concentrate upon the role and impact of those committees as the principal scrutiny mechanism, though as is made clear in Part II, EC business has also featured prominently in proceedings on the floors of the two houses, in questions, ministerial statements and debates.

The establishment of a European Communities Committee was a particularly innovative move for the House of Lords. As Donald Shell comments in Chapter 5, as the House had no investigatory select committees prior to the early 1970s, the ECC and its sub-committees represented a very considerable investment by the Lords in what was for them a new form of parliamentary activity.[12] It has provided an opportunity for participation for many peers who do not otherwise contribute to the work of the House.

The initial method of operation established by the ECC has stood the test of time and the Committee itself has established an extremely high reputation for the quality of its work. Shell observes that within the House it 'has been widely viewed as a resounding success'[13], and he quotes the Jellicoe Report's generous tribute to the Committee as having made 'a unique contribution to the process of European scrutiny by national parliaments'[14] (though the Report recommended that it should be streamlined). So far as the House of Lords itself is concerned, most of the Committee's reports are recommended for debate, and receive one

---

[11] Select Committee on Procedures for Scrutiny of Proposals for European Instruments: First Report, 1972–73, HL 67, March 1973; Second Report, 1972–73, HL 194, July 1973.

[12] p 97, *ante.*

[13] p 109, *ante.*

[14] p 104, *ante, Report from the Select Committee on the Committee Work of the House,* 1991–92, HL 35–ii, para 137.

relatively quickly. A debate helps to bring a report to the attention of other peers and requires front-bench spokesmen to state their position. Whilst the government now invariably produces a written response, ministerial positions can be elaborated in debate, particularly if there have been later developments. On the other hand, almost half of the speeches in such debates are made by members of the sub-committees concerned and it is rarely the case that much is added to what has already been written in a report. Such debates are not occasions for changing minds.

The reports also have an impact on Whitehall, in that civil servants are required to digest the reports in order to decide what advice to give to their minister and draft the government's reply. However, Donald Shell suggests, in his analysis of the Committee's work in 1990–91, that once that task has been accomplished, reports tend to fade quickly from the official mind.[15]

Arguably the most important target for the ECC's work should be the institutions of the Community. Copies of reports are always sent to the relevant section of the Commission and there is some evidence that they are a useful resource for desk officers. Reports are also sent to selected members of the European Parliament and to the clerk of the counterpart EP Committee. According to Sir Christopher Prout, former Chairman of the Democratic Group, they have earned a high reputation there, and are particularly influential in the relevant EP committees.[16]

The ECC seldom hits the headlines but, from the point of view of peers themselves, it has been a success. One commentator has suggested that its reports 'have long been required reading in Brussels and other national capitals as well as in Whitehall'.[17] However, as Donald Shell notes, the committee appointed to review the House's committee work during 1991 expressed concerns about the very large proportion of peers' and clerks' time taken by the committee and scepticism about its real impact. Lord Bancroft, former head of the civil service, for example, whilst acknowledging the 'extremely high reputation' of the committee's work and its 'powerful influence on Brussels' felt that 'the effect it has on our own Ministers and Government seems much smaller than would

---

[15] p 183, *ante*.

[16] Evidence to the Select Committee on the Committee Work of the House, 1991–92, HL 35-ii.

[17] S George, ed, *Britain and the European Community*, Oxford, Clarendon Press, 1992, p 101.

correspond to the amount of resources devoted to it and the influence which it has outside this country'.[18]

The review committee concluded that the ECC's scrutiny function should be exercised with greater speed and more selectivity and accordingly called for a reduction in the number of sub-committees so that the number of peers involved could be cut from eighty to fifty. This would mean that instead of consuming some three-quarters of the resources of the house available for committee work, the ECC would consume only two-thirds. Although these proposals elicited considerable opposition from the ECC's supporters, they were approved after a tied vote and implemented in January 1993.

So far as the House of Commons is concerned, British membership of the EC has always been a deeply controversial matter and that controversy runs within as well as between the major parties. That controversy has been an important factor in determining the form of the Commons' arrangements for scrutinising Euro-business and the manner in which members of parliament have approached their task.

At the heart of those arrangements, described in Chapter 4, is a European select committee, but one that is quite different from its counterpart in the House of Lords. The Select Committee on European Legislation (set up in 1974 as the Committee on European Secondary Legislation, following the recommendations of the Foster Committee[19]) is a sifting committee. It examines EC legislative proposals, including draft directives, and assigns them to one of four categories: of sufficient legal or political importance to require further consideration by the House; of importance, but not important enough to warrant debate; of no legal or political importance; and documents concerning which it is not yet clear whether they are important enough to require debate.

In its response to a report by the Select Committee on Procedure in 1989, the government resisted proposals that it saw as a major shift of the Scrutiny Committee's work into the examination of broad policy areas, particularly since 'this might tend to detract from the Committee's present effectiveness in its primary scrutiny function'.[20]

---

[18] Cited by D Shell, p 186, *ante*.

[19] Select Committee on European Community Secondary Legislation: First Report, 1972–73, HC 143, 13 February 1973; Final Report, 1972–73, HC 463, 25 October 1973.

[20] Cm 1081, May 1990.

In spite of some early procedural and documentary teething troubles the revised system seems to have worked well. Fewer late-night debates are held and the ministerial statement and 'question time' at the start of the standing committee session seem to be widely appreciated. Attendance at the committees of non-members continues to be low, even though the meetings feature in the Leader of the House's weekly business statement. In the 1992–93 session the maximum number of non-members present was 8 (on one occasion) and the total non-member appearances 160, an average of 3 per sitting.

The analysis by Priscilla Baines in Chapter 4 concludes that 'the Committee has been not only durable and resilient but also able to adapt its proceedings to changing circumstances both in the EC and at Westminster and to handle an ever-increasing volume of paper.'[21] However, she also notes the government's resistance (see above) to relinquishing its own power of initiative in EC scrutiny by extending the Committee's terms of reference. And she identifies the unusual constitutional position of parliament in relation to scrutiny of EC legislation, discussed at the beginning of this chapter, when she explains why the Committee on European Legislation differs so markedly from other select committees.

... it is an essential element in the Houses's legislative processes, but its role relates to legislation which is not of domestic origin and over which the government has very little direct control. This is in distinct contrast to the tight control which governments normally exercise both over the domestic legislative programme and the rest of the House's business.[22]

Moreover, the undertaking to allow debates on documents recommended by the Committee for consideration by the House means that any extension of the Committee's remit would weaken government control over an important part of the Commons' agenda.

What of the other Commons select committees? As Priscilla Baines points out, the 1988–89 Procedure Committee inquiry found that the Commons' departmentally-related select committees devoted surprisingly little time and resources to European issues. Although for a few

---

[21] p 86, *ante*.
[22] p 88, *ante*.

Committees European documents formed a central part of wider investigations of policy issues, the majority saw little prospect of being able to devote more effort to considering European legislation and several doubted whether this would be desirable anyway. Nevertheless it was the Procedure Committee's view that the House would benefit from an increased contribution by select committees to the scrutiny process. Although it stopped short of recommending that the House should so direct the Committees, it argued that endorsement of their report would 'send a strong signal to (them) that it wishes to see them adopt a higher profile in this area'.[23]

As it happened, several select committee inquiries in the 1990–91 and 1991–92 sessions were concerned with specific EC legislative proposals (see Chapter 6). The Agriculture Committee's report on *Animals in Transit*[24] was a direct response to draft European legislation as well as reflecting widespread concern amongst the British public about the issue. The Environment Committee's inquiry into *The EC Draft Directive on the Landfill of Waste*[25] combined the Committee's long-standing interest in landfill with a recognition of the growing importance of the European Commission's role in the formulation of environmental protection policy. Similarly, the Employment Committee reported on *The European Community Social Charter*[26] and the Transport Committee on *Developments in European Air Transport Policy*,[27] considering the impact of earlier measures as well as some draft proposals for further ones.

Taken as a whole, the total amount of time and resources which the departmentally related select committees devote to matters European is still not great and there are some odd gaps—such as the fact that the Trade and Industry Committee conducted only one inquiry into any aspect of the single market during the whole of the 1987–92 parliament. Committees prefer to choose their own agendas and are reluctant to tie up time and resources in routine scrutiny exercises. Moreover, the vagaries of the timetables of EC draft legislation make timing—the essence of effective committee influence—very difficult.

---

[23] Fourth Report from the Commons Select Committee on Procedure, 1988–89, HC 622, para 103.

[24] 1990–91, HC 45 (see also Chapter 9).

[25] 1990–91, HC 263.

[26] 1990–91, HC 509.

[27] 1991–92, HC 147.

In addition to formal legislative scrutiny and the work of select committees, analysis in Chapter 6 of the 1990–91 session in the House of Commons also shows the importance for European issues of questions, particularly written questions, and ministerial statements and the question periods which follow them. That session was particularly interesting as it showed how the House grappled with three controversial issues—reform of the CAP; the common fisheries policy; and the inter-governmental conferences.

In pursuing those issues, MPs were carrying out three classic parliamentary functions. Primarily, they were carrying out the basic constitutional function of scrutiny, both of the decisions and actions of British ministers and of the activities of the European Community. Secondly, MPs were performing their classic representative role: representing the interests of their constituencies—particularly evident in the debates on the common fisheries policy (see Chapter 6) and the CAP (see Chapter 8); of other interests affected by EC decisions (evident in, for example, Early Day Motions, drawing attention to particular concerns); and acting as political and partisan advocates on social and economic issues, as for example, in the controversies about the welfare of farm animals (see Chapter 9) and the debates about the social chapter in the long running Maastricht saga (see Chapters 10 and 11). The House of Commons provided a forum in which these various interests could be expressed—and challenged. The third function which MPs were performing was legislating—directly, as when considering statutory instruments implementing EC directives; and indirectly when considering EC proposals about to be debated in the Council of Ministers.

However, these classic parliamentary roles also serve wider political purposes. For the government they can strengthen its negotiating position in Brussels by demonstrating the weight and vigour of opinion 'at home'. For the opposition parties, they provide an opportunity both to develop their own distinctive policy positions—of particular importance in the run-up to a general election—and also to demonstrate and exploit divisions within the governing party, which at that time were acute. And for Euro-sceptics on both sides of the House these continuing opportunities to deploy their case against the European project.

**Conclusion**

The 'impact' of United Kingdom membership of the EC on Westminister can be analysed at one level by examining the novel constitutional problems that have been posed for parliament and how it has responded to them. At a more basic level, impact also has to do with the extent to which the substantive content of day to day parliamentary business has changed.

We have described at some length the arrangements that have developed for the discussion and scrutiny of EC business in both Houses—and the unique characteristics of those arrangements. New European scrutiny committees have come into being in both Houses, forming the basis of a completely new, and widely esteemed, committee structure in the Lords. As for the second level of impact, we have seen that membership of the Community has impinged substantially—and increasingly, as the range of Community competence has expanded—on all traditional forms of business, such as parliamentary questions, ministerial statements and debates; it has also impinged significantly though unevenly on the agendas of departmental select committees. To employ the famous metaphor used by Lord Denning in the early 1970s,[28] the 'incoming tide' of Community law has flowed not just into the courtroom but also into every nook and cranny of parliamentary business.

As noted at the beginning of this chapter, political rhetoric has made much play with the notion of parliamentary sovereignty having ebbed away from Westminster to Brussels. For Euro-sceptics, there is gloom about what they perceive to be the flooding out of the domestic legislative agenda; for pro-Europeans, the European tide has washed in new ideas and policies to augment and complement exclusively home-grown ones.

Our earlier chapters have underlined the extent to which parliamentarians have made use of their opportunities to debate European issues in key areas—and the fierce controversies that have emerged, particularly in the context of the Maastricht debates. Parliament has been the arena, not just for day to day scrutiny of European policy but also for some important debates about the wider issues of Community development.

It is apparent that EC membership has generated a lot of new parliamentary activity. But what has all this activity actually achieved? Our

---

[28] *Bulmer Ltd v Bollinger SA* [1974] Ch 401, 418–9.

answer must be a cautious one. For one thing it is impossible to know whether outcomes would have been different without it, given the absence of reliable accounts of the deliberations of the Council. But it seems that parliamentary scrutiny seldom harmed the Government's negotiating position and may well, in many cases, have strengthened it—particularly when there were no major differences between the main parties: a good illustration can be found in the UK's response to the MacSharry proposals for reform of the Common Agricultural Policy, described in Chapter 8.[29]

The broad picture that emerges from the chapters in Part II of this book is one of parliament performing its classic roles of scrutiny and representation in a policy context in which the final decisions were clearly going to be made away from Westminster, in international negotiating fora —a context in which a national parliament could at best exercise only influence, not power.

There are conflicting views on the effectiveness of Westminster's scrutiny arrangements. In 1988 Jacques Delors identified Britain and Germany as the only two member states whose parliaments had fully recognised the implications for national sovereignty of the 1992 Single Market project.[30] However, in a memorandum to the Commons Procedure Committee in 1989, Juliet Lodge suggested that 'the House of Commons scrutiny of EC legislation has been seriously deficient and weaker than that of its counterparts in other EC states'.[31]

In a memorandum to the Hansard Society Commission on the Legislative Process in January 1992 the Institute of Directors concluded:

> the Institute sees the legislative process as much wider than Parliament. It is a long drawn out process involving interactions at many levels and today, particularly with the growing scope of the competence of the European Community, the Westminster Parliament (Ministers apart) is a residual, last-stage focus of pressure. This conclusion must have very serious implications for our traditional views of Parliament as a legislator.[32]

---

[29] p 220, *ante*.

[30] S George, op cit, p 101.

[31] 1988–89, HC 622-ii, p 154.

[32] *Making the Law*: The Report of the Hansard Society Commission on the Legislative Process, London: Hansard Society, 1992, pp 256–7.

In Michael Mezey's terminology the Westminster Parliament is considered overall as a reactive legislature.[33] But it is clear from this account of its relationship with the European Community that both formally and practically its position is more marginal. Its power to affect outcomes in Brussels or Strasbourg is at best negative, and exercised through British ministers (ie with the concurrence of the executive) in those areas of decision-making in which unanimity is required. Otherwise, it is a matter of influence, an influence again exercised through ministers rather than independently.

Moreover, the political culture of the European Community is significantly different from that in which British parliamentarians are accustomed to operate. Britain is used to majority party government. That means government ministers, and their supporters, and those who would replace them (the opposition), are accustomed to getting their way, if necessary simply by mobilising their parliamentary majority via the whips. Whilst there are exceptions when this does not apply (of which the Maastricht Treaty proceedings are a recent example), ministers in Britain are accustomed to getting their way, as long as they retain the support of their party. This is particularly true of legislative and budgetary matters. But in the European context, the culture is consensual and coalitionist, not adversarial and majoritarian in the Westminster tradition:[34] majorities, or blocking minorities, in the Council of Ministers or the European Parliament have to be constructed; they cannot be assumed as they are at Westminster.

It is a culture of negotiation, persuasion and influence, a culture in which the sensitivities of one national parliament are but one of a host of factors to be taken into account in complex process of Community decision-making. And alongside the sensitivities of national governments, the Commission, the European Parliament and the many interests and lobbies directly represented in Brussels, the concerns of one national parliament are likely to be distinctly marginal.

What can the Westminster parliament do to extend its influence or deploy such influence as it has more effectively? There are four possibilities:

First, the existing scrutiny system at Westminster could be made more effective by detailed improvements to its mode of operation, particularly

---

[33] M Mezey, *Comparative Legislatures*, Duke University Press, 1979.
[34] See A Lijphart, *Democracies: Patterns of Majoritarian and Consensual Government in Twenty One Countries*, Yale University Press, 1984.

in the Commons. Broadening the remit of the Commons scrutiny committee, so that it is equivalent in scope to the Lords' ECC, would help. So would continuing the process of enhancing the European content of the work of the departmentally-related select committees and integrating it with the specifically European committees. But the biggest difference would be a behavioural one, leading to a shift in focus, a shift away from continually re-running the debate about Britain's relationship with the EC towards detailed consideration of the substance of the proposals contained in the European documents.

Secondly, given the pressure of business at Westminster, which now affects both chambers, it is surely time to re-consider the question of a joint European scrutiny committee to make more effective use of limited resources. It transpired that the Commons could not man more than two standing committees. Many peers were disturbed at the proposal to reduce the number of ECC sub-committees. Putting the two together would seem to offer a way of increasing the amount of effective scrutiny without inhibiting other parliamentary activities.

Thirdly, it is time for Westminster to recognise fully the key role of the European Parliament and to explore ways of linking the activities of the two institutions. This line of argument was strongly supported in the Procedure Committee's 1989 Report. In particular, linkages need to be made between British MEPs and MPs at Westminster, perhaps through involving the former in party and (more radically) Commons committees. Similarly, regular linkages between departmentally-related committees at Westminster and their functional equivalents in the European Parliament would enhance the role of both.[35] The practice of several other member states (Italy, the Netherlands, Belgium and Germany—see Appendix) might provide useful models for Westminster.

Fourthly, Westminster needs to recover and enhance its representational role. Many interest groups are now directly represented in Brussels as well as in Whitehall/Westminster. Indeed, there is some cause for concern that the more important interest groups bypass Westminster and go instead to the European institutions at Brussels, Strasbourg and Luxembourg. The Commons' initial negativity towards the EC has encouraged this marginalising of the British parliament. As we have seen from our accounts of Westminster at work, parliamentarians are often expressing the concerns of their constituents and other interests. Part of the purpose of

---

[35] See Fourth Report from the Commons Select Committee on Procedure, 1988–89, HC 622, paras 105–115.

a parliament is to legitimise the process of interest representation. As the EU develops, there is an opportunity for national parliaments to develop their representational role in conjunction with interests, national and local, and with MEPs in order to ensure that those interests are effectively heard at the European level. This would complement the work of the Economic and Social Committee and the new Committee of the Regions.

In the absence of a written constitution, the Westminster parliament has demonstrated great adaptability in responding to changes in the political, social and economic context over the centuries. As a parliament it has at different times been the English, British, United Kingdom and Imperial Parliament. It has been the parliament of a feudal, limited and constitutional monarchy and is now the parliament of a liberal democracy with universal suffrage and a highly developed party system. It has, in short, proved to be a highly adaptable institution. And British membership of the European Union provides it with the opportunity to demonstrate that adaptability once again. Will it be taken?

# 13

# The Way Forward?

*David Millar*

## Introduction

This book looks at the methods of dealing with the European Community which the Westminster Parliament has developed over the first 20 years of UK membership. It also examines the impact on Westminster of the negotiations and ratification debates which led up to the creation of the European Union in 1993. These absorbed much time and energy in the House of Commons and sparked intense debates inside and outside parliament about the nature of Britain's involvement with Europe, but did not greatly change the established procedures for scrutinising European legislation or monitoring the intergovernmental mechanisms now transformed into the second and third pillars of the Union.

However, another round of treaty changes is already on the horizon. The Maastricht Treaty contained within it, in Article N(2), a commitment to hold another inter-governmental conference (IGC) beginning in 1996. The agenda has still to be finalised, but certain items on it have already been fixed. The European Union is already committed to considering new applications for membership, including those submitted or anticipated from the central and eastern European states which now have 'Europe Agreements'; and the European Council laid down at Corfu in June 1994 that the IGC must look at institutional issues 'in the perspective of the future enlargement of the Union'. The Maastricht Treaty also committed the member states to looking again in 1996 at expanding the scope of the 'co-decision' procedure in Article 189b, which would give more power to the European Parliament. A revision of the arrangements for conducting security and defence policy was also foreseen by the Treaty. There have also been many informal proposals for structural changes to the Union— such as a clearer division of powers on a federal model or a new second chamber of the European Parliament—which may find their way onto the IGC agenda. The possibility of a single currency from 1997 or 1999 is also now being intensively discussed across Europe and this has prompted a lively debate at Westminster as to whether Britain, which reserved its position at Maastricht, would experience fundamental political and constitutional changes were it ever to join a single European currency system.

The question posed by this chapter is therefore whether the two Houses at Westminster are capable of preparing for the inter-governmental conference by adapting their procedures in collaboration so as to provide for the British people an effective service of scrutiny of EC legislation and activities, and of information thereupon, coupled with discerning examination of British policies towards the European Union.

Many lessons can be learned from the process of ratification by national parliaments of the Treaty on European Union (TEU). The negative result of the Danish referendum of June 1992 and the narrow victory for the 'Yes' campaign in the French referendum of September 1992 were matched by open public scepticism in the United Kingdom and even in Germany, hitherto strongly supportive of the cause of European integration. While it is true that the result of the Irish referendum of 1992 was firmly affirmative of ratification, as was that of the second Danish referendum of May 1993, the adverse public reaction in several member states to the treaty (and in Britain to the ratification process) has given rise to a campaign by the European Parliament and some national parliaments for more effective parliamentary powers to monitor and scrutinise EC legislative proposals.

## Reform of the ratification procedure

The first lesson to be learned from the ratification process of the Maastricht Treaty in national parliaments is that the procedures used by the House of Commons stand in need of reform. These procedures are described in detail in Chapter 11 above. Conclusions can be drawn here regarding the need for reform and the lessons to be learnt from the ratification process.

All national parliaments stand to benefit from a treaty emerging from the inter-governmental conference commencing in 1996 which is simpler in structure and clearer in content than the TEU. While it is too much to expect that the three-pillar structure will revert to the unitary nature of the Treaty of Rome, which covered only EEC policies and activities as such, the success of the forthcoming enlargement of the European Union to include countries of East and Central Europe will in part depend on the simplicity and clarity of the treaties then in force. The contrast is stark between the comprehensive and structured character of those sections of the treaty dealing with monetary union, and the other sections which either amend the existing treaties or set up new pillars alongside them.

While political compromises during the negotiation of such treaties are inevitable, the advantage for national parliaments would seem to lie along the path to differentiated integration or, colloquially, opt-outs on the one hand, matched on the other by agreements between a core of states to proceed to further integration. From the point of view of effective parliamentary procedures a clear opt-out is preferable to a series of ill-composed compromises within the treaty.

In any event governments should perhaps be reminded, as they approach the negotiation of the 1996 Conference, that the complexity and non-unitary nature of the TEU contributed significantly to the difficulties experienced in winning ratification for it.

A second desirable reform would be to provide, if necessary by statute, that all parts of future EC treaties should be subject to approval by both Houses at Westminster by primary legislation. Such a procedure would be modelled on the precedent set in Section 6 of the European Parliamentary Elections Act 1978, under which any provisions in EC treaties which serve to increase the powers of the European Parliament can only be ratified by the British government if they have been incorporated in an Act of Parliament and so formally approved by both Houses.

A reform in this sense would avoid the confusion caused generally during proceedings on the European Communities (Amendment) Bill in 1992 and 1993 by the fact that some sections of the TEU did not legally require to be approved by Act of Parliament, as is explained in Chapter 11.

A further useful reform making for simplicity and clarity would be to subject all future EC treaties in their entirety to the parent Act in this field, that is the European Communities Act of 1972. The possibilities for the drafting of and for debate upon amendments to the new treaty would be considerably clearer if this simple change could be agreed.

## Openness in EC decision-making

The second lesson to be learned from the Maastricht ratification process is the need to secure more openness in the decision-making process of the EC. The TEU includes a Declaration stating that the member states consider that 'transparency of the decision-making process strengthens the democratic nature of the institutions and the public's confidence in the administration'. The European Council of Edinburgh in December 1992 arrived at Conclusions on openness which *inter alia* foresaw certain debates in the Council being televised for viewing in the press area of the Council building, publication of records of formal votes in the Council, a full description in press releases of the Council's conclusions, background information (mainly for the press) on decisions on EC matters and also on the CFSP and Justice and Home Affairs. All written material was to be made available rapidly in all official languages.[1]

For the purposes of this study the importance of these attempts to secure more openness in decision-making in the EC lies in their impact on the role of national parliaments in that decision-making process. Obviously the more information is made available about the stance and voting record of each national government in the various sectoral Councils, the more effective can national parliaments be in rendering their own ministers accountable to them, and in monitoring the activities of the Council as a whole. Equally, the wider their access to documentary information held by all the institutions, the sharper can scrutiny by national parliaments become.

In order to implement the conclusions on openness agreed at Edinburgh an inter-institutional Declaration on Democracy, Transparency and Subsidiarity was agreed between the European Parliament (EP), the Council and the Commission in October 1993.[2] The Council and Commission subsequently agreed upon a code of conduct on public access to Council and Commission documents,[3] which was implemented by a Council Decision[4] and a Commission Decision[5] and Communication.[6]

These commitments to openness on the part of the three institutions have already shown results, in that the Commission is publishing more information, more EP committees are open to the public, and the Council has moved towards partial implementation of the Edinburgh Conclusions,

---

[1] European Council, Edinburgh, Presidency Conclusions, Part A, Annex 3, Transparency. Information on the Role of the Council, Agence Europe, Special Edition, 13–14 December 1992.
[2] OJ C 329, 6.12.93, p 133.
[3] OJ L 340, 31.12.93, p 41.
[4] OJ L 340, 31.12.93, p 43.
[5] OJ L 46, 18.2.94, p 58.
[6] OJ C 67, 4.3.94, p 5.

as embodied in these formal undertakings. But in many respects the Council has not yet fulfilled its commitments.

Openness has a special significance for the three new members of the European Union. The Finnish government, in a Declaration attached to its Accession Treaty, affirmed that 'open government, including public access to official records, is a principle of fundamental legal and political importance'. The Swedish government made a like Declaration; the question of openness was an issue in both the Finnish and Swedish referendums in Autumn 1994 on accession.

However, these two acceding member states, with openness in government enshrined in their constitutions, must have been at the least disappointed by the inclusion both in the Council Decisions and in the Code of Conduct of a proviso restricting access to Council documents in order to protect the confidentiality of Council proceedings. These provisos were invoked in order to deny access to documents in two cases, which had led to actions taken in the European Court of Justice. In the first case the government of the Netherlands, supported by the European Parliament, in March 1994 challenged the validity of the legal base of the Code of Conduct and the Council Decision—referred to above.[7] The Danish government, mindful of the criticisms of Council secrecy made during the referendum campaigns, supported the Dutch stand in Council.

In the second action, *The Guardian* newspaper of London, having been refused Council documents giving information on three sittings of the Council, took an action in 1994 before the Court of First Instance, asking it to annul the Council's refusal to provide the information sought.[8] The Dutch and Danish governments are known to have voted against the Council's decision to refuse to supply the documents requested. The Danish government subsequently decided to support the case brought by *The Guardian* newspaper, as did the EP. The Court is not expected to give its judgement on these two actions until late 1995.

In a wider focus, the attempts of the Council to block full implementation of the Declarations and Decisions adopted by it or by the European Council serve to increase public disillusionment with the Council and, by extension with the EC. This public feeling in turn lends weight to the claims by the national parliaments for a substantive role in EC decision-making, as a means of reducing the democratic deficit therein.

---

[7] OJ C 90, 26.3.94, p 11. Case C 58/94.
[8] OJ C 202, 23.7.94. Case T—194/94.

## National parliaments' role in the EC

The third lesson to be drawn from the Maastricht ratification process concerns therefore the role of national parliaments, not just in ratifying Treaties agreed by the governments, but in the process of legislation in the EC. The TEU included two Declarations on national parliaments, one of which foresaw the use of Conferences of Parliaments, comprising both MPs and MEPs, to afford national parliaments an opportunity for influencing EC legislation. The other Declaration exhorted national parliaments to collaborate with the EP in order to gain information about projected legislation so as to sharpen their procedures for scrutiny of Commission proposals.[9]

Regrettably, neither of these Declarations has to date been taken to heart. On the one hand, six national parliaments, in the course of ratifying the TEU, extracted assurances from their respective governments that more ample information about Commission proposals and other EC projects would be supplied to them, more expeditiously than in the past. However, there is to date little evidence of improvements in this field.

On the other hand, as the Appendix indicates, several national parliaments before ratifying the TEU exacted from their government increased accountability in regard to European legislation and to major decisions on European policy, particularly as regards economic and monetary union. Discussions have been held regarding the possibility that national parliaments might be represented in the Group of Reflection, which is to meet in June 1995 to prepare the IGC of 1996. But there are few signs of consensus among the national chambers in favour of a Conference of Parliaments, as foreseen in the TEU Declaration.

Given the sceptical, if not indeed hostile, mood of the public in many member states both to the TEU and to further European integration, it is surprising that national parliaments, severally and individually, have not, as it were, put themselves at the head of public opinion as regards the EC. They might have been expected, having won concessions from governments during the ratification process, to have followed up the advantage gained by pressing for more information, by greater collaboration with each other and with the European Parliament to improve

---

[9] Council and Commission of the EC, *Treaty on European Union*, Luxembourg: Office for Official Publications of the EC, 1992: Declaration on the Role of National Parliaments in the EU; Declaration on the Conference of the Parliaments.

their scrutiny procedures, and even by seeking, through a Conference of Parliaments, to influence the EC institutions.

But governments in the Council of Ministers are resisting demands for more openness and to date only the British and French parliaments have responded to the leaders of the Christian Democratic Union parliamentary party in the Bundestag, who have launched a debate on the future of the European Union.[10] Unless parliaments and governments take positive steps to explain and justify to the electors the preparations for the IGC, the course of the negotiations, and their outcome, it seems likely that there will be irresistible—and probably justified—demands for referendums, either on the outcome of the inter-governmental conference 1996 or on the text of any treaty agreed by it.

## More influence in Westminster

Should Westminster not therefore regard public disenchantment with the parliamentary ratification process, and the threat of a referendum on the IGC of 1996 as a spur to reforming its procedures for meeting the impact of membership of the EC? Before examining procedures already in use in other national parliaments for scrutiny of EC affairs, which might be adapted for use at Westminster, it is logical to set in context four proposals made in the preceding chapter. Each seeks, by reforming the existing scrutiny system, and adapting it to the EC as it exists post-Maastricht, to extend the influence of the Westminster parliament or to deploy more effectively such influence as it already has.

Specifically, the House of Commons should strengthen the terms of reference of the EC Legislation Committee in the Commons by aligning them to those enjoyed by the Lords Committee on the European Communities. The select committees monitoring government departments should continue to devote more of their resources to scrutiny of EC proposals and policies, which impinge ever increasingly on UK domestic administration. They should do this in collaboration with the EC select and standing committees.

Co-ordination of attempts by the two Houses to oversee EC activities has always existed, but has never been sufficiently close. Accepting that claims upon the time of MPs are heavy, EC scrutiny could be accorded a

---

[10] Karl Lamers, *A German Agenda for the European Union*, London: Federal Trust and Konrad Adenauer Foundation, 1994.

higher priority in the national interest, and also much more could be done to husband resources. For example, if too few MPs are available to man more than two European Standing Committees, would time and energy not be saved by creating a joint Committee of both Houses on the European Communities? Commons and Lords combine effectively to operate the Joint Committee on Statutory Instruments and other joint committees: this procedure could usefully be called upon to meet the challenge posed by the need for closer scrutiny of EC legislation.

A Declaration annexed to the TEU called for greater collaboration between the European Parliament and national parliaments. This could extend from the Conference of Parliaments to joint meetings of EP committees with national committees, joint meetings of European affairs committees, and use by Westminster of the knowledge and expertise of British MEPs, some of whom hold leading positions in the EP. Westminster would benefit by learning from the practice and procedure of other national parliaments in working with the EP, which is described in the Appendix.

A decisive referendum on continued British membership of the EC was held in 1975. For a short period ending in 1983 the Labour party nevertheless espoused a policy of withdrawal from the EC, but apart from this both major parties and the Liberal Democrat party have since 1975 favoured British membership. Despite this, a small group of MPs has, as earlier chapters have shown, used the opportunity of debates on EC legislation and policies to deploy arguments, either implicit or explicit, against British membership of the EC. While they had every right so to do, their interventions limited the opportunities of MPs representing the majority view to advance constructive criticism of the EC on a basis of continuing membership. This train of events, coupled with the lack of interest in the EC shown by a large number of MPs, has militated against the development by the Commons of co-ordinated and constructive procedures (such as were introduced for the new select committees in 1979) for EC scrutiny.

In particular, as industrial, commercial and financial interests campaigned constructively for the creation of a single EC market in the 1980s and 1990s, an objective also sought by all political parties, Commons debates on the floor and in committees were—as earlier chapters reveal conclusively—often dominated by negative and repetitive assertions of the case for withdrawal from the European Community.

The results have been dramatic: as the major actors in the British economy perceived that on EC matters the Commons was bent on self-marginalisation while the European Parliament's powers continued to expand, they have increasingly concentrated their efforts to influence EC legislation on the Strasbourg Parliament rather than on that at Westminster. The irony of this process is that, had the House of Commons, from accession to the EC in 1973, directed its energies towards exerting influence and oversight over both EC institutions and policies and the British government's activities in relation to them, it could have performed these functions better than any other national parliament (save perhaps that of Denmark). At the same time this would have helped to maintain its status, relevance and utility within the British constitutional structure.

## Action at a pre-legislative stage

The committees of the European Parliament enjoy unrivalled opportunities for questioning the Commission as to its legislative intentions, long before a proposal is published. The challenge to Westminster is to persuade EP committees to share with Westminster committees their information as to the avenues of eventual legislation under exploration by the Commission in each area of EC policy. The former President of the Commission, Jacques Delors, told the EP that not more than five per cent of Commission proposals originate from the Commission: the remaining 95 per cent are foisted on the Commission by the Council, by the EP, and by the member states. Westminster must so organise itself (profiting from the glimmerings of openness emerging from the Council, and from contacts with other parliaments and the EP) as to identify the sources of Commission proposals at an early and pre-legislative stage, the better to prepare considered opinions thereon. For example, a national parliament with active scrutiny procedures should be able, by questioning ministers, to ascertain what legislative proposals its own government is putting to the Commission.

In a drive for openness, the Commission since 1985 has increasingly sought the views of parliaments and others by publishing at a pre-legislative stage Communications and White and Green Papers; this practice is of great assistance to parliaments. Again, since the signing of the SEA in 1986 the Commission has been persuaded by the EP to publish, usually in February of each year, its legislative programme for that calendar year; the Council has regrettably not yet agreed to do likewise. This programme is thus available to committees at Westminster as a basis not only for scrutiny by the Commons and Lords EC committees, but also by select committees of both Houses.

For example, the Trade and Industry Committee of the House of Commons, or the Select Committee on the European Communities of the House of Lords, could take note in March of any year that the Commission intended to put forward in October a proposal under an Article of the TEU. Each Committee would then have the opportunity to seek advance information from the Commission and from the appropriate committee of the EP about the main thrust and likely scope of the proposal and could, based perhaps on previous reports by them, submit observations to the Commission about the projected proposal. In this way Westminster committees could influence the Commission at a pre-legislative stage and assist interested parties in Britain to do likewise.

Two further initiatives by the European Parliament can be drawn upon by national parliaments anxious to monitor Commission legislation as effectively as possible. The first is a computerised system called OEIL, which offers an overview of the stage reached within the EP or the Council by any proposal at any given moment; this is available to national parliaments.

In second place the EP has created a new service for close monitoring of legislative proposals. Each proposal will be monitored by a staff member of the relevant parliamentary committee, and the Commission and Council will also nominate a member of their secretariats whose responsibility is to follow the progress of the proposal. If the national parliament staff were able to tap into this inter-institutional network, their monitoring work would be greatly simplified.[11]

If Westminster was prepared to invest in monitoring systems of this type, it could facilitate the work of Library and other staff not only in reacting to legislative proposals but in anticipating them, so providing an even better service for Members of both Houses. Although by 1996 the Commons Library hopes to have sufficient resources in staff and equipment to introduce an awareness service on EC legislation, ie a type of 'early warning system', this is years too late and will probably be too limited to be fully effective.

---

[11] Information from the EP secretariat, 1994.

## Scrutiny of the EC by select committees

Some continental parliaments have drawn upon the experience and expertise of their permanent committees to assist in the scrutiny and control of European proposals, legislative and otherwise. The Bundestag has followed this procedure since 1991, the Danish Folketing introduced it in 1993, and the Assemblée Nationale of France in 1990, with further refinement in 1992.

Earlier chapters have discussed the reluctance of the Commons departmentally-related select committees to give priority to enquiries into prospective EC legislation or policy areas. The difficulty may lie in the refusal of successive governments to include in the terms of reference of such select committees the power to appoint sub-committees. If those committees in whose fields of enquiry the EC plays a major role were each free to appoint a sub-committee on EC policies and proposals, the overall capability of the House to monitor EC activities would be greatly enhanced.

Such sub-committees could examine proposals and projects at a pre-legislative stage, including those embodied in Commission communications and White and Green Papers and those in its legislative programme, and they could be charged with drawing up reports on legislative proposals, reporting to their parent committee. An advantage of scrutiny at a pre-legislative stage is that more time is normally available than is the case once a proposal has been put forward formally by the Commission. Collaboration with the work of the Commons EC Legislation Committee and with the Lords EC Committee could be assured by regular meetings between the chairmen and clerks of the committees in question. The sub-committees' reports to their parent committees would also serve to inform the members of European Standing Committees, other Members of the House and the general public.

Once the Commission has put forward a formal proposal, the existing scrutiny procedures are engaged in each House. The success of the European Standing Committees in providing for questions to be put to a minister followed by debate on proposals would seem to call for at least one more such committee to be created to buttress the existing two.[12] In 1991 the government proposed three committees, but Members could only be found to operate two: a sad reflection on Members' perception at that

---

12 See Chapter 4.

time of their duty to monitor EC legislation. The subsequent proceedings on the European Communities Bill in 1992 and 1993, and the debate on the future of the European Union launched in September 1994 by members of the Bundestag, and taken up by the Prime Ministers of Britain and France and others, may serve to convince MPs that a higher priority should be accorded to this duty. Closer to home, recognition by parliamentary parties of the invaluable contribution to Commons scrutiny made by members of the European Standing Committees would encourage more members to undertake this taxing, but essential work.

British MEPs, if offered the access to Westminster and reasonable use of its facilities at present denied to them by the House of Commons, could render considerable assistance to Commons committees in their oversight of EC activities.

### Danish and Dutch innovations

But however effective these suggestions—and those advanced in the preceding chapters—prove to be for sharpening the scrutiny procedures in the Commons, a bolder approach is now essential if, on the one hand, the House is to re-assert itself in its role of overseeing EC proposals and policies and, on the other, is to persuade the government into much greater openness in regard both to its EC policies and the activities of the Council of Ministers.

Using the Danish government's embarrassment following the adverse vote in the 1992 referendum on the TEU, the Folketing introduced several innovations in its procedures for scrutinising EC proposals and Danish government policy thereon.[13]

The two relevant to Westminster are the creation within the Folketing of a parliamentary information and documentation service on the EC proposals and their progress. The Folketing decided that it, as well as the government, was an appropriate body to provide information about the EC, which had so plainly been lacking before the first (negative) referendum in Denmark.

The second innovation was the launching of a 'European Council', convened by the Folketing, to meet twice per year. This is intended to provide an opportunity for Danish groupings or associations with a special

---

[13] See Appendix.

interest in European affairs to give their views directly to the parliamentary EC committee and to Danish MEPs. At one and the same time this enables informed views on the EC to be put directly to MPs and MEPs, alerts the public to the special case being put to MPs by interest groups, and creates a point of contact (one of the few) between the Folketing and Danish MEPs.

There appears to be no reason why the Lords and Commons EC select committees, together with members from other select committees and British MEPs, should not meet jointly in this way to hear the views of British associations and groupings with a particular interest in EC affairs in a public forum. The advantages of creating a parliamentary information and documentation service on the lines of that established by the Folketing would appear to be manifold. It would fulfil a clamant need, inadequately met at present by MEPs and MPs, by the government, by the offices in Britain of the EU institutions and by the European documentation centres for information on EC activities. For example, in a Gallup survey of EU information needs in Britain, published in November 1994, 77% of those interviewed said they would like to be better informed on what the EU was doing in their region, 76% on employment/job opportunities and 73% on the environment and environmental legislation.[14] The same survey showed that while 82% of respondents thought that their local MEP should 'be making greater efforts to provide the general public in Britain with information about Britain and the EU,' 73% thought that their MP should do this. For parliament to establish an information and documentation service would demonstrate the will and ability of parliament to meet a public need and thus to contribute to re-establishing the relevance of parliament in the eyes of the British people.

The States General is the Parliament of the Netherlands, and is composed of the First (Upper) Chamber and the Second (Lower) Chamber. In the course of ratification of the TEU the States General obliged the government to accept a notable constraint upon its freedom of action.[15] Before any decision of the Council of Ministers is taken in the field of justice and home affairs (Title VI of the Treaty), the prior assent of the States General is necessary before the government of the Netherlands can participate in such a decision. As most Council decisions under Title VI are taken by unanimity, this new provision endows the

---

[14] Gallup: 'Survey of EU information needs in Britain', London: European Commission press release, 20 November 1994, ISEC/20/94.

[15] See Appendix.

States General with a virtual veto over Council decisions on justice and home affairs matters.

From the point of view of the EC this may be regarded as 'one constraint too far' and one not to be imitated by other national parliaments. On the other hand as the governments at Maastricht specifically excluded the EP from exercising democratic surveillance and control of justice and home affairs (Article K.6 of the TEU), the Council can scarcely cavil if national parliaments use their best endeavours at least to mitigate this further exemplar of the democratic deficit. Indeed the British government goes so far as to believe 'that national governments of member states should be accountable to national parliaments, not to the European Parliament, on business under these pillars'.[16]

The House of Lords Select Committee on the European Communities, reporting on scrutiny of the common foreign and security policy (CFSP) and justice and home affairs pillars, stated, in cases where urgency or secrecy was not paramount: 'We believe that the objective should be a system under which the government undertake, wherever possible, not to agree to a proposal in the Council until parliamentary scrutiny has been completed'.[17] In response, the government stated that they 'are not persuaded that a formal scrutiny reserve is appropriate for cooperation carried out under the justice and home affairs pillar'. No scrutiny reserve is offered for CFSP matters.[18]

The Foreign Affairs Committee of the House of Commons recommended in 1993 that 'the government make it its policy to consult the House before important decisions are taken under the CFSP,' and under the justice and home affairs pillar of the TEU.[19] In its reply the government recalled that, as was the case with European Political Co-operation, much CFSP business 'will be fast moving and subject to the normal confidentiality and security considerations of foreign policy'. Ministers, however, were very willing to brief the relevant Committees in

---

[16] Observations by the Secretaries of State for Foreign and Commonwealth and for Home Affairs on the report from the Lords Select Committee on the European Communities on *House of Lords Scrutiny of the inter-governmental pillars of the European Union*, London: HMSO, Cm 2471, February 1994, para 2 (i).

[17] 28th report from the Select Committee on the European Communities, 1992–93, *House of Lords Scrutiny of the inter-governmental pillars of the European Union*, HL Paper 124, November 1993, para 62.

[18] Observations, op cit supra, para 2 (vii).

[19] Second report from the Foreign Affairs Committee, 1992–93, *Europe after Maastricht*, London: HMSO, April 1993, HC 642, vol I, paras 95 and 96.

both Houses on an *ad hoc* basis on particularly important CFSP issues, and the Foreign Secretary or his deputy would be willing to see the Foreign Affairs Committee from time to time before Foreign Affairs Councils of particular importance.[20]

Thus although the Lords Committee failed to win a scrutiny reserve on the two pillars in question, the Commons Committee won undertakings on prior briefings on particularly important CFSP Council meetings and issues. It remains to be seen whether the two Houses will attempt further to improve their scrutiny machinery in regard to the two pillars to the level of other national parliaments. One initiative which they should take immediately is to insist that the government furnishes the Library of each House with copies of the documents on which decisions by the Council of Ministers under the two pillars are being based.

Both Committees recognised that Council decisions under the CFSP might have to be taken rapidly, and that considerations of security and confidentiality might inhibit prior consultation of either House. But such considerations apply with much less force—if indeed at all—to decisions in the field of justice and home affairs. Taking this view, the States General required the Dutch government, in cases where urgency or secrecy was not paramount, at least to submit its draft approach to the Council decision confidentially for information to members of the States General. Neither House at Westminster has dared to go so far. But for the Lords and Commons to secure the agreement of the British government to seek prior parliamentary assent before it participated in a Council decision in the justice and home affairs field would constitute a major advance in parliamentary scrutiny of EC decision-making, would enable both Houses to consult informed opinion and would in many cases strengthen the arm of the government in discussions and decision-making in the Council.

## Conclusion

This volume includes a description of the evolution of the scrutiny system at Westminster; detailed studies of the work of both Houses in certain sessions; analysis of the European Communities Committees in both Houses; case studies of the treatment of agricultural policy and animal

---

[20] Observations by the Secretary of State for Foreign and Commonwealth Affairs on *Europe after Maastricht,* report from the Foreign Affairs Committee, 1992–93, London: HMSO, Cm 2287, July 1993, para 2 (ii).

welfare questions; an analysis of parliament's scrutiny of the IGCs of 1990–91; a detailed study of the passage of the European Communities (Amendment) Act 1993; and an assessment of the impact of the EC on the Westminster Parliament.

This closing chapter has sought to draw upon the conclusions and suggestions which have emerged from these chapters, to set them against a wider background, and to make further proposals designed to reduce the democratic deficit in the EC. National parliaments have a major part to play in achieving this latter objective. Although the British parliament is acknowledged as being among the leading parliaments in scrutinising the EC, many opportunities exist for improving its procedures. As the European Union moves forward towards economic and monetary union and closer political union, and the powers of the EP remain too limited for it to monitor these areas adequately, national parliaments will increasingly be called upon to develop, adapt and sharpen their scrutiny procedures. Public opinion will demand no less.

That is the challenge: the authors of this book hope that Westminster will rise to it.

# Appendix

## Scrutiny of European Community Affairs by National Parliaments

### David Millar

### Introduction

The purpose of this appendix is to indicate briefly the framework within which relations between the European Parliament and the national parliaments are conducted. Thereafter the impact of the Treaty on European Union is noted, and the procedures used by a representative selection of national parliaments to oversee European Union activities are discussed in some detail. By way of conclusion, various proposals are made as to which continental scrutiny procedures are worthy of study and of application by the British Parliament.

The Treaty of Rome made but limited provision for the national parliaments of the six original member states of the European Economic Community (EEC) to exercise any functions in regard to the Community. Indeed, it endowed the European Parliament (EP) itself with limited powers and competences. During the two decades from 1958 to 1978, the EP succeeded in extending its competences and influence but, except for the budgetary field, was unable to win a substantive increase in its powers.

The first election by direct, universal suffrage to the EP in 1979 marked the beginning of its sustained effort to win both greater power and wider influence. During this period, the EP adopted a resolution in July 1981, contained in the report of M. Andre Diligent, on its relations with the national parliaments.[1] The resolution sought closer co-operation with national parliaments and made specific suggestions in order to secure it. But it excited little response from the national parliaments which, to the extent that they scrutinised legislative proposals by the Commission and other EEC documents, did so chiefly in relation to the activities of the representatives of their own government in the Council of Ministers. It should also be recalled that the decade 1973–83 saw little progress in

---

[1] OJ C 234, 14.9.81, p 58.

333

European integration such as might awaken the interest of national parliaments.

## Creation of European Affairs Committees

National parliaments reacted to the challenge posed to their fields of competence by the signing of the Treaty of Rome in various ways and over a long period. Perhaps understandably, the parliaments of the three Northern European countries which acceded to the EEC in 1973 moved more rapidly than did those of the 'Old Six' to establish instruments through which they could carry out scrutiny and oversight of EC activities. Thus, by 1974 the Danish, Irish and British parliaments had all set up committees on the EEC and/or its legislation.

Of the Six, the Bundesrat acted promptly, in 1957, to set up a Committee for EEC Matters but the Italian Senate did not follow suit until eleven years later. In 1970, the First Chamber of the Dutch States-General set up its Standing Committee on Organisations for European Co-operation. This is not to say, however, that, among the Parliaments of the Six, EC questions had been neglected in the 1960s and 1970s. In most cases the Foreign Affairs Committee of each parliament included in its remit matters relating to the EEC.

Notwithstanding this situation, the first direct election of the EP in 1979, followed by the signature of the Single European Act (SEA) in 1986 launching the single market, spurred eleven chambers of the national parliaments, between 1985 and 1991, to establish 'European committees' of one type or another. They were notably (in chronological order) the Belgian Chamber, both Houses of the Spanish Cortes, the Dutch Second Chamber, the Portuguese Assembly, the Bundesrat, the Belgian Senate, the Greek Assembly, the Chamber of Deputies in Italy, and the Bundestag.[2]

The motives for the establishment by so many chambers of specialised committees on European affairs were probably three. First, the realisation that many of the 285 legislative proposals contained in the Commission's

---

[2] The Bundestag set up a Europe Committee in 1984, which in 1987 was replaced by the sub-committee on European Affairs of the Foreign Affairs Committee. This was in turn replaced by the European Community Committee in 1991. In December 1992 new Article 45 of the Basic Law provided for the creation of a committee for European Union Affairs of the Bundestag. The Bundesrat added a new body to scrutinise EC documents to is existing mechanism for scrutinising European integration 1988.

White Paper of 1985 on the internal market impinged directly upon policy sectors hitherto the preserve of national governments and monitored by national parliaments.

Second, the calculation that the introduction in the SEA of qualified majority voting to aid decision-making in the Community would at the least weaken the unanimity rule imposed by the Luxembourg Compromise of 1966; in the event it virtually destroyed it.[3] Majority voting has also weakened national parliaments' oversight of the activities of ministers in the Council, as they can always plead that they have been out-voted when they are unable to secure the adoption of policies predicated by their national parliament.

Third, as the EP made a bid to increase its influence with the adoption of the Draft Treaty on European Union 1984, its repeated assertion of its budgetary powers against the Council in the early 1980s, and its increased legislative powers arising from the SEA, national parliaments reacted by seeking to sharpen their oversight of EC activities.

## Conference of Presidents

Even before the first European elections in 1979, however, and well before the creation of European affairs committees in the late 1980s, the presidents of European parliamentary assemblies had begun to meet in conference. These assemblies included the parliaments of the member states of the Council of Europe, together with the EP, the Parliamentary Assembly of the Council of Europe and the Assembly of Western European Union. The conferences were launched by the EP and met every two years to discuss European matters of particular interest to parliamentary leaders. Discussions took place on the basis of reports prepared and circulated in advance, and a final declaration was usually drawn up and distributed to the media by the President of the host Parliament.[4]

By 1981, the need was felt by the presidents of the assemblies of the (then) ten EC member states to meet more frequently to debate matters specific to the Community. Thereafter, the 'large' Presidents' Conferences

---

[3] Anthony Teasdale: 'The Life and Death of the Luxembourg Compromise', *Journal of Common Market Studies*, vol 31, no 4, Dec 1993.

[4] F Jacobs, R Corbett and M Shackleton, *The European Parliament* (2nd edition), Harlow: Longman, 1992, pp 259–262.

alternated with 'small' conferences, comprising the President of the EP and those of the chambers of the parliaments of the EC states; the conferences were conducted on similar lines.

Since 1977 all these conferences have been prepared and organised by senior officials of the EP and the Parliamentary Assembly of the Council of Europe, acting as joint directors of the European Centre for Parliamentary Research and Documentation. The Centre runs a network for exchanges of information, documentation and research papers between officials of the European Assemblies and the parliaments of the member states of the Council of Europe. Thus a research study done on a European matter by one assembly has, since 1977, been available to all the others, except where a member of an assembly has insisted on confidentiality.

The importance of the Conferences of Presidents and of the Centre for the present study is that they assisted in forming habits and manifold practices of collaboration and co-operation between assemblies, on the basis of which European affairs committees were established in the 1980s and the 'Assizes' held in Rome in November 1990 (see below).

At this point, a brief notice is required of the status at the Conferences of Presidents of the Lord Chancellor and the Speaker of the House of Commons.

The Lord Chancellor, in his capacity as Speaker of the House of Lords, and the Speaker of the House of Commons, find themselves in an anomalous position. The reason is that the primary role of the former is as a senior Cabinet Minister, while the latter is the non-party servant and spokesman of the Commons. Neither officer is able to represent his or her House as do presidents of parliaments in continental countries, whose function is to represent their chambers not only in a formal but also in an effective—and, if necessary—political manner. The difference in status of the British presiding officers has, over the years, acted to diminish the influence of both Lords and Commons at such conferences. This is significant because it was the Conferences of Presidents which launched the first joint meeting of representatives of the national parliaments with the EP (the Assizes, Rome, November 1990) and also regular meetings between the European affairs committees of the parliaments.

## Impact of the IGCs and Maastricht Treaty

Speaking to the European Parliament in October 1989, President Mitterrand, President-in-office of the European Council, proposed that a conference be held between the EP and national parliaments, to which he gave the title 'Assises' (Assizes). One year later a 'small' Conference of Presidents of the EC Parliaments and the EP accepted this proposal. The Assizes were held in Rome in November 1990.

The motivation for the proposal had been the prospect of inter-governmental conferences (IGCs) being held to amend the Treaties: President Mitterrand was concerned lest the powers of national parliaments be further eroded by decisions taken at the IGCs, and that these parliaments should therefore review their relations with their own governments, with the EP and other Community institutions, and among themselves.

The Assizes (or Conference of the Parliaments) adopted a final Declaration which owed much to reports adopted by the EP in July 1990 in the perspective of the forthcoming IGCs. In fact, the Declaration incorporated a large part of the EP's position, and was adopted by a large majority.

The two relevant paragraphs in the Declaration are these:

13. Supports enhanced co-operation between the national parliaments and the European Parliament, through regular meetings of specialized committees, exchanges of information and by organizing Conferences of Parliaments of the European Community when the discussion of guidelines of fundamental importance to the Community justifies it, in particular when Intergovernmental Conferences are being held;

14. Takes the view that each national parliament must be able to exert its influence on the shaping of its government's policy stances on the Community.[5]

The success of the Assizes prompted the IGCs to include in the Maastricht Treaty two Declarations: on the Role of National Parliaments in the European Union, and on the Conference of the Parliaments.[6] The former calls for 'greater involvement of national parliaments in the activities of the European Union', and for a stepping-up of exchanges of

---

[5] European Parliament: *The New Treaties 1993 (EP Proposals)*, Luxembourg: Office for Official Publications of the EC, 1991, Part III.

[6] Council and Commission of the European Union, *Treaty on European Union*, Luxembourg: Office for Official Publications of the EC, 1992, pp 225–226.

information between national parliaments and the EP. The governments undertook *inter alia* that national parliaments should receive Commission proposals for legislation in good time.

The IGC also considered that contacts between the EP and national parliaments should be intensified. The second Declaration invited the EP and national parliaments to meet 'as necessary' in a Conference of Parliaments. This conference would be consulted on the main features of the European Union; the presidents of the European Council and the Commission agreed to report on the state of the Union to each session of the conference.

The significance of these Declarations lies in their recognition of the rôle that national parliaments have to fulfil in the European Union, mainly in collaboration with the EP. This is the first acknowledgement in any EC Treaty of this role; national parliaments are thus challenged to make good use of the opportunities now offered to them to influence the development of the European Union.

One indication of their eagerness to do so, and another manifestation of the impact of intensifying European integration on national parliaments, was the creation of yet another co-operative body. In November 1989, at the invitation of the President of the French National Assembly, M. L Fabius, representatives of the European affairs committees of the national parliaments, together with a delegation from the EP, launched the conference of bodies specialising in EC affairs. The aim of this conference, which holds one meeting every six months at the invitation of the parliament of the country holding the presidency of the Union, is to exchange information upon, and to assess, major themes of European integration. Many delegations make a formal report to their parliament after each meeting, thus further informing them about the progress of European integration in general, and of EC legislative proposals in particular.

It is now appropriate to describe the principal characteristics of European affairs committees of certain national parliaments.

## European Affairs Committees of National Parliaments

The character of specialised committees in national parliaments, created to enquire into and to monitor European Community or European affairs, has varied according to the nature of the parliament or assembly concerned. For example, bicameral parliaments faced the option of creating joint committees of both chambers, or one for each. Traditions and conventions regarding the scope and strength of the powers normally exercised by a committee of parliament varied between one chamber and another, and attitudes towards the EC and Council of Europe Assemblies and institutions were as diverse as the member states of these bodies.

Of the parliaments of the twelve Community states, eight are bicameral; of these, only those of Ireland and Spain have set up joint EC committees. In selecting some parliaments for particular study, more useful criteria would be the date of their accession to the EC, whether they hail from North Europe or Mediterranean Europe, and the extent of these committees' powers and influence.

### Denmark

Pride of place should be given to the Market Committee, now the 'EEC Committee', of the Folketing of Denmark[7], by reason of its unique powers in relation to those ministers who represent Denmark in the Council of Ministers of the European Union (formerly the EC).

The committee was created by a law in October 1972. The government has a duty to inform it of Commission proposals which will either be directly applicable in Denmark or will require national legislation for their implementation. The government is obliged to consult the committee on EC policy questions of major importance. Prior to each EC Council meeting, the government presents all the items on the Council's agenda for discussion by the committee; written reports of all Council meetings are submitted to the committee by the government. Prior to negotiations thereon, the government must give an oral explanation of its initial stance. If a majority of the committee does not disapprove of this standpoint, it becomes the government's mandate for the negotiations. If however, during the negotiations, it appears possible that the Council of Ministers may adopt a standpoint essentially different from that of the Danish government, the committee must be afforded another opportunity to approve or disapprove this new solution.

---

[7] Details of the creation, structure and operation of European Affairs Committees were derived from European Parliament, DG for Committees and Delegations, 'Bodies within national Parliaments specialising in EC affairs'. Luxembourg: European Parliament, March 1992, Doc W.1.

Co-operation between the government and the committee must, however, be based on mutual recognition of the necessity of respecting both the influence of the Folketing and the freedom of the government to act during negotiations. The law of 1972 obliges the government to keep the committee fully informed on EC legislative proposals, which are normally accompanied by a government explanatory memorandum.

The adoption of the SEA has inspired the introduction of a new procedure, by which the committee may decide that certain Commission proposals relating to the internal market should be set down on the agenda of the House itself for a reading, equivalent to the first (in UK terms, second) reading of a Bill. This procedure has not yet been used, however.

The EEC Committee has 17 members and 11 alternate members and meets weekly, except in August. It acts as an external relations instrument of the Folketing insofar as it co-ordinates all meetings between its committees and delegations, and the corresponding bodies in the European Parliament. The committee itself visits the EC institutions every year for detailed discussions. Despite, or perhaps because of, this close relationship, Danish MEPs cannot even attend committee meetings, much less speak or vote, unless they are also members of the Folketing and have been elected to the committee.

Not only do its terms of reference endow the EEC Committee with a position of influence vis-à-vis the Danish government's activities in the Council of Ministers, the multiplicity of parties in the Folketing and the decline in the 1970s and 1980s in the number of seats held by the Social Democratic Party have resulted in a series of minority governments, whose comparative weakness, especially on EC issues, has strengthened the rôle of the committee in guiding and monitoring the stance of the government in the Council of Ministers.

In 1992 the Folketing sharpened its oversight of EC affairs by various measures.[8] The EEC Committee and the other committees of the Folketing now exchange documents, the committees are entitled to consider EC documents and to report their conclusions thereupon to the EEC Committee, and they may hold hearings on EC topics within their competence. In addition, EC policies may be debated in plenary more frequently than hitherto.

---

[8] For details of the changes in national parliaments' procedures consequent upon the signature of the Treaty of Maastricht, see DG for Research, European Parliament, 'Recent changes in oversight by national Parliaments of the EC activities of their governments', Luxembourg: European Parliament, 1994 (PE.207.163).

In order better to inform the public, the Market Committee now holds a press conference after every meeting to explain the mandate it has given to Danish ministers. The Folketing has created a documentation service to inform the public about EC proposals and their progress. Finally, a 'European Council' will meet twice per year to offer citizens with special interests in European affairs the chance to inform the EEC Committee and Danish MEPs of their views. These three measures are an interesting response to the 'No' vote in the Danish referendum of June 1992 on ratification of the Maastricht Treaty.

In contrast to the restrictive rules in Denmark, in two EC member states, Belgium and Germany, a number of MEPs are full members of the European Affairs Committees of the Chamber and of the Bundestag, but only in Belgium do they have full voting rights.

## Belgium

Certain members of the Chamber of Representatives of Belgium had, for some time in the 1980s, sought a majority on the floor for their proposal to set up a committee on European questions. After protracted negotiations, the Advisory Committee on European Questions was set up in April 1985, composed of 10 members of the Chamber and 10 Belgian members of the EP. This composition (as also other aspects of the Committee's procedure) was influenced by the Europa Kommission (Europe Committee) of the Bundestag (see below).

In addition to the 20 appointed Members, one Member of the Chamber per political group not represented on the committee, and one Belgian MEP per political group not represented on the committee may sit, but not speak or vote, at meetings of the Advisory Committee.

The committee's function is to deliver opinions, on its own initiative or at the request of a Member of the Chamber or a Belgian MEP, on institutional and major political matters relating to the European Union, on co-operation between the Chamber and the EP, and on questions relating to the status of Belgian MEPs. To assist the other committees of the Chamber to examine matters within their competence, both on the agenda of the Council of Ministers of the EC, and arising from decisions of the Council, the Advisory Committee keeps committees informed as to the Council's activities.

The committee summons members of the government to appear before it, and meets monthly during sittings of the House. It also possesses a major power, that of having its draft resolutions tabled directly in the Chamber for debate.

The Belgian Senate set up an Advisory Committee on European questions in 1990, comprising 22 Members of the Senate. Belgian MEPs who are not members of the committee are invited to speak, but not vote, at committee meetings. The committee delivers opinions on European questions at the request of the President, or of a Committee, of the Senate. It summons members of the government and is kept informed by the government about EC matters.

## Germany

In Germany, the Bundestag has tried three approaches to the problem of scrutinising EC affairs, but a common element in each has been the admission of German MEPs to full membership of each committee, but without the right to vote.

The Bundestag was the first chamber of a national parliament to offer full membership of its European Committee to MEPs. Its Europa Kommission was established in 1984 as an independent committee, half the members being from the Bundestag and half German MEPs. The Kommission drew up detailed reports on issues of European integration but worked too slowly to be able to influence either the Bundestag itself, the Council of Ministers or the European Parliament.

The Kommission was therefore replaced in 1987 by the Sub-Committee for EC Affairs of the Committee on Foreign Affairs (CFA). This marked a partial return to the pre-1984 arrangement by which EC matters were covered by the CFA. In its time that system worked well, and German MEPs who were members of the CFA were often better briefed on EC issues in the EP's committees than MEPs from other countries. But the increasing pace of progress towards European integration—marked by the internal market programme and the SEA and its associated policies—demanded the creation of a specialised body on EC matters.

The Committee on European Affairs was set up in 1991. It comprised 44 full, and 44 substitute Members, including 11 MEPs in each category. The need for specialist knowledge from other committee areas was recognised by the inclusion of members of other Bundestag committees. This demonstrates the value of the unitary, all-purpose committee, whose members acquire expertise in other fields in overseeing EC affairs.

The German MEPs (and substitutes) had the right to speak in the EC Committee, but not to vote or to present motions.

The European Affairs Committee had competence on European questions for which no other committee was clearly competent, such as:

(a)   to discuss all proposed amendments to the Treaties;
(b)   to discuss the institutional affairs of the EC;
(c)   to act on its right to be informed by the federal government of all government proposals with a European dimension, and in particular to scrutinise government activity closely in the period preceding a meeting of the European Council.

Alongside the European Affairs Committee, the Committee on Budgets and the Committees on Legal and Economic Affairs constituted sub-committees on EC affairs. Such sub-committees were limited to their specific field of responsibility however, in order to avoid clashes of competence. These rather complex and interlocking scrutiny procedures in the event proved cumbersome and slow. Partly for this reason, and partly for major constitutional reasons, in the course of ratification of the Maastricht Treaty both the Bundestag and Bundesrat acquired the power to subject all future transfers of power to the European Union to approval of each House by a two-thirds majority (Constitution, Article 23). Article 45 of the Constitution provided for the creation of a new Committee on the European Union in the Bundestag which at the time of writing had yet to be appointed.

As has been noted, the Federal Council of Germany, the Bundesrat, was the first chamber of a national parliament to establish a Committee for EC Affairs in 1957. As a federal representative body, the Bundesrat is unique in the EC, and its particular character must be borne in mind. It is composed of ministers of Land (provincial) governments, who may be represented by Land civil servants. Its function is to protect the interests of the Laender in the light of the activities of the federal government and the EU. This function is exercised in the perspective of the responsibility of the Land governments for implementation of much of the body of federal law and also of EU law.

The Committee for EU Affairs of the Bundesrat is comprised therefore of 22 delegates from the 16 Laender in a number proportionate to the size of each Land. German MEPs may participate only in individual cases. The German treaties ratifying the Treaty of Rome and the SEA laid upon the federal government the duty of referring to the Bundesrat all Commission legislative proposals, communications, reports, and similar documents. These are in turn referred to committees of the Bundesrat, and the EU Committee considers the documents, and the other committees' recommendations thereon, from the point of view of European integration. It seeks to co-ordinate these recommendations to the Bundesrat, which may embody them in opinions to the federal government.

The EU Committee also receives reports from the federal government on European integration, and discusses the activities of the EC institutions and the policies of the federal government. It meets every three weeks to prepare the decisions of the Bundesrat.

By a decision of June 1988, the Bundesrat created a second body related to EC Affairs, namely, the Chamber for scrutiny of EC documents. Each Land delegates one member to the Chamber, but may also appoint any number of substitute members from the Bundesrat. MEPs may participate in debate, but have no right of membership of the Chamber. It meets only rarely.

The function of the Chamber is to discuss, and take decisions on, urgent or confidential documents relating to the activities of the EC. This includes sending representatives to negotiations in EC bodies, such as the Commission and Council, in cases where the documents concern exclusively legislative matters or the vital interests of the Laender.

The most important characteristic of the Chamber is that its decisions are equivalent to decisions of the Bundesrat; thus Chamber decisions can be referred directly to the federal government. In urgent cases, and where the relevant documents are confidential, the Chamber acts in place of the federal council in plenary sitting. As a consequence, the Chamber shares the right of the Bundesrat to require the attendance of Federal ministers at its deliberations, and is a potentially powerful scrutiny body.

### France

In France, as in Denmark and Germany, the debates on ratification of the Maastricht Treaty provided an opportunity for the legislature to reinforce significantly its power of scrutiny of the EC policy-making process.

The first direct election to the European Parliament in 1979 provoked both chambers of the French Parliament to appoint 'Delegations' for the European Communities. EC issues were previously treated by the Committee on External Affairs of each chamber.

In 1990 the number of members of each delegation was doubled from 18 to 36. Deputies or Senators elected also to the EP may belong to either delegation, which in turn may invite other French MEPs to participate in their work in a consultative rôle.

The delegations may be consulted by the committees of each chamber on any EC draft act or legislative proposal. Equally, the delegations refer information and proposals from the Community to other committees. They publish information reports, usually with conclusions, which may be debated on the floor of each chamber.

At least once every six months the two delegations hold a joint hearing with the Minister for European Affairs and invite other ministers to provide information.

In 1992 the process of ratification of the Maastricht Treaty afforded the French Parliament the opportunity to strengthen its oversight of EC legislative proposals and government policy towards the Community. A constitutional amendment (new Article 88.4) was adopted at a joint Congress of the National Assembly and the Senate, which reads:

> The Government will transmit to the National Assembly and the Senate, at the time of their submission to the EC Council, proposals for EC acts which include legislative elements.

During or outwith sessions, resolutions within the scope of this Article may be adopted by either chamber.

Although such resolutions do not bind the government, this amendment constitutes a substantive constitutional change with two effects. First, it removes EC policy-making from the field of foreign policy hitherto reserved by the constitution to the Head of State or of Government, and passes it to parliamentary scrutiny, even to a limited degree. Second, it assures the provision of information on EC legislative proposals to both chambers.

The rules of procedure of the National Assembly and the Senate set out the detailed arrangements for the exercise of this new parliamentary power:

(a) EC legislative proposals are transmitted to the chambers.
(b) A deputy or senator may table a motion for resolution on any proposal.

(c)   The motions are referred to the competent committee, are considered
      by them and may be amended. The European 'Delegation' may
      submit its opinion thereon.

(d)   Under a new procedure, the competent committee may, on behalf of
      the chamber, adopt any resolution definitively, with or without
      amendment, unless the president of a committee or of a political
      group requests that the resolution be debated in plenary.

(e)   Resolutions, once adopted either in committee or in plenary, are
      transmitted to the government.

## Netherlands

Just as the SEA provoked the creation in 1986, for the first time, of a
Standing Committee on European Affairs in the Dutch Tweede Kamer
(Second or Lower Chamber), the ratification of the Maastricht Treaty
stimulated further measures. In line with the Parliaments of Denmark,
France and Germany, the States General of the Netherlands used the
opportunity to strengthen its oversight of government participation in
decision-making in the EC or European Union.

The Dutch law ratifying the treaty specifies that before any decision by
the Council of the Union on Title VI (Co-operation in the fields of justice
and home affairs), the relevant draft order must be submitted to the States
General. The latter must approve the draft order before the government
can implement it.

In the monetary field, the States General has in two areas advanced its
powers of oversight of government action. The first case applies when,
under Article 103(4) of the Maastricht Treaty, the Council decides to make
a recommendation to the Dutch government advocating measures to be
taken either to secure economic convergence or, under Article 104C, to
reduce an excessive government deficit; or if, in the latter case, the
Council requires the member state to act to reduce its deficit. If any of
these situations arises, the government must inform the States General
fully of the Council decision.

In the second case, parliamentary oversight is considerably stricter. In
the third stage of EMU, the States General must give its prior approval to
the position adopted by the government in its evaluation of the four
economic and monetary criteria set out in Article 109J of the Treaty on
European Union. These criteria measure the achievement or otherwise by
any member state of a high degree of convergence, and are the rate of

inflation; the amount of any deficit; the stability of the exchange rate; and the levels of long-term interest rates.

Thus the States General have acquired a veto—like the Bundestag, the Bundesrat and the House of Commons—over any action by their respective governments to implement the decisive phase of stage three of EMU.

Apart from these new powers in relation to European Union, the Standing Committee on European Affairs employs a battery of procedures for effective scrutiny, which make it one of the most effective of all those in national parliaments.

The Committee has six tasks:

(a)  to consult, at every stage of the decision-making procedure in the EU institutions, the Foreign Minister and his State Secretary (head of the ministry), and to inform other committees and the chamber about these consultations;

(b)  to oversee the activities of the EP in monitoring the implementation of EC policies;

(c)  in collaboration with other parliamentary committees, to assess the implications of EC policy for the Netherlands;

(d)  to maintain contacts with the EP, in particular with Dutch MEPs and EP committees, and with European committees of other Parliaments;

(e)  to ensure that the Chamber and its committees are fully informed and documented on EU policy;

(f)  to ascertain that each government bill submitted to the chamber contains a clause describing the relationship between the bill and existing EC legislation in that field.

In addition to the consultations under (a) above, before—and where appropriate, after—meetings of the Council of Ministers and the European Council, the European Affairs Committee meets the State Secretary for Foreign Affairs and the Prime Minister, or other ministers, respectively. Further meetings with government ministers arise in relation to the form and content of detailed agendas of Council meetings; and at least once a year the committee meets the government for a wide-ranging discussion, which can lead to a debate in the chamber.

Finally, the European Affairs Committee seeks a meeting with its counterpart in the parliament of the member state currently holding the Presidency of the Council of the EU, ie every six months.

## A traditional approach: Spain

In order to achieve a balance in this survey of procedures deployed by certain national parliaments in order to oversee the policy of their governments towards the EC, the case of Spain should be considered. Spain became a member of the EC in 1986 having only ten years previously thrown off the totalitarian régime of General Franco.

The Spanish Cortes created in 1985 the Joint Committee on the European Communities (Law 47/1985), comprising 21 members from the Congreso de Los Diputados, and 16 from the Senado. By Law 18/1988 the Committee was empowered to hold joint meetings with Spanish MEPs, and has done so.

The same law endowed the committee with the following rights and tasks:

(1)    to be informed by the government of EC legislative proposals which encroach on matters on which the Cortes has the right to legislate;
(2)    to be informed by the government of its EC policies and of decisions taken by the EC Council;
(3)    to draw up reports on legislative proposals by the Commission.

Thus, almost all the activities of the committee consist of questioning ministers and senior officials on EC matters. Although the Joint Committee itself meets only monthly, in 1990 it set up three sub-committees, which meet several times per month.

Some of the 'autonomous regions' of Spain (eg the Basque country, the Canary Islands) have set up European affairs committees in their regional parliaments.

## Conferences of Committees on European Affairs

The process of negotiation within the inter-governmental conferences of 1990–91, culminating in the Treaty of Maastricht; the subsequent referendums in Denmark and France; and the widespread public resistance to the secrecy governing discussions of the IGCs and to the 'democratic deficit' in the EU have had salutary effects. In Denmark, Germany, France and the Netherlands, parliamentary scrutiny of national government activities in regard to the EC has been substantially strengthened. In addition to these procedural changes, and to co-operation among national parliaments and between them and the EP at the levels of Conferences of Presidents, as noticed above, the Conference of bodies specialising in European affairs (ie European affairs committees) is becoming increasingly active and effective.

For example, the Conference met at the invitation of the Belgian Parliament in Brussels in November 1993 to discuss the subjects of employment and immigration, and the Schengen Agreement on free movement of persons.[9] Exceptionally, the Belgian Prime Minister and Minister for Foreign Affairs, representing the Belgian Presidency of the EC, were invited. The Belgian ministers specialising in the subjects under discussion (and thus Presidents of the appropriate groupings of the Council of Ministers) and the Member of the Commission concerned with these subjects also attended; the Commission were thus represented for the first time. As regards the EP, its appropriate rapporteurs were invited to form part of its normal delegation of six Members to meetings of the Conference.

This is an excellent example of the intensified efforts made by one EU Presidency to inform those national MPs most closely implicated in parliamentary proceedings about major subjects of concern both to the institutions of the Union and to national parliaments and governments.

On the level of the permanent committees of parliaments (in the UK, select committees), contacts with the EP have been stepped up between 1991 and 1993. In this period the total of multi-lateral meetings, round table meetings, visits of specialised committees and bilateral meetings and hearings increased from 20 to 36. The EP has noted that requests for meetings have been particularly numerous from those national parliaments which have achieved closer oversight of their governments' EC policies (Denmark, Germany, France, Netherlands).[10]

## Conclusion

The aim of this Appendix is to offer concise information on the procedures used by national parliaments to scrutinise the EC and national government activities in regard to it. It is clear that Denmark, Germany, the Netherlands and the UK have been the most successful in reinforcing their

---

[9] Internal EP document, 1993.
[10] Internal EP document, 1994.

procedures for monitoring the EC policies and activities of their own governments. The principal improvements have been:

(1)  introduction of formal votes in parliament to sanction government proposals for participation in stage three of Economic and Monetary Union (Germany, Netherlands, UK).

(2)  in the Netherlands, a new power of control of government action has been granted to the States General to the effect that its assent is required before the Kingdom of the Netherlands participates in any decision of the Council of Ministers relating to Co-operation on justice and home affairs (Title VI of the Maastricht Treaty).

(3)  measures in Denmark to increase 'openness'. These include press conferences held after every EEC committee meeting to give the public details of the mandate given by the committee to Danish representatives in the Council of Ministers, and an information section in the Folketing specifically to inform the public about EC proposals and their progress and sources of further information thereupon. Finally, an innovatory procedure has been launched by which a 'European Council' comprising Danish MEPs and members of the public closely interested in EC matters (such as interest groups, trades unions and employers) meets twice a year to advise the EEC Committee.

(4)  the adoption of resolutions relating to government action on EC affairs (France).

(5)  commitments by governments to provision of information to European affairs committees (all parliaments).

The British Parliament has used the process of ratification of the Maastricht Treaty to sharpen its oversight and control of government action in regard to the European Union.

Nevertheless, the descriptions of scrutiny procedures adopted by some national parliaments set out earlier in this text, and summarised above, indicate that Westminster might usefully study the new Dutch and Danish procedures with a view to their adoption. Perhaps the most interesting is the prior assent claimed by the States General to government action in regard to justice and home affairs. Such action is not normally subject to considerations of confidentiality and urgency such as might prevent effective parliamentary scrutiny of actions within the field of common foreign and security policy.

Finally, the national parliaments have still ample scope for improving their collaboration with the European Parliament, which has on several occasions made proposals in this sense, only to be greeted with silence or disdain.

# Bibliography

(**Note**: this bibliography includes only a small number of the many select committee reports that are cited in footnotes to the text).

H Arbuthnott and G Edwards, *A Common Man's Guide to the Common Market*, London: Macmillan, 1989.

D Arter, *The Politics of European Integration in the Twentieth Century*, London: Dartmouth, 1993.

D Baker, A Gamble and S Ludlam, 'Whips or Scorpions? The Maastricht Vote and the Conservative Party', *Parliamentary Affairs*, vol 46, April 1993, pp 151–166.

D Baker, A Gamble and S Ludlam, 'The Parliamentary Siege of Maastricht', *Parliamentary Affairs*, vol 47, January 1994, pp 37–60.

V Bogdanor, 'Britain and The European Community'. In J Jowell and D Oliver (eds), *The Changing Constitution*, 3rd edition, Oxford: Clarendon Press, 1994, pp 3–31.

C J Boulton (ed), Erskine May's *Treatise on the Law, Privileges, Proceedings and Usages of Parliament*, 21st edition. London: Butterworths, 1989.

A Bressand, 'The 1992 Breakthrough and the Global Economic Agenda'. In J Story (ed), *The New Europe*, Oxford: Blackwell, 1993, pp 314–327.

C Carstairs and R Ware (eds) *Parliament and International Relations* Buckingham: Open University Press, 1991

A Clark, *Diaries*, London: Weidenfeld and Nicolson, 1993.

M Clarke, *British External Policy Making in the 1990s*, London: Macmillan, 1992.

N Colchester and D Buchan, *Europe Relaunched: Truths and Illusions on the Way to 1992,* London: Hutchinson, 1990.

D Coombes et al, *European Integration, Regional Devolution and National Parliaments* London: European Centre for Political Studies, 1979

D Coombes, M Beloff and N Johnson for the Study of Parliament Group *The Consequences for Parliament of British Membership of the European Communities* London: Hansard Society for Parliamentary Government, 1972

D Coombes (introduction) *Westminster to Brussels: the significance for Parliament of Accession to the European Community* London: PEP in Association with the Hansard Society and the Study of Parliament Group, Volume XXXIX Broadsheet 540, January 1973

R Corbett, *The Treaty of Maastricht. From Conception to Ratification: A Comprehensive Reference Guide,* Longman, 1993.

P J Cullen, *The United Kingdom and the Ratification of the Maastricht Treaty: the Constitutional Position,* University of Edinburgh Europa Institute, July 1993.

T Daintith, 'Regulation'. In *The International Encyclopedia of Comparative Law,* vol xvii, 'Law State and Economy'; Tubingen: Mohr, 1995, para 53.

Department of Trade and Industry, *Review of the Implementation and Enforcement of EC Law in the UK,* 1993.

A V Dicey, *An Introduction to the Study of the Law of the Constitution,* 10th edition, London and Basingstoke: Macmillan, 1959.

G Edwards, 'Britain and Europe'. In J Story (ed), *The New Europe,* Oxford: Blackwell, 1993, pp 187–227.

N Emiliou, 'Subsidiarity: Panacea or Fig-Leaf?' In D O'Keefe and P Twomey (eds), *Legal Issues of the Maastricht Treaty,* London: Chancery Lane Publishing, 1994, pp 65–83.

Foster Report: *First Report from the Select Committee on European Community Secondary Legislation* (Chairman: Sir John Foster QC, MP), 1972–73, HC 143

Foster Report: *Second Report from the Select Committee on European Community Secondary Legislation* (Chairman: Sir John Foster QC, MP), 1972–73, HC 463–I–II

M Franklin and P Norton (eds), *Parliamentary Questions*, Oxford: Clarendon Press, 1993.

D Freestone and J Davidson, *The Institutional Framework of the European Communities*, London: Croom Helm, 1988.

P Fussell, *The Great War and Modern Memory*, Oxford University Press, 1975.

S George, *An Awkward Partner: Britain in the European Community*, Oxford: The University Press, 1990.

S George (ed), *Britain and the European Community*, Oxford: Clarendon Press, 1992.

J A G Griffith and M Ryle, *Parliament: Functions, Practice and Procedures*, London: Sweet and Maxwell, 1989.

Hansard Society for Parliamentary Government *The British People: their Voice in Europe* Farnborough, Hants: Saxon House, 1977

*Making the Law: The Report of The Hansard Commission on The Legislative Process*, London: The Hansard Society, 1993.

T Hartley, 'Constitutional and institutional aspects of the Maastricht agreement' *International and Comparative Law Quarterly*, vol 42, 1992, pp 213–237.

G Howe, 'The European Communities Act 1972' *International Affairs*, vol 49, January 1973, pp 1–13.

R Jennings & A Watts (eds), *Oppenheim's International Law*, 9th edition, Harlow: Longman, 1992.

P Jones, 'Playing the Westminster Numbers Game' *Scottish Affairs*, no 5, Autumn 1993, pp 26–40.

D Judge, *The Parliamentary State*, London: Sage, 1993.

M Kolinsky 'Parliamentary Scrutiny of European Legislation' *Government and Opposition*, volume 10, Winter 1975, pp 46–69.

A Lijphart, *Democracies: Patterns of Majoritarian and Consensual Government in Twenty One Countries*, New Haven, CT: Yale University Press, 1984.

J Lodge (ed) *The European Community and the Challenge of the Future*, 2nd Edition, London: Pinter, 1993.

G Marshall, 'The Maastricht proceedings', *Public Law*, Autumn 1993, pp 402–407.

P Mathijsen, *A Guide to European Community Law*, London: Sweet and Maxwell, 1990.

Maybray-King Report: *First Report by the Select Committee on Procedures for Scrutiny of Proposals for European Instruments* (Chairman Lord Maybray-King), 1972–73, HL 67, March 1973.

Maybray-King Report: *Second Report by the Select Committee on Procedures for Scrutiny of Proposals for European Instruments* (Chairman Lord Maybray-King), 1972–73, HL 194, July 1973.

F W Mayer, 'Managing domestic differences in international negotiations: the strategic use of internal side-payments', *International Organization*, vol 46, Autumn 1992, pp 793–818.

M Mezey, *Comparative Legislatures*, Durham NC: Duke University Press, 1979.

D Miers and A Page, *Legislation,* 2nd Edition, London: Sweet and Maxwell, 1990.

J D B Mitchell, 'British Law and British Membership' *Europarecht,* vol 6, April 1971, pp 97–118.

J D B Mitchell, 'The Sovereignty of Parliament and Community Law: the Stumbling Block that isn't there', *International Affairs,* vol 55, January 1979, pp 33–46.

J D B Mitchell, 'What Happened to the Constitution on 1st January 1973?' *Cambrian Law Review,* vol 11, 1980, pp 69–86.

J Mitchell, S Kuipers and B Gall, 'Constitutional Aspects of the Treaty and Legislation Relating to British Membership' *Common Market Law Review,* vol 9, 1972, pp 134–151.

W Nicoll and T Salmon, *Understanding the European Communities,* London: Philip Allan, 1990.

N Nugent, *The Government and Politics of the European Community,* London: Macmillan, 1989.

D O'Keefe and P Twomey, *Legal Issues of the Maastricht Treaty,* London: Chancery Lane Publishing, 1994.

Procedure Committee: *First Report from the Select Committee on Procedure,* 1977–78, HC 588-I-III.

Procedure Committee: *Fourth Report from the Select Committee on Procedure,* 1988–89, HC 622-I-II, *The Scrutiny of European Legislation.*

Procedure Committee: *Fourth Report from the House of Commons Select Committee on Procedure Session 1988–89: The Scrutiny of European Legislation—Government Response,* Cm 1081; May 1990.

Procedure Committee: *First Report from the Select Committee on Procedure,* 1991–92, HC 31, *Review of European Standing Committees.*

R D Putnam, 'Diplomacy and Domestic Politics: the Logic of Two-Level Games', *International Organization*, vol 43, Summer 1988, 427-460.

R Rawlings, 'Legal Politics: The United Kingdom and Ratification of the Treaty on European Union (in two parts), *Public Law*, Summer 1994, pp 254-278 and Autumn 1994, pp 367-391.

E Regelsberger, 'European Political Cooperation'. In J Story (ed), *The New Europe*, Oxford: Blackwell, 1993, pp 270-291.

M Ryle and P G Richards (eds) *The Commons under Scrutiny* London: Routledge, 1988

D Shell, *The House of Lords*, 2nd Edition, London: Philip Allan, 1992.

D Shell and D Beamish (eds), *The House of Lords at Work*, Oxford: Clarendon Press, 1993.

M Smith, 'The Agricultural Community: Maintaining a Closed Relationship'. In D Marsh and R A W Rhodes (eds), Policy Networks in British Government, Oxford: Clarendon Press, 1992, pp 27-50.

F Snyder, *New Directions in European Community Law*, London: Weidenfeld and Nicolson, 1990.

J Steiner, 'Subsidiarity under the Maastricht Treaty'. In D O'Keefe and P Twomey (eds), *Legal Issues of the Maastricht Treaty*, London: Chancery Lane Publishing, 1994, pp 49-64.

J Story, 'Europe: from One Containment to Another'. In J Story (ed), *The New Europe*, Oxford: Blackwell, 1993, pp 493-514.

J Story and M de Cecco, 'The Politics of Monetary Union: 1985-1991'. In J Story (ed), *The New Europe*, Oxford: Blackwell, 1993, pp 328-354.

A Toth, 'A Legal Analysis of Subsidiarity'. In D O'Keefe and P Twomey (eds), *Legal Issues of the Maastricht Treaty*, London: Chancery Lane Publishing, 1994, pp 37-48.

H Wallace, 'European Governance in Turbulent Times', *Journal of Common Market Studies*, vol 31, no 3, 1993, pp 293–303.

R Ware and V Miller, *European Political Union*, House of Commons Library Background Paper 271, 23 May 1991.

S Woodcock, 'Trade Diplomacy and the European Community'. In J Story (ed), *The New Europe*, Oxford: Blackwell, 1993, pp 292–313.

# Index

Italics have been used for titles and in locations containing a table

agricultural policy making,
EC 192–4
Agriculture Council 197–8,
201–2
Assizes, final Declaration 337

Belgium 334, 341–2
Biffen, John 65–6, 75, 85–6
Bridge, Lord, European Court of
Justice 46–7
Bruges Group 251–2

Cairns Group 193–4
CAP *see* Common Agricultural
Policy
CFSP *see* EC, common foreign &
security policy
Cockfield report 23
Commission of the EC 11, 72, 131,
277, 302, 320, 325–6, 335
Committee of the Regions 262,
277–81, 316
Common Agricultural Policy (CAP)
17 Chapter 8 *passim*
agricultural price proposals 197,
212
*Development & Future of the
CAP* 171, 216–17
expenditure 193, 206
financing arrangements 22
*Perspectives for the CAP* 179,
215
reform 194–5, 197, 199–221,
311
Treaty on European Union 191
Commons, House of
adjournment debates 123
debates, general 58, 74, 125,
134–6, 244, 245,

248–9, 253–6, 281–96
Consolidated Fund debates
121, 208
early day motions 123–5,
156–8
Committees *see also* European
Legislation Committee,
European Standing
Committees, and select
committees
European Legislation Committee
37–8, 57, 61, 63–75,
78–88, 109, 138–44, 197,
199–201, 205, 211, 218–221,
245, 308–9, 315
terms of reference 65, 70, 74,
77, 88, 86, 96
European Secondary Legislation
Committee 51–60, 82, 87–8,
120–1, 304–5
European Standing Committees 80,
144–8, 198, 205, 229
Financial procedures 121–2
Library 247, 326
Questions 58, 115–19, 195,
199, 311
Select Committees
departmentally-related
148–54, 309–10, 315,
323, 327
Agriculture 151–2, 154,
197, 204, 209–10,
219, 224, 232
Defence 154
Education, Science &
Arts 150
Employment 150, 153–4
Environment 151–2
Foreign Affairs 132, 151,

*Index*

245-6, 330
Health 150, 154
Home Affairs 151
Social Services 154
Trade & Industry 151,
154, 310, 326
Transport 153-4
Treasury & Civil Service
151-2, 154, 245
Procedure Committee 50-1,
55, 58, 60-3, 73-82,
85-6, 145-9, 306,
309-10
reports
(1973) 51, 94-6
(1977-78) 58, 61, 73
(1983-84) 85
(1988-89) 86, 138
(1989) 58, 76-7, 315
(1991-92) 81-2, 145,
149
statements 119-20, 155, 201,
272, 311
Conference of Parliaments 143,
322-24, 338
Conference of Presidents 335-6
Conferences of Committees on
European Affairs 142-3, 170,
348-9
Constitution, British
background and principles
31-48, 302
implications of EC membership
Chapter 3 *passim* 262-8,
296, 301-11
treaty process 32-6, 42, 45,
318-9
Council of Europe 335
Council of Ministers 2, 11, 19-21,
55, 73, 107, 114, 212,
232-4, 246-7, 277, 302,
320-1
Court of Auditors 131, 196, 206-7,
216, 241

Court of First Instance 321
Court of Justice of the European
Communities (CJEC) 11, 23,
43-7, 131, 135, 273, 282, 301,
321
Courts, UK, impact of membership
43-48
Cyprus, application for membership
(1990) 14
de Gaulle, Charles 13, 18, 21-2
Delors Committee report on Economic
& Monetary Union 72, 245
Delors, Jacques 313, 325
Denmark 19, 95, 303, 321, 327-9,
339-41
referendums 248, 259, 261, 268,
271, 276, 318, 328
Denning, Lord, community & national
laws 47
Dicey, AV 32, 43, 300-3
Diplock, Lord, UK treaty obligations
45
Dooge Report 19

Eastern Europe 15, 16
EC (European Community) accession
and enlargement
Austria, Finland & Sweden
13-14
Denmark 13, 49
Greece 13
Ireland 13, 19, 49
Portugal 13, 16
Spain 13, 16
UK 9, 13, 49, 56-7, 192,
266-7
aims, structure & legal
characteristics 10
animal welfare 223-240
budgets, 15, 19, 200, 241
common foreign & security
policy (CFSP) 108, 320,
330-1
competence 26-7, 34

decision-making procedures 17, 26, 49 , 107, 319–20, 323

Economic & Social Committee 277, 316

enlargement 12–17, 21, 317–18

federalism 28, 136

fishing industry
British 46, 128
common fisheries policy 18, 126–30, 311
Spanish 46

foreign policy (see CFSP) 24–5, 108, 241

heads of governments meetings *see* European Council meetings

internal market 19–20, 23

Justice & Home Affairs 108, 320, 329–31

law 12, 267, 273, 277, 301
supremacy over national law 43, 47, 49, 54
legislation, scrutiny of 33–4, 73 192, 241, 305, 327
legislative process 41, 68, 78
political culture 314
qualified majority voting 20–3, 40, 73–4, *see also* Single European Act; Treaty of European Union

regional policies 19, 277

single European currency 317–18

Structural Funds 277

summit meetings *see* European Council

transport of live animals 223–33

ECOFIN 134

Economic & Monetary Union 25, 28, 36, 37, 241
Delors Committee report 72

EEA *see* European Economic Area

EFTA *see* European Free Trade Association

EMS *see* European Monetary System

EP *see* European Parliament

Euro-sceptics 93, 132, 136, 299, 312

European Affairs Committees 75–6, 334–9
conferences 142–3, 170, 348–9

European Assembly *see* European Parliament

European Assembly Elections Act 289

European Communities, *see* EC

European Communities Act (1972) 3, 33, 51, 167, 222, 266–8, 273, 282, 290, 292, 319
domestic laws 35, 44, 304
Section 2(2) 38–40
Section 2(4) 44–5

European Communities (Amendment) Act (1993) 9, 36, 261–96, 332

European Communities (Amendment) Bill (1985–86) 69

European Communities (Amendment) Bill (1992–93) Chapter 11 *passim*

European Communities Bill (1971–72) 50–2, 242, 262–3, 292, 301

European Convention on Human Rights 108

European Council
meetings 17, 19–20, 78, 217
(1969) The Hague 13, 18
(1983) Stuttgart 18
(1989) Madrid 75, 87
(1990) Rome 131–32, 201
(1990–91) Luxembourg 131, 246
(1992) Edinburgh 27, 261, 320
(1994) Corfu 317

European Court of Justice *see* Court of Justice of the European Communities (CJEC)

European Economic Area (EEA)

13–14, 35
European Economic Community
(EEC) *see* European
Community (EC)
European Free Trade Association
(EFTA) 13, 14
European Monetary System (EMS)
25
European Monetary Union (EMU),
proposals 241–2
European Parliament (EP) 11, 67
budget, control 22
committees 325
Conference of Presidents 335–6
Council of Ministers 26, 107
decision-making role 19
direct elections 15, 334
law-making functions 12
legislative proposals, monitoring
326
powers 19–20, 35, 37, 131, 135,
317, 319, 333
public accessibility 320
UK Parliament, comparisons
11–12, 316
European Parliamentary Elections
Act (1978) 265, 274, 290–1,
319
European Political Co-operation 330

European Political Union (EPU) 42,
241–2
European Union *see* European
Community
European Union Treaty *see*
Treaties, Treaty on European
Union
Exchange Rate Mechanism (ERM),
crisis 261, 268

*Factortame case* 45–7
Farm Animal Welfare Council
235–6
Fisheries Council 127, 130, *see also*

EC, fishing industry
Fontainebleau resolution (June 1984)
19
Foreign Affairs Councils 58, 331
Foster Committee Report *see* HC,
Select Committees, European
Secondary Legislation
Committee
France 327, 344–6
boycott of Council 22
European Parliament, direct election
334–5
federal goal 28
referendum 261, 276, 318

GATT (General Agreement on
Tariffs & Trade) 14–15, 113,
193–4, 199–213, 215–16
Germany 327, 342–4
European committees 334, 342–4
federal goal 28
Greece
accession 13, 15, 16, 18
Committee of the Regions 278
European committees 334

Hansard Society Commission 313
Hungary, application for
membership (1994) 14

Inter-governmental Conferences
(IGC) 130–8, 311, 336–38, *see
also* Treaty on European
Union
(1985) 19, 70
(1991) 25, 241–260, 332
(1996) 103, 317–19, 323
Ireland 19, 293, 318
Italy 17, 334

Joint Committee, UK Parliament
315, 324, 327, 329

Labour government

EC legislative proposals 60
Foster report 59
renegotiations (1974 & 1975) 18,
    56-7
Lords, House of
    character of the House 92-6,
        159-60
    committee work 97
    Committees, *see also* European
        Communities Committee
        (ECC), Select Committees
    Common Agricultural Policy
        (CAP) reform 213-21
    Debates 187-8
    EC agriculture & rural
        society 213-15
    Future of the Community
        164-7
    Regulations on welfare of
        calves & pigs 238
    European Communities
        Committee (ECC) 70,
        91-110, 170, 182,
        186-7, 323 , 326
        enquiries 173-82, 219, 306-8
        reports 99-102, 106, 171-3,
            175, 184-5, *189-90*, 198,
            213, 216-17, 245, 307-8,
            330
    GATT negotiations 214
    Jellicoe Report 94-5, 97-8,
        103-4, 107, 306
    Questions 91-2, 160-4
    Select Committees 94-8, 102-5,
        107-8, 172, 183-6, 306
        *see also* European
        Communities Committee
        (ECC), and Jellicoe
        Report
    Procedures for Scrutiny of
        Proposals for European
        Instruments 95-6,
        105
    Select Committees, sub-committees

97, 99, 102, 108, 168,
    170-1, 173-82, 198, 214-6
    session 1990-91, work of the House
        167-86
    Statements 164
Luxembourg Compromise (1966) 19,
    21-2, 303, 335

MacSharry proposals 179-180, 194,
    197-98, 201-203, 206-212,
    215-218, 313
Malta, application for membership
    (1990) 14
Maybray-King, Committee Report *see*
    Lords, Select Committees,
    Procedures for Scrutiny
Mezey, Michael 314
Mitchell, JDB 31, 36

National Farmers' Union 180, 206
national parliaments 1, 49, 107, 302,
    316, 322-3, 327, 332-351
Netherlands 346-7
    Committee of the Regions 278
    European committees 334
    openness 321
    Presidency 231, 247
    States-General 329, 331, 334,
        346-7
    Treaty on European Union
        329-30
Norway, referendum 21

Parliamentary reserve Chapter 4
    *passim* 99, 303
parliamentary sovereignty 31-2,
    49 Chapter 12 *passim*
Poland, application for membership
    (1994) 14
Ponsonby Rule 264-6
Portugal 13, 15, 210-11, 334

Royal Agricultural Society 180

*The Scrutiny of European
    Legislation* 73
SEA *see* Treaties, Single European
    Act
Social Chapter 28, 176, 243
Social Policy Agreement 273, 275,
    283
Social Protocol 262, 266, 269,
    272–5, 281–9, 292
Spain 13, 15–16, 21, 334, 348
Sweden 321

TEU *see* Treaties, Treaty on
    European Union
Thatcher, Margaret 15, 23–5, 29,
    113, 276
Treaties
    Maastricht Treaty *see* Treaty on
        European Union
    Single European Act (SEA)
        (1986) 9–10, 12, 17–24,
        34–5, 37, 40, 67, 73, 83,
        87, 114, 223, 226, 242,
        267, 273, 282, 290,
        302–3, 334–5
    Treaty on European Union
        (TEU) 2, 9, 12, 14, 19,
        22, 24–9,37, 69, 73, 107,
        113, 243–5, 247–53,262,
        267, 272, 290, 303,
        317–20, 330
        effect 34–5, 302, 335–8
        ratification 105, 261, 271,
            318–9, 322
    Treaty of Paris 9
    Treaty of Rome 12–13, 17–19,
        242, 263, 267, 290–1,
        293, 318–9
Turkey, application for membership
    (1987) 14

UK membership 13, 31, 33, 42, 50,
    300, 302, 312
Uruguay Round, *see* GATT